GW00630532

IFRS Guidebook

2016 Edition

Steven M. Bragg

Copyright © 2015 by AccountingTools, Inc. All rights reserved.

Published by AccountingTools, Inc., Centennial, Colorado.

No part of this publication may be reproduced, stored in a retrieval system, or transmitted in any form or by any means, except as permitted under Section 107 or 108 of the 1976 United States Copyright Act, without the prior written permission of the Publisher. Requests to the Publisher for permission should be addressed to Steven M. Bragg, 6727 E. Fremont Place, Centennial, CO 80112.

Limit of Liability/Disclaimer of Warranty: While the publisher and author have used their best efforts in preparing this book, they make no representations or warranties with respect to the accuracy or completeness of the contents of this book and specifically disclaim any implied warranties of merchantability or fitness for a particular purpose. No warranty may be created or extended by written sales materials. The advice and strategies contained herein may not be suitable for your situation. You should consult with a professional where appropriate. Neither the publisher nor author shall be liable for any loss of profit or any other commercial damages, including but not limited to special, incidental, consequential, or other damages.

For more information about AccountingTools® products, visit our Web site at www.accountingtools.com.

ISBN-13: 978-1-938910-61-6

Printed in the United States of America

Table of Contents

Preface

The accounting by businesses throughout the world is largely governed by International Financial Reporting Standards (IFRS). The source documents for IFRS cover several thousand pages, so their heft alone makes them difficult to research. The *IFRS Guidebook* lightens the research chore by presenting the essential elements of IFRS in a single volume, with an emphasis on key accounting requirements and disclosures. These essential elements are closely supported by several hundred examples and tips.

Following an introduction to IFRS in Chapter 1, the *Guidebook* covers in Chapters 2 through 9 all aspects of the presentation of financial statements, including accounting changes and error corrections, earnings per share, interim reporting, and operating segments. We then move on to the accounting for assets, liabilities, and equity in Chapters 10 through 19, which encompasses investments in other entities, inventories, fixed assets, asset impairment, assets held for sale, provisions, and contingent liabilities. Chapters 20 through 23 address a number of income statement topics – revenue recognition, employee benefits, share-based payments, income taxes, and more. Chapters 24 through 32 delve into a number of major transaction types, including business combinations, fair value measurements, foreign currency, leases, subsequent events, and insurance contracts. Finally, Chapters 33 through 38 describe industry-specific accounting for agriculture, construction, mineral resources, and more. The chapters include tips, podcast references, and a variety of illustrations.

You can find the answers to many accounting questions in the *Guidebook* that might otherwise require extensive research in the original IFRS source documents, such as:

- What is the proper presentation of a balance sheet?
- How do I calculate diluted earnings per share?
- What information must be included in interim financial statements?
- How do I use the equity method to account for investments?
- How do I use a cost layering system to account for inventory?
- What is the process for testing intangible assets for impairment?
- How do I account for fixed assets acquired in a business combination?
- When can I recognize revenue?
- How do I account for a defined benefit pension plan?
- How do I account for a business combination?

The *IFRS Guidebook* is designed for both professionals and students. Professionals can use it as a handy reference tool that reduces research time, while students will find that it clarifies many of the more arcane accounting topics.

Centennial, Colorado
October 2015

The *IFRS Guidebook* is also available as a continuing professional education (CPE) course. You can purchase the course (and many other courses) and take an on-line exam at:

www.accountingtools.com/cpe

About the Author

Steven Bragg, CPA, has been the chief financial officer or controller of four companies, as well as a consulting manager at Ernst & Young. He received a master's degree in finance from Bentley College, an MBA from Babson College, and a Bachelor's degree in Economics from the University of Maine. He has been a two-time president of the Colorado Mountain Club, and is an avid alpine skier, mountain biker, and certified master diver. Mr. Bragg resides in Centennial, Colorado. He has written the following books and courses:

Accountants' Guidebook	Financial Analysis
Accounting Changes and Error Corrections	Financial Forecasting and Modeling
Accounting Controls Guidebook	Fixed Asset Accounting
Accounting for Derivatives and Hedges	Foreign Currency Accounting
Accounting for Earnings per Share	GAAP Guidebook
Accounting for Inventory	Hospitality Accounting
Accounting for Investments	Human Resources Guidebook
Accounting for Managers	IFRS Guidebook
Accounting for Stock-Based Compensation	Interpretation of Financial Statements
Accounting Procedures Guidebook	Inventory Management
Bookkeeping Guidebook	Investor Relations Guidebook
Budgeting	Lean Accounting Guidebook
Business Combinations and Consolidations	Mergers & Acquisitions
Business Insurance Fundamentals	New Controller Guidebook
Business Ratios	Nonprofit Accounting
Capital Budgeting	Payables Management
CFO Guidebook	Payroll Management
Closing the Books	Project Accounting
Constraint Management	Public Company Accounting
Corporate Cash Management	Purchasing Guidebook
Corporate Finance	Real Estate Accounting
Cost Accounting Fundamentals	Revenue Recognition
Cost Management Guidebook	The Soft Close
Credit & Collection Guidebook	The Year-End Close
Enterprise Risk Management	Working Capital Management
Fair Value Accounting	

On-Line Resources by Steven Bragg

Steven maintains the accountingtools.com web site, which contains continuing professional education courses, the Accounting Best Practices podcast, and over a thousand articles on accounting subjects.

Chapter 1
Introduction

Introduction

In this chapter, we provide an introduction to the nature of IFRS, the IFRS conceptual framework, and how to use this book and other source materials to research IFRS topics. We also provide brief descriptions of the accounting principles upon which much of the IFRS elsewhere in this book is based.

What is IFRS?

IFRS is short for International Financial Reporting Standards. IFRS is comprised of a group of accounting standards that have been developed over a number of years. IFRS is used by businesses to properly organize their financial information into accounting records and summarize it into financial statements, as well as disclose certain supporting information.

One of the reasons for using IFRS is so that anyone reading the financial statements of multiple companies has a reasonable basis for comparison, since all companies using IFRS have created their financial statements using the same set of rules.

IFRS covers a broad array of topics, which are aggregated into the following major categories:

- *Presentation.* Covers the proper formatting and presentation of the financial statements, and includes the following topic areas:
    - Presentation of financial statements
    - Statement of cash flows
    - Consolidated and separate financial statements
    - Accounting policies, estimate changes and errors
    - Financial reporting in hyperinflationary economies
    - Earnings per share
    - Interim financial reporting
    - Operating segments
- *Assets, liabilities, and equity.* Describes the accounting for assets, liabilities, and equity, and includes the following topic areas:
    - Joint arrangements
    - Investments in associates and joint ventures
    - Disclosure of interests in other entities
    - Inventories
    - Property, plant, and equipment
    - Intangible assets
    - Investment property

- o Impairment of assets
- o Assets held for sale and discontinued operations
- o Provisions, contingent liabilities and contingent assets
- *Revenue and expenses.* Covers the accounting issues related to revenue and several key expense areas. The following topics are included:
  - o Revenue
  - o Employee benefits and retirement plans
  - o Share-based payment
  - o Income taxes
- *Broad transactions.* Describes several transaction types that cannot be classified within one of the preceding areas, and which has broad applicability to many industries. The following topic areas are included:
  - o Business combinations
  - o Financial instruments
  - o Fair value measurement
  - o Effects of changes in foreign exchange rates
  - o Borrowing costs
  - o Leases
  - o Related party disclosures
  - o Events after the reporting period
  - o Insurance contracts
- *Specific industries.* Includes accounting that is specific to certain industries, and includes the following topic areas:
  - o Agriculture
  - o Construction contracts
  - o Government grants
  - o Mineral resources
  - o Service concessions
  - o Other topics

IFRS is used by businesses reporting their financial results in those parts of the world that accept this framework. The main competing accounting framework is Generally Accepted Accounting Principles (GAAP), which is used in the United States. GAAP is much more rules-based than IFRS. IFRS focuses more on general principles than GAAP, which makes the IFRS body of work much smaller, cleaner, and easier to understand than GAAP.

There are several working groups that are gradually reducing the differences between the IFRS and GAAP accounting frameworks, so eventually there should be only minor differences in the reported results of a business if it switches between the two frameworks. The working groups are proceeding diligently, but there are still many issues to reconcile, so it may require a number of years before the two accounting frameworks are in approximate alignment. There have been occasional statements that the two frameworks (and presumably their supporting organizations) will eventually be merged, but this has not yet occurred.

The IFRS Conceptual Framework

A generalized conceptual framework has been released by the International Accounting Standards Board, which is responsible for the creation and maintenance of IFRS. This framework lays out the concepts that underlie how financial statements are to be prepared and presented. The main subject areas addressed by the framework are as follows:

- *Objective of financial reporting.* The objective is to provide financial information about the reporting organization that is useful to readers in making decisions about providing resources to the organization. This means that information must be provided concerning its assets, liabilities, and efficiency of use of resources. Accrual accounting is mandated when financial information is prepared.
- *Qualitative characteristics of financial reporting.* Certain types of information are likely to be most useful to the readers of financial information. This information should be relevant, so that it makes a difference in decision making, either by having predictive value or by confirming existing information. The information should also faithfully represent the condition and results of an entity by being complete, neutral in how information is presented, and free from error. In addition, the following qualitative characteristics of financial information should be enhanced to the extent possible, given the constraint of the cost of financial reporting:
    - *Comparability.* The information should be comparable to similar information released by other entities.
    - *Verifiability.* Multiple parties can reach a consensus that the information presented is a faithful representation of the reporting entity.
    - *Timeliness.* The information should be presented quickly enough to assist in decision-making.
    - *Understandability.* The information is clearly classified and presented.
- *Definition, recognition, and measurement of the financial statement components.* The key financial statements used to portray an entity are the balance sheet and income statement. The balance sheet is comprised of assets, liabilities, and equity, while the income statement is comprised of income and expenses. These components of the financial statements are defined as follows:
    - *Assets.* These are resources controlled by an organization, and from which it expects to derive future economic benefits. These benefits may involve operational activities or convertibility into cash.
    - *Liabilities.* These are obligations arising from past events. A liability may also arise from an irrevocable agreement to acquire an asset on a future date. Some liabilities can only be measured

through estimation, since the exact amounts of these liabilities have not yet been settled.

- o *Equity.* This is the residual interest in an organization's assets after deducting all liabilities. This interest may include invested funds and reserves against future expenditures.
- o *Income.* This is increases in economic benefits that are derived from either inflows of assets or decreases of liabilities, other than investor contributions. The income concept can be split further into revenue and gains, where revenue arises from ordinary activities and gains are a catchall phrase arising from other activities. An example of a gain is from the sale of a long-term asset.
- o *Expenses.* This is decreases in economic benefits that are derived from outflows or the usage of assets, or the incurrence of liabilities, other than distributions to investors. The expenses concept can be split further into expenses and losses, where expenses arise from ordinary activities and losses are a catchall phrase arising from other activities. An example of a loss is the destruction caused by flood damage.

- *Concepts of capital and capital maintenance.* A financial concept of capital means that the net assets of the business contribute to performance. Under a physical concept of capital, the productive capacity of the business is emphasized. The financial concept of capital is most commonly used, as it emphasizes maintenance of invested capital and/or the purchasing power of that capital. Under the financial concept of capital, a profit is only earned when the net assets at the end of a period exceed the amount at the beginning of the period, excluding the effects of owner distributions and contributions. Under the physical concept of capital, a profit is only earned when the physical productive capacity at the end of a period exceeds the amount at the beginning of the period, excluding the effects of owner distributions and contributions. Changes in prices under the financial concept of capital are recognized as a profit or loss (depending on the circumstances), while such changes under the physical concept are considered to be adjustments to equity.

In addition to these basic conceptual topics, the framework also addresses the recognition concept. Recognition is the process of incorporating an item into the financial statements if it meets the criteria for recognition, and can be defined as an element of the financial statements. More specifically, recognition occurs when the following conditions are met:

- *Probable benefit.* It is probable that the organization will derive a benefit from the item.
- *Measurable.* The item has a cost or benefit that can be reliably measured. The use of reasonable estimates is allowable.

For example, a favorable outcome of a lawsuit cannot be recognized until such time as the settlement has been approved and the amount to be paid has been determined. Prior to that date, there is no way to recognize the gain.

The framework also includes a discussion of the measurement bases that are used to compile the financial statements. Measurement bases are needed to derive the monetary amounts at which the various elements of the financial statements are recognized. The following measurement bases may be used to varying extents in financial statements:

- *Historical cost.* Assets are recorded at the amounts paid for them, and liabilities are recorded at the amount of proceeds received in exchange for incurring each obligation. This is the most commonly used basis of measurement.
- *Current cost.* Assets are recorded at the amount that would be paid if these assets were to be acquired in the current period. Liabilities are recorded at the undiscounted amount of cash that would be needed to settle these obligations in the current period.
- *Settlement value.* Assets are recorded at the amount that could be obtained from their sale in the current period in an orderly sale. Liabilities are carried at the undiscounted amount of cash expected to be paid in the current period to settle these obligations in the normal course of business. This measurement basis is also known as realizable value.
- *Present value.* Assets are recorded at the present discounted value of their future net cash inflows. Liabilities are recorded at the present discounted value of their future net cash outflows.

How this Book is Organized

This book is designed to provide a streamlined view of IFRS that can also be used for training purposes.

The IFRS source document is several thousand pages long. Within those pages, IFRS follows a rigid format that provides for each topic a set of sections covering an introduction, objective, scope, definitions, recognition, presentation, disclosure, and transition information. A companion volume delves into the basis for conclusions reached, dissenting opinions, and sometimes examples of how guidance can be used. Because of the highly sub-divided nature of the presentation, it may be necessary to wade through a substantial amount of information before finding the desired guidance. The *IFRS Guidebook* condenses IFRS to provide only the information that is most likely to be needed, and in far fewer sections. The book does so by focusing on recognition, measurement, and disclosures, while eliminating much of the implementation guidance that is less likely to be referenced by the mainstream user.

The chapter layout of the *IFRS Guidebook* is structured to roughly adhere to the names of the accounting standards used in IFRS. This means that the chapters listed in the table of contents approximate the topics used in IFRS, though the *Guidebook* consolidates some topics. We have chosen to use this chapter format so that the reader can more easily cross-reference IFRS topics in the *Guidebook* with the underlying IFRS pronouncements for more detailed research.

How to Use this Book

There are multiple tools available in this book for researching IFRS topics. The primary challenge is simply locating the correct topic, since there are hundreds of them in the book. To make searching easier in the *Guidebook*, we have added dozens of sub-topics, which appear in the table of contents beneath the chapter titles. We have also endeavored to expand the index to the greatest extent possible, using a number of alternative index terms. Several other sources of information are:

- *Podcast episodes*. The author manages the Accounting Best Practices podcast, which provides information about a variety of accounting topics, and which has been downloaded over two million times. When there is a podcast episode relevant to a chapter, it is noted in a text box at the beginning of the chapter.
- *Tips*. A variety of accounting management tips are sprinkled throughout the book, usually immediately after a related IFRS topic.
- *Glossary*. The book contains a lengthy glossary of accounting terminology.

In addition, consider researching accounting topics on the accountingtools.com website. The site contains articles, blog posts, podcasts, and other information on over a thousand accounting topics. Use of the site is completely free.

Accounting Principles

Almost all of this book contains descriptions of the accounting rules and disclosures required by IFRS. However, the other chapters do not address the general accounting principles that provide structure to the IFRS accounting framework. These accounting principles have been described somewhat in the conceptual framework that accompanies the IFRS pronouncements, and are also based on common usage. The principles are:

- *Accrual principle*. The concept that accounting transactions should be recorded in the accounting periods when they actually occur, rather than in the periods when there are cash flows associated with them. This is the foundation of the accrual basis of accounting. It is important for the construction of financial statements that show what actually happened in an accounting period, rather than being artificially delayed or accelerated by the associated cash flows. For example, if an entity were to ignore the accrual principle, it would record an expense only after paying for it, which might incorporate a lengthy delay caused by the payment terms for the associated supplier invoice.
- *Conservatism principle*. The concept that a business should record expenses and liabilities as soon as possible, but record revenues and assets only when it is certain that they will occur. This introduces a conservative slant to the

financial statements that may yield lower reported profits, since revenue and asset recognition may be delayed for some time. This principle tends to encourage the recordation of losses earlier, rather than later. This concept can be taken too far, where a business persistently misstates its results to be worse than is realistically the case.

- *Consistency principle*. The concept that, once an accounting principle or method is adopted, an organization should continue to use it until a demonstrably better principle or method comes along. Not following the consistency principle means that a business could continually jump between different accounting treatments of its transactions that make its long-term financial results extremely difficult to discern.
- *Cost principle*. The concept that a business should only record its assets, liabilities, and equity investments at their original purchase costs. This principle is becoming less valid, as a host of accounting standards are heading in the direction of adjusting to fair value.
- *Economic entity principle*. The concept that the transactions of a business should be kept separate from those of its owners and other businesses. This prevents intermingling of assets and liabilities among multiple entities.
- *Full disclosure principle*. The concept that one should include in or alongside the financial statements of a business all of the information that may impact a reader's understanding of those financial statements. The accounting standards have greatly amplified upon this concept in specifying an enormous number of informational disclosures.
- *Going concern principle*. The concept that a business will remain in operation for the foreseeable future. This means that the accountant would be justified in deferring the recognition of some expenses, such as depreciation, until later periods. Otherwise, it would be necessary to recognize all expenses at once and not defer any of them.
- *Matching principle*. The concept that, when revenue is recorded, all related expenses should be recorded at the same time. Thus, inventory is charged to the cost of goods sold at the same time that revenue is recorded from the sale of those inventory items. This is a cornerstone of the accrual basis of accounting.
- *Materiality principle*. The concept that a transaction should be recorded in the accounting records if not doing so might have altered the decision making process of someone reading the company's financial statements. This is quite a vague concept that is difficult to quantify, which has led some of the more picayune controllers to record even the smallest transactions.
- *Monetary unit principle*. The concept that a business should only record transactions that can be stated in terms of a unit of currency. Thus, it is easy enough to record the purchase of a fixed asset, since it was bought for a specific price, whereas the value of the quality control system of a business is not recorded. This concept keeps a business from engaging in an excessive level of estimation in deriving the value of its assets and liabilities.

- *Reliability principle.* The concept that only those transactions that can be proven should be recorded. For example, a supplier invoice is solid evidence that an expense has been recorded. This concept is of prime interest to auditors, who are constantly in search of the evidence supporting transactions.
- *Revenue recognition principle.* The concept that revenue should only be recognized when a business has substantially completed the earnings process. So many people have skirted around the fringes of this concept to commit reporting fraud that a variety of standard-setting bodies have developed a massive amount of information about what constitutes proper revenue recognition. Being principles-based, IFRS coverage of this topic remains at a relatively high level.
- *Time period principle.* The concept that a business should report the results of its operations over a standard period of time. This may qualify as the most glaringly obvious of all accounting principles, but is intended to create a standard set of comparable periods, which is useful for trend analysis.

When there is a question about IFRS that could result in several possible treatments of an accounting transaction or disclosure, it is sometimes useful to resolve the question by viewing the IFRS guidance in light of these accounting principles. Doing so may indicate that one solution more closely adheres to the general intent of the accounting framework, and so is a better solution.

Summary

The *IFRS Guidebook* is intended to be what the name implies – a guide to IFRS. We expect it to be used as a handy reference when there is a specific question about IFRS, not as a book to be read from cover to cover. The immense amount of material that was condensed into this book inevitably means that there is little room for some of the explanatory comments typically found in an introductory accounting textbook concerning why a particular accounting rule was established. Instead, we assume that the reader already has a working knowledge of the general structure of accounting, and only need clarification on a particular accounting issue. If more information is required about how accounting works, rather than the rules stated in the *Guidebook*, consider buying the author's other books on accounting management, such as *Closing the Books* and *The New Controller Guidebook*. All of the author's books can be purchased at the accountingtools.com website.

Chapter 2
Presentation of Financial Statements

Introduction

IFRS sets forth standards of presentation that are designed to keep the financial statements of a business as comparable as possible, both between its own reports across multiple periods and between the financial reports of multiple entities. These standards of presentation focus on the structure and content of financial statements.

In this chapter, we address the requirements for the statements of financial position, profit or loss, and changes in equity, along with relevant examples. The requirements for the statement of cash flows are addressed in the next chapter.

IFRS Source Document

- IAS 1, *Presentation of Financial Statements*

Overview of the Financial Statements

Financial statements are designed to show the financial results and financial position of a business. This information can be evaluated by users to make decisions about how to manage or interact with a business. Only a complete set of financial statements can provide the full range of information needed. A complete set of financial statements includes the following items:
- A statement of financial position (the balance sheet)
- A statement of profit or loss (the income statement) and other comprehensive income
- A statement of changes in equity
- A statement of cash flows
- Notes that describe significant accounting policies and other information

The following issues apply to the presentation of financial statements:
- *Accrual basis.* Financial statements shall be prepared using the accrual basis of accounting, so that revenues are recognized when earned and expenses recognized as incurred.
- *Aggregation.* Do not reduce the understandability of the financial statements by aggregating material items that have different natures. Also, do not obscure material information by aggregating it with immaterial information.
- *Comparative information.* Disclose comparative information for the previous period for all amounts included in the financial statements for the most recent period. If relevant, also disclose comparative narrative information in the accompanying notes. This means that a complete set of finan-

cial statements should include two of each type of financial statement. Further, if there has been a retrospective change in accounting policy, a retrospective restatement, or a reclassification, there should be three balance sheets, of which the additional one is stated as of the beginning of the earliest comparative period.

- *Compliance.* If the financial statements comply with IFRS, disclose in the accompanying notes that this is the case.
- *Consistency.* Continue to use the same presentation of information within the financial statements from period to period, unless another presentation would be more appropriate, or IFRS requires a change in presentation.
- *Departures.* In the rare cases where management believes that following IFRS will result in misleading information, disclose management's conclusion, the name of the IFRS from which the company has departed, the circumstances of the departure, and the effect of the departure on the financial statements. Also note that the financial statements are a fair presentation of the company's financial position, performance, and cash flows. If IFRS does not allow a departure from a reporting requirement, disclose the name of the IFRS, the nature of the requirement, why management believes that following the requirement yields misleading information, and the adjustments that would be needed to correct the issue.
- *Frequency.* A complete set of financial statements should be issued at least once a year.
- *Going concern.* A business should prepare financial statements on a going concern basis, unless management intends to liquidate the business or has no other realistic alternative. If there is uncertainty about being able to continue as a going concern, disclose the relevant uncertainties. If the financial statements are not prepared on a going concern basis, disclose this fact, why the business is not considered a going concern, and the basis on which the financial statements were prepared.
- *Identification.* Clearly identify each financial statement and distinguish it from other information being presented within the same document. In particular, state the following information prominently:
  - The name of the entity
  - Whether the financial statements apply to one entity or a group of entities
  - The period covered by the financial statements, or the date as of the end of the reporting period
  - The currency in which the financial statements are presented
  - The level of rounding (if any) used to present amounts in the financial statements
- *Materiality.* It may not be necessary to provide a disclosure required by IFRS if the resulting information is not material. Conversely, it may be necessary to provide disclosures beyond what is mandated by IFRS, if the IFRS requirements are not sufficient to provide users with a complete understanding of the impact of certain transactions.

- *Offsetting.* The netting of assets against liabilities, or of income against expenses, is not allowed unless specifically permitted under IFRS. In brief, netting is typically only allowed when the substance of the underlying transaction also allows for the same netting. Netting against an offsetting valuation allowance (such as netting the allowance for doubtful accounts against accounts receivable) is allowed.
- *Other comprehensive income.* Other comprehensive income may be included in the statement of profit or loss, or it may be presented separately. In either case, the statement of profit or loss should be presented first.
- *Prominence.* All of the financial statements shall be presented with equal prominence.
- *Similarity.* A business should aggregate similar items for presentation purposes. A materially different class of items should be presented separately. An item that is not individually material can be aggregated with other items, though a possibility is to present such items separately in the accompanying notes.
- *Titles.* It is allowable to apply a different title to a financial statement than the ones used by IFRS. Thus, a statement of financial position could be entitled a balance sheet.

The Statement of Financial Position

A statement of financial position (also known as a balance sheet) presents information about an entity's assets, liabilities, and shareholders' equity, where the compiled result must match this formula:

$$Total\ assets = Total\ liabilities + Equity$$

The balance sheet reports the aggregate effect of transactions as of a specific date. The balance sheet is used to assess an entity's liquidity and ability to pay its debts. IFRS requires that the following line items be included in the balance sheet:

Asset items:
- Assets classified as held for sale
- Biological assets
- Cash and cash equivalents
- Current tax assets
- Deferred tax assets
- Financial assets
- Intangible assets
- Inventories
- Investment property
- Investments accounted for under the equity method
- Property, plant, and equipment

- Trade and other receivables

Liability items:
- Current tax liabilities
- Deferred tax liabilities
- Financial liabilities
- Liabilities classified as held for sale
- Provisions
- Trade and other payables

Equity items:
- Issued capital
- Non-controlling interests

These IFRS requirements are the minimum amount of information that should be imparted. Other line items can be added, as well as headings and subtotals, if doing so will improve a user's understanding of a balance sheet. The decision to add other items can include an assessment of the nature, liquidity, and function of assets, as well as the nature, timing, and amounts of liabilities. Examples of additional line items are for:
- Individual classes of property, plant, and equipment
- Individual types of receivables, such as trade receivables and receivables from related parties
- Individual classes of inventory, such as for materials, work in process, and finished goods

A *current asset* is one that will be sold or consumed within the normal operating cycle of a business or the next 12 months, or which is a cash or cash equivalent. This classification can also include assets held for the purpose of trading. A *current liability* is one that will be settled within the normal operating cycle of a business or the next 12 months. The presentation of classifications within the balance sheet for current and non-current assets and liabilities is required; the only alternative is to present assets and liabilities in order of liquidity, which can be used when doing so provides information that is more reliable and relevant. The following rules apply to the current and non-current distinction:
- *Deferred taxes.* If there is an election to present line items as current or non-current assets or liabilities within the balance sheet, IFRS prohibits the classification of deferred tax assets as current assets. It also prohibits the classification of deferred tax liabilities as current liabilities.
- *Lending breach.* If a business breaches the terms of a lending arrangement and the result is that the loaned funds are payable on demand, classify the loan as a current liability, even if the lender agrees not to demand payment. This rule does not apply if the lender provides a grace period of at least one year after the reporting period.

- *Obligation rollover.* If a business has the discretion to roll over an obligation for at least one year after the reporting period, classify the obligation as non-current. However, if this action is not at the discretion of the business, classify the obligation as a current liability.
- *Settlement period.* Separately disclose the amount of an asset or liability line item expected to be recovered or settled within 12 months from the amount that will be recovered or settled at a later date.

There is no requirement within IFRS for presenting line items in a certain order or format.

The Standard Balance Sheet Format

Here is an example of a balance sheet which presents information as of the end of two fiscal years:

Lowry Locomotion
Balance Sheet
As of December 31, 20X2 and 20X1

	12/31/20X2	12/31/20x1
ASSETS		
Current assets		
Cash and cash equivalents	£270,000	£215,000
Trade receivables	147,000	139,000
Inventories	139,000	128,000
Other current assets	15,000	27,000
Total current assets	£571,000	£509,000
Non-current assets		
Property, plant, and equipment	551,000	529,000
Goodwill	82,000	82,000
Intangible assets	143,000	143,000
Total non-current assets	£776,000	£754,000
Total assets	£1,347,000	£1,263,000
LIABILITIES AND EQUITY		
Current liabilities		
Trade and other payables	£217,000	£198,000
Short-term borrowings	133,000	202,000
Current portion of long-term borrowings	5,000	5,000
Current tax liabilities	26,000	23,000
Accrued expenses	9,000	13,000
Total current liabilities	£390,000	£441,000
Non-current liabilities		
Long-term debt	85,000	65,000

	12/31/20X2	12/31/20x1
Deferred tax liabilities	19,000	17,000
Total non-current liabilities	£104,000	£82,000
Total liabilities	£494,000	£523,000
Shareholders' equity		
Issued capital	853,000	740,000
Total equity	£853,000	£740,000
Total liabilities and equity	£1,347,000	£1,263,000

The Common Size Balance Sheet

A common size balance sheet presents not only the standard information contained in a balance sheet, but also a column that notes the same information as a percentage of the total assets (for asset line items) or as a percentage of total liabilities and shareholders' equity (for liability or shareholders' equity line items).

It is extremely useful to construct a common size balance sheet that itemizes the results as of the end of multiple time periods, so that trend lines can be constructed to ascertain changes over longer time periods. The common size balance sheet is also useful for comparing the proportions of assets, liabilities, and equity between different companies, particularly as part of an industry or acquisition analysis.

For example, if you were comparing the common size balance sheet of an acquirer to that of a potential acquiree, and the acquiree had 40% of its assets invested in accounts receivable versus 20% by the acquirer, this may indicate that aggressive collection activities might reduce the acquiree's receivables if the acquirer were to buy it.

The common size balance sheet is not required under IFRS. However, being a useful document for analysis purposes, it is commonly distributed within a company for review by management.

There is no mandatory format for a common size balance sheet, though percentages are nearly always placed to the right of the normal numerical results. If balance sheet results are being reported as of the end of many periods, it is even possible to dispense with numerical results entirely, in favor of just presenting the common size percentages.

EXAMPLE

Lowy Locomotion creates a common size balance sheet that contains the balance sheet as of the end of its fiscal year for each of the past two years, with common size percentages to the right:

Lowry Locomotion
Common Size Balance Sheet
As of 12/31/20x02 and 12/31/20x1

	(£) 12/31/20x2	(£) 12/31/20x1	(%) 12/31/20x2	(%) 12/31/20x1
Current assets				
Cash	£1,200	£900	7.6%	7.1%
Accounts receivable	4,800	3,600	30.4%	28.3%
Inventories	3,600	2,700	22.8%	21.3%
Total current assets	£9,600	£7,200	60.8%	56.7%
Total fixed assets	6,200	5,500	39.2%	43.3%
Total assets	£15,800	£12,700	100.0%	100.0%
Current liabilities				
Accounts payable	£2,400	£41,800	15.2%	14.2%
Accrued expenses	480	360	3.0%	2.8%
Short-term debt	800	600	5.1%	4.7%
Total current liabilities	£3,680	£2,760	23.3%	21.7%
Long-term debt	9,020	7,740	57.1%	60.9%
Total liabilities	£12,700	£10,500	80.4%	82.7%
Issued capital	3,100	2,200	19.6%	17.3%
Total liabilities and equity	£15,800	£12,700	100.0%	100.0%

How to Construct a Balance Sheet

If an accounting software package is being used, it is quite easy to construct a balance sheet. Just access the report writing module, select the time period needed for the balance sheet, and print it. If it is necessary to construct the balance sheet manually, follow these steps:

1. Create the trial balance report.
2. List each account pertaining to the balance sheet in a separate column of the trial balance.
3. Add the difference between the revenue and expense line items on the trial balance to a separate line item in the equity section of the balance sheet.
4. Aggregate these line items into those you want to report in the balance sheet as a separate line item.
5. Shift the result into the company's preferred balance sheet format.

The following example illustrates the construction of a balance sheet.

EXAMPLE

The accounting software for Lowry Locomotion breaks down at the end of July, and the controller has to create the financial statements by hand. He has a copy of Lowry's trial balance, which is shown below. He transfers this information to an electronic spreadsheet, creates separate columns for accounts to include in the balance sheet, and copies the account balances into these columns. This leaves a number of accounts related to the income statement, which he can ignore for the purposes of creating the balance sheet. However, he *does* include the net loss for the period in the "Current year profit" row, which is included in the equity section of the balance sheet.

Lowry Locomotion Extended Trial Balance

	Adjusted Trial Balance		Balance Sheet		Aggregation	
	Debit	Credit	Debit	Credit	Debit	Credit
Cash	£60,000		£60,000		£60,000	
Accounts receivable	230,000		230,000		230,000	
Inventories	300,000		300,000		300,000	
Fixed assets (net)	210,000		210,000		210,000	
Accounts payable		£90,000		£90,000		£165,000
Accrued liabilities		75,000		75,000		
Notes payable		420,000		420,000		420,000
Equity		350,000		350,000		215,000
Current year profit			135,000			
Revenue		450,000				
Cost of goods sold	290,000					
Salaries expense	225,000					
Payroll tax expense	20,000					
Rent expense	35,000					
Other expenses	15,000					
Totals	£1,385,000	£1,385,000	£935,000	£935,000	£800,000	£800,000

In the "Aggregation" columns of the extended trial balance, the controller has aggregated the liabilities for accounts payable and accrued liabilities in the accounts payable line, and aggregated equity and current year profit into the equity line. He then transfers this information into the following condensed balance sheet:

Lowry Locomotion
Balance Sheet
For the month ended July 31, 20X1

Assets	
Cash	£60,000
Accounts receivable	230,000
Inventories	300,000
Fixed assets	210,000
Total assets	£800,000
Liabilities	
Accounts payable	£165,000
Notes payable	420,000
Total liabilities	£585,000
Equity	£215,000
Total liabilities and equity	£800,000

Overview of the Statement of Profit or Loss

The statement of profit or loss is a financial report that summarizes an entity's revenue, expenses, and net income or loss. The intent of the statement is to show the financial results of a business over a specific period of time, such as a month, quarter, or year. The statement of profit or loss is also known as the *income statement*.

A related concept that is sometimes reported alongside the income statement is *other comprehensive income*. This classification contains all changes that are not permitted to be recorded within the income statement, because they have not yet been realized. Examples of other comprehensive income items are unrealized gains and losses on securities that have not yet been sold, as well as foreign currency translation adjustments.

When combined with other comprehensive income, the income statement provides the following information:
- The derivation of profit or loss
- Total other comprehensive income
- Comprehensive income for the period (which is the sum of the last two items)

Within this financial statement, you must also present an allocation of profit or loss and other comprehensive income to each of the following items:
- Non-controlling interests
- Owners of the parent entity

The following items must be included in the income statement:
- Revenue
- Interest revenue, calculated using the effective interest method
- Gains and losses due to the derecognition of financial assets that are measured at their amortized cost
- Financing costs
- Impairment losses
- Any shares of the profits and losses of associates and joint ventures that the entity accounts for using the equity method
- Gains and losses due to a reclassified financial asset that is now measured at its fair value, based on the difference between its former carrying amount and its fair value on the reclassification date
- Tax expense
- The total amount of discontinued operations

The following additional items apply to either the income statement or other comprehensive income, or both:
- *Income taxes.* Disclose the amount of income tax associated with each line item included in other comprehensive income, either within this portion of the financial statements, or in the accompanying notes. It is permissible to present other comprehensive income line items net of any related taxes; an alternative presentation is to state these items before tax effects, and then include the aggregate amount of income taxes relating to all of these items in a separate line item. In the latter case, allocate income taxes between those items that will eventually be reclassified to the income statement, and those that will not be reclassified.
- *Offsetting.* In nearly all cases, IFRS does not allow the offsetting of revenue and expense items, which would thereby present only the residual amount. The primary exception is when the underlying agreement with a third party actually allows the company to offset revenue and expense items.
- *Other comprehensive income line items.* Present line items in the other comprehensive income section that are classified by nature. Also, classify items separately that will not be reclassified to profit or loss at a later date, and those which *will* be so classified.
- *Reclassification adjustments.* If there are any reclassification adjustments (when items are shifted from other comprehensive income to profit or loss) in the income statement, disclose both the reclassification adjustments and the amount of income tax related to them. This disclosure can be made within the income statement or in the accompanying notes.
- *Additional items.* Add other line items, headings, and subtotals to the income statement when doing so improves users' understanding of the company's financial performance. Consider the materiality and nature of revenue and expense items when determining whether to include or exclude a line item. Examples of circumstances that may trigger such additional dis-

closures are inventory write-downs, the disposal of fixed assets or investments, the settlement of litigation, and the restructuring of a business.

Several variations on the layout of the income statement are shown later in this section.

Presentation by Nature or Function

A key additional item is to present an analysis of the expenses in profit or loss, using a classification based on their nature or functional area; the goal is to maximize the relevance and reliability of the presented information. If expenses are being presented by their nature, the format looks similar to the following (not including other comprehensive income):

Sample Presentation by Nature of Items

Revenue		£xxx
Expenses		
Direct materials	£xxx	
Direct labor	xxx	
Salaries expense	xxx	
Payroll taxes	xxx	
Employee benefits	xxx	
Depreciation expense	xxx	
Telephone expense	xxx	
Other expenses	xxx	
Total expenses		£xxx
Profit before tax		£xxx
Total comprehensive income attributable to:		
Owners of the parent	£xxx	
Non-controlling interests	xxx	
		£xxx

Alternatively, if expenses are presented by their functional area, the format looks similar to the following, where most expenses are aggregated at the department level (not including other comprehensive income):

Sample Presentation by Function of Items

Revenue	£xxx
Cost of goods sold	xxx
Gross profit	xxx
Administrative expenses	£xxx
Distribution expenses	xxx
Research and development expenses	xxx
Sales and marketing expenses	xxx
Other expenses	xxx
Total expenses	£xxx
Profit before tax	£xxx
Total comprehensive income attributable to:	
Owners of the parent	£xxx
Non-controlling interests	xxx
	£xxx

If expenses are classified by function, IFRS requires that additional disclosures be made for depreciation and amortization expense, as well as for employee benefits expense.

Of the two methods, presenting expenses by their nature is easier, since it requires no allocation of expenses between functional areas. Conversely, the functional area presentation may be more relevant to users of the information, who can more easily see where resources are being consumed. IFRS simply suggests that management select the format that is more reliable and relevant.

An example follows of an income statement that presents expenses by their nature, rather than by their function.

EXAMPLE

Lowry Locomotion presents its results in two separate statements by their nature, resulting in the following format, beginning with the income statement:

Lowry Locomotion
Income Statement
For the years ended December 31

	20x2	20x1
Revenue	£900,000	£850,000
Expenses		
Direct materials	£270,000	£255,000
Direct labor	90,000	85,000
Salaries	300,000	275,000
Payroll taxes	27,000	25,000
Depreciation expense	45,000	41,000
Telephone expense	30,000	20,000
Other expenses	23,000	22,000
Finance costs	29,000	23,000
Other income	-25,000	-20,000
Profit before tax	£111,000	£124,000
Income tax expense	38,000	43,000
Profit from continuing operations	£73,000	£81,000
Loss from discontinued operations	42,000	0
Profit	£31,000	£81,000
Profit attributable to:		
Owners of the parent	£21,700	£56,700
Non-controlling interests	9,300	24,300
	£31,000	£81,000

Lowry Locomotion then continues with the following statement of comprehensive income:

Lowry Locomotion
Statement of Comprehensive Income
For the years ended December 31

	20x2	20x1
Profit	£31,000	£81,000
Other comprehensive income (items that may be reclassified subsequently to profit or loss)		
Exchange differences on translating foreign operations	£5,000	£9,000
Available-for-sale financial assets	10,000	-2,000
Cash flow hedges	-2,000	-12,000
Other comprehensive income, net of tax	£13,000	-£5,000
Total comprehensive income	£18,000	£76,000
Total comprehensive income attributable to:		
Owners of the parent	£12,600	£53,200
Non-controlling interests	5,400	22,800
	£18,000	£76,000

The Single-Step Income Statement

The simplest format in which an income statement can be constructed is the single-step income statement. In this format, present a single subtotal for all revenue line items, and a single subtotal for all expense line items, with a net gain or loss appearing at the bottom of the report. A sample single-step income statement follows:

Sample Single-Step Income Statement

Revenues	£1,000,000
Expenses:	
Cost of goods sold	350,000
Advertising	30,000
Depreciation	20,000
Rent	40,000
Payroll taxes	28,000
Salaries and wages	400,000
Supplies	32,000
Travel and entertainment	50,000
Total expenses	950,000
Net income	£50,000

The single-step format is not heavily used, because it forces the reader of an income statement to separately summarize subsets of information within the income statement. For a more readable format, try the following multi-step approach.

The Multi-Step Income Statement

The multi-step income statement involves the use of multiple sub-totals within the income statement, which makes it easier for readers to aggregate selected types of information within the report. The usual subtotals are for the gross margin, operating expenses, and other income, which allow readers to determine how much the company earns just from its manufacturing activities (the gross margin), what it spends on supporting operations (the operating expense total) and which components of its results do not relate to its core activities (the other income total). A sample format for a multi-step income statement follows:

Sample Multi-Step Income Statement

Revenues	£1,000,000
Cost of goods sold	350,000
Gross margin	£650,000
Operating expenses	
Advertising	30,000
Depreciation	20,000
Rent	40,000
Payroll taxes	28,000
Salaries and wages	380,000
Supplies	32,000
Travel and entertainment	50,000
Total operating expenses	£580,000
Other income	
Interest income	-5,000
Interest expense	25,000
Total other income	£20,000
Net income	£50,000

The Contribution Margin Income Statement

A contribution margin income statement is an income statement in which all variable expenses are deducted from sales to arrive at a contribution margin, from which all fixed expenses are then subtracted to arrive at the net profit or loss for the period. This income statement format is a superior form of presentation, because the contribution margin clearly shows the amount available to cover fixed costs and generate a profit or loss.

In essence, if there are no sales, a contribution margin income statement will have a zero contribution margin, with fixed costs clustered beneath the contribution margin line item. As sales increase, the contribution margin will increase in conjunction with sales, while fixed costs remain approximately the same.

A contribution margin income statement varies from a normal income statement in the following three ways:

- Fixed production costs are aggregated lower in the income statement, after the contribution margin;
- Variable selling and administrative expenses are grouped with variable production costs, so that they are a part of the calculation of the contribution margin; and
- The gross margin is replaced in the statement by the contribution margin.

Thus, the format of a contribution margin income statement is:

Sample Contribution Margin Income Statement

+	Revenues
-	Variable production expenses (such as materials, supplies, and variable overhead)
-	Variable selling and administrative expenses
=	Contribution margin
-	Fixed production expenses (including most overhead)
-	Fixed selling and administrative expenses
=	Net profit or loss

In many cases, direct labor is categorized as a fixed expense in the contribution margin income statement format, rather than a variable expense, because this cost does not always change in direct proportion to the amount of revenue generated. Instead, management needs to keep a certain minimum staffing in the production area, which does not vary even if there are lower production volumes.

The key difference between gross margin and contribution margin is that fixed production costs are included in the cost of goods sold to calculate the gross margin, whereas they are not included in the same calculation for the contribution margin. This means that the contribution margin income statement is sorted based on the variability of the underlying cost information, rather than by the functional areas or expense categories found in a normal income statement.

It is useful to create an income statement in the contribution margin format when there is a need to determine that proportion of expenses that truly varies directly with revenues. In many businesses, the contribution margin will be substantially higher than the gross margin, because such a large proportion of production costs are fixed and few of its selling and administrative expenses are variable.

The Multi-Period Income Statement

A variation on any of the preceding income statement formats is to present them over multiple periods, preferably over a trailing 12-month period. By doing so, readers of the income statement can see trends in the information, as well as spot changes in the trends that may require investigation. This is an excellent way to present the income statement, and is highly recommended. The following sample shows the layout of a multi-period income statement over a four-quarter period, with key items noted in bold.

Sample Multi-Period Income Statement

	Quarter 1	Quarter 2	Quarter 3	Quarter 4
Revenues	£1,000,000	£1,100,000	£1,050,000	£1,200,000
Cost of goods sold	350,000	385,000	368,000	**480,000**
Gross margin	£650,000	£715,000	£682,000	£720,000
Operating expenses				
Advertising	30,000	**0**	**60,000**	30,000
Depreciation	20,000	21,000	22,000	24,000
Rent	40,000	40,000	**50,000**	50,000
Payroll taxes	28,000	28,000	28,000	26,000
Salaries and wages	380,000	385,000	385,000	370,000
Supplies	32,000	30,000	31,000	33,000
Travel and entertainment	50,000	45,000	40,000	60,000
Total operating expenses	£580,000	£549,000	£616,000	£593,000
Other income				
Interest income	-5,000	-5,000	-3,000	-1,000
Interest expense	25,000	25,000	30,000	**39,000**
Total other income	£20,000	£20,000	£27,000	£38,000
Net income	£50,000	£146,000	£39,000	£89,000

The report shown in the sample reveals several issues that might not have been visible if the report had only spanned a single period. These issues are:

- *Cost of goods sold.* This cost is consistently 35% of sales until Quarter 4, when it jumps to 40%.
- *Advertising.* There was no advertising cost in Quarter 2 and double the amount of the normal £30,000 quarterly expense in Quarter 3. The cause could be a missing supplier invoice in Quarter 2 that was received and recorded in Quarter 3.
- *Rent.* The rent increased by £10,000 in Quarter 3, which may indicate a scheduled increase in the rent agreement.
- *Interest expense.* The interest expense jumps in Quarter 3 and does so again in Quarter 4, while interest income declined over the same periods. This indicates a large increase in debt.

In short, the multi-period income statement is an excellent tool for spotting anomalies in the presented information from period to period.

How to Construct the Income Statement

If an accounting software package is being used, it is quite easy to construct an income statement. Just access the report writing module, select the needed time period for the income statement, and print it.

> **Tip:** If a report writer is being used to create an income statement in the accounting software, there is a good chance that the first draft of the report will be wrong, due to some accounts being missed or duplicated. To ensure that the income statement is correct, compare it to the default income statement report that is usually provided with the accounting software, or compare the net profit or loss on the report to the current year earnings figure listed in the equity section of the balance sheet. If there is a discrepancy, the income statement is incorrect.

The situation is more complex if the income statement is to be created by hand. This involves the following steps:

1. Create the trial balance report.
2. List each account pertaining to the income statement in a separate column of the trial balance.
3. Aggregate these line items into those to be reported in the income statement as a separate line item.
4. Shift the result into the company's preferred income statement format.

The following example illustrates the construction of an income statement.

EXAMPLE

The accounting software for Lowry Locomotion breaks down at the end of July, and the controller has to create the financial statements by hand. He has a copy of Lowry's trial balance, which is shown below. He transfers this information to an electronic spreadsheet, creates separate columns for accounts to include in the income statement, and copies those balances into these columns. This leaves a number of accounts related to the balance sheet, which he can ignore for the purposes of creating the income statement.

Lowry Locomotion Extended Trial Balance

	Adjusted Trial Balance		Income Statement		Aggregation	
	Debit	Credit	Debit	Credit	Debit	Credit
Cash	£60,000					
Accounts receivable	230,000					
Inventory	300,000					
Fixed assets (net)	210,000					
Accounts payable		£90,000				
Accrued liabilities		75,000				
Notes payable		420,000				
Equity		350,000				
Revenue		450,000		£450,000		£450,000
Cost of goods sold	290,000		£290,000		£290,000	
Salaries expense	225,000		225,000		245,000	
Payroll tax expense	20,000		20,000			
Rent expense	35,000		35,000			
Other expenses	15,000		15,000		50,000	
Totals	£1,385,000	£1,385,000	£585,000	£450,000	£585,000	£450,000

In the "Aggregation" columns of the extended trial balance, the controller has aggregated the expenses for salaries and payroll taxes into the salaries expense line, and aggregated the rent expense and other expenses into the other expenses line. He then transfers this information into the following condensed income statement:

Lowry Locomotion
Income Statement
For the month ended July 31, 20X1

Revenue	£450,000
Cost of goods sold	290,000
Salaries expenses	245,000
Other expenses	50,000
Net loss	-£135,000

Overview of the Statement of Changes in Equity

The statement of changes in equity reconciles changes in the equity classification in the balance sheet within an accounting period. The statement has a more specialized use than the income statement and balance sheet, and so tends to be the least-read of the financial statements. The statement of changes in equity should include the following line items:

- Total comprehensive income for the period attributable to owners of the parent entity
- Total comprehensive income for the period attributable to non-controlling interests (if any)

- The effects of retrospective application or restatement for each component of equity with separate line items for changes in accounting policies and from the correction of errors
- Changes due to profit or loss, other comprehensive income, and owner transactions for each component of equity, in a reconciliation format

The following example shows a simplified format for the statement.

EXAMPLE

The controller of Lowry Locomotion assembles the following statement of changes in equity to accompany his issuance of the financial statements of the company:

Lowry Locomotion
Statement of Changes in Equity
For the year ended 12/31/20X3

	Share Capital	Retained Earnings	Cash Flow Hedges	Total Equity
Balance at 1/1/20X3	£1,000,000	£450,000	-£20,000	£1,430,000
Changes in accounting policy		-30,000		-30,000
Restated balance	1,000,000	420,000	-20,000	1,400,000
Changes in equity for 20X3				
Dividends		-100,000		-100,000
Total comprehensive income		85,000	5,000	90,000
Balance at 12/31/20X3	£1,000,000	£405,000	-£15,000	£1,390,000

Income Statement Disclosures

The financial statements should include a set of disclosures, commonly called *notes*, that further clarify the contents of the information presented within the statements. These notes can include a broad range of information, depending upon the types of transactions in which a business engages. The minimum set of information that should be included in the notes is as follows:

- *Accounting policies*. Describe those accounting policies of the entity that are relevant to user understanding of the financial statements.
- *Basis of preparation*. Note the basis under which the financial statements were prepared. Examples of measurement bases are historical cost, current cost, and fair value. If multiple bases are used, indicate the categories of assets and liabilities to which each basis applies.
- *Capital management*. Describe how the business manages its capital, for which the following items are required:
  - The company's objectives, policies, and processes for managing capital
  - The nature of any externally-imposed capital requirements

- o The consequences of non-compliance when the business has not complied with externally-imposed capital requirements
- o A quantitative summary of what the company considers to be capital (some companies choose to include debt in their definition of capital)
- o Any changes in the capital base or management policies from the previous period
- *Change of period.* If a business alters its fiscal year end, it must disclose the reason for the change, and note that comparable-period amounts presented in the financial statements are not entirely comparable.
- *Dividends.* Note the amount of dividends recognized as distributions to owners, as well as the related amount of dividends per share. Also note the amount of any cumulative preference shares not recognized, and the amount of any dividends proposed or declared that were not recognized as a distribution during the period.
- *Domicile.* Note the domicile of the business and its legal form, and the address of its registered office.
- *Estimation uncertainty.* Describe any estimates made about which there is uncertainty that could lead to a material adjustment in the carrying amount of the entity's assets or liabilities within the next year, including their nature and carrying amount. The disclosure could include the range of possible outcomes and the expected resolution. Examples of these estimates are the amount of inventory obsolescence that may be triggered by technology changes, and provisions related to the outcome of a lawsuit.
- *Judgments.* Describe the judgments management has made (other than estimations) in order to apply accounting policies, and which have a significant impact on the amounts recognized in the period. For example, a judgment may be involved in the proper recognition of revenue when a company is providing lease financing to a buyer.
- *Life span.* If the entity has a limited life, state the expected duration of its life.
- *Other comprehensive income.* Present an analysis of other comprehensive income by item, for each component of equity.
- *Nature of operations.* Describe the nature of the operations and principal activities of the business.
- *Parent.* Note the name of the corporate parent, and the ultimate parent of the group owning the business.
- *Puttable financial instruments.* If there are any puttable financial instruments that are classified as equity, disclose the amount classified as equity, the company's objectives for redeeming these instruments, the related amount of cash flow caused by the redemption, and how the cash outflow related to the redemption was determined.
- *Reclassification.* When there is a reclassification of items in the financial statements and this includes reclassification of the comparative periods,

disclose the nature of and reason for the change, as well as the amount of each line item reclassified. If it is impracticable to reclassify comparative periods, disclose the reason why, and the nature of the adjustments that would have been made if reclassification had occurred.

- *Reclassified financial instrument.* If a financial instrument has been reclassified between the liability and equity classifications, disclose the amount reclassified, as well as the timing of and reason for the change.
- *Reserves.* Describe the nature and purpose of each equity reserve (if any).
- *Share capital.* For each class of share capital that has been issued, disclose the following items:
  - The number of authorized shares
  - The number of shares issued and fully paid
  - The number of shares issued and not fully paid
  - The par value per share
  - A reconciliation of the number of shares outstanding at the beginning and end of the period
  - Any rights or restrictions associated with the shares
  - The number of shares held by the entity or its subsidiaries or associates
  - The number of shares reserved for later issuance under the terms of any agreements for the sale of shares, as well as the details of those agreements

EXAMPLE

The Close Call Company discloses the following information about its management of capital:

> The company's objective when managing capital is to expand the business as rapidly as possible in additional cities, which involves the aggressive use of all available funds, including maximization of the amount of available debt. The management team realizes that such an aggressive stance puts the business at increased risk of a liquidity crisis, but it believes that the rapid expansion enhances the long-term value of the company to its shareholders.

> The strategy for capital management precludes the payment of dividends in the short term. Also, if there is an immediate opportunity to profitably employ additional funds, the company is prepared to sell additional shares, though only if the opportunity is likely to result in a net increase in value per share.

> The company monitors its debt-to-equity ratio on an ongoing basis. The objective of management is to maintain a debt-to-equity ratio of between 3:1 and 4:1. The actual ratio at the end of 20X4 was 3.2:1, and 3.6:1 in 20X5.

In addition to the preceding disclosures, note any other items required under IFRS that are not presented anywhere else in the financial statements, as well as any items that are *not* required, but which are relevant to understanding the financial statements.

Finally, IFRS mandates that notes be cross-referenced in a systematic manner, so that users can easily refer from financial statement line items to the relevant explanatory text in the notes. The following order of presentation is recommended by IFRS for notes:

1. A statement that the business complies with IFRS
2. A summary of significant accounting policies used
3. Supporting discussions of information presented in the financial statements, presented in the order in which each of the financial statements were presented
4. Other disclosures

Summary

IFRS is not overly rigorous in requiring a specific form of presentation for the financial statements. However, this does not mean that a business should routinely modify the layouts of its financial reports, since doing so may confuse readers, and will certainly require significant restatements in all comparable periods that are presented. Consequently, the best approach to developing a financial statement presentation is to settle upon a reasonable format early, and to only make subsequent changes following lengthy deliberation regarding how those changes will improve the content of the financial statements.

The presentation of the statement of cash flows is included in the Statement of Cash Flows chapter. This separate treatment is used in order to match the separate treatment given by IFRS to the statement of cash flows in its IAS 7, *Statement of Cash Flows*.

Chapter 3
Statement of Cash Flows

Introduction

The statement of cash flows is the least used of the financial statements, and may not be issued at all for internal financial reporting purposes. The recipients of financial statements seem to be mostly concerned with the profit information on the income statement, and to a lesser degree with the financial position information on the balance sheet. Nonetheless, the cash flows on the statement of cash flows can provide valuable information, especially when combined with the other elements of the financial statements.

This chapter addresses the two formats used for the statement of cash flows, related disclosures, and how to assemble the information needed for the statement.

IFRS Source Document

- IAS 7, *Statement of Cash Flows*

Overview of the Statement of Cash Flows

The statement of cash flows contains information about the flows of cash into and out of a company during the same period covered by the income statement; in particular, it shows the extent of those company activities that generate and use cash and cash equivalents. It is particularly useful for assessing the differences between net income and the related cash receipts and payments. IFRS requires that a statement of cash flows be presented as an integral part of the financial statements for all periods in which the statements are presented. The following general requirements apply to the statement of cash flows:

- *Classifications.* Report net cash provided or used in the categories of operating, investing, and financing activities.
- *Format.* Entities are encouraged to use the direct method of report presentation (see the next section).

The primary activities reported on the statement of cash flows are:

- *Operating activities.* These are an entity's primary revenue-producing activities. Examples of cash inflows from operating activities are cash receipts from the sale of goods or services, royalties, and commissions, as well as tax refunds. Examples of cash outflows for operating activities are payments to employees and suppliers, taxes paid, and insurance premium payments. Loans made by financial institutions are considered operating activities, since lending is the primary revenue-generating activity of these entities.

- *Investing activities.* These generally involve the acquisition and disposal of resources that will generate future income and cash flows for a business. Only an expenditure that results in a recorded asset can qualify as an investing activity. Examples of cash inflows from investing activities are cash receipts from the sale of fixed assets, the sale of the debt or equity instruments issued by other entities, the repayment of loans by third parties, and payments under forward contracts and futures contracts. Examples of cash outflows from investing activities are cash payments to purchase fixed assets, acquire debt or equity instruments, make loans to other parties, and payments made under forward contracts and futures contracts.

- *Financing activities.* These are the activities resulting in alterations to the amount of contributed equity and an entity's borrowings. Examples of cash inflows from financing activities are cash receipts from the sale of an entity's own equity instruments or from issuing debt. Examples of cash outflows from financing activities are cash outlays for share repurchases and the pay-down of outstanding debt.

EXAMPLE

Mole Industries has a rent-to-purchase feature on its line of trench digging equipment, where customers can initially rent the equipment and then apply the rental payments to an outright purchase. The rental of equipment could be considered an investing activity. However, since the company earns the bulk of its cash flow from the sale of equipment, the cash flows are placed within the operating activities classification.

Tip: Create a policy regarding how certain items are to be classified within the statement of cash flows. Otherwise, there may be some variation from period to period in categorizing items as cash equivalents or investments.

When a futures contract, forward contract, or some similar arrangement is accounted for as a hedge, the cash flows associated with the hedge are given the same classification as the asset or liability being hedged.

When there are cash flows arising from certain activities, they can be reported in the statement of cash flows on a net basis, rather than separately showing cash inflows and outflows. The following items can be reported on a net basis:

- Cash payments and receipts made on behalf of customers, where the cash flows relate to the activities of the customer, rather than the activities of the reporting entity. An example is rents collected on behalf of a property owner, and which are then remitted to the property owner.

- Cash payments and receipts related to items where there is a short maturity, rapid turnover, and large amounts. An example is borrowings having a maturity of three months or less.

- Cash payments and receipts related to the acceptance and repayment of fixed-maturity deposits by a financial institution.
- Deposits placed by a financial institution with other financial institutions, and the subsequent withdrawal of those deposits.
- Loans made to customers by a financial institution, and the repayment of those loans.

The following situations are accorded special treatment under IFRS:

- *Cash and cash equivalents.* Present a reconciliation of the amount of ending cash and cash equivalents shown in the statement of cash flows to the same items appearing in the balance sheet.
- *Control change.* If there is a change in control of another entity, classify the related cash flows, in aggregate, as investing activities. If there are cash flows related to a change in ownership interest, but which does not result in a loss of control, classify them as financing activities.
- *Foreign currency gains and losses.* There may be unrealized gains and losses on changes in foreign currency exchange rates. If so, report these amounts in the statement of cash flows within a reconciliation of the beginning and ending balances of cash and cash equivalents.
- *Foreign currency reporting.* Record transactions in a foreign currency in the reporting entity's functional currency, using the exchange rate on the date of each cash flow. Similarly, the cash flows of a subsidiary that are recorded in a foreign currency should be translated at the exchange rate on the date of each cash flow. The weighted average exchange rate for a reporting period may be used as a reasonable substitute for the exchange rate on the date of each cash flow.
- *Income taxes.* Separately disclose income taxes. It is normally classified within the operating activities section, unless it can be specifically associated with one of the other two sections of the statement of cash flows.
- *Interest and dividends.* Separately disclose cash flows related to interest and dividends, and consistently record them within either the operating, investing, or financing activities sections. Also, the total amount of interest paid in the period should be disclosed within the statement of cash flows; the amount disclosed should include any interest that may have been capitalized during the period.
- *Non-cash transaction.* The effects of a non-cash transaction are excluded from the statement of cash flows. Examples of such transactions are the conversion of debt to equity and paying for an acquiree with stock.

Either the *direct method* or the *indirect method* can be used to present the statement of cash flows. These methods are described in the following sections.

The Direct Method

The direct method of presenting the statement of cash flows shows specific cash flows in the operating activities section of the report. IFRS does not rigidly enforce a specific set of line items within this type of report, but consider using the presentation format shown in the following example.

EXAMPLE

Lowry Locomotion constructs the following statement of cash flows using the direct method:

Lowry Locomotion
Statement of Cash Flows
For the year ended 12/31/20X1

Cash flows from operating activities		
Cash receipts from customers	£45,800,000	
Cash paid to suppliers	-29,800,000	
Cash paid to employees	-11,200,000	
Cash generated from operations	4,800,000	
Interest paid	-310,000	
Income taxes paid	-1,700,000	
Net cash from operating activities		£2,790,000
Cash flows from investing activities		
Purchase of fixed assets	-580,000	
Proceeds from sale of equipment	110,000	
Net cash used in investing activities		-470,000
Cash flows from financing activities		
Proceeds from issuance of share capital	1,000,000	
Proceeds from issuance of long-term debt	500,000	
Principal payments under capital lease obligation	-10,000	
Dividends paid	-450,000	
Net cash used in financing activities		1,040,000
Net increase in cash and cash equivalents		3,360,000
Cash and cash equivalents at beginning of period		1,640,000
Cash and cash equivalents at end of period		£5,000,000

A company should report the cash inflows and outflows for investing and financing activities separately within the statement of cash flows. Thus, cash payments for the purchase of fixed assets should be reported on a separate line item from cash receipts from the sale of fixed assets.

IFRS encourages the use of the direct method, but it is rarely used, for the excellent reason that the information in it is difficult to assemble; companies simply do not collect and store information in the manner required for this format. Instead, they use the indirect method, which is described in the following section.

The Indirect Method

Under the indirect method of presenting the statement of cash flows, the presentation begins with net income or loss, with subsequent additions to or deductions from that amount for non-cash revenue and expense items, resulting in cash generated from operating activities. This means that the effects of the deferral or accrual of expenses in the income statement must be removed, as well as such non-cash expenses as depreciation and amortization, so that cash flows can be more readily observed.

The format of the indirect method appears in the following example.

EXAMPLE

Lowry Locomotion constructs the following statement of cash flows using the indirect method:

Lowry Locomotion
Statement of Cash Flows
For the year ended 12/31/20X2

Cash flows from operating activities		
Net income		£3,000,000
Adjustments for:		
Depreciation and amortization	£125,000	
Provision for losses on accounts receivable	20,000	
Gain on sale of facility	-65,000	
		80,000
Increase in trade receivables	-250,000	
Decrease in inventories	325,000	
Decrease in trade payables	-50,000	
		25,000
Cash generated from operations		3,105,000
Cash flows from investing activities		
Purchase of fixed assets	-500,000	
Proceeds from sale of equipment	35,000	
Net cash used in investing activities		-465,000
Cash flows from financing activities		
Proceeds from issuance of share capital	150,000	
Proceeds from issuance of long-term debt	175,000	
Dividends paid	-45,000	
Net cash used in financing activities		280,000
Net increase in cash and cash equivalents		2,920,000
Cash and cash equivalents at beginning of period		2,080,000
Cash and cash equivalents at end of period		£5,000,000

The indirect method is very popular, because the information required for it is relatively easily assembled from the accounts that a business normally maintains.

How to Prepare the Statement of Cash Flows

The most commonly-used format for the statement of cash flows is the indirect method (as described in the preceding section). The general layout of an indirect method statement of cash flows is shown below, along with an explanation of the source of the information in the statement.

Company Name
Statement of Cash Flows
For the year ended 12/31/20XX

Line Item	Derivation
Cash flows from operating activities	
Net income	From the net income line on the income statement
Adjustment for:	
Depreciation and amortization	From the corresponding line items in the income statement
Provision for losses on accounts receivable	From the change in the allowance for doubtful accounts in the period
Gain/loss on sale of facility	From the gain/loss accounts in the income statement
Increase/decrease in trade receivables	Change in trade receivables during the period, from the balance sheet
Increase/decrease in inventories	Change in inventories during the period, from the balance sheet
Increase/decrease in trade payables	Change in trade payables during the period, from the balance sheet
Cash generated from operations	Summary of the preceding items in this section
Cash flows from investing activities	
Purchase of fixed assets	Itemized in the fixed asset accounts during the period
Proceeds from sale of fixed assets	Itemized in the fixed asset accounts during the period
Net cash used in investing activities	Summary of the preceding items in this section
Cash flows from financing activities	
Proceeds from issuance of share capital	Net increase in the share capital and additional paid-in capital accounts during the period
Proceeds from issuance of long-term debt	Itemized in the long-term debt account during the period
Dividends paid	Itemized in the retained earnings account during the period
Net cash used in financing activities	Summary of the preceding items in this section
Net change in cash and cash equivalents	Summary of all preceding subtotals

A less commonly-used format for the statement of cash flows is the direct method. The general layout of this version is shown below, along with an explanation of the source of the information in the statement.

Statement of Cash Flows

Company Name
Statement of Cash Flows
For the year ended 12/31/20XX

Line Item	Derivation
Cash flows from operating activities	
Cash receipts from customers	Summary of the cash receipts journal for the period
Cash paid to suppliers	Summary of the cash disbursements journal for the period (less the financing and income tax payments noted below)
Cash paid to employees	Summary of the payroll journal for the period
Cash generated from operations	Summary of the preceding items in this section
Interest paid	Itemized in the cash disbursements journal
Income taxes paid	Itemized in the cash disbursements journal
Net cash from operating activities	Summary of the preceding items in this section
Cash flows from investing activities	
Purchase of fixed assets	Itemized in the fixed asset accounts during the period
Proceeds from sale of fixed assets	Itemized in the fixed asset accounts during the period
Net cash used in investing activities	Summary of the preceding items in this section
Cash flows from financing activities	
Proceeds from issuance of share capital	Net increase in the share capital and additional paid-in capital accounts during the period
Proceeds from issuance of long-term debt	Itemized in the long-term debt account during the period
Principal payment under capital leases	Itemized in the capital leases liability account during the period
Dividends paid	Itemized in the retained earnings account during the period
Net cash used in financing activities	Summary of the preceding items in this section
Net change in cash and cash equivalents	Summary of all preceding subtotals

As can be seen from the explanations for either the indirect or direct methods, the statement of cash flows is more difficult to create than the income statement and balance sheet. In fact, a complete statement may require a substantial supporting spreadsheet that shows the details for each line item in the statement.

If the company's accounting software contains a template for the statement of cash flows, use it. The information may not be aggregated quite correctly, and it may not contain all of the line items required for the statement, but it *will* produce most of the information needed, and is much easier to modify than the alternative of creating the statement entirely by hand.

Disclosures for the Statement of Cash Flows

The following disclosures are required by IFRS, and are associated with the statement of cash flows:

- *Cash not available for use*. Disclose the amount of any cash and cash equivalent balances that are not available for use. An example is when cash is held by a subsidiary in a foreign country that does not allow the repatriation of cash.
- *Control changes*. If there is a change in control of another entity, disclose:
  - The total consideration paid or received
  - The amount paid or received in cash and cash equivalents
  - The amount of cash and cash equivalents over which control has been gained or lost
  - The amount of other assets and liabilities over which control has been gained or lost (summarized by category)
- *Policy*. Disclose the accounting policy used to determine the composition of the cash and cash equivalent line items. If there is a change in this policy, disclose the effects of the change.

IFRS also encourages, but does not require, the following disclosures:

- *Investments in capacity*. Separately state the amount of cash invested in the expansion of operating capacity, and in the maintenance of operating capacity. This disclosure reveals whether a business is re-investing a sufficient amount in its operations.
- *Segments*. Expand upon the segment requirements for publicly-held companies by stating cash flows from operating, investing, and financing activities at the reportable segment level.
- *Unused debt*. If there are unused borrowing facilities, note the amount and any restrictions on their use.

EXAMPLE

Lowry Locomotion discloses the following reconciliation of its cash and cash equivalents, as well as other issues related to its cash balances and available debt:

Cash and cash equivalents consist of cash on hand and in demand deposits, and in investments in overnight repurchase agreements. The cash and cash equivalents included in the statement of cash flows is derived from the following amounts in Lowry's balance sheet:

(000s)	20X1	20X0
Cash on hand	£950	£720
Cash in overnight repurchase agreements	4,000	3,500
Cash and cash equivalents as previously reported	4,950	4,220
Effect of exchange rate changes	50	-80
Cash and cash equivalents as restated	£5,000	£4,300

At the end of 20X1 and 20X0, £220,000 of cash equivalents were held by a subsidiary in a country that does not allow the repatriation of cash.

At December 31, 20X1, the company had £3,000,000 of unused borrowing facilities available under a line of credit arrangement that expires on June 30, 20X3.

EXAMPLE

The Close Call Company reports the following cash flow information for its two segments:

(000s)	Pedestrian Delivery	Aerial Delivery	Total
Cash flows from:			
Operating activities	£2,080	£3,460	£5,540
Investing activities	375	-120	255
Financing activities	-850	275	-575
	£1,605	£3,615	£5,220

Summary

The statement of cash flows is a useful ancillary statement that sometimes accompanies the income statement and balance sheet for internal reporting, but which is nearly always included in financial statements issued to outside parties. The report can be difficult to assemble, unless it is available as an accounting software template, which is why it tends to be treated as an occasional add-on to the other elements of the financial statements. If it will be issued, we strongly recommend using the indirect method instead of the direct method, since the information required for the direct method of presentation is not easily gathered from the accounting records.

Chapter 4
Consolidated and Separate
Financial Statements

Introduction

When a company controls one or more entities, it should consolidate the results of these entities into a set of financial statements. In this chapter, we pay particular attention to deciding whether consolidation is necessary, and then address the methodology for preparing and presenting consolidated financial statements. There is also coverage of the circumstances under which a company presents separate financial statements, and the related disclosures.

IFRS Source Documents

- IFRS 10, *Consolidated Financial Statements*
- IAS 27, *Consolidated and Separate Financial Statements*

The Control Concept

Consolidated financial statements are the financial statements of a group of entities that are presented as being those of a single economic entity. The related concepts are:
- A group is a parent entity and all of its subsidiaries
- A subsidiary is an entity that is controlled by a parent company

In short, consolidated financial statements are the combined financial statements for a parent company and its subsidiaries.

Consolidated financial statements are useful for reviewing the financial position and results of an entire group of commonly-owned businesses. Otherwise, reviewing the results of individual businesses within a group does not give an indication of the financial health of the group as a whole.

EXAMPLE

Pensive Corporation has £5,000,000 of revenues and £3,000,000 of assets appearing in its own financial statements. However, Pensive also controls five subsidiaries, which in turn have revenues of £50,000,000 and assets of £82,000,000. Clearly, it would be extremely misleading to show the financial statements of just the parent company, when the consolidated results reveal that it is really a £55 million company that controls £85 million of assets.

To decide if consolidation is necessary, a business must first determine the level of control that it exercises over another entity (the investee). Control exists only when all of the following are present:

- *Power over investee.* The business has power over the investee, which gives it the right to direct those investee activities that alter the investee's returns. Power typically comes from voting rights, but can also be based on a historical record of having exercised power over the investee. If there are several investors, the one who has power is the one who can most significantly affect the returns of the investee.
- *Returns from investee.* The business is exposed to variable returns from its investment in the investee. Multiple parties can qualify under this criterion.
- *Alter investee returns.* The business can exercise its power over the investee to alter the amount of its investment returns. An investor that acts as an agent for the investee does not control the investee.

EXAMPLE

Three companies form an investee entity that will specialize in bridge building for local governments. One of the investor companies will be responsible for preparing bid proposals to the relevant governments, while the second investor will oversee the work, and the third investor will oversee ongoing maintenance. Thus, each of the entities exercises a certain amount of control over the investee during different stages of the projects that will be performed. For consolidation purposes, each of the investors must decide whether it directs those activities of the investee that most significantly affect its returns. Factors to consider include who controls the profit margins of the investee, the difficulty of winning bids, and who controls bridge construction and maintenance.

There may be situations where the preceding indicators of control are not present, but there is evidence that the investor has a special relationship with the investee that essentially gives it control. The following factors may indicate the presence of a control relationship:

- *Close linking.* A large part of investee activities involve the investor, or are conducted on its behalf.
- *Dependency.* The investee is dependent on the investor in such areas as funding, guarantees, technology, raw materials, licenses, and technical expertise.
- *Return on investment.* The returns of the investor are greater than its ownership share of the investee.
- *Shared managers.* The investee has key managers who used to be or still are employees of the investor.

An investor may not have control over an investee if there are barriers to the practical exercise of the rights of the investor. Any of the following examples could keep control from being exercised:

- Legal or regulatory requirements
- No mechanism for exercising rights held
- Penalties or financial incentives
- The conversion price or terms associated with convertible instruments
- Tightly defined conditions under which control can be exercised

EXAMPLE

Ligature Corporation has entered into an agreement to buy the shares of an investor in Malleable Manufacturing. When combined with Ligature's existing 25% ownership of Malleable, the company will have outright majority ownership. However, for tax reasons, the sale will not take place until the beginning of the next calendar year, which is four months away. Since Ligature does not have the current ability to direct the activities of Malleable, it does not exercise control.

An investor may effectively have control over an investee, even in the absence of outright majority ownership, if the remaining ownership of the investee is widely dispersed. This means that many other investors would have to act in concert to override the wishes of the primary investor.

EXAMPLE

Ligature Corporation acquires 44% of the outstanding common shares of Linden Limited. Linden is publicly held, which has contributed to the wide dispersal of its remaining share holdings across several hundred additional investors. The other investors have no mechanism for coordinating their actions, and have no history of doing so. Under these conditions, the 44% ownership stake of Ligature may very well give it effective control over Linden.

EXAMPLE

Ligature Corporation owns 40% of the outstanding common shares of Suture Corporation. Two other investors each own 30% of the remaining shares of Suture. Since the two other investors can combine to block any efforts by Ligature to control Suture, it does not appear that Ligature has control over Suture.

An investor with a minority interest in an investee may exercise control over an investee if it has the right to acquire additional shares. This situation may arise through a contractual arrangement with another investor, or through the investor's holdings of debt instruments that can be converted into investee shares. However, this determination depends on the circumstances, since the right to acquire shares may also be unlikely, if the price at which they can be purchased is substantially higher than their current market price.

EXAMPLE

Smithy Ironworks currently holds 25% of the shares of Alum Smelters, and has the right to buy an additional 40% of the outstanding shares from the current owner of Alum at any point during the next year. However, the price at which Smithy can purchase these additional shares is double the current market price. Consequently, Smithy does not have substantive control over Alum.

An investor that has control over an investee may choose to delegate its authority to another party. This other party is considered an agent of the investor, and so should not consolidate its results with those of the investee. When the right to make decisions is shifted to an agent, the investor is considered to retain control over the investee via its agent.

An agent relationship is definitively proven to exist when the investor can remove the agent without cause. An agent relationship is likely when the party making decisions on behalf of investors must obtain their consent for certain actions. Also, an agent relationship is not considered to exist unless the party making decisions is being paid in accordance with the services provided, and the compensation agreement contains those terms normally found in an agent relationship. Conversely, if the party making decisions holds a significant interest in the investee, it may not be acting in the role of an agent.

A parent company does not have to present consolidated financial statements under the following circumstances:
- If the parent is a subsidiary of another entity;
- All of the owners of the parent have been notified that consolidated financial statements will not be produced; and
- The owners do not object to not receiving financial statements.
- In addition, the entity cannot be publicly held.
- In addition, either the entity's parent or the ultimate parent of the group must produce consolidated financial statements that are available to the public.

If the parent entity loses control over a subsidiary, the parent should take the following steps to account for the change:
- Remove (derecognize) the former subsidiary's assets and liabilities from the consolidated financial statements. Assets and liabilities are derecognized at their carrying amounts on the date when control is lost.
- If a gain or loss had previously been recognized in other comprehensive income, reclassify it to profit or loss when the related assets and liabilities are disposed of.
- Recognize any remaining investment in the subsidiary that was retained, at its fair value on the date when control was lost.
- If there is a gain or loss associated with the loss of control of the former subsidiary, recognize it at this time.

Consolidation Accounting

Consolidation accounting is the process of combining the financial results of several subsidiary companies into the combined financial results of the parent company. The following steps document the consolidation accounting process flow:

1. *Adjust for dates.* If the reporting period of a subsidiary varies from that of the parent, the subsidiary prepares additional information to effectively match the dates of its reported results to those of the parent. If this is impracticable, the parent instead adjusts the financial statements of the subsidiary for any significant transactions occurring during the period in question. Under no circumstances can the date differential be longer than three months.

2. *Adjust for accounting policies.* If a subsidiary records transactions using a different accounting policy than that used by the parent entity, adjust the recognition to match the accounting policy of the parent.

3. *Combine similar items.* Combine similar assets, liabilities, equity, revenue, expense, and cash flow items from the various subsidiaries and the parent entity.

4. *Record intercompany loans.* If the parent company has been consolidating the cash balances of its subsidiaries into an investment account, record intercompany loans from the subsidiaries to the parent company. Also record an interest income allocation for the interest earned on consolidated investments from the parent company down to the subsidiaries.

5. *Charge corporate overhead.* If the parent company allocates its overhead costs to subsidiaries, calculate the amount of the allocation and charge it to the various subsidiaries.

6. *Charge payables.* If the parent company runs a consolidated payables operation, verify that all accounts payable recorded during the period have been appropriately charged to the various subsidiaries.

7. *Charge payroll expenses.* If the parent company has been using a common paymaster system to pay all employees throughout the company, ensure that the proper allocation of payroll expenses has been made to all subsidiaries.

8. *Complete adjusting entries.* At the subsidiary and corporate levels, record any adjusting entries needed to properly record revenue and expense transactions in the correct period.

9. *Investigate asset, liability, and equity account balances.* Verify that the contents of all asset, liability, and equity accounts for both the subsidiaries and the corporate parent are correct, and adjust as necessary.

10. *Review subsidiary financial statements.* Print and review the financial statements for each subsidiary, and investigate any items that appear to be unusual or incorrect. Make adjustments as necessary.

11. *Eliminate intercompany transactions.* If there have been any intercompany transactions, reverse them at the parent company level to eliminate their effects from the consolidated financial statements.

12. *Eliminate investments.* Reverse the parent's recorded investment amount in each of the subsidiaries, as well as the parent's portion of the equity recorded in the accounting records of each subsidiary.

13. *Present non-controlling interests.* Present the amount of non-controlling interests in the equity section of the consolidated balance sheet, in a line item separate from other items. If there were changes in the amounts of these interests, adjust the carrying amounts of the controlling and non-controlling interests to reflect the changes.

14. *Attribute profits and losses.* When there are non-controlling interests, separately attribute profit or loss and all line items within other comprehensive income to non-controlling interests and the owners of the parent.

15. *Review parent financial statements.* Print and review the financial statements for the parent company, and investigate any items that appear to be unusual or incorrect. Make adjustments as necessary.

16. *Record income tax liability.* If the company earned a profit, record an income tax liability. It may be necessary to do so at the subsidiary level, as well.

17. *Close subsidiary books.* Depending upon the accounting software in use, it may be necessary to access the financial records of each subsidiary and flag them as closed. This prevents any additional transactions from being recorded in the accounting period being closed.

18. *Close parent company books.* Flag the parent company accounting period as closed, so that no additional transactions can be reported in the accounting period being closed.

19. *Issue financial statements.* Print and distribute the financial statements of the parent company.

Tip: If losses have been recorded on intercompany transactions, it is possible that an asset impairment exists. If so, recognize the related loss on impairment in the consolidated financial statements.

If a subsidiary uses a different currency as its operating currency, an additional consolidation accounting step is to convert its financial statements into the reporting currency of the parent company.

When creating consolidated financial statements, the following accounting rules apply:

- *Policies.* Ensure that uniform accounting policies are being used across the various subsidiaries in the treatment of similar transactions and events.

- *Relevant dates.* Consolidation should only be performed from the date when the investor gains control over the investee, and stops when control over the investee ceases.

- *Loss of control.* If the parent loses control over the investee, the parent completes the following tasks:
    - Removes the assets and liabilities of the former subsidiary from its consolidated financial statements.

    o Removes the carrying amounts of any non-controlling interests and those elements of other comprehensive income attributable to the non-controlling interests from its consolidated financial statements.

    o Recognizes any retained interest in the subsidiary at its fair value.

    o Recognizes any amounts in other comprehensive income that relate to the subsidiary, as though the parent had directly disposed of the underlying assets and liabilities. In some cases, recognition means that a balance in other comprehensive income is shifted directly into retained earnings.

    o Depending on the circumstances of the preceding items, the parent may recognize a gain or loss in profit or loss that relates to the loss of control.

Separate Financial Statements

A parent entity may sometimes elect or be required to issue separate financial statements. Separate financial statements are the financial statements of a parent entity, in which investments in subsidiaries are recorded at their cost, as financial instruments, or using the equity method. Thus, consolidated financial statements are not presented. The following accounting applies under these circumstances:

- The same investment accounting methodology must be applied consistently to each category of investments.
- If an investment is held for sale, record it as per the guidance in the Assets Held for Sale and Discontinued Operations chapter.
- If an investment is recorded at its fair value or cost, record it as per the guidance in the Financial Instruments chapter.
- The parent recognizes a dividend from another entity when the parent's right to receive the dividend has been established. The dividend is recognized in profit or loss, unless the parent has elected to use the equity method; in the latter case, the dividend reduces the carrying amount of the parent's investment.

When a parent entity does not present consolidated financial statements, it should disclose the following information in the notes accompanying its financial statements:

- *Status*. The fact that separate financial statements have been issued, and the exemption under which they were issued.
- *Identification*. The name and principal place of business of the entity whose consolidated financial statements are available for public use, and where these statements can be obtained.
- *Investments*. An itemization of the significant investments of the parent in subsidiaries, joint ventures, and associates, including their names, principal places of business, and the parent's ownership percentages.
- *Methodology*. The methodology upon which the accounting for these investments is based.

Summary

The bulk of this chapter has been concerned with the determination of whether an investor has control over an investee, which then triggers consolidation accounting. In reality, this is usually an easy matter to discern, and is based on a simple majority of shares held. If such is not the case, and management wishes to proceed with consolidation accounting, it is possible that the consolidation will be challenged by the investor's auditors. In anticipation of such a challenge, be sure to fully document the reasons why control is considered to have been established, and any changes in this determination over successive reporting periods. If the issue of control appears to be unusually difficult to discern, consult with the company's auditors in advance, to gain their perspective on the issue.

Chapter 5
Accounting Policies, Estimate Changes
and Errors

Introduction

From time to time, a company will find that it must alter its accounting policies to reflect the impact of a new IFRS, or change a policy for internal reasons. There may also be an ongoing series of changes to the accounting estimates needed to formulate financial statements. Finally, there may be occasional accounting errors from prior periods that must be corrected. In this chapter, we describe how to account for and disclose these situations. Consistent treatment of these issues is needed to ensure that a company's financial statements remain comparable over time.

IFRS Source Document

- IAS 8, *Accounting Policies, Changes in Accounting Estimates and Errors*

Accounting Policies

Many accounting policies are derived internally from the nature of a business and the types of accounting transactions that it routinely records. However, an accounting policy may also be externally imposed. When an IFRS specifically applies to a transaction, the accounting policies that are defined for that transaction must incorporate IFRS. The incorporation of IFRS into accounting policies is only required when the effect of doing so is material to the resulting financial statements.

In a situation where there is no IFRS upon which an accounting policy can be based, management should develop policies that result in relevant and reliable financial information. In particular, the policies should yield unbiased information that reflects the economic substance of transactions, and which faithfully represent the financial performance, position, and cash flows of a business.

In the development of accounting policies, when IFRS does not provide guidance, management can consider the pronouncements of other standard-setting bodies, accounting literature, and industry practices.

Once accounting policies have been developed, a business should apply them consistently for similar transactions. Doing so also makes sense from an efficiency perspective, since having a smaller set of broadly-applicable accounting policies makes it easier to manage the accounting function.

In general, accounting policies are not changed, since doing so alters the comparability of accounting transactions over time. Only change a policy when the update is required by IFRS, or when the change will result in more reliable and relevant information.

If the initial application of an IFRS mandates that a business change an accounting policy, account for the change under the transition requirements stated in the IFRS. When there are no transition requirements that accompany an IFRS, a business should apply the change retrospectively. Retrospective application means that the accounting records be adjusted as though the new accounting policy had always been in place, so that the opening equity balance of all periods presented incorporates the effects of the change.

There are cases where it may be impracticable to determine the retrospective effect of a change in accounting policy. If so, apply the new policy to the carrying amounts of affected assets and liabilities as of the beginning of the earliest period to which the policy can be applied, along with the offsetting equity account. If the effect of a policy change cannot be determined for any prior period, then do so from the earliest date on which it is practicable to apply the new policy. When making policy changes, adjust all other affected information in the notes that accompany the financial statements.

Tip: Thoroughly document the reason for any change in an accounting policy, since it will likely be reviewed by the company's auditors.

EXAMPLE

Armadillo Industries changes from the last in, first out method of inventory accounting to the first in, first out method. Doing so results in an increase in the cost of ending inventory in the preceding period, which in turn increases net profits for that period. Altering the inventory balance is a direct effect of the change in policy. The calculation of the change in the prior period income statement, net of income tax effects, is:

(000s)	Original Balances	Adjustment	Restated Balances
Revenue	£17,980		£17,980
Cost of goods sold	13,450	-£450	13,000
Selling and administrative expenses	3,605		3,605
Net profit	£925	-£450	£1,375

Changes in Accounting Estimates

When financial statements are produced, a common element of the production process is to estimate a number of items, such as the amount of the reserves for bad debt and inventory obsolescence, as well as fixed asset useful lives and the fair value of various assets and liabilities. It is entirely possible, if not expected, that these estimates will change over time as new information is received and business conditions change. Consequently, there will be an ongoing series of changes in accounting estimates.

Because changes to accounting estimates are a natural and ongoing adjustment to the process of creating financial statements, they are not considered to relate to prior periods. Consequently, changes in accounting estimates are only dealt with on a prospective (go-forward) basis. This means that these items are recorded in the period of the change in estimate and future periods. There is no change to the financial statements for prior periods.

EXAMPLE

The credit manager of Close Call Company reviews all open accounts receivable, and concludes that the allowance for doubtful accounts is overstated by £50,000. The allowance is therefore reduced by that amount, which is a change in accounting estimate that only impacts the current period.

The fixed asset accountant reviews the projected useful lives of the company's fixed assets, and concludes that several assets will have shorter useful lives than had previously been estimated. Their useful lives are therefore reduced in the depreciation calculations, which results in an increase in the amount of depreciation expense recognized in the financial statements for both the current period and future periods.

In both cases, there is no retrospective change to the financial statements for prior periods.

Errors

There can be a number of errors in a set of financial statements. For example, there can be incorrect transaction measurements, incorrect presentation, and incorrect or missing disclosures in the accompanying notes. If financial statements contain material errors, or immaterial errors made with the intent of achieving a particular financial statement result, they are not considered to be in compliance with IFRS.

EXAMPLE

The preliminary income statement of the Close Call Company shows profits of £999,995. The controller makes an intentional immaterial error of £5 to increase the amount of profits to £1,000,000, at which point the management team qualifies for the company's bonus plan. In this case, the financial statements do not comply with IFRS, despite the minimal size of the error.

When material errors are made, they should be corrected under one of the following scenarios:
- If the impacted financial statement is still being reported as a comparative period, restate the financial statement in the period in which it occurred.
- If the impacted financial statement is in a prior period that is no longer being reported as a comparative period, restate the relevant opening balances for the earliest period presented.

It may not be possible to make a retrospective correction of an error if it is impracticable to determine the effect of the error. If this is the case for a prior comparative period, make the adjustment to the relevant opening balances for the current period. If it is not possible to even make the adjustment to the relevant opening balances, correct the error in the current period.

EXAMPLE

During 20X3, Rapunzel Hair Products discovers that goods on consignment with a large hair products distributor were accidentally not included in the company's ending inventory balance for 20X2, resulting in profits of £100,000 not being reported. The tax rate for the company in 20X2 was 35%. Accordingly, Rapunzel discloses the following information:

Inventory items in the amount of £180,000 that were held at a distributor under a consignment agreement were incorrectly withheld from the ending inventory balance on December 31, 20X2. The 20X2 financial statements have been restated to correct this error. The effect of the restatement is summarized below.

	Effect on 20X2
Decrease in cost of goods sold	£180,000
Increase in income tax expense	63,000
Increase in profit	£117,000
Increase in inventory	£180,000
Increase in income taxes payable	63,000
Increase in equity	£117,000

Impracticability of Application

There are a number of circumstances that make it impracticable to adjust the financial statements for prior periods to account for policy changes or error corrections. For example, the chart of accounts may not have been structured in earlier periods to collect certain types of information. While it may be possible to eventually reconstruct the necessary information from historical records, doing so may not be cost-effective.

Another concern with restatements is that they should only be made based on evidence that existed in the prior accounting period(s), and which would have been available when those statements were authorized for issuance. Conversely, it is *not* allowable to make prior period adjustments based on information that was not available at that time.

Disclosures for Policies, Estimate Changes, and Errors

There are a number of variations on the disclosures required for the different types of accounting policies, estimate changes, and errors, so we address each one within the following sub-sections.

Accounting Policies

When a new IFRS is initially applied and its application impacts prior periods, the current period, or future periods, disclose the following information:
- The name of the IFRS
- Whether the change in accounting policy is in accordance with the transitional guidance in the IFRS
- The transition guidance in the IFRS (if any), and any effect on future periods
- The nature of the policy change
- The amount of the adjustment caused by the policy change for specific financial statement line items, both for the current period and each prior period
- If practicable, the adjustment amount relating to periods prior to those presented
- If retrospective application is impracticable, the reason for this situation and a description of when and how the policy was applied

When a new IFRS is not yet effective, and has not been applied, disclose the following:
- The fact that the IFRS is not yet effective and has not yet been applied by the business
- The impact that the new IFRS will have on the financial statements when it is initially applied
- Though not required, consider disclosing the name of the new IFRS, the nature of the change, the date when application is required, and the date when the company plans to apply it

For a voluntary change to an accounting policy, disclose the following:
- The nature of the change, and why the change provides more reliable and relevant information
- The amount of the adjustment caused by the policy change for specific financial statement line items, both for the current period and each prior period
- If practicable, the adjustment amount relating to periods prior to those presented
- If retrospective application is impracticable, the reason for this situation and a description of when and how the policy was applied

Once these disclosures have been made for a change in accounting policy, it is not necessary to repeat the disclosures in future periods, as long as the policy is not changed again.

Changes in Accounting Estimates

If there is a change in accounting estimate, disclose the following information:
- The nature and amount of the change, including the effect on future periods
- If it is impracticable to estimate the impact of the change in future periods, disclose this issue

Errors

If an accounting error is discovered, disclose the following information:
- The nature of the error
- The amount of the error correction applied to the periods presented, by line item
- The amount of the error correction included in the beginning balances of the earliest period presented
- If it is impracticable to restate financial statements for a prior period, note the circumstances and how the error was corrected

Once these disclosures have been made for an accounting error, it is not necessary to repeat the disclosures in future periods.

For the preceding disclosures of changes caused by policies and errors, if the reporting entity is publicly-held, also note the impact of the change on basic and diluted earnings per share.

Summary

Retrospective changes can require a large amount of detective accounting work, judgment, and thorough documentation of the changes made. Given the amount of labor involved, it is cost-effective to find justifiable reasons for not making retrospective changes. Two valid methods for doing so are to question the materiality of the necessary changes, or to find reasons to instead treat issues as changes in accounting estimate.

If retrospective application is completely unavoidable, it may make sense to have the company's auditors review proposed retrospective changes in advance. Doing so minimizes the risk that an issue will be discovered by the auditors during the annual audit, which will require additional retrospective changes.

Chapter 6
Financial Reporting in Hyperinflationary Economies

Introduction

When a business issues financial statements, the information contained within those statements is likely to be based on a mix of historical and current costs. When there is a rapid increase in prices, which is known as hyperinflation, it is impossible to use the traditional approach to compiling financial statements and still issue reports that are comparable across multiple time periods. Instead, the rapid and ongoing changes in price make it appear as though a business is experiencing an ongoing acceleration of its revenues, expenses, assets, and liabilities. In this chapter, we address the methods required under IFRS to adjust the financial statements of a business that is located in a hyperinflationary economy.

IFRS Source Documents

- IAS 29, *Financial Reporting in Hyperinflationary Economies*
- IFRIC 7, *Applying the Restatement Approach under IAS 29*

Overview of Hyperinflationary Reporting

A business may operate within a country where the currency is losing its purchasing power at a rapid rate. If so, reporting the financial results and financial position of the business in that local currency is not useful, since it is impossible to compare the resulting financial statements with those of prior periods in any meaningful way. Even comparing transactions occurring at the beginning and end of a single reporting period may be difficult.

There is no single trigger point above which hyperinflation is considered to be present. Instead, a final determination is based on a mix of the following conditions:

- The country's population prefers to store its wealth outside of the currency, such as in non-monetary assets or in a foreign currency.
- Prices tend to be quoted in a foreign currency.
- Credit sales are at elevated prices, to account for the expected loss of currency value during the credit period.
- Prices, wages, and interest rates are linked to a price index.
- Over the past three years, the cumulative inflation rate has approached or exceeded 100%.

Apply the following guidance from the beginning of the reporting period in which the determination is made that hyperinflation exists:

- *Primary rule.* The financial statements must be stated in terms of the measuring unit current at the *end* of the reporting period.
- *Comparative information.* Restate any comparative information presented for a prior period in terms of the measuring unit current at the end of the reporting period.
- *Restatement gain or loss.* Include any gain or loss on the net monetary position in profit or loss. See the Net Monetary Position sub-section later in this chapter for more information.

> **Tip:** It is essential to rigidly follow the same restatement procedure when preparing the financial statements for every reporting period. Otherwise, it will be difficult to create reports that can be compared to those of prior periods.

In addition to the preceding set of general rules, apply the following more specific points to the restatement of financial statements:

Balance sheet:

- *General price index.* If a balance sheet item is not already stated in the measuring unit current at the end of the reporting period, restate it using a general price index.
- *No general price index.* If there is no general price index available for the required periods, estimate the amount of the index. One way to create such an estimate is to base it on changes in the exchange rate between the functional currency and a more stable foreign currency.
- *Current cost items.* When a business is already updating certain line items in its financial statements at their current cost, there is no need to restate these line items, since they are already presented using the measuring unit current at the end of the reporting period.
- *Index-linked assets and liabilities.* If an asset or liability is linked to a change in prices under the terms of an agreement, adjust its amount as per the contract terms to determine the amount at which it will be recorded at the end of the reporting period.
- *Monetary items.* Do not restate monetary items, since they are already expressed in the measuring unit current at the end of the reporting period.
- *Non-monetary items.* If a non-monetary item is carried at its net realizable value or fair value at the end of the period, do not adjust this amount. Restate all other non-monetary items; to do so, apply to the historical cost and any accumulated depreciation the change in the general price index from the date of acquisition to the end of the reporting period. Non-monetary assets to which restatement should probably be applied include:
    - Property, plant, and equipment
    - Inventories

    ○ Goodwill, patents, and trademarks
- *Constructed inventory.* Restate work-in-process inventory and finished goods based on the change in the price index from the dates on which these items were purchased and converted to their present state.
- *Missing acquisition dates.* If there is no record of the acquisition date of an asset, obtain an independent assessment of its value, which becomes the starting value and date for any subsequent restatements.
- *Revalued assets.* Some assets may have been revalued at regular intervals (such as property, plant, and equipment). If so, revalue their recorded amounts from the date of the last revaluation.
- *Recoverable amount limitation.* If the restated amount of an asset is greater than its recoverable amount, reduce the restated amount to its recoverable amount.
- *Investee results.* A business may report its investment in an investee using the equity method. If the investee is located in a hyperinflationary economy, a business using the equity method should calculate its share of the investee's net assets and profit or loss only after restating the financial statements of the investee.
- *Equity (initial restatement).* When hyperinflationary restatements are initiated, apply a general price index to the components of owners' equity (not including retained earnings and revaluation surplus) from the dates when these items were originally contributed or arose in some other manner to the beginning of the first period of application. Eliminate any revaluation surplus that arose in a prior period.
- *Equity (subsequent restatement).* At the end of each subsequent period, restate all elements of owners' equity by applying a general price index from the beginning of the reporting period. If equity items were contributed during the period, the general price index is applied from the date of contribution.

EXAMPLE

The Close Call Company opens a subsidiary in Byjerkistan, whose economy subsequently experiences hyperinflation. Close Call converts the line items in the year-end balance sheet of its Byjerkistan subsidiary as noted in the following table, and based on a general price index that increased from 100 to 300 in the past year. The subsidiary's inventory turns over twice a year.

(000s)	Balance Sheet (Pre-adjustment)	Adjustment Calculation	Balance Sheet (Post-adjustment)
Cash	3,870	Monetary item	3,870
Accounts receivable	6,210	Monetary item	6,210
Inventory	5,450	5,450 × (300 ÷ 150)	10,900
Property, plant, and equipment	2,080	2,080 × (300 ÷ 100)	6,240
Total assets	17,610		27,220
Accounts payable	7,390	Monetary item	7,390
Notes payable	4,140	Monetary item	4,140
Share capital	3,250	3,250 × (300 ÷ 100)	9,750
Retained earnings	2,830	Remaining balance	5,940
Total liabilities and equity	17,610		27,220

Statement of comprehensive income:

- *Basis of restatement.* Express all items in the statement of comprehensive income using the measuring unit current at the end of the reporting period. The restatement should be applied using the change in the general price index from those dates when revenue and expense items were initially recorded.
- *Current cost items.* When transactions are recorded at their current cost, it is as of the date when revenues are earned or costs consumed. Since the effects of hyperinflation must be adjusted for as of the *end* of a reporting period, these amounts must still be restated to the measuring unit current at the end of the reporting period with a general price index.

Statement of cash flows:

All line items in the statement of cash flows must be expressed using the measuring unit current at the end of the reporting period.

Net Monetary Position

A result of the various restatements just noted is that there will probably be a net gain or loss on the *net monetary position* of a business. This gain or loss arises because a net balance of monetary assets over monetary liabilities will lose purchasing power, while a net balance of monetary liabilities over monetary assets will gain purchasing power. The amount of this net gain or loss can be approximated by multiplying the change in the applicable general price index by the difference between monetary assets and monetary liabilities. Any gain or loss on the net monetary position is to be recorded within profit or loss. Examples of monetary assets and liabilities are:

Examples of Monetary Assets

Accounts receivable	Loans to employees
Advances to suppliers	Notes receivable
Cash	Refundable deposits
Cash surrender value of life insurance	Time deposits
Foreign currency holdings	Trading investments

Examples of Monetary Liabilities

Accounts payable	Deposit liabilities of financial institutions
Accrued expenses payable	Life insurance policy reserves
Advances from customers	Notes payable
Capital stock subject to mandatory redemption	Property and casualty insurance loss reserves
Cash dividends payable	Refundable deposits

Comparative Information

IFRS mandates that comparative information from a prior period be included in a set of financial statements. These comparative amounts are to be restated using a general price index, so that the information is presented in terms of the measuring unit current at the end of the current reporting period. Further, all comparative information stated in the accompanying notes must also be restated in the same manner.

Initial Restatement

When a business restates its financial statements for the first time because of a hyperinflationary economy, the basic rule is to apply the restatement requirements as though the economy had always been hyperinflationary. This means that non-monetary items remeasured at their historical cost must be restated at the beginning of the earliest period presented to reflect the effects of inflation, through the end of the latest reporting period. Non-monetary items carried on the books since that date must also be adjusted for inflationary effects.

After the initial restatement has been completed, restate all figures in subsequent periods only from the previous reporting period.

Consolidation Issues

When a parent company consolidates the financial statements of its subsidiaries, and a subsidiary reports its financial statements in the currency of a hyperinflationary economy, the parent must first restate the financial statements of the subsidiary using a general price index for that currency. After doing so, the parent may then consolidate the financial statements of its subsidiaries.

When a subsidiary states its results in a foreign currency, its restated financial statements are then translated to the reporting currency of the parent company at the closing exchange rate at the end of the reporting period.

Termination of Hyperinflationary Period

When it is determined that an economy is no longer hyperinflationary, a business shall terminate the restatement of its financial statements from that point onward. At that point, the company should consider the amounts stated in its financial statements at the end of the most recent reporting period to be the basis for the carrying amounts stated in its subsequent financial statements.

Historical Presentation

IFRS does not allow a business to present the information required within this chapter as a supplement to financial statements that have not been restated. It also discourages separate presentation of the financial statements prior to their restatement.

Hyperinflationary Reporting Disclosures

IFRS requires that the following disclosures be made regarding financial reporting in a hyperinflationary environment:

- Note that all periods presented in the financial statements have been restated for changes in the purchasing power of the entity's functional currency as of the end of the reporting period.
- State whether the information in the financial statements is based on historical or current costs.
- Identify the price index used for the restatement, as well as the level of the index at the end of the reporting period. Also note the change in the index in both the current and previous reporting periods.

Summary

The solution to financial reporting in hyperinflationary economies is to restate the financial statements using a general price index. However, it can be quite difficult to obtain a reliable price index, especially when the index is needed for periods of less than one month. Accordingly, it may be necessary to create an alternative measure of price changes, probably based on changes in the country's exchange rate in relation to one or more other currencies. If it is necessary to use such an internally-derived price index, be sure to thoroughly document how the information is collected and used. This may call for a policy that describes which exchange rate shall be used, how often the exchange information will be collected, the source of this information, how the price index is to be derived from this information, and how the price index is to be calculated for shorter periods within a reporting period. A stringently-applied policy is needed to ensure that financial statements are restated in a consistent manner.

Chapter 7
Earnings per Share

Introduction

If the reporting entity is publicly-held, it must report two types of earnings per share information within the financial statements. In this chapter, we describe how to calculate both basic and diluted earnings per share, as well as how to present this information within the financial statements. The information presented in this chapter only applies to entities whose ordinary shares are traded in a public market.

IFRS Source Document

- IAS 33, *Earnings per Share*

Basic Earnings per Share

Basic earnings per share is the amount of a company's profit or loss for a reporting period that is available to its ordinary shares that are outstanding during a reporting period. If a business only has ordinary shares in its capital structure, it presents only its basic earnings per share for income from continuing operations and net income. This information is reported on its income statement.

The formula for basic earnings per share is:

$$\frac{\text{Profit or loss attributable to ordinary equity holders of the parent business}}{\text{Weighted average number of ordinary shares outstanding during the period}}$$

In addition, subdivide this calculation into:

- The profit or loss from continuing operations attributable to the parent company
- The total profit or loss attributable to the parent company

When calculating basic earnings per share, incorporate into the numerator adjustments for the following items:

- The after-tax amounts of preference dividends. This is the after-tax amount of preference dividends on noncumulative preference shares declared in the period, and the after-tax amount of preference dividends required in the period, even if not declared.
- Differences caused by the settlement of preference shares. In general, any difference between the consideration paid by a business to acquire preference shares and their carrying amount is included in the calculation of profit or loss that is attributable to the holders of ordinary shares.

- Other similar effects of preference shares

Also, incorporate the following adjustments into the denominator of the basic earnings per share calculation:
- *Contingent shares.* If there are contingently issuable shares, treat them as though they were outstanding as of the date when there are no circumstances under which the shares would *not* be issued. If shares are contingently returnable, do not include them in this calculation.
- *Weighted-average shares.* Use the weighted-average number of shares during the period in the denominator. This is done by adjusting the number of shares outstanding at the beginning of the reporting period for ordinary shares repurchased or issued in the period. This adjustment is based on the proportion of the days in the reporting period that the shares are outstanding.

EXAMPLE

Lowry Locomotion earns a profit of £1,000,000 net of taxes in Year 1. In addition, Lowry owes £200,000 in dividends to the holders of its cumulative preference shares. Lowry calculates the numerator of its basic earnings per share as follows:

£1,000,000 Profit - £200,000 Dividends = £800,000

Lowry had 4,000,000 ordinary shares outstanding at the beginning of Year 1. In addition, it sold 200,000 shares on April 1 and 400,000 shares on October 1. It also issued 500,000 shares on July 1 to the owners of a newly-acquired subsidiary. Finally, it bought back 60,000 shares on December 1. Lowry calculates the weighted-average number of ordinary shares outstanding as follows:

Date	Shares	Weighting (Months)	Weighted Average
January 1	4,000,000	12/12	4,000,000
April 1	200,000	9/12	150,000
July 1	500,000	6/12	250,000
October 1	400,000	3/12	100,000
December 1	-60,000	1/12	-5,000
			4,495,000

Lowry's basic earnings per share is:

£800,000 adjusted profits ÷ 4,495,000 weighted-average shares = £0.18 per share

Diluted Earnings per Share

Diluted earnings per share is the profit for a reporting period per ordinary share outstanding during that period; it includes the number of shares that would have been outstanding during the period if the company had issued ordinary shares for all potential dilutive ordinary shares outstanding during the period.

If a company has more types of shares than ordinary shares in its capital structure, it must present both basic earnings per share and diluted earnings per share information; this presentation must be for both income from continuing operations and net income. This information is reported within the company's income statement.

To calculate diluted earnings per share, include the effects of all dilutive potential ordinary shares. This means that the number of shares outstanding is increased by the weighted average number of additional ordinary shares that would have been outstanding if the company had converted all dilutive potential ordinary shares to ordinary shares. This dilution may affect the profit or loss in the numerator of the dilutive earnings per share calculation. The formula is:

$$\frac{\text{(Profit or loss attributable to ordinary equity holders of parent company} + \text{After-tax interest on convertible debt} + \text{Convertible preferred dividends)}}{\text{(Weighted average number of ordinary shares outstanding during the period} + \text{All dilutive potential ordinary shares)}}$$

It may be necessary to make two adjustments to the *numerator* of this calculation. They are:

- *Interest expense.* Eliminate any interest expense associated with dilutive potential ordinary shares, since the assumption is that these shares are converted to ordinary shares. The conversion would eliminate the company's liability for the interest expense.
- *Dividends.* Adjust for the after-tax impact of dividends or other types of dilutive potential ordinary shares.

Further adjustments may be required for the *denominator* of this calculation. They are:

- *Anti-dilutive shares.* If there are any contingent share issuances that would have an anti-dilutive impact on earnings per share, do not include them in the calculation. This situation arises when a business experiences a loss, because including the dilutive shares in the calculation would reduce the loss per share.
- *Dilutive shares.* If there are potential dilutive ordinary shares, add them to the denominator of the diluted earnings per share calculation. Unless there is more specific information available, assume that these shares are issued at the beginning of the reporting period.
- *Dilutive securities termination.* If a conversion option lapses during the reporting period for dilutive convertible securities, or if the related debt is extinguished during the reporting period, the effect of these securities should still be included in the denominator of the diluted earnings per share calculation for the period during which they were outstanding.

In addition to these adjustments to the denominator, also apply all of the adjustments to the denominator already noted for basic earnings per share.

> **Tip:** The rules related to diluted earnings per share appear complex, but they are founded upon one principle – that the absolute worst-case scenario is being established to arrive at the smallest possible amount of earnings per share. If there is an unusual situation involving the calculation of diluted earnings per share and are not sure what to do, that rule will likely apply.

In addition to the issues just noted, here are a number of additional situations that could impact the calculation of diluted earnings per share:

- *Most advantageous exercise price.* When the number of potential shares that could be issued is calculated, do so using the most advantageous conversion rate from the perspective of the person or entity holding the security to be converted.
- *Settlement assumption.* If there is an open contract that could be settled in ordinary shares or cash, assume that it will be settled in ordinary shares, but only if the effect is dilutive. The presumption of settlement in stock can be overcome if there is a reasonable basis for expecting that settlement will be partially or entirely in cash.
- *Effects of convertible instruments.* If there are convertible instruments outstanding, include their dilutive effect if they dilute earnings per share. Consider convertible preference shares to be anti-dilutive when the dividend on any converted shares is greater than basic earnings per share. Similarly, convertible debt is considered anti-dilutive when the interest expense on any converted shares exceeds basic earnings per share. The following example illustrates the concept.

EXAMPLE

Lowry Locomotion earns a net profit of £2 million, and it has 5 million ordinary shares outstanding. In addition, there is a £1 million convertible loan that has an eight percent interest rate. The loan may potentially convert into 500,000 of Lowry's ordinary shares. Lowry's incremental tax rate is 35 percent.

Lowry's basic earnings per share is £2,000,000 ÷ 5,000,000 shares, or £0.40/share. The following calculation shows the compilation of Lowry's diluted earnings per share:

Net profit	£2,000,000
+ Interest saved on £1,000,000 loan at 8%	80,000
- Reduced tax savings on foregone interest expense	-28,000
= Adjusted net earnings	£2,052,000
Ordinary shares outstanding	5,000,000
+ Potential converted shares	500,000
= Adjusted shares outstanding	5,500,000
Diluted earnings per share (£2,052,000 ÷ 5,500,000)	**£0.37/share**

- *Option exercise.* If there are any dilutive options and warrants, assume that they are exercised at their exercise price. Then, convert the proceeds into the total number of shares that the holders would have purchased, using the average market price during the reporting period. Then use in the diluted earnings per share calculation the difference between the number of shares assumed to have been issued and the number of shares assumed to have been purchased. The following example illustrates the concept.

> **Tip:** The average market price is usually considered to be a simple average of closing weekly or monthly prices. However, if prices fluctuate markedly, it may be necessary to instead use an average of the high and low prices.

EXAMPLE

Lowry Locomotion earns a net profit of £200,000, and it has 5,000,000 ordinary shares outstanding that sell on the open market for an average of £12 per share. In addition, there are 300,000 options outstanding that can be converted to Lowry's ordinary shares at £10 each.

Lowry's basic earnings per share is £200,000 ÷ 5,000,000 ordinary shares, or £0.04 per share.

Lowry's controller wants to calculate the amount of diluted earnings per share. To do so, he follows these steps:
1. *Calculate the number of shares that would have been issued at the market price.* Thus, he multiplies the 300,000 options by the average exercise price of £10 to arrive at a total of £3,000,000 paid to exercise the options by their holders.
2. *Divide the amount paid to exercise the options by the market price to determine the number of shares that could be purchased.* Thus, he divides the £3,000,000 paid to exercise the options by the £12 average market price to arrive at 250,000 shares that could have been purchased with the proceeds from the options.

3. *Subtract the number of shares that could have been purchased from the number of options exercised.* Thus, he subtracts the 250,000 shares potentially purchased from the 300,000 options to arrive at a difference of 50,000 shares.

4. *Add the incremental number of shares to the shares already outstanding.* Thus, he adds the 50,000 incremental shares to the existing 5,000,000 to arrive at 5,050,000 diluted shares.

Based on this information, the controller arrives at diluted earnings per share of £0.0396, for which the calculation is:

£200,000 Net profit ÷ 5,050,000 Ordinary shares

- *Put options.* If there are purchased put options, only include them in the diluted earnings per share calculation if the exercise price is higher than the average market price during the reporting period.

- *Written put options.* If there is a written put option that requires a business to repurchase its own stock, include it in the computation of diluted earnings per share, but only if the effect is dilutive. If the exercise price of such a put option is above the average market price of the company's stock during the reporting period, this is considered to be "in the money," and the dilutive effect is to be calculated using the following method, which is called the *reverse treasury stock method*:

    1. Assume that enough shares were issued by the company at the beginning of the period at the average market price to raise sufficient funds to satisfy the put option contract.
    2. Assume that these proceeds are used to buy back the required number of shares.
    3. Include in the denominator of the diluted earnings per share calculation the difference between the numbers of shares issued and purchased in steps 1 and 2.

EXAMPLE

A third party exercises a written put option that requires Armadillo Industries to repurchase 1,000 shares from the third party at an exercise price of £30. The current market price is £20. Armadillo uses the following steps to compute the impact of the written put option on its diluted earnings per share calculation:

1. Armadillo assumes that it has issued 1,500 shares at £20.
2. The company assumes that the "issuance" of 1,500 shares is used to meet the repurchase obligation of £30,000.
3. The difference between the 1,500 shares issued and the 1,000 shares repurchased is added to the denominator of Armadillo's diluted earnings per share calculation.

- *Call options*. If there are purchased call options, only include them in the diluted earnings per share calculation if the exercise price is lower than the market price.

> **Tip:** There is only a dilutive effect on the diluted earnings per share calculation when the average market price is greater than the exercise prices of any options or warrants.

- *Contingent shares in general*. Treat ordinary shares that are contingently issuable as though they were outstanding as of the beginning of the reporting period, but only if the conditions have been met that would require the company to issue the shares. If the conditions were not met by the end of the period, then include in the calculation, as of the beginning of the period, any shares that would be issuable if the end of the reporting period were the end of the contingency period, and the result would be dilutive.
- *Contingent shares dependency*. If there is a contingent share issuance that is dependent upon the future market price of the company's ordinary shares, include the shares in the diluted earnings per share calculation, based on the market price at the end of the reporting period; however, only include the issuance if the effect is dilutive. If the shares have a contingency feature, do not include them in the calculation until the contingency has been met.
- *Issuances based on future earnings and stock price*. There may be contingent stock issuances that are based on future earnings and the future price of a company's stock. If so, the number of shares to include in diluted earnings per share should be based on the earnings to date and the current market price as of the end of each reporting period. If both earnings and share price targets must be reached in order to trigger a stock issuance and both targets are not met, do not include any related contingently issuable shares in the diluted earnings per share calculation.

Always calculate the number of potential dilutive ordinary shares independently for each reporting period presented in the financial statements.

Disclosure of Earnings per Share

The basic and diluted earnings per share information is normally listed at the bottom of the income statement, and is listed for every period included in the income statement. Also, if diluted earnings per share is reported in *any* of the periods included in a company's income statement, it must be reported for *all* of the periods included in the statement. The following sample illustrates the concept.

Sample Presentation of Earnings per Share

Earnings per Share	20x3	20x2	20x1
From continuing operations			
Basic earnings per share	£1.05	£0.95	£0.85
Diluted earnings per share	1.00	0.90	0.80
From discontinued operations			
Basic earnings per share	£0.20	£0.17	£0.14
Diluted earnings per share	0.15	0.08	0.07
From total operations			
Basic earnings per share	£1.25	£1.12	£0.99
Diluted earnings per share	1.15	0.98	0.87

Note that, if the company reports a discontinued operation, it must present the basic and diluted earnings per share amounts for the discontinued operation. The information can be included either as part of the income statement or in the accompanying notes. The preceding sample presentation includes a disclosure for earnings per share from discontinued operations.

> **Tip:** If the amounts of basic and diluted earnings per share are the same, it is allowable to have a dual presentation of the information in a single line item within the income statement.

In addition to the earnings per share reporting format just noted, a company is also required to report the following information:
- *Reconciliation.* State the differences between the numerators and denominators of the basic and diluted earnings per share calculations for income from continuing operations. This should include the individual effect of each class of instruments that impact earnings per share.
- *Potential effects.* Describe the terms and conditions of any securities not included in the computation of diluted earnings per share due to their antidilutive effects, but which could potentially dilute basic earnings per share in the future.
- *Subsequent events.* Describe any transactions occurring after the latest reporting period but before the issuance of financial statements that would have a material impact on the number of ordinary or potential ordinary shares if they had occurred prior to the end of the reporting period. Examples of such transactions are the issuance of shares for cash, the issuance of warrants, and the redemption of ordinary shares outstanding.

If the number of ordinary shares or potential ordinary shares changes because of a share split or similar transaction, retrospectively adjust both basic and diluted earnings per share for all of the periods presented. Also disclose the fact that the revision has been made to the earnings per share information. The same changes should be made if there are retrospective updates caused by changes in accounting policies.

Summary

It will have been evident from the discussions of earnings per share that the computation of diluted earnings per share can be quite complex if there is a correspondingly complex equity structure. In such a situation, it is quite likely that diluted earnings per share will be incorrectly calculated. To improve the accuracy of the calculation, create an electronic spreadsheet that incorporates all of the necessary factors impacting diluted earnings per share. Further, save the calculation for each reporting period on a separate page of the spreadsheet; by doing so, there will be an excellent record of how these calculations were managed in the past.

Chapter 8
Interim Financial Reporting

Introduction

When a company issues financial statements for reporting periods of less than one year, the statements are said to cover an interim period. When preparing financial information for these periods, consider whether to report information assuming that quarterly results are stand-alone documents, or part of the full-year results of the business. This chapter discusses the disparities that these different viewpoints can cause in the financial statements, as well as other requirements mandated under IFRS. The guidance in this chapter is not specific to any particular type of reporting entity, but is most commonly applicable to publicly-held businesses that are required to report their quarterly results.

IFRS Source Documents

- IAS 34, *Interim Financial Reporting*
- IFRIC 10, *Interim Financial Reporting and Impairment*

Overview of Interim Financial Reporting

A business will periodically create financial statements for shorter periods than the full fiscal year, which are known as *interim periods*. The most common examples of interim periods are monthly or quarterly financial statements, though any period of less than a full fiscal year can be considered an interim period. The concepts related to interim periods are most commonly applicable to the financial statements of publicly-held companies, since they are required to issue quarterly financial statements that must be reviewed by their outside auditors; these financials must account for certain activities in a consistent manner, as well as prevent readers from being misled about the results of the business on an ongoing basis. IFRS encourages publicly-traded businesses to issue interim financial reports for at least the first half of their fiscal years, and to make those reports available not more than 60 days after the end of every reported interim period.

Content of an Interim Financial Report

An interim financial report should contain the following financial statements:
- *Balance sheet*. Presented as of the end of the current interim period and as of the end of the preceding fiscal year.
- *Statement of comprehensive income*. Presented for the current interim period and the fiscal year-to-date, as well as for the same interim period and fiscal year-to-date for the preceding year.

- *Statement of changes in equity.* Presented for the current fiscal year-to-date, as well as for the same period in the preceding year.
- *Statement of cash flows.* Presented for the current fiscal year-to-date, as well as for the same period in the preceding year.
- Disclosures of significant accounting policies and other explanatory items.

In addition, if an accounting policy is applied retrospectively or there is a reclassification of items, include an adjusted balance sheet for the earliest comparative period.

Reduced Information Requirements

Interim financial reports are typically prepared and issued within time frames that are more compressed than the time periods that apply to annual financial reports. Because of this time compression, companies may elect to provide less information in their interim reports than in their annual reports. If they do so, the amount of information provided should at least give an update on the information in the latest annual financial report. Thus, the focus of a reduced set of information is to reveal significant new activities, events, and circumstances. The following are examples of such items that may require disclosure if they are significant:

- Asset impairment losses or the reversal of these losses
- Contingent liability or contingent asset changes
- Fair value changes in financial assets or liabilities
- Fair value hierarchy transfers
- Financial asset classification changes
- Fixed asset acquisitions or disposals
- Fixed asset purchase commitments
- Inventory write-down or the reversal of a write-down
- Litigation settlements
- Loan defaults that have not been remedied
- Prior period error corrections
- Related party transactions
- Restructuring provision reversals

For the purposes of interim reporting, consider the materiality of an item in relation to its impact on the interim period financial information, rather than its impact on the annual financial report. Doing so means that more items will likely be considered material, and will therefore be included in interim financial reports. This approach makes it less likely that the users of interim financial reports will be misled by the absence of key information.

EXAMPLE

Close Call Company records revenues of £10,000,000 and profits of £300,000 in its first quarter. The company's budget, which management has a reliable history of attaining, projects full-year revenues of £45,000,000 and profits of £1,800,000. The company's controller considers a material item to represent at least five percent of net income. In the first quarter, the company experiences an obsolete inventory loss of £18,000. Since this amount exceeds the materiality limit for the first quarter results, it should be separately reported within the interim financial report for that quarter. However, the amount is too small to be material for the company's full-year results, and so should not be separately reported within the year-end financial report.

The following additional disclosures must be included in each interim financial report:

- *Compliance*. If the financial report complies with all IFRS requirements, disclose that fact.
- *Dividends*. Separately note the amount of dividends paid for ordinary shares and other shares.
- *Estimates*. Disclose and quantify the amount of any changes in estimate reported from prior interim periods or prior fiscal years.
- *Fair value*. Include all related fair value disclosures for financial instruments.
- *Investment entities*. When an entity is becoming or ceasing to be an investment entity, disclose the change in status and reason for the change. If the entity has become an investment entity, also note the fair value of those entities no longer being consolidated, the total gain or loss, and the line item in which the gain or loss is recognized.
- *Policies*. State that the existing accounting policies and computation methods used in the interim financial report were the same ones used in the preparation of the last annual financial report. If this was not the case, describe the change and its effect on the financial statements.
- *Revenue disaggregation*. Note the disaggregation of revenue from contracts with customers, as noted in the Revenue chapter.
- *Seasonality*. Describe the seasonality or cyclicality of interim operations.
- *Securities*. Note any issuances, repurchases, or repayments of debt and equity securities.
- *Segments*. If segment reporting is required (usually just for publicly-held entities), report by segment the revenues from external customers, intersegment revenues, profit or loss, total assets where there has been a material change since the last annual financial report, a reconciliation of segment-level profit or loss to the consolidated profit or loss (with separate identification of material reconciling items), and a description of changes in the basis of segmentation or profit/loss measurement since the last annual financial report.

- *Structure*. Note any changes in the composition of the business during the period from changes in control, restructurings, discontinued operations, and/or business combinations.
- *Subsequent events*. Note events that occurred after the interim reporting period that are not included in the financial statements.
- *Unusual items*. Describe and quantify any unusual items affecting assets, liabilities, equity, net income, or cash flows.

If a business elects to make a significant change to an estimate during the final interim period of a fiscal year, but does not issue a separate interim financial report for that period, it should describe and quantify the change in the annual financial report for that year.

If a business elects to provide a condensed set of financial statements in an interim financial report, those statements are subject to the following presentation rules:

- Include the same headings and subtotals used in the most recent annual financial statements.
- Include any line items or disclosures needed to keep the financial statements from being misleading.
- Present basic and diluted earnings per share, if the company is publicly-held.
- Prepare consolidated financial statements if the last annual financial report contained consolidated statements.

IFRS merely sets forth the low-end boundaries for the minimum amount of information that must be presented in interim financial reports. A business may elect to provide a complete set of financial information that greatly expands upon the minimum requirements set forth by IFRS.

General Interim Reporting Rule

The general rule for interim period reporting is that the same accounting principles and practices be applied to interim reports that are used for the preparation of annual financial reports. The following bullet points illustrate revenues and expenses that follow the general rule, and which therefore do not change for interim reporting:

- *Revenue*. Revenue is recognized in the same manner that is used for annual reporting, with no exceptions. Do not anticipate or defer revenues based on anticipated seasonal changes in sales in future periods.
- *Costs associated with revenue*. If a cost is typically assigned to a specific sale (such as cost of goods sold items), expense recognition is the same as is used for annual reporting.
- *Direct expenditures*. If an expense is incurred in a period and relates to that period, it is recorded as an expense in that period. An example is salaries expense.
- *Accruals for estimated expenditures*. If there is an estimated expenditure to be made at a later date but which relates to the current period, it is recorded

as an expense in the current period. An example is accrued wages. Generally, accrue expenses in an interim period if this would also be done at the end of the fiscal year.

- *Inventory.* If an inventory item is written down to its net realizable value during an interim period, it is permissible to reverse the entry in a later interim period if it would be appropriate to do so at the end of the fiscal year. Also, do not defer the recognition of any cost variances arising from a standard costing system; instead, charge them to expense as incurred.

Tip: It is permissible to estimate inventory valuations as of the end of interim reporting periods, usually based on historical sales margins.

In addition, there are cases where a company is accustomed to only making a year-end adjustment, such as to its reserves for doubtful accounts, obsolete inventory, and/or warranty claims, as well as for year-end bonuses. Where possible, these adjustments should be made in the interim periods, thereby reducing the amount of any residual adjustments still required in the year-end financial statements.

EXAMPLE

Armadillo Industries incurs an annual property tax charge of £60,000. Also, Armadillo has historically earned an annual volume discount of £30,000 per year, based on its full-year purchases from a major supplier.

Since the property tax charge is applicable to all months in the year, the controller accrues a £5,000 monthly charge for this expense. Similarly, the volume discount relates back to volume purchases throughout the year, not just the last month of the year, in which the discount is retroactively awarded. Accordingly, the controller creates a monthly credit of £2,500 to reflect the expected year-end volume discount of £30,000.

Goodwill Impairment Losses

A business may recognize a goodwill impairment loss in an interim period. In some cases, the circumstances will have changed in a later interim period to such an extent that the impairment charge would not have been made. In such cases, IFRS does not allow for the reversal of a goodwill impairment loss that had been recognized in a prior interim period.

Interim Period Restatements

If there is a change in accounting policy prior to the end of a fiscal year, restate the financial statements for all presented current-year and comparative interim periods to incorporate the change. This involves the following steps:
1. Include that portion of the item that relates to the current interim period in the results of the current interim period.

2. Restate the results of prior interim periods of the current year to include that portion of the item relating to each interim period.
3. Restate the results of any comparison interim periods in prior years.

If it is impracticable to do so for all presented periods, then do so from the earliest date at which it is practicable to do so.

The Integral View

Under the integral view of producing interim reports, the assumption is that the results reported in interim financial statements are an integral part of the full-year financial results (hence the name of this concept). This viewpoint produces the following accounting issues:

- *Accrue expenses not arising in the period*. If an expense will be paid later in the year that is incurred at least partially in the current interim reporting period, accrue some portion of the expense in the current period. Here are several examples of the concept:
    - o *Accumulating paid absences*. If a company pays its employees for absences from work, and this right is carried forward in time, the expense accrual should be updated in each interim financial report.
    - o *Advertising*. If payment is made in advance for advertising that is scheduled to occur over multiple time periods, recognize the expense over the entire range of time periods.
    - o *Bonuses*. If there are bonus plans that contain a legal or constructive obligation to pay, accrue the expense in all accounting periods. Only accrue this expense if it is possible to reasonably estimate the amount of the bonus obligation, which may not always be possible during the earlier months covered by a performance contract.
    - o *Contingencies*. If there are contingent liabilities that will be resolved later in the year, and which are both probable and reasonably estimated, then accrue the related expense. An example is a contingent lease payment that is based on the annual sales achieved by the lessee.
    - o *Depreciation and amortization*. If there is a fixed asset, depreciation (for tangible assets) or amortization (for intangible assets) is ratably charged to all periods in its useful life. Do not depreciate or amortize an asset that will not be acquired until a later interim period.
    - o *Insurance contributions*. If assessments are made into a government-sponsored insurance fund once a year, accrue the expense in all interim periods.
    - o *Profit sharing*. If employees are paid a percentage of company profits at year-end, and the amount can be reasonably estimated, then accrue the expense throughout the year as a proportion of the profits recognized in each period.

- o *Property taxes.* A local government entity issues an invoice to the company at some point during the year for property taxes. These taxes are intended to cover the entire year, so accrue a portion of the expense in each reporting period.
  - o *Purchase price changes.* If there is a contractually-mandated purchase price change that has been earned and will take effect, accrue it in the relevant prior interim periods. This recordation is not allowed if the price change is discretionary.
- *Tax rate.* A company is usually subject to a graduated income tax rate that incrementally escalates through the year as the business generates more profit. Under the integral view, use the expected tax rate for the entire year in every reporting period, rather than the incremental tax rate that applies only to the profits earned for the year to date. If it is practicable to do so, estimate and apply the expected full-year tax rate at the level of each individual tax jurisdiction and category of income.

EXAMPLE

The board of directors of Lowry Locomotion approves a senior management bonus plan for the upcoming year that could potentially pay the senior management team a maximum of £240,000. It initially seems probable that the full amount will be paid, but by the third quarter it appears more likely that the maximum amount to be paid will be £180,000. In addition, the company pays £60,000 in advance for a full year of advertising in *Locomotive Times* magazine. Lowry recognizes these expenses as follows:

	Quarter 1	Quarter 2	Quarter 3	Quarter 4	Full Year
Bonus expense	£60,000	£60,000	£30,000	£30,000	£180,000
Advertising	15,000	15,000	15,000	15,000	60,000

The accounting staff spreads the recognition of the full amount of the projected bonus over the year, but then reduces its recognition of the remaining expense starting in the third quarter, to adjust for the lowered bonus payout expectation.

The accounting staff initially records the £60,000 advertising expense as a prepaid expense, and recognizes it ratably over all four quarters of the year, which matches the time period over which the related advertisements are run by *Locomotive Times*.

One problem with the integral view is that it tends to result in a significant number of expense accruals. Since these accruals are usually based on estimates, it is entirely possible that adjustments should be made to the accruals later in the year, as the company obtains more precise information about the expenses that are being accrued. Some of these adjustments could be substantial, and may materially affect the reported results in later periods.

Summary

When creating interim financial reports, judiciously apply the integral view to the reports – that is, the integral method increases the comprehensiveness of the information presented, but at the cost of maintaining a large number of accruals and estimates. Since a key factor in closing the books for an interim period is the reduced amount of time in which to complete closing activities, it may be necessary to emphasize efficiency over comprehensiveness and restrict the use of accruals to material items.

Chapter 9
Operating Segments

Introduction

If a company is publicly-held, it needs to report segment information, which is part of the disclosures attached to the financial statements. This information is used to give the readers of the financial statements more insights into the operations and prospects of a business, as well as to allow them to make more informed judgments about the entity as a whole, and the business environment within which it operates. In this chapter, we describe how to determine which business segments to report separately, and how to report that information.

IFRS Source Document

- IFRS 8, *Operating Segments*

Overview of Segment Reporting

An operating segment is a component of a public entity, and which possesses the following characteristics:

- *Business activities*. It has business activities that can generate revenues and cause expenses to be incurred. This can include revenues and expenses generated by transactions with other operating segments of the same public entity. In addition, a start-up operation that has yet to earn revenues may have operating segments.
- *Results reviewed*. The chief operating decision maker (typically the chief executive officer or chief operating officer) of the public entity regularly reviews its operating results, with the intent of assessing its performance and making decisions about allocating resources to it.
- *Financial results*. Financial results specific to it are available.

Generally, an operating segment has a manager who is accountable to the chief operating decision maker, and who maintains regular contact with that person, though it is also possible that the chief operating decision maker directly manages one or more operating segments. A segment manager may manage more than one operating segment.

Some parts of a business are not considered to be reportable business segments under the following circumstances:

- *Corporate overhead*. The corporate group does not usually earn outside revenues, and so is not considered a segment.

- *Post-retirement benefit plans.* A benefit plan can earn income from investments, but it has no operating activities, and so is not considered a segment.

The primary issue with segment reporting is determining which business segments to report. The rules for this selection process are quite specific. Segment information should be reported if a business segment passes *any one* of the following three tests:

1. *Revenue.* The revenue of the segment from both external and intercompany sales is at least 10% of the combined internal and external revenue of all operating segments; or
2. *Profit or loss.* The absolute amount of the profit or loss of the segment is at least 10% of the greater of the combined profits of all the operating segments that did not report a loss, or of the combined losses of all operating segments reporting a loss (see the following example for a demonstration of this concept); or
3. *Assets.* The assets of the segment are at least 10% of the combined assets of all the operating segments of the business.

If you run the preceding tests and arrive at a group of reportable segments whose combined revenues are not at least 75% of the consolidated revenue of the entire business, then add more segments until the 75% threshold is surpassed.

If there is a business segment that used to qualify as a reportable segment and does not currently qualify, but which is expected to qualify in the future, continue to treat it as a reportable segment.

It is acceptable to report the results and assets of additional segments, if management believes that doing so will provide useful information to the readers of the financial statements.

If there are operating segments that have similar economic characteristics, their results can be aggregated into a single operating segment, but only if they are similar in *all* of the following areas:

- The nature of their products and services
- The nature of their systems of production
- The nature of their regulatory environments (if applicable)
- Their types of customers
- Their distribution systems

The number of restrictions on this type of reporting makes it unlikely that you would be able to aggregate reportable segments.

After all of the segment testing has been completed, it is possible that there will be a few residual segments that do not qualify for separate reporting. If so, combine the information for these segments into an "other" category and include it in the segment report for the entity. Be sure to describe the sources of the revenues included in this "other" category.

Tip: The variety of methods available for segment testing makes it possible that there will be quite a large number of reportable segments. If so, it can be burdensome to create a report for so many segments, and it may be confusing for the readers of the company's financial statements. Consequently, consider limiting the number of reportable segments to ten; the information for additional segments can be aggregated for reporting purposes.

EXAMPLE

Lowry Locomotion has six business segments whose results it reports internally. Lowry's controller needs to test the various segments to see which ones qualify as being reportable. He collects the following information:

Segment	(000s) Revenue	(000s) Profit	(000s) Loss	(000s) Assets
Diesel locomotives	£120,000	£10,000	£--	£320,000
Electric locomotives	85,000	8,000	--	180,000
Maglev cars	29,000	--	-21,000	90,000
Passenger cars	200,000	32,000		500,000
Toy trains	15,000	--	-4,000	4,000
Trolley cars	62,000	--	-11,000	55,000
	£511,000	£50,000	-£36,000	£1,149,000

In the table, the total profit exceeds the total loss, so the controller uses the total profit for the 10% profit test. The controller then lists the same table again, but now with the losses column removed and with test thresholds at the top of the table that are used to determine which segments are reported. An "X" mark below a test threshold indicates that a segment is reportable. In addition, the controller adds a new column on the right side of the table, which is used to calculate the total revenue for the reportable segments.

Segment	(000s) Revenue	(000s) Profit	(000s) Assets	75% Revenue Test
Reportable threshold (10%)	**£51,100**	**£5,000**	**£114,900**	
Diesel locomotives	X	X	X	£120,000
Electric locomotives	X	X	X	85,000
Maglev cars				
Passenger cars	X	X	X	200,000
Toy trains				
Trolley cars	X			62,000
			Total	£467,000

This analysis shows that the diesel locomotive, electric locomotive, passenger car, and trolley car segments are reportable, and that the combined revenue of these reportable segments easily exceeds the 75% reporting threshold. Consequently, the company does not need to separately report information for any additional segments.

Segment Disclosure

This section contains the disclosures for various aspects of segment reporting that are required under IFRS. At the end of each set of requirements is a sample disclosure containing the more common elements of the requirements.

Segment Disclosure

The key requirement of segment reporting is that the revenue, profit or loss, and assets of each segment be separately reported for any period for which an income statement is presented. In addition, reconcile this segment information back to the company's consolidated results, which requires the inclusion of any adjusting items. Also disclose the methods by which it was determined which segments to report, and note the judgments made by management in applying the aggregation criteria noted earlier in this chapter. The essential information to include in a segment report includes:

- The types of products and services sold by each segment
- The basis of organization (such as by geographic region or product line)
- Revenues from external customers
- Revenues from inter-company transactions
- Interest revenue
- Interest expense
- Depreciation and amortization expense
- Material income and expense items
- Any interest in the profit or loss of associates or joint ventures accounted for using the equity method
- Income tax expense or income
- Other material non-cash items
- Profit or loss

The following two items must also be reported if they are included in the determination of segment assets, or are routinely provided to the chief operating decision maker:

- Equity method interests in other entities.
- The total expenditure for additions to fixed assets. Expenditures for most other long-term assets are excluded from this requirement.

The company should also disclose the following information about how it measures segment information:

- How any transactions between reportable segments were accounted for.
- The nature of any differences between reported segment profits or losses and the consolidated profit or loss for the entity, before the effects of income taxes and discontinued operations.
- The nature of any differences between the assets and/or liabilities reported for segments and for the consolidated entity.

- The nature of any changes in the measurement of segment profits and losses from prior periods, and their effect on profits and losses.
- A discussion of any asymmetrical allocations, such as the allocation of depreciation expense to a segment without a corresponding allocation of assets.

The preceding disclosures should be presented along with the following reconciliations, which should be separately identified and described:

Category	Reconciliation
Revenues	Total company revenues to reportable segment revenues
Profit or loss	Total consolidated income before income taxes and discontinued operations to reportable segment profit or loss
Assets	Consolidated assets to reportable segment assets
Liabilities	Consolidated liabilities to reportable segment liabilities (if liabilities were reported)
Other items	Consolidated amounts to reportable segment amounts for every other significant item of disclosed segment information

If an operating segment qualifies for the first time as being reportable, also report the usual segment information for it in any prior period segment data that may be presented for comparison purposes, even if the segment was not reportable in the prior period. An exemption is allowed for this prior period reporting if the required information is not available, or if it would be excessively expensive to collect the information.

The operating segment information reported should be the same information reported to the chief operating decision maker for purposes of assessing segment performance and allocating resources. This may result in a difference between the information reported at the segment level and in the public entity's consolidated financial results. If so, disclose the differences between the two figures.

If a public entity alters its internal structure to such an extent that the composition of its operating segments is altered, restate its reported results for earlier periods, as well as interim periods, to match the results and financial position of the new internal structure. This requirement is waived if it is impracticable to obtain the required information. The result may be the restatement of some information, but not all of the segment information. If an entity *does* alter its internal structure, it should disclose whether there has also been a restatement of its segment information for earlier periods. If the entity does not change its prior period information, it must report segment information in the current period under both the old basis and new basis of segmentation, unless it is impracticable to do so.

EXAMPLE

The controller of Lowry Locomotion produces the following segment report for the segments identified in the preceding example:

(000s)	Diesel	Electric	Passenger	Trolley	Other	Consolidated
Revenues	£120,000	£85,000	£200,000	£62,000	£44,000	£511,000
Interest income	11,000	8,000	28,000	8,000	2,000	57,000
Interest expense	--	--	--	11,000	39,000	50,000
Depreciation	32,000	18,000	50,000	6,000	10,000	116,000
Income taxes	4,000	3,000	10,000	-3,000	-7,000	7,000
Profit	10,000	8,000	32,000	-11,000	-25,000	14,000
Assets	320,000	180,000	500,000	55,000	94,000	1,149,000

Tip: IFRS does not require that a business report information that it does not prepare for internal use, if the information is not available and obtaining it would be excessively expensive.

Revenue Disclosure

A publicly-held entity must report the sales garnered from external customers for each product and service or group thereof, unless it is impracticable to compile this information.

The entity must also describe the extent of its reliance on its major customers. In particular, if revenues from a single customer exceed 10% of the entity's revenues, this fact must be disclosed, along with the total revenues garnered from each of these customers and the names of the segments in which these revenues were earned. It is not necessary to disclose the name of a major customer.

If there is a group of customers under common control (such as different departments of the federal government), the revenues from this group should be reported in aggregate as though the revenues were generated from a single customer.

EXAMPLE

Armadillo Industries reports the following information about its major customers:

Revenues from one customer of Armadillo's home security segment represented approximately 12% of the company's consolidated revenues in 20X2, and 11% of consolidated revenues in 20X1.

Geographic Area Disclosure

A publicly-held entity must disclose the following geographic information, unless it is impracticable to compile:

- *Revenues*. All revenues generated from external customers, and attributable to the entity's home country, and all revenues attributable to foreign countries. Foreign-country revenues by individual country shall be disclosed if these country-level sales are material. There must also be disclosure of the basis under which revenues are attributed to individual countries.
- *Assets*. All long-lived assets (for which the definition essentially restricts reporting to fixed assets) that are attributable to the entity's home country, and all such assets attributable to foreign countries. Foreign-country assets by individual country shall be stated if these assets are material.

It is also acceptable to include in this reporting the subtotals of geographic information by groups of countries.

Geographic area reporting is waived if providing it is impracticable. If so, the entity must disclose the fact.

EXAMPLE

Armadillo Industries reports the following geographic information about its operations:

	Revenues	Long-Lived Assets
United Kingdom	£27,000,000	£13,000,000
Mexico	23,000,000	11,000,000
Chile	14,000,000	7,000,000
Other foreign countries	8,000,000	2,000,000
Total	£72,000,000	£33,000,000

Tip: A company may choose to disclose segment information that is not compliant with IFRS. If so, do not describe the information as being segment information.

Summary

The determination of whether a business has segments is, to some extent, based upon whether information is tracked internally at the segment level. Thus, if a company's accounting systems are sufficiently primitive, or if management is sufficiently disinterested to not review information about business segments, it is possible that even a publicly-held company will have no reportable business segments.

If there are a number of reportable segments, consider using the report writing software in the accounting system to create a standard report that automatically generates the entire segment report for the entity's disclosures. By using this approach, no time will be wasted manually compiling the information, which avoids the risk of making a mistake while doing so. However, if the reportable segments change over time, the report structure must be modified to match the new group of segments.

Chapter 10
Joint Arrangements

Introduction

When two entities decide to engage in mutually beneficial activities through a joint arrangement, the accounting for the arrangement will vary, depending upon its structure. In this chapter, we focus on the rules that trigger the classification of a joint arrangement as either a joint operation or a joint venture, as well as the accounting for each type of arrangement.

IFRS Source Document

- IFRS 11, *Joint Arrangements*

Overview of Joint Arrangements

A joint arrangement is one in which several parties exercise joint control under a contractual arrangement. Such arrangements may be created to share costs or risks, or to share access to certain types of technology, import arrangements, and so forth. They may be established under any number of legal structures, such as corporations or various types of limited liability entities.

Joint control is considered to be when decisions about certain activities require unanimous consent by those parties contractually entitled to share control. Thus, a joint arrangement requires that the controlling parties must act together to direct certain activities. Viewed from a negative perspective, a party participating in a joint arrangement has the ability to prevent the other parties from controlling the arrangement.

EXAMPLE

Kilo Corporation, Lima Limited, and Mike Manufacturing establish an arrangement under which Kilo has 50% of the voting rights, Lima has 40%, and Mike has 10%. The arrangement between these entities specifies that at least 90% of the voting rights are required to make valid decisions concerning the activities conducted by the joint arrangement. Given these terms, Kilo does not control the arrangement, because it must obtain the agreement of Lima for any decision. The implication of the arrangement is that Kilo and Lima exercise joint control over the arrangement. Mike does not have joint control, since its approval is not required in order to make decisions concerning the arrangement, and it cannot block decisions.

An arrangement could still be considered a joint arrangement even in the absence of unanimous consent among those parties having joint control, if the contractual arrangement includes a provision for dealing with dispute resolution, such as the use of an arbitrator.

The treatment of a joint venture depends upon its classification as either a *joint operation* or a *joint venture*. The operators of a joint operation have rights to the assets and obligations for the liabilities related to the arrangement, while the operators of a joint venture have rights to the net assets of the arrangement.

A joint operation exists when it is not structured as a separate legal entity, with only a contractual arrangement stating the rights and responsibilities of the parties. In this situation, the parties recognize in their own financial statements their respective shares of the related revenues and expenses, as well as any assets and liabilities.

A joint arrangement may also be structured through a separate entity, which holds the assets and liabilities used to conduct the operations of the arrangement. This type of arrangement can be considered either a joint operation or a joint venture, depending upon the rights and obligations of the parties. An arrangement that gives the operators rights to the assets and liabilities of the separate entity is a joint operation, while an arrangement that gives the operators rights to the net assets of the arrangement is a joint venture. The following flowchart shows the decision points in deciding whether an arrangement is a joint operation or a joint venture.

When an interest is acquired in a joint operation whose activities are considered to be a business, the investing entity should apply the principles of business combination accounting to the arrangement, based on its share in the joint operation, but only to the extent that these principles do not conflict with the accounting for joint arrangements. The applicable principles of business combinations include:

- Measuring assets and liabilities at their fair values
- Recognizing acquisition-related expenses as the costs are incurred
- Recognizing deferred tax assets and liabilities caused by the initial recognition of assets and liabilities
- Recognizing as goodwill any amount of consideration paid out that exceeds the net amount of assets and liabilities acquired and assumed, respectively
- Testing goodwill for impairment at least annually and when there is an indication of impairment

See the Business Combinations chapter for more information.

Joint Arrangement Decision Path

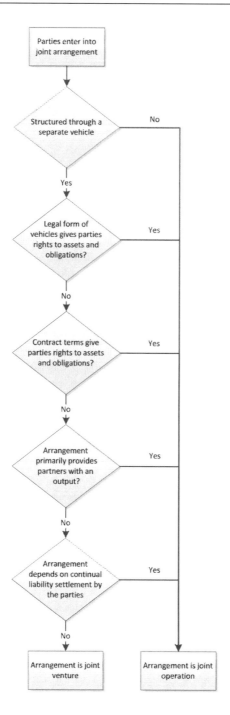

EXAMPLE

Oscar Corporation and Papa Manufacturing enter into a joint arrangement, whereby they create Quebec Company, with each of the owners taking a 50% stake in the new business. By using the legal form of the corporation, Oscar and Papa separate themselves from the assets and liabilities of Quebec. This means that both parties have rights to the net assets of the arrangement, which classifies the arrangement as a joint venture.

However, Oscar and Papa alter the corporate structure of the Quebec entity, so that each one has an ongoing interest in the assets and liabilities of Quebec. By making this change to the corporate structure, Oscar and Papa have essentially altered the form of the transaction to be a joint operation.

EXAMPLE

Romeo Inc. and Sierra Corporation enter into a joint arrangement by creating Tango Company, in which Romeo and Sierra each hold a 50% interest. The legal form of the arrangement indicates that the owners have rights to the net assets of the arrangement, which would logically lead to the classification of the arrangement as a joint venture.

However, the arrangement was specifically created to supply both Romeo and Sierra with equal proportions of a rare earth mineral, which Tango extracts from a mine. Romeo and Sierra take virtually all of the output of the mine, and also set the price at which they purchase it to match the costs incurred by Tango. Because this arrangement means that Tango is exclusively dependent upon Romeo and Sierra for its cash flows, the owners essentially have an obligation to fund the settlement of Tango's liabilities. Also, since they take all of Tango's output, they essentially have rights to all of the economic benefits of Tango.

Thus, the facts and circumstances indicate that the arrangement is actually a joint operation.

It is possible that the facts and circumstances under which an arrangement was originally classified as a joint operation or joint venture will change over time. If so, adjust the classification to meet the circumstances.

Financial Statement Presentation of Joint Arrangements

If an entity classifies its participation in a joint arrangement as a joint operation, it should recognize the following information in its financial statements:

- *Assets*. The entity's assets in the joint operation, as well as its share of any jointly-held assets.
- *Liabilities*. The entity's liabilities incurred through the joint operation, as well as its share of any jointly-incurred liabilities.
- *Revenues from share of output*. The amount of any revenues recognized from the sale of the entity's share of any output generated by the joint operation.

- *Revenues from allocation.* The amount of any revenues sold by the joint venture and allocated to the entity.
- *Expenses.* The entity's expenses incurred in relation to the joint operation, and its share of any expenses that were jointly incurred.

When a party to a joint arrangement that is classified as a joint operation enters into a transaction with the joint operation, it is essentially doing business with the other parties to the arrangement. The following accounting applies to such a transaction:

- *Asset purchase.* If the party purchases assets from the joint operation, the party cannot recognize its share of the resulting gains or losses until it has resold the assets to a third party.
- *Gains and losses.* The party should recognize any gains and losses generated by the transaction only to the extent of the interests of the other parties in the joint operation.
- *Impairment.* If the transaction reduces the net realizable value of the assets of the joint operation, the party should recognize its full share of the loss.

If an entity classifies its participation in a joint arrangement as a joint venture, it should recognize in its financial statements the entity's investment in the joint venture, using the equity method of accounting. See the Investments in Associates and Joint Ventures chapter for more information.

Summary

The flowchart in this chapter might make it appear as though most joint arrangements will, by default, be classified as joint operations. However, the overriding factor is the presence of a separate legal entity to house a jointly-controlled entity. In most cases, barring the presence of a joint arrangement that definitively states otherwise, most joint arrangements that make use of a legal entity will probably be classified as joint ventures.

Chapter 11
Investments in Associates and Joint Ventures

Introduction

Most of the guidance in this chapter is applicable to those situations where a business is an investor with either significant or joint control over an investee, and needs to record its initial and ongoing investment in the investee. We also address a related topic, which is the proper classification of member investments in a cooperative enterprise.

IFRS Source Documents

- IAS 28, *Investments in Associates and Joint Ventures*
- IFRIC 2, *Members' Shares in Cooperative Entities and Similar Instruments*

Investments in Associates and Joint Ventures

The proper type of accounting to use for an investment in an associate or joint venture depends upon the level of control that an investor exercises over the investee. The assumption in this section is that significant control is being exercised, which leads to a requirement to use the equity method of accounting for an investment. In this section, we address the concept of significant influence, as well as how to account for an investment using the equity method.

Significant Influence

The key element in determining whether to use the equity method is the extent of the influence exercised by an investor over an investee. The essential rules governing the existence of significant influence are:

- *Voting power.* Significant influence is presumed to be present if an investor and its subsidiaries hold at least 20 percent of the voting power of an investee. When reviewing this item, consider the impact of potential voting rights that are currently exercisable, such as warrants, stock options, and convertible debt. This is the overriding rule governing the existence of significant influence.
- *Board seat.* The investor controls a seat on the investee's board of directors.
- *Personnel.* Managerial personnel are shared between the entities.
- *Policy making.* The investor participates in the policy making processes of the investee. For example, the investor can affect decisions concerning distributions to shareholders.

- *Technical information.* Essential technical information is provided by one party to the other.
- *Transactions.* There are material transactions between the entities.

These rules should be followed unless there is clear evidence that significant influence is not present. Conversely, significant influence can be present when voting power is lower than 20 percent, but only if it can be clearly demonstrated.

An investor can lose significant control over an investee, despite the presence of one or more of the preceding factors. For example, a government, regulator, or bankruptcy court may gain effective control over an investee, thereby eliminating what had previously been the significant influence of an investor.

The Equity Method

If significant influence is present, an investor should account for its investment in an investee using the equity method. In essence, the equity method mandates that the initial investment be recorded at cost, after which the investment is adjusted for the actual performance of the investee. The following table illustrates how the equity method operates:

+	Initial investment recorded at cost
+/-	Investor's share of investee profit or loss after the acquisition date
-	Distributions received from the investee
=	Ending investment in investee

The investor's share of the investee's profits and losses are recorded within profit or loss for the investor. Also, if the investee records changes in its other comprehensive income, the investor should record its share of these items within other comprehensive income, as well.

EXAMPLE

Armadillo Industries purchases 30% of the common stock of Titanium Barriers, Inc. Armadillo controls two seats on the board of directors of Titanium as a result of this investment, so it uses the equity method to account for the investment. In the next year, Titanium earns £400,000. Armadillo records its 30% share of the profit with the following entry:

	Debit	Credit
Investment in Titanium Barriers	120,000	
Equity in Titanium Barriers income		120,000

A few months later, Titanium issues a £50,000 cash dividend to Armadillo, which the company records with the following entry:

	Debit	Credit
Cash	50,000	
Investment in Titanium Barriers		50,000

The percentage of investee profits and losses that an investor recognizes is based on the investor's actual ownership interest in the investee. The impact of potential voting rights, as evidenced by warrants, stock options, convertible debt, and so forth, is not included in the calculation of this percentage.

When the equity method is in use, the investor should periodically examine its investment to see if there has been any impairment of the recorded amount. The impairment test is to compare the recoverable amount of the investment with its carrying amount. If impairment has occurred, the investor records an impairment loss in the amount by which the recoverable amount is less than the carrying amount; this is used to reduce the recorded investment in the investee. If the value of an investment subsequently increases, the impairment loss can be reversed, to the extent that the recoverable amount of the investment increases. Objective evidence of impairment can result from one or more of the following loss events:

- Significant financial difficulties experienced by the joint venture or associate
- A breach of contract by the joint venture or associate
- A concession is granted to the joint venture or associate due to financial difficulties
- The joint venture or associate will probably require financial reorganization
- There is no active market for the investment, due to the financial difficulties of the joint venture or associate

If an investee reports a large loss, or a series of losses, it is possible that recording the investor's share of these losses will result in a substantial decline of the investor's recorded investment in the investee. If so, the investor should stop using the equity method when its investment reaches zero. If an investor's investment in an investee has been written down to zero, but it has other investments in the investee (such as loans), the investor should continue to recognize its share of any additional investee losses, and offset them against the other investments, in sequence of the seniority of those investments (with offsets against the most junior items first). Any further share of investee losses is only recorded if the investor has committed to obligations on behalf of the investee. If the investee later begins to report profits again, the investor does not resume use of the equity method until such time as its share of investee profits have offset all investee losses that were not recognized during the period when use of the equity method was suspended.

EXAMPLE

Armadillo Industries has a 35% ownership interest in the common stock of Arlington Research. The carrying amount of this investment has been reduced to zero because of previous losses. To keep Arlington solvent, Armadillo has purchased £250,000 of Arlington's preferred stock, and extended a long-term unsecured loan of £500,000.

During the next year, Arlington incurs a £1,200,000 loss, of which Armadillo's share is 35%, or £420,000. Since the next most senior level of Arlington's capital after common stock is its preferred stock, Armadillo first offsets its share of the loss against its preferred stock investment. Doing so reduces the carrying amount of the preferred stock to zero, leaving £170,000 to be applied against the carrying amount of the loan. This results in the following entry by Armadillo:

	Debit	Credit
Equity method loss	420,000	
Preferred stock investment		250,000
Loan		170,000

In the following year, Arlington records £800,000 of profits, of which Armadillo's share is £280,000. Armadillo applies the £280,000 first against the loan write-down, and then against the preferred stock write-down with the following entry:

	Debit	Credit
Preferred stock investment	110,000	
Loan	170,000	
Equity method income		280,000

The result is that the carrying amount of the loan is fully restored, while the carrying amount of the preferred stock investment is still reduced by £140,000 from its original level.

There may be a reduction in the ownership interest of an investor in an investee, where the equity method is already in use. If the reduction still allows the investor to have significant influence over the investee, the investor should continue to use the equity method. However, this change means that the investor has effectively disposed of a portion of its share of the assets and liabilities of the investee. Therefore, the investor should reclassify to profit or loss a portion of those amounts related to the activities of the investee that are currently reported in the other comprehensive income of the investor.

If an investor classifies an equity method investee as held for sale, it freezes use of the equity method while the investment is so classified. If, at a later date, the held for sale classification is no longer valid, the investor must retroactively apply the equity method from the date when the held for sale classification was first applied to the investment.

Use of the equity method should be discontinued as of the date when the investee can no longer be classified as an associate or a joint venture. Specifically, the following circumstances cancel use of the equity method:

- The investee becomes a subsidiary, in which case its financial statements are consolidated with those of the parent entity.
- The investment is classified as a financial asset, in which case the investment is measured and recognized at its fair value.

When use of the equity method is discontinued, and if the investor had previously recorded its share of investee transactions in other comprehensive income, these items should be reclassified to profit or loss.

EXAMPLE

Armadillo Industries is a 25% investor in Titanium Housings Ltd., and so is considered to have significant influence over Titanium. Titanium is currently holding short-term investments in commercial paper for which it has recorded an unrecognized gain of £100,000 in other comprehensive income. Armadillo records its 25% share of this gain in other comprehensive income. The next month, Armadillo loses significant influence over Titanium when a federal regulator takes control of the entity. On the date of the loss of control, Armadillo should reclassify the £25,000 gain to profit or loss.

The following additional rules apply to the use of the equity method:
- *Accounting policies.* The accounting policies used by the investee should be the same as those used by the investor. If not, adjust the financial statements of the investee so that they present information in accordance with the policies used by the investor.
- *Cumulative preference shares.* The investee may have cumulative preference shares outstanding that are held by other parties than the investor. If so, the investor calculates its share of investee profits or losses after adjusting for the dividends on these shares, even if the dividends have not yet been declared.
- *Financial statements used.* To record the equity method, the investor uses the most recent financial statements of the investee. If the reporting period closing dates of the investor and investee are different, the investee should prepare financial statements through the date used by the investor, unless this is impracticable to do so. If there is a difference in dates, adjust the financial statements of the investee for significant transactions and events that occurred after the date of the investee's financial statements and through the ending date of the investor's financial statements. The upper limit on the difference in the reporting periods of the entities is three months. For consistency, any differences between the ending dates of the reporting periods of the two entities should be the same from period to period.
- *Impairments.* When an investor sells assets to associates or joint ventures, and there is an impairment loss or a reduction in net realizable value on the assets sold, the investor recognizes these losses in full.

- *Inter-entity transactions.* The investor only recognizes transactions with an investee to the extent of the interests of any unrelated investors in the investee. Thus, the investor's share in the gains and losses recorded by an investee for these transactions is eliminated.
- *Non-monetary contribution.* If the investor contributes a non-monetary asset to an associate or joint venture in exchange for an equity interest, and also receives assets in exchange, the investor can recognize the full amount of any gain or loss on that portion of the contribution relating to the assets received.

EXAMPLE

Armadillo Industries sells £200,000 of raw materials to its 25 percent owned associate, Titanium Housings Ltd. The cost to Armadillo of these raw materials is £125,000.

Armadillo initially records a profit of £75,000 on this transaction, but must reduce the profit by its 25 percent stake in Titanium, which results in a £56,250 profit.

Members' Shares in Cooperative Entities

Groups of individuals or businesses sometimes work together to create cooperatives that represent their interests. Members typically hold shares or interests in these cooperatives. These shares or interests may contain a redemption clause that requires a cooperative to buy back member shares or interests.

A cooperative may not have to classify these shares or interests as financial liabilities, despite the presence of a redemption clause. Proper classification will depend upon the exact terms and conditions of the shares or interests, as well as local laws and regulations, and the charter of the cooperative. If there is no right of redemption or the cooperative can refuse redemption, shares and interests are most likely classified as equity. If certain conditions must be met before a redemption can take place, the related shares or interests should not be treated as equity.

If there is a prohibition on redemptions above a certain number of shares or interests, the shares and interests that can be redeemed are classified as liabilities, while the other shares and interests are classified as equity. If the proportion of shares or interests subject to this prohibition changes over time, this can trigger a transfer between the equity and financial liability accounts of the cooperative.

When measuring the amount of a financial liability related to a redemption feature, a cooperative should initially do so at the fair value of the redemption. Fair value is considered to be no less than the maximum redemption amount payable from the first possible payment date.

If a member acts as a customer, the transactions related to that activity, such as depositing funds in a deposit account, are considered operational assets and liabilities of the cooperative.

EXAMPLE

The Ethanol Cooperative is run by a regional group of farmers, who have pooled their assets to create an ethanol production facility that uses their produce as input to the production process. Local regulations mandate that cooperatives cannot redeem member shares if doing so reduces paid-in capital below 60 percent of the highest amount of paid-in capital. The highest amount of paid-in capital has been £10,000,000. At the end of the current reporting period, the amount of paid-in capital is £8,400,000.

Based on these facts, £6,000,000 of the paid-in capital can be classified as equity, and the remaining £2,400,000 as a financial liability.

Disclosures

An investment in an associate or joint venture should be classified as a non-current asset. However, if the intent of the investor is to sell the investment, the proper classification is to list the investment as held for sale.

When there is a transfer between the equity and financial liability accounts of a cooperative that is caused by a change in the amount of member shares or interests that may be redeemed, disclose the amount, timing, and reason for the change.

Summary

The equity method is one of the more difficult methods for measuring an investment, especially if a share of both profit and loss and other comprehensive income transactions of the investee must be recognized, and when losses place an investment on the cusp of terminating or restarting use of the method. Accordingly, the best option is to closely examine the presence of significant influence over an investee, and to make a persuasive case that such influence is not present. If this argument is sufficiently convincing, the investor can avoid use of the equity method, and instead treat the situation as a simple investment.

Chapter 12
Disclosure of Interests in Other Entities

Introduction

A business may own an interest in another entity. If so, the business should disclose a sufficient amount of information about that interest to inform readers of its financial statements about the nature of the relationship. This chapter outlines a number of required disclosures, which are segregated by type of interest.

IFRS Source Document

- IFRS 12, *Disclosure of Interests in Other Entities*

Overview of Interests in Other Entities

A company may have an interest in another entity, which means that the company is exposed to a certain amount of variability in returns from the other entity. The nature of a company's interests in other entities could be critical to its success, since these other entities may generate a substantial amount of the profits or losses reported by the company. Consequently, the readers of a company's financial statements should be given sufficient information to evaluate the nature of these interests and the risks associated with them, as well as how these interests affect the financial performance, position, and cash flows of the company. The following general types of information are considered to represent sufficient disclosure:
- The judgments made to determine the nature of a relationship.
- Information about interests in specific types of entities, such as subsidiaries, joint arrangements and associates, and structured entities over which the company does not exercise control.

These disclosures may include a discussion of:
- Why a business does not control another entity, even though it owns over half of the voting rights of the entity, or why it *does* control an entity, despite having a lower ownership percentage.
- Why a business is considered an agent of another entity for certain transactions, or why it considers itself to be acting as a principal.
- Why a business has significant influence over another entity, despite holding less than 20% of its voting rights, or why the business does *not* have significant influence despite holding more than 20% of its voting rights.

The level and type of these disclosures will vary, depending upon the nature of the relationships that a business has with other entities. In the following sections, we will address the disclosures required for specific types of interests in other entities.

Interests in Subsidiaries

When a business has subsidiaries, the general goals of disclosure are to enable users of the information to understand the composition of the group of companies, the involvement of non-controlling interests, any restrictions on the use of subsidiary assets and liabilities, and risks. Users must also comprehend the consequences of changes in ownership interests or the loss of control over subsidiaries during a reporting period.

More specifically, the following information relating to subsidiaries must be disclosed in the notes accompanying the financial statements:

- *Reporting dates.* When the financial statements of a subsidiary are rolled into the parent company's consolidated statements, and the period encompassed by the financials of the subsidiary are different from the reporting period of the parent, note the ending date of the subsidiary's reporting period and the reason for using the different reporting period.

- *Non-controlling interests.* If there is a non-controlling interest in a subsidiary, disclose the subsidiary's name and principal place of business, the proportions of the non-controlling interests' ownership interest and voting rights, any profit or loss allocated to the non-controlling interests, and the accumulated amount of non-controlling interests in the subsidiary as of the end of the period. Also disclose dividends paid to the non-controlling interests, and summarized financial information about the subsidiary in such areas as current assets, non-current assets, current liabilities, non-current liabilities, revenue, profit or loss, and total comprehensive income.

- *Restrictions.* Disclose any significant restrictions on the ability of the parent entity to access or use the assets of the subsidiary, or settle its liabilities, such as restrictions on cash transfers, or the presence of guarantees that prevent dividends from being paid. Also note the carrying amounts of the assets and liabilities to which these restrictions apply.

- *Risks.* Note the terms of any contractual arrangements that may require financial support to a consolidated structured entity, including the circumstances under which the reporting entity could be exposed to a loss. If the parent or another entity in the reporting group has provided support to a consolidated structured entity in the absence of a contractual obligation to do so, describe the type and amount of support provided, and the reasons for doing so. If the provision of support resulted in the control of a structured entity, disclose the reasons for extending support. Finally, if the reporting entity intends to provide support to a consolidated structured entity, disclose this fact.

- *Changes in ownership interest.* Present a schedule showing the effects of changes in the ownership interest in a subsidiary on the equity attributable to owners of the parent, where the changes do not result in a loss of control.
- *Loss of control.* If the parent entity loses control over a subsidiary, disclose the gain or loss attributable to the fair value measurement of the investment in the former subsidiary on the date when control was lost, as well as the line item within which this information is classified in the income statement.

Interests in Joint Arrangements and Associates

A *joint arrangement* is one in which several parties exercise joint control under a contractual arrangement, while an *associate* is an entity over which another party exercises significant control. When a business has interests in joint arrangements or in associates, it should disclose enough information for users of its financial statements to evaluate the nature and financial effects of these interests, as well as any related risks. Consequently, the following disclosures should be made in the notes that accompany the financial statements.

For each material joint arrangement and associate, disclose:
- The name of the joint arrangement or associate, and its principal place of business.
- The nature of the relationship with the joint arrangement or associate.
- The ownership interest percentage in the joint arrangement or associate.

For each material joint venture and associate, disclose:
- Whether the investment is measured under the equity method or using fair value.
- Dividends received from the joint venture or associate.
- Summarized financial information that includes current assets, non-current assets, current liabilities, non-current liabilities, revenue, profit or loss from continuing operations, post-tax profits or losses from discontinued operations, other comprehensive income, and total comprehensive income.
- For each material joint venture, the cash and cash equivalents, current financial liabilities, non-current financial liabilities, depreciation and amortization, interest income, interest expense, and income taxes.
- The fair value of the investment, if a quoted market price is available from which to derive the fair value, and if the investment is accounted for under the equity method.
- For all individually immaterial joint ventures that are accounted for using the equity method, the carrying amount of these investments, as well as the aggregate share of profit or loss from continuing operations, post-tax profit or loss from discontinued operations, other comprehensive income, and total comprehensive income. The same information should be provided separately for all individually immaterial associates that are accounted for using the equity method.

Other disclosures that may apply to joint arrangements and associates are:

- The nature of any significant restrictions on the ability of the joint venture or associate to transfer funds to the business, such as in the form of dividends, loan repayments, or advances. Examples of possible restrictions are loan covenants or contractual arrangements.
- The ending date of the reporting period of the joint venture or associate, if it varies from that of the business, and the reason for using this different date.
- Any unrecognized share of the losses of a joint venture or associate, both for the period and in total, if the business has ceased recognizing its share of losses under the equity method.
- Commitments relating to joint ventures, as well as total commitments made but not recognized relating to joint ventures, and which may cause a future outflow of cash. Examples of unrecognized commitments are unconditional purchase obligations, commitments to provide loans, and commitments to acquire the interest of another party in a joint venture that is based on a future event.

Interests in Unconsolidated Structured Entities

A *structured entity* is one that has been structured in such a manner that voting rights are not the key determinant of who controls it. A structured entity tends to engage in a tightly restricted set of activities that support a specific objective, such as conducting certain research and development activities. It may also be insufficiently capitalized to fund its own activities, and so depends on financial support from other parties. Examples of structured entities are investment funds and asset-backed financings.

If a business consolidates the results of such a structured entity, it should provide sufficient supporting information that users of the financial statements can understand the nature of the interest, as well as evaluate the nature of any risks associated with that interest. Accordingly, include the following disclosures in the notes accompanying the financial statements:

- The nature of the relationship with unconsolidated structured entities, including the purpose, size, activities, and financing of these entities.
- If the business does not have an interest in an unconsolidated structured entity at the reporting date, disclose the carrying amount of any assets transferred to the structured entity in the period, the income amount and types of income from the entity, and the method for determining which structured entities the business has sponsored. This information should be presented in a tabular format.
- A tabular summary of the following information related to the nature of risks related to structured entities:
    - The carrying amounts of assets and liabilities recognized by the company, relating to its interests in any unconsolidated structured

entities, as well as the line items in the balance sheet where they are located.

- o The maximum exposure to loss from the structured entities, as well as how this amount is determined. If it is not possible to quantify this information, state the reasons why.
- o A comparison of the first two items, matching carrying amounts to maximum exposure.
- If the business has provided support to a structured entity that it was not obligated to provide, state the amount and type of support, and the reason for doing so. Further, disclose situations in which the business assisted the entity in procuring financial support.
- If the business intends to provide support to an unconsolidated structured entity, disclose the nature of this support, as well as any intended assistance in obtaining financial support.

The discussion of risk should include any remaining risk exposures related to structured entities with which the business no longer has any contractual involvement.

In order to provide complete disclosure of risk information pertaining to structured entities, it may be necessary to disclose additional information, such as the terms of an arrangement to provide financial support, the types of profits or losses related to structured entities, whether there is a requirement to absorb the losses of an unstructured entity, any difficulties experienced by a structured entity in securing funding, the forms of funding obtained, and so forth.

Summary

In order to fully understand the disclosure requirements in this chapter, it is useful to peruse the Joint Arrangements chapter and the Investments in Associates and Joint Ventures chapter, which precede this chapter. Some of the disclosure requirements noted in those chapters duplicate the requirements stated in this chapter; when this happens, a single disclosure of the required information is sufficient to satisfy the disclosure requirements stated in both chapters.

Chapter 13
Inventories

Introduction

Inventory is one of the most important asset classifications, for it may represent the largest asset investment by a manufacturer or seller of goods. As a major asset, it is imperative that inventory be properly valued, as well as those goods designated as having been sold. This chapter discusses the IFRS requirements for inventory, and then expands upon them with discussions of inventory tracking systems, costing methodologies, and a variety of related topics. The guidance in this chapter does not apply to work in progress under construction contracts, financial instruments, or agricultural assets.

> **Related Podcast Episodes:** Episodes 56, 66, and 119 of the Accounting Best Practices Podcast discuss inventory record accuracy, obsolete inventory, and overhead allocation, respectively. They are available at: **accounting-tools.com/podcasts**

IFRS Source Document

- IAS 2, *Inventories*

Overview of Inventory

In general, inventory is to be accounted for at cost, which is considered to be the sum of those expenditures required to bring an inventory item to its present condition and location. There are three types of costs to apply to inventory, which are:

- *Direct costs.* If a cost was directly incurred to produce or acquire a specific unit of inventory, this is called a direct cost, and is recorded as a cost of inventory. Typical direct costs are the purchase price, import duties, sales taxes, transport charges, and site preparation, less any trade discounts or rebates.
- *Variable overhead costs.* If there are any factory costs that are not direct, but which vary with production volume, they are assigned to inventory based on actual usage of a company's production facilities. There are usually not many variable overhead costs.
- *Fixed overhead costs.* If there are any factory costs that are not direct, and which do not vary with production volume, they are assigned to inventory based on the normal capacity of a company's production facilities.

The accounting for overhead costs is particularly critical, given the large amount of such costs that are allocated in many production facilities. The basic IFRS rules for fixed overhead allocation are:

- *Normal capacity allocation basis.* Only allocate fixed overhead costs to produced units based on the normal capacity of the company's production process. Normal capacity is the average production level expected over multiple periods under normal operating circumstances.
- *Low-production periods.* During periods of abnormally low production, the overhead allocation per produced unit is *not* increased. This means that an excess amount of overhead cannot be charged to produced units because production levels are unusually low; instead, the excess amount of unallocated overhead is to be charged to expense as incurred.
- *High-production periods.* During periods of abnormally high production, the overhead allocation per produced unit should be reduced in order to keep from recording an inventory amount that is above its actual cost.

In addition, variable overhead is to be allocated to produced units based on the actual level of usage of the manufacturing facility.

If some costs are incurred to produce more than one product, and where the costs of production can be directly associated with specific products (such as a primary product and a by-product), allocate the production cost between the resulting products on a rational and consistent basis, which is typically based on their relative sales values. An alternative approach is to measure by-products whose sales values are immaterial at their net realizable values, and to then deduct this amount from the cost of the primary product.

Tip: Though overhead must be allocated to inventory, this does not mean that an inordinate amount of time should be spent compiling an exquisitely designed allocation system. Instead, focus on a simple and efficient allocation methodology that allows the books to be closed quickly.

Several other rules have been developed regarding inventory costs, most of which are designed to keep certain costs from being allocated to inventory. They are:

- *Abnormal expenses.* If unusually high costs are incurred, such as abnormal freight, spoilage, or scrap charges, they are to be charged to expense in the period incurred.
- *Administrative expenses.* Administrative costs can only be allocated to inventory when they are clearly related to production. In nearly all cases, these costs are charged to expense as incurred.
- *Deferred payment terms.* When a business purchases inventories that have delayed payment terms associated with them, the financing element is recognized as interest expense over the financing period, rather than a cost of inventory.

- *Selling expenses.* All costs related to selling are charged to expense as incurred; they are never allocated to inventory.
- *Storage costs.* Charge storage costs to expense as incurred, unless these costs are required as part of the production process.

Once costs have initially been apportioned to inventory, IFRS requires that any decline in the utility of goods below their cost result in the recognition of a loss in the current period. This decline in utility is most commonly caused by the deterioration or obsolescence of inventory items. The Accounting for Obsolete Inventory section describes how to account for this type of loss. A decline in utility may also be caused by a decline in the price of inventory items. The Net Realizable Value section describes how to calculate and account for this type of loss.

The *inventory cost flow* assumption is the concept that the cost of an inventory item changes between the time it is acquired or built and the time when it is sold. Because of this cost differential, a company needs to adopt a cost flow assumption regarding how it treats the cost of goods as they move through the company.

For example, a company buys a widget on January 1 for £50. On July 1, it buys an identical widget for £70, and on November 1 it buys yet another identical widget for £90. The products are completely interchangeable. On December 1, the company sells one of the widgets. It bought the widgets at three different prices, so what cost should it report for its cost of goods sold? There are several ways to interpret the cost flow assumption. For example:

- *FIFO cost flow assumption.* Under the first in, first out method, assume that the first item purchased is also the first one sold. Thus, the cost of goods sold would be £50. Since this is the lowest-cost item in the example, profits would be highest under FIFO.
- *Weighted average cost flow assumption.* Under the weighted average method, the cost of goods sold is the average cost of all three units, or £70. This cost flow assumption tends to yield a mid-range cost, and therefore also a mid-range profit.

The cost flow assumption does not necessarily match the actual flow of goods (if that were the case, most companies would use the FIFO method). Instead, it is allowable to use a cost flow assumption that varies from actual usage. For this reason, companies tend to select an assumption that either minimizes profits (in order to minimize income taxes) or maximize profits (in order to increase share value).

The cost flow assumption is a minor item when inventory costs are relatively stable over the long term, since there will be no particular difference in the cost of goods sold, no matter which assumption is used. Conversely, dramatic changes in inventory costs over time will yield a notable difference in reported profit levels, depending on the assumption used. Therefore, be especially aware of the financial impact of the inventory cost flow assumption in periods of fluctuating costs.

In the following sections, we describe the more commonly-used methods for inventory costing, several of which are based on cost flow assumptions. First, however, we address the two main record-keeping systems needed to accurately track inventory, which are the periodic inventory system and the perpetual inventory system.

The Periodic Inventory System

The periodic inventory system only updates the ending inventory balance when a physical inventory count is conducted. Since physical inventory counts are time-consuming, few companies complete them more than once a quarter or year. In the meantime, the inventory account continues to show the cost of the inventory that was recorded as of the last physical inventory count.

Under the periodic inventory system, all purchases made between physical inventory counts are recorded in a purchases account. When a physical inventory count is done, shift the balance in the purchases account into the inventory account, which in turn is adjusted to match the cost of the ending inventory.

The calculation of the cost of goods sold under the periodic inventory system is:

Beginning inventory + Purchases = Cost of goods available for sale

Cost of goods available for sale – Ending inventory = Cost of goods sold

---

EXAMPLE

Milagro Corporation has beginning inventory of £100,000, has paid £170,000 for purchases, and its physical inventory count reveals an ending inventory cost of £80,000. The calculation of its cost of goods sold is:

£100,000 Beginning inventory + £170,000 Purchases - £80,000 Ending inventory

= £190,000 Cost of goods sold

The periodic inventory system is most useful for smaller businesses that maintain minimal amounts of inventory. For them, a physical inventory count is easy to complete, and they can estimate cost of goods sold figures for interim periods. However, there are several problems with the system:

- It does not yield any information about the cost of goods sold or ending inventory balances during interim periods when there has been no physical inventory count.
- The cost of goods sold must be estimated during interim periods, which will likely result in a significant adjustment to the actual cost of goods whenever a physical inventory count is eventually completed.
- There is no way to adjust for obsolete inventory or scrap losses during interim periods, so there tends to be a significant (and expensive) adjustment for these issues when a physical inventory count is eventually completed.

A more up-to-date and accurate alternative to the periodic inventory system is the perpetual inventory system, which is described in the next section.

The Perpetual Inventory System

Under the perpetual inventory system, an entity continually updates its inventory records to account for additions to and subtractions from inventory for such activities as received inventory items, goods sold from stock, and items picked from inventory for use in the production process. Thus, a perpetual inventory system has the advantages of both providing up-to-date inventory balance information and requiring a reduced level of physical inventory counts. However, the calculated inventory levels derived by a perpetual inventory system may gradually diverge from actual inventory levels due to unrecorded transactions or theft, so periodically compare book balances to actual on-hand quantities.

EXAMPLE

This example contains several journal entries used to account for transactions in a perpetual inventory system. Milagro Corporation records a purchase of £1,000 of widgets that are stored in inventory:

	Debit	Credit
Inventory	1,000	
Accounts payable		1,000

Milagro records £250 of inbound freight cost associated with the delivery of widgets:

	Debit	Credit
Inventory	250	
Accounts payable		250

Milagro records the sale of widgets on credit from inventory for £2,000, for which the associated inventory cost is £1,200:

	Debit	Credit
Accounts receivable	2,000	
Revenue		2,000
Cost of goods sold	1,200	
Inventory		1,200

Milagro records a downward inventory adjustment of £500 caused by inventory theft, and detected during an inventory count:

	Debit	Credit
Inventory shrinkage expense	500	
Inventory		500

Inventory Costing

Several methods for calculating the cost of inventory are shown in this section. Of the methods presented, only the first in, first out method and the weighted average method have gained worldwide recognition. Standard costing is an acceptable alternative to cost layering, as long as any associated variances are properly accounted for. The retail inventory method and gross profit method should be used only to derive an approximation of the ending inventory cost, and so should be used only in interim reporting periods when a company does not intend to issue any financial results to outside parties.

The First In, First Out Method

The first in, first out (FIFO) method of inventory valuation operates under the assumption that the first goods purchased are also the first goods sold. In most companies, this accounting assumption closely matches the actual flow of goods, and so is considered the most theoretically correct inventory valuation method.

Under the FIFO method, the earliest goods purchased are the first ones removed from the inventory account. This results in the remaining items in inventory being accounted for at the most recently incurred costs, so that the inventory asset recorded on the balance sheet contains costs quite close to the most recent costs that could be obtained in the marketplace. Conversely, this method also results in older historical costs being matched against current revenues and recorded in the cost of goods sold, so the gross margin does not necessarily reflect a proper matching of revenues and costs.

EXAMPLE

Milagro Corporation decides to use the FIFO method for the month of January. During that month, it records the following transactions:

	Quantity Change	Actual Unit Cost	Actual Total Cost
Beginning inventory (layer 1)	+100	£210	£21,000
Sale	-75		
Purchase (layer 2)	+150	280	42,000
Sale	-100		
Purchase (layer 3)	+50	300	15,000
Ending inventory	= 125		

The cost of goods sold in units is calculated as:

100 Beginning inventory + 200 Purchased – 125 Ending inventory = 175 Units

Milagro's controller uses the information in the preceding table to calculate the cost of goods sold for January, as well as the cost of the inventory balance as of the end of January.

	Units	Unit Cost	Total Cost
Cost of goods sold			
FIFO layer 1	100	£210	£21,000
FIFO layer 2	75	280	21,000
Total cost of goods sold	175		£42,000
Ending inventory			
FIFO layer 2	75	280	£21,000
FIFO layer 3	50	300	15,000
Total ending inventory	125		£36,000

Thus, the first FIFO layer, which was the beginning inventory layer, is completely used up during the month, as well as half of Layer 2, leaving half of Layer 2 and all of Layer 3 to be the sole components of the ending inventory.

Note that the £42,000 cost of goods sold and £36,000 ending inventory equals the £78,000 combined total of beginning inventory and purchases during the month.

The Last In, First Out Method

The last in, first out (LIFO) method operates under the assumption that the last item of inventory purchased is the first one sold. Picture a store shelf where a clerk adds items from the front, and customers also take their selections from the front; the remaining items of inventory that are located further from the front of the shelf are rarely picked, and so remain on the shelf – that is a LIFO scenario. IFRS does not permit the use of LIFO as a method for measuring the cost of inventory.

The Weighted Average Method

When using the weighted average method, divide the cost of goods available for sale by the number of units available for sale, which yields the weighted-average cost per unit. In this calculation, the cost of goods available for sale is the sum of beginning inventory and net purchases. Use this weighted-average figure to assign a cost to both ending inventory and the cost of goods sold.

The singular advantage of the weighted average method is the complete absence of any inventory layers, which avoids the record keeping problems that would be encountered with either the FIFO or LIFO methods that were described earlier.

EXAMPLE

Milagro Corporation elects to use the weighted-average method for the month of May. During that month, it records the following transactions:

	Quantity Change	Actual Unit Cost	Actual Total Cost
Beginning inventory	+150	£220	£33,000
Sale	-125		
Purchase	+200	270	54,000
Sale	-150		
Purchase	+100	290	29,000
Ending inventory	= 175		

The actual total cost of all purchased or beginning inventory units in the preceding table is £116,000 (£33,000 + £54,000 + £29,000). The total of all purchased or beginning inventory units is 450 (150 beginning inventory + 300 purchased). The weighted average cost per unit is therefore £257.78 (£116,000 ÷ 450 units).

The ending inventory valuation is £45,112 (175 units × £257.78 weighted average cost), while the cost of goods sold valuation is £70,890 (275 units × £257.78 weighted average cost). The sum of these two amounts (less a rounding error) equals the £116,000 total actual cost of all purchases and beginning inventory.

In the preceding example, if Milagro used a perpetual inventory system to record its inventory transactions, it would have to recompute the weighted average after every purchase. The following table uses the same information in the preceding example to show the recomputations:

	Units on Hand	Purchases	Cost of Sales	Inventory Total Cost	Inventory Moving Average Unit Cost
Beginning inventory	150	£--	£--	£33,000	£220.00
Sale (125 units @ £220.00)	25	--	27,500	5,500	220.00
Purchase (200 units @ £270.00)	225	54,000	--	59,500	264.44
Sale (150 units @ £264.44)	75	--	39,666	19,834	264.44
Purchase (100 units @ £290.00)	175	29,000	--	48,834	279.05
Total			£67,166		

Note that the cost of goods sold of £67,166 and the ending inventory balance of £48,834 equal £116,000, which matches the total of the costs in the original example. Thus, the totals are the same, but the moving weighted average calculation results in slight differences in the apportionment of costs between the cost of goods sold and ending inventory.

Standard Costing

The preceding methods (FIFO and weighted average) operate under the assumption that some sort of cost layering is used, even if that layering results in nothing more than a single weighted-average layer. The standard costing methodology arrives at inventory valuation from an entirely different direction, which is to set a standard cost for each item and to then value those items at the standard cost – not the actual cost at which the items were purchased.

Standard costing is clearly more efficient than any cost layering system, simply because there are no layers to keep track of. However, its primary failing is that the resulting inventory valuation may not equate to the actual cost. The difference is handled through several types of variance calculations, which may be charged to the cost of goods sold (if minor) or allocated between inventory and the cost of goods sold (if material).

At the most basic level, a standard cost is created simply by calculating the average of the most recent actual cost for the past few months. An additional factor to consider when deriving a standard cost is whether to set it at a historical actual cost level that has been proven to be attainable, or at a rate that should be attainable, or one that can only be reached if all operations work perfectly. Here are some considerations:

- *Historical basis.* This is an average of the costs that a company has already experienced in the recent past, possibly weighted towards just the past few months. Though clearly an attainable cost, a standard based on historical results contains all of the operational inefficiencies of the existing production operation.
- *Attainable basis.* This is a cost that is more difficult to reach than a historical cost. This basis assumes some improvement in operating and purchasing efficiencies, which employees have a good chance of achieving in the short term.
- *Theoretical basis.* This is the ultimate, lowest cost that the facility can attain if it functions perfectly, with no scrap, highly efficient employees, and machines that never break down. This can be a frustrating basis to use for a standard cost, because the production facility can never attain it, and so always produces unfavorable variances.

Of the three types of standards noted here, use the attainable basis, because it gives employees a reasonable cost target to pursue. If standards are continually updated on this basis, a production facility will have an incentive to continually drive down its costs over the long term.

Standard costs are stored separately from all other accounting records, usually in a bill of materials for finished goods, and in the item master file for raw materials.

At the end of a reporting period, the following steps show how to integrate standard costs into the accounting system (assuming the use of a periodic inventory system):

1. *Cost verification.* Review the standard cost database for errors and correct as necessary. Also, if it is time to do so, update the standard costs to more accurately reflect actual costs.
2. *Inventory valuation.* Multiply the number of units in ending inventory by their standard costs to derive the ending inventory valuation.
3. *Calculate the cost of goods sold.* Add purchases during the month to the beginning inventory and subtract the ending inventory to determine the cost of goods sold.
4. *Enter updated balances.* Create a journal entry that reduces the purchases account to zero and which also adjusts the inventory asset account balance to the ending total standard cost, with the offset to the cost of goods sold account.

EXAMPLE

A division of the Milagro Corporation is using a standard costing system to calculate its inventory balances and cost of goods sold. The company conducts a month-end physical inventory count that results in a reasonably accurate set of unit quantities for all inventory items. The controller multiplies each of these unit quantities by their standard costs to derive the ending inventory valuation. This ending balance is £2,500,000.

The beginning balance in the inventory account is £2,750,000 and purchases during the month were £1,000,000, so the calculation of the cost of goods sold is:

Beginning inventory	£2,750,000
+ Purchases	1,000,000
- Ending inventory	(2,500,000)
= Cost of goods sold	£1,250,000

To record the correct ending inventory balance and cost of goods sold, the controller records the following entry, which clears out the purchases asset account and adjusts the ending inventory balance to £2,500,000:

	Debit	Credit
Cost of goods sold	1,250,000	
Purchases		1,000,000
Inventory		250,000

IFRS mandates that standard costs be regularly reviewed and adjusted to bring them into alignment with the company's normal levels of capacity utilization and efficiency, as well as the current costs of materials and labor.

The Retail Inventory Method

The retail inventory method is sometimes used by retailers that resell merchandise to estimate their ending inventory balances. This method is based on the relationship between the cost of merchandise and its retail price. To calculate the cost of ending inventory using the retail inventory method, follow these steps:

1. Calculate the cost-to-retail percentage, for which the formula is (Cost ÷ Retail price).
2. Calculate the cost of goods available for sale, for which the formula is (Cost of beginning inventory + Cost of purchases).
3. Calculate the cost of sales during the period, for which the formula is (Sales × Cost-to-retail percentage).
4. Calculate ending inventory, for which the formula is (Cost of goods available for sale - Cost of sales during the period).

EXAMPLE

Milagro Corporation sells home coffee roasters for an average of £200, and which cost it £140. This is a cost-to-retail percentage of 70%. Milagro's beginning inventory has a cost of £1,000,000, it paid £1,800,000 for purchases during the month, and it had sales of £2,400,000. The calculation of its ending inventory is:

Beginning inventory	£1,000,000	(at cost)
Purchases	+ 1,800,000	(at cost)
Goods available for sale	= 2,800,000	
Sales	- 1,680,000	(sales of £2,400,000 × 70%)
Ending inventory	= £1,120,000	

The retail inventory method is a quick and easy way to determine an approximate ending inventory balance. However, there are also several issues with it:

*   The retail inventory method is only an estimate. Do not rely upon it too heavily to yield results that will compare with those of a physical inventory count.
*   The retail inventory method only works if there is a consistent mark-up across all products sold. If not, the actual ending inventory cost may vary wildly from what was derived using this method.
*   The method assumes that the historical basis for the mark-up percentage continues into the current period. If the mark-up was different (as may be caused by an after-holidays sale), the results of the calculation will be incorrect.

IFRS points out that the retail method is often calculated separately for each retail department of a business; this can lead to a more accurate estimation of inventory cost.

The Gross Profit Method

The gross profit method can be used to estimate the amount of ending inventory. This is useful for interim periods between physical inventory counts, or when inventory was destroyed and you need to back into the ending inventory balance for the purpose of filing a claim for insurance reimbursement. Follow these steps to estimate ending inventory using the gross profit method:

1. Add together the cost of beginning inventory and the cost of purchases during the period to arrive at the cost of goods available for sale.
2. Multiply (1 - expected gross profit %) by sales during the period to arrive at the estimated cost of goods sold.
3. Subtract the estimated cost of goods sold (step #2) from the cost of goods available for sale (step #1) to arrive at the ending inventory.

The gross profit method is not an acceptable method for determining the year-end inventory balance, since it only estimates what the ending inventory balance may be. It is not sufficiently precise to be reliable for audited financial statements.

EXAMPLE

Mulligan Imports is calculating its month-end golf club inventory for March. Its beginning inventory was £175,000 and its purchases during the month were £225,000. Thus, its cost of goods available for sale is:

£175,000 beginning inventory + £225,000 purchases

= £400,000 cost of goods available for sale

Mulligan's gross margin percentage for all of the past 12 months was 35%, which is considered a reliable long-term margin. Its sales during March were £500,000. Thus, its estimated cost of goods sold is:

(1 - 35%) × £500,000 = £325,000 cost of goods sold

By subtracting the estimated cost of goods sold from the cost of goods available for sale, Mulligan arrives at an estimated ending inventory balance of £75,000.

There are several issues with the gross profit method that make it unreliable as the sole method for determining the value of inventory, which are:

- *Applicability.* The calculation is most useful in retail situations where a company is simply buying and reselling merchandise. If a company is instead manufacturing goods, the components of inventory must also include labor and overhead, which make the gross profit method too simplistic to yield reliable results.
- *Historical basis.* The gross profit percentage is a key component of the calculation, but the percentage is based on a company's historical experi-

ence. If the current situation yields a different percentage (as may be caused by a special sale at reduced prices), the gross profit percentage used in the calculation will be incorrect.

- *Inventory losses*. The calculation assumes that the long-term rate of losses due to theft, obsolescence, and other causes is included in the historical gross profit percentage. If not, or if these losses have not previously been recognized, the calculation will likely result in an inaccurate estimated ending inventory (and probably one that is too high).

Overhead Allocation

The preceding section was concerned with charging the direct costs of production to inventory, but what about overhead expenses? In many businesses, the cost of overhead is substantially greater than direct costs, so considerable attention must be expended on the proper method of allocating overhead to inventory.

There are two types of overhead, which are administrative overhead and manufacturing overhead. *Administrative overhead* includes those costs not involved in the development or production of goods or services, such as the costs of front office administration and sales; this is essentially all overhead that is *not* included in manufacturing overhead. *Manufacturing overhead* is all of the costs that a factory incurs, other than direct costs.

The costs of manufacturing overhead should be allocated to any inventory items that are classified as work-in-process or finished goods. Overhead is not allocated to raw materials inventory, since the operations giving rise to overhead costs only impact work-in-process and finished goods inventory. The following items are usually included in manufacturing overhead:

Depreciation of factory equipment	Quality control and inspection
Factory administration expenses	Rent, facility and equipment
Indirect labor and production supervisory wages	Repair expenses
Indirect materials and supplies	Rework labor, scrap and spoilage
Maintenance, factory and production equipment	Taxes related to production assets
Officer salaries related to production	Uncapitalized tools and equipment
Production employees' benefits	Utilities

The typical procedure for allocating overhead is to accumulate all manufacturing overhead costs into one or more cost pools, and to then use an activity measure to apportion the overhead costs in the cost pools to produced units. Thus, the overhead allocation formula is:

Cost pool ÷ Total activity measure = Overhead allocation per unit

EXAMPLE

Mulligan Imports has a small production operation for an in-house line of golf clubs. During April, it incurs costs for the following items:

Cost Type	Amount
Building rent for production line	£65,000
Building utilities	12,000
Factory equipment depreciation	8,000
Production equipment maintenance	7,000
Total	£92,000

All of these items are classified as manufacturing overhead, so Mulligan creates the following journal entry to shift the costs into an overhead cost pool:

	Debit	Credit
Overhead cost pool	92,000	
Depreciation expense		8,000
Maintenance expense		7,000
Rent expense		65,000
Utilities expense		12,000

Overhead costs can be allocated by any reasonable measure, as long as it is consistently applied across reporting periods. Common bases of allocation are direct labor hours charged against a product, or the amount of machine hours used during the production of a product. The amount of allocation charged per unit is known as the *overhead rate*.

The overhead rate can be expressed as a proportion, if both the numerator and denominator are stated in a currency. For example, Armadillo Industries has total indirect costs of £100,000 and it decides to use the cost of its direct labor as the allocation measure. Armadillo incurs £50,000 of direct labor costs, so the overhead rate is calculated as:

$$\frac{\text{£100,000 Indirect costs}}{\text{£50,000 Direct labor}}$$

The result is an overhead rate of 2.0.

Alternatively, if the denominator is not stated in a currency, the overhead rate is expressed as a cost per allocation unit. For example, Armadillo decides to change its allocation measure to hours of machine time used. The company has 10,000 hours of machine time usage, so the overhead rate is now calculated as:

$$\frac{\text{£100,000 Indirect costs}}{\text{10,000 Machine hours}}$$

The result is an overhead rate of £10.00 per machine hour.

EXAMPLE

Mulligan Imports has a small golf shaft production line, which manufactures a titanium shaft and an aluminum shaft. Considerable machining is required for both shafts, so Mulligan concludes that it should allocate overhead to these products based on the total hours of machine time used. In May, production of the titanium shaft requires 5,400 hours of machine time, while the aluminum shaft needs 2,600 hours. Thus, 67.5% of the overhead cost pool is allocated to the titanium shafts and 32.5% to the aluminum shafts.

In May, Mulligan accumulates £100,000 of costs in its overhead cost pool, and allocates it between the two product lines with the following journal entry:

	Debit	Credit
Finished goods – Titanium shafts	67,500	
Finished goods – Aluminum shafts	32,500	
Overhead cost pool		100,000

This entry clears out the balance in the overhead cost pool, readying it to accumulate overhead costs in the next reporting period.

If the basis of allocation does not appear correct for certain types of overhead costs, it may make more sense to split the overhead into two or more overhead cost pools, and allocate each cost pool using a different basis of allocation. For example, if warehouse costs are more appropriately allocated based on the square footage consumed by various products, then store warehouse costs in a warehouse overhead cost pool, and allocate these costs based on square footage used.

Thus far, we have assumed that only actual overhead costs incurred are allocated. However, it is also possible to set up a standard overhead rate that is used for multiple reporting periods, based on long-term expectations regarding how much overhead will be incurred and how many units will be produced. If the difference between actual overhead costs incurred and overhead allocated is small, charge the difference to the cost of goods sold. If the amount is material, allocate the difference to both the cost of goods sold and inventory.

EXAMPLE

Mulligan Imports incurs overhead of £93,000, which it stores in an overhead cost pool. Mulligan uses a standard overhead rate of £20 per unit, which approximates its long-term experience with the relationship between overhead costs and production volumes. In September, it produces 4,500 golf club shafts, to which it allocates £90,000 (allocation rate of £20 × 4,500 units). This leaves a difference between overhead incurred and overhead absorbed of £3,000. Given the small size of the variance, Mulligan charges the £3,000 difference to the cost of goods sold, thereby clearing out the overhead cost pool.

A key issue is that overhead allocation is not a precisely-defined science – there is plenty of latitude in how to allocate overhead. The amount of allowable diversity in practice can result in slipshod accounting, so be sure to use a standardized and well-documented method to allocate overhead using the same calculation in every reporting period. This allows for great consistency, which auditors appreciate when they validate the supporting calculations.

Net Realizable Value

IFRS requires that inventories be measured at the lower of cost or net realizable value. This becomes an issue when the original cost of inventory is no longer recoverable, which can occur when inventory is damaged or becomes obsolete, or its selling price declines.

The cost of inventory is normally written down to its net realizable value on an individual-item basis, though it is permissible to do so for groups of similar items. A group write-down should not be used for an entire class of inventory, such as finished goods.

When there are materials or supplies that are being stored in expectation of being used to manufacture finished goods, it is not necessary to write down their cost if the finished goods into which they will be incorporated will be sold at cost or above.

The net realizable value of inventory should be reassessed in every reporting period. If there is clear evidence that there has been an increase in net realizable value in one of these subsequent periods, the original amount of the write-down should be reversed to the extent of the increase in net realizable value.

Accounting for Obsolete Inventory

A materials review board is used to locate obsolete inventory items. This group reviews inventory usage reports or physically examines the inventory to determine which items should be disposed of. Then review the findings of this group to determine the most likely disposition price of the obsolete items, subtract this projected amount from the book value of the obsolete items, and set aside the difference as a reserve. As the company later disposes of the items, or the estimated amounts to be received from disposition change, adjust the reserve account to reflect these events.

EXAMPLE

Milagro Corporation has £100,000 of excess home coffee roasters it cannot sell. However, it believes there is a market for the roasters through a reseller in China, but only at a sale price of £20,000. Accordingly, the controller recognizes a reserve of £80,000 with the following journal entry:

	Debit	Credit
Cost of goods sold	80,000	
Reserve for obsolete inventory		80,000

After finalizing the arrangement with the Chinese reseller, the actual sale price is only £19,000, so the controller completes the transaction with the following entry, recognizing an additional £1,000 of expense:

	Debit	Credit
Reserve for obsolete inventory	80,000	
Cost of goods sold	1,000	
Inventory		81,000

The example makes inventory obsolescence accounting look simple enough, but it is not. The issues are:

- *Timing.* A company's reported financial results can be improperly altered by changing the timing of the actual dispositions. As an example, if a supervisor knows that he can receive a higher-than-estimated price on the disposition of obsolete inventory, he can either accelerate or delay the sale in order to shift gains into whichever reporting period needs the extra profit.
- *Timely reviews.* Inventory obsolescence is a minor issue as long as management reviews inventory on a regular basis, so that the incremental amount of obsolescence detected is small in any given period. However, if management does not conduct a review for a long time, this allows obsolete inventory to build up to quite impressive proportions, along with an equally impressive amount of expense recognition. To avoid this issue, conduct frequent obsolescence reviews, and maintain a reserve based on historical or expected obsolescence, even if specific inventory items have not yet been identified.

EXAMPLE

Milagro Corporation sets aside an obsolescence reserve of £25,000 for obsolete roasters. However, in January the purchasing manager knows that the resale price for obsolete roasters has plummeted, so the real reserve should be closer to £35,000, which would call for the immediate recognition of an additional £10,000 of expense. However, since this would result in an overall reported loss in Milagro's financial results in January, he waits until April, when Milagro has a very profitable month, and completes the sale at that time, thereby incorrectly delaying the additional obsolescence loss until the point of sale.

Work in Process Accounting

Work in process (WIP) is goods in production that have not yet been completed. It typically involves the full amount of raw materials needed for a product, since that is usually included in the product at the beginning of the manufacturing process. During production, the cost of direct labor and overhead is added in proportion to the amount of work done.

In prolonged production operations, there may be a large amount of investment in work in process. Conversely, the production of some products occupies such a brief period of time that the accounting staff does not bother to track it at all; instead, the items in production are considered to still be in the raw materials inventory. In this latter case, inventory essentially shifts directly from the raw materials inventory to the finished goods inventory, with no separate work in process tracking.

Work in process accounting involves tracking the amount of WIP in inventory at the end of an accounting period and assigning a cost to it for inventory valuation purposes, based on the percentage of completion of the WIP items.

In situations where there are many similar products in process, it is more common to follow these steps to account for work in process inventory:

1. *Assign raw materials.* We assume that all raw materials have been assigned to work in process as soon as the work begins. This is reasonable, since many types of production involve kitting all of the materials needed to construct a product and delivering them to the manufacturing area at one time.

2. *Compile labor costs.* The production staff can track the time it works on each product, which is then assigned to the work in process. However, this is painfully time-consuming, so a better approach is to determine the stage of completion of each item in production, and assign a standard labor cost to it based on the stage of completion. This information comes from labor routings that detail the standard amount of labor needed at each stage of the production process.

3. *Assign overhead.* If overhead is assigned based on labor hours, it is assigned based on the labor information compiled in the preceding step. If overhead is assigned based on some other allocation methodology, the basis of allocation (such as machine hours used) must first be compiled.

4. *Record the entry.* This journal entry involves shifting raw materials from the raw materials inventory account to the work in process inventory account, shifting direct labor expense into the work in process inventory account, and shifting factory overhead from the overhead cost pool to the WIP inventory account.

It is much easier to use standard costs for work in process accounting. Actual costs are difficult to trace to individual units of production.

The general theme of WIP accounting is to always use the simplest method that the company can convince its auditors to accept, on the grounds that a complex costing methodology will require an inordinate amount of time by the accounting staff, which in turn interferes with the time required to close the books at the end of each month.

Inventory Measurement by Commodity Broker-Traders

A broker-trader that deals in commodities can measure its inventory at fair value, less any remaining costs to sell. If this approach is used, the broker-trader should record any change in the fair value less costs to sell in profit or loss in the period in which the fair value change occurs.

Inventory Disclosures

The following information should be disclosed about a company's inventory practices in its financial statements:

- *Basis*. The basis on which inventories are stated, including the cost formula used.
- *Carrying amount*. The total carrying amount of inventory, and for any relevant inventory classifications, such as merchandise, materials, work-in-process, and finished goods. Also note the amount of any inventories being carried at their fair value, less any costs to sell.
- *Charge to expense*. The amount of inventory charged to expense during the period.
- *Pledges*. The carrying amount of any inventories that have been pledged as security for liabilities.
- *Reversals*. The amount of any reversal of an inventory write-down during the period, and the circumstances leading to the reversal.
- *Write-downs*. The amount of any write-downs of inventory to net realizable value.

Summary

When designing systems that will properly account for inventory, the key consideration is the sheer volume of transactions that must be tracked. It can be extremely difficult to consistently record these transactions with a minimal error rate, so tailor the accounting system to reduce the record keeping work load while still producing results that are in accordance with IFRS. In particular, be watchful for any additional accounting procedures that only refine the inventory information to a small degree, and eliminate or streamline them whenever possible. In essence, this is *the* accounting area in which having a cost-effective recordkeeping system is of some importance.

Chapter 14
Property, Plant, and Equipment

Introduction

One of the central functions of accounting is the proper classification and measurement of fixed assets, which can comprise a substantial part of the balance sheets of many companies. In this chapter, we discuss which costs can be capitalized into fixed assets, how these costs may be altered or revalued over time, which depreciation methods to use, how to derecognize an asset, and other topics related to the costs of decommissioning certain assets.

In the following sections, we use the term *fixed assets* interchangeably with property, plant and equipment.

> **Related Podcast Episode:** Episode 109 of the Accounting Best Practices Podcast discusses fixed asset accounting differences between GAAP and IFRS. They are available at: **accountingtools.com/podcasts**

IFRS Source Documents

- IAS 16, *Property, Plant and Equipment*
- IFRIC 1, *Changes in Existing Decommissioning, Restoration and Similar Liabilities*
- IFRIC 5, *Rights to Interests Arising from Decommissioning, Restoration and Environmental Rehabilitation Funds*

Recognition of Property, Plant and Equipment

A fixed asset is a tangible item that is to be used in multiple reporting periods, and which is used for production, administration, or rentals. When a business expends funds, it can recognize a fixed asset in the amount of the expenditure if it is probable that there will be future economic benefits flowing to the business, or for safety or environmental reasons, and if the cost can be measured reliably. From a practical perspective, it may be easier to charge such expenditures directly to expense if their benefits will be consumed within just a few months. Also, given the increase in accounting documentation required for a fixed asset (which will become evident later in this chapter), it is more efficient to set a *capitalization limit*, below which expenditures that would normally qualify for treatment as fixed assets are charged directly to expense as incurred. These best practices should result in a vastly smaller number of expenditures being accounted for as fixed assets.

The following additional rules and suggestions apply to the recognition of expenditures as fixed assets:

- *Abnormal costs.* If unusually large amounts of wasted costs are incurred in the construction of a fixed asset, these wasted costs should not be capitalized into the cost of the fixed asset. Instead, charge them to expense as incurred.
- *Aggregation.* Depending on the circumstances, it may be acceptable to aggregate a number of low-value items for the purposes of recognizing a single fixed asset, such as a group of desks.
- *Assets constructed for sale.* If a company capitalizes an asset that it normally constructs for sale, the capitalized cost of the asset should be the same as the cost of the units constructed for sale.
- *Bearer plants.* These are living plants that are used in the production of agricultural produce. They are accounted for in the same manner as self-constructed assets, where the cost to cultivate the plants is considered part of the asset.
- *Cash price equivalent.* The capitalized cost of a purchased asset is its cash price equivalent. Thus, if lengthy credit terms are associated with a purchase, do not capitalize the interest cost implied by the difference between the cash price and credit price of the asset.
- *Inspections.* If a major inspection is required as a condition of continuing to operate a fixed asset (such as a passenger plane), recognize the cost of the inspection as a fixed asset, and derecognize the carrying amount of any remaining asset from the preceding inspection. This derecognition is required, even if the cost of the preceding inspection was never separately identified; thus, it may be necessary to estimate the amount of the preceding inspection and derecognize it.
- *Interest.* Interest expense may be included in the capitalized cost of a fixed asset. See the Borrowing Costs chapter for more information.
- *Minor spare parts.* Low-value spare parts are usually treated as part of inventory, rather than as fixed assets, and so are carried as assets without any associated depreciation. They are charged to expense when consumed.
- *Non-monetary exchange.* When an asset is acquired through a non-monetary exchange, the asset acquired is measured at the fair value of the asset given up. If it is not possible to derive that fair value, the fair value of the asset obtained can be used instead. If this fair value also cannot be derived, use the carrying amount of the asset given up. Such an exchange is only considered to have taken place if it has commercial substance, which means that the future cash flows of the entity are expected to change as a result of the transaction.
- *Replacement parts.* If a major part is replaced in a fixed asset, recognize the cost of the part as a fixed asset, and derecognize the carrying amount of the part that was replaced. This derecognition is required, even if the cost of the replaced part was never separately identified. If it is not possible to determine the carrying amount of the replaced part, use the cost of the replacement as an indicator of the original cost of the item being replaced.

- *Servicing costs.* The ongoing servicing costs of a fixed asset are charged to expense as incurred, rather than being included in the capitalized cost of the asset.
- *Spare parts.* Spare parts and servicing equipment can only be classified as fixed assets if they meet all of the requirements for fixed assets. If not, they are instead classified as inventory.
- *Targeted parts and equipment.* If servicing equipment and spare parts are only used in connection with a specific fixed asset, they are accounted for as fixed assets (subject to the capitalization limit noted above).

EXAMPLE

Universal Airlines acquires a twin engine commuter plane from a failed carrier and initially accounts for it as a single asset, with a purchase price of £750,000. Two years later, both engines reach the end of their allowed service lives of 6,000 hours. Each new engine costs £100,000.

The original invoice for the commuter plane did not itemize the cost of the engines, so Universal instead uses the cost of the replacement engines as the basis for estimating the cost of the original engines. To do so, Universal uses its 10% cost of capital to discount the £200,000 cost of the engines for two years, resulting in a discounted cost of £165,290 (calculated as £200,000 × 0.82645).

Universal then subtracts the £165,290 cost of the existing engines from the asset record for the commuter plane and adds the cost of the new engines. The resulting change in the gross carrying amount of the plane is:

£750,000 Purchase price + £200,000 New engines - £165,290 Old engines
= £784,710 Gross carrying amount

A fixed asset is initially recognized at its cost. These costs can include any of the following items, which include those costs needed to bring the asset to the location and condition intended for it by management:

Benefits of employees constructing the asset	Purchase price
Dismantling of items on asset site	Site preparation
Import duties	Testing costs
Installation and assembly costs	Transport costs
Non-refundable purchase taxes	Wages
Professional fees	

Also, trade discounts and rebates should be deducted from the capitalized cost of a fixed asset, as well as the proceeds from the sale of any items produced during asset testing.

Conversely, the following costs should be charged to expense as incurred, and *not* be capitalized into a fixed asset:

- Administration
- Conducting business in a new location
- General overhead costs
- Introducing a new product
- Opening a new facility

The costs associated with a fixed asset should continue to be capitalized until the asset is in the location and condition intended for it by management. At that point, no further costs are capitalized. This means that shifting a fixed asset to a new location cannot be capitalized, nor can any subsequent operating losses.

Subsequent Fixed Asset Recognition

Once a fixed asset has initially been measured, you have a choice of continuing to measure it at cost (the cost model), or of revaluing it on a regular basis (the revaluation model). Both models are addressed in this section.

The Cost Model

Under the cost model, continue to carry the cost of a fixed asset, minus any accumulated depreciation and accumulated impairment losses. This is the simplest approach, since the least amount of accounting is required.

When the cost model is selected, it should be applied to an entire class of fixed assets; thus, you cannot shift between the cost and revaluation models for individual items within a class of assets.

The Revaluation Model

If it is possible to measure the fair value of an asset reliably, there is an option to carry the asset at its revalued amount. Subsequent to the revaluation, the amount carried on the books is the fair value, less subsequent accumulated depreciation and accumulated impairment losses. Under this approach, fixed assets must be revalued at sufficiently regular intervals to ensure that the carrying amount does not differ materially from the fair value in any period.

The fair values of some fixed assets may be quite volatile, necessitating revaluations as frequently as once a year. In most other cases, IFRS considers revaluations once every three to five years to be acceptable.

When a fixed asset is revalued, there are two ways to deal with any depreciation that has accumulated since the last revaluation. The choices are:

- Force the carrying amount of the asset to equal its newly-revalued amount by proportionally restating the amount of the accumulated depreciation; or
- Eliminate the accumulated depreciation against the gross carrying amount of the newly-revalued asset. This method is the simpler of the two alternatives, and is used in the example later in this section.

Tip: Though all of the assets in an asset class must be revalued at the same time, you can stretch the requirement and revalue them on a rolling basis, as long as the revaluation is completed within a short period of time and the revaluation analysis is subsequently kept up to date.

Use a market-based appraisal by a qualified valuation specialist to determine the fair value of a fixed asset. If a fixed asset is of such a specialized nature that a market-based fair value cannot be obtained, use an alternative method to arrive at an estimated fair value. Examples of such methods are using discounted future cash flows or an estimate of the replacement cost of an asset.

If you elect to use the revaluation model and a revaluation results in an increase in the carrying amount of a fixed asset, recognize the increase in other comprehensive income, as well as accumulate it in equity in an account entitled "revaluation surplus." However, if the increase reverses a revaluation decrease for the same asset that had been previously recognized in profit or loss, recognize the revaluation gain in profit or loss to the extent of the previous loss (thereby erasing the loss).

If a revaluation results in a decrease in the carrying amount of a fixed asset, recognize the decrease in profit or loss. However, if there is a credit balance in the revaluation surplus for that asset, recognize the decrease in other comprehensive income to offset the credit balance. The decrease recognized in other comprehensive income decreases the amount of any revaluation surplus already recorded in equity.

The following table summarizes the proper recognition of revaluation changes just described:

Asset Revaluation Change	Recognition
Value increases	Recognize in other comprehensive income and in the "revaluation surplus" equity account
Value increases, and reverses a prior revaluation decrease	Recognize gain in profit or loss to the extent of the previous loss, with the remainder in other comprehensive income
Value decreases	Recognize in profit or loss
Value decreases, but there is a credit in the revaluation surplus	Recognize in other comprehensive income to the extent of the credit, with the remainder in profit or loss

In essence, IFRS requires the prominent display of any revaluation losses, and gives less reporting stature to revaluation gains.

If a fixed asset is derecognized, transfer any associated revaluation surplus to retained earnings. The amount of this surplus transferred to retained earnings is the difference between the depreciation based on the original cost of the asset and the depreciation based on the revalued carrying amount of the asset.

EXAMPLE

Nautilus Tours elects to revalue one of its tourism submarines, which originally cost £12,000,000 and has since accumulated £3,000,000 of depreciation. It is unlikely that the fair value of the submarine will vary substantially over time, so Nautilus adopts a policy to conduct revaluations for all of its submarines once every three years. An appraiser assigns a value of £9,200,000 to the submarine. Nautilus creates the following entry to eliminate all accumulated depreciation associated with the submarine:

	Debit	Credit
Accumulated depreciation	3,000,000	
Submarines		3,000,000

At this point, the net cost of the submarine in Nautilus' accounting records is £9,000,000. Nautilus also creates the following entry to increase the carrying amount of the submarine to its fair value of £9,200,000:

	Debit	Credit
Submarines	200,000	
Other comprehensive income – gain on revaluation		200,000

Three years later, on the next scheduled revaluation date, the appraiser reviews the fair value of the submarine, and determines that its fair value has declined by £350,000. Nautilus uses the following journal entry to record the change:

	Debit	Credit
Other comprehensive income – gain on revaluation	200,000	
Loss on revaluation	150,000	
Submarines		350,000

This final entry eliminates all of the revaluation gain that had been recorded in other comprehensive income, and also recognizes a loss on the residual portion of the revaluation loss.

When the revaluation model is selected, it should be applied to an entire class of fixed assets; thus, it is not possible to shift between the revaluation and cost models for individual items within a class of assets. Examples of asset classes are land, machinery, motor vehicles, furniture and fixtures, and office equipment.

Depreciation

The purpose of depreciation is to charge to expense a portion of an asset that relates to the revenue generated by that asset. This is called the matching principle, where revenues and expenses both appear in the income statement in the same reporting period, which gives the best view of how well a company has performed in a given accounting period. There are three factors to consider in the calculation of depreciation, which are:

- *Useful life.* This is the time period over which an asset is expected to be productive, or the number of units of production expected to be generated from it. Useful life can also be defined by the expected amount of wear and tear, the level of expected technical obsolescence of an asset, as well as by any legal limitation on the usage period of an asset. Past its useful life, it is no longer cost-effective to continue operating the asset, so you would dispose of it or stop using it. Depreciation is recognized over the useful life of an asset.

Tip: Rather than recording a different useful life for every asset, it is easier to assign each asset to an asset class, where every asset in that asset class has the same useful life. This approach may not work for very high-cost assets, where a greater degree of precision may be needed.

- *Salvage value.* When a company eventually disposes of an asset, it may be able to sell the asset for a reduced amount, which is the salvage value. Depreciation is calculated based on the asset cost, less any estimated salvage value. If salvage value is expected to be quite small, it is generally ignored for the purpose of calculating depreciation. Salvage value is not discounted to its present value. In those rare cases where the estimated salvage value equals or exceeds the carrying amount of an asset, perhaps due to an increase in the estimated amount of salvage value, do not depreciate the asset further, unless the estimated salvage value subsequently declines.

Tip: If the amount of salvage value associated with an asset is estimated to be minor, it is easier from a calculation perspective to not reduce the depreciable amount of the asset by the salvage value. Instead, assume that the salvage value is zero.

EXAMPLE

Pensive Corporation buys an asset for £100,000, and estimates that its salvage value will be £10,000 in five years, when the company plans to dispose of the asset. This means that Pensive will depreciate £90,000 of the asset cost over five years, leaving £10,000 of the cost remaining at the end of that time. Pensive expects to then sell the asset for £10,000 and eliminate the asset from its accounting records.

- *Depreciation method.* Depreciation expense can be calculated using an accelerated depreciation method, or evenly over the useful life of the asset. The advantage of using an accelerated method is that more depreciation can be recognized early in the life of a fixed asset, which defers some income tax expense recognition into a later period. The advantage of using a steady depreciation rate is the ease of calculation. Examples of accelerated depreciation methods are the double declining balance and sum-of-the-years' digits methods. The primary method for steady depreciation is the straight-line method. No matter which method is used, the depreciation of an asset should begin when it is ready for use. Depreciation does not stop when an asset is idle, except under the units of production method (as described later in this section).

IFRS mandates that the useful life and salvage value of an asset be evaluated at least once a year, to see if these estimates have changed. If so, alter the remaining depreciation to account for the changes.

EXAMPLE

Pensive Corporation acquires production equipment for £240,000, and initially concludes that the equipment should be depreciated over 10 years and have a salvage value of £40,000. This results in annual depreciation of £20,000.

At the end of the fifth year, the production manager reviews the situation and decides that the declining serviceability of the equipment will result in its sale at the end of the eighth year, rather than the tenth year. Also, its salvage value will only be £20,000. At this point, the remaining carrying amount of the asset has declined to £140,000. The remaining depreciable amount is now £120,000, which should be depreciated over just three more years, which is £40,000 per year.

The *mid-month convention* states that, no matter when a fixed asset was purchased in a month, it was assumed to have been purchased in the middle of the month for depreciation purposes. Thus, if a fixed asset was bought on January 5th, assume that it was bought on January 15th; or, if it was bought on January 28, still assume that it was bought on January 15th. By doing so, you can more easily calculate a standard half-month of depreciation for that first month of ownership.

If the mid-month convention is used, this also means that a half-month of depreciation must be recorded for the *last* month of the asset's useful life. By doing so, the two half-month depreciation calculations equal one full month of depreciation.

Many companies prefer to use full-month depreciation in the first month of ownership, irrespective of the actual date of purchase within the month, so that they can slightly accelerate their recognition of depreciation, which in turn reduces their taxable income in the near term.

IFRS mandates that each part of a fixed item with a cost that is significant in relation to the total cost be tracked and depreciated separately. This requirement should be followed with caution, since the accounting department may find itself tracking a plethora of additional items. The best interpretation of this rule is to separately depreciate those portions of a fixed asset that have different useful lives than the rest of an asset. For example, the jet engines in a passenger jet should be depreciated separately from the airframe, since the useful life of the airframe should substantially exceed that of the engines. Similarly, the roof of a building could be depreciated separately, since it may be replaced several times over the life of the building.

IFRS mandates that fixed assets be depreciated using whichever depreciation method most closely reflects the expected pattern of consumption of their future economic benefits, and to apply that method consistently across reporting periods. Fixed assets are to be reviewed at least annually to see if the depreciation method in use continues to reflect this pattern of consumption. If not, the most relevant depreciation method is to be applied for the remaining useful life of the assets. Realistically, it is difficult to ascertain the pattern of consumption of future economic benefits, so the accounting department tends to instead rely upon the simplest possible depreciation method, which is the straight-line method. In the following sub-sections, we describe the most commonly-used depreciation methods, and where their use is most applicable.

Straight-Line Method

Under the straight-line method of depreciation, recognize depreciation expense evenly over the estimated useful life of an asset. The straight-line calculation steps are:

1. Subtract the estimated salvage value of the asset from the amount at which it is recorded on the books.
2. Determine the estimated useful life of the asset. It is easiest to use a standard useful life for each class of assets.
3. Divide the estimated useful life (in years) into 1 to arrive at the straight-line depreciation rate.
4. Multiply the depreciation rate by the asset cost (less salvage value).

EXAMPLE

Pensive Corporation purchases the Procrastinator Deluxe machine for £60,000. It has an estimated salvage value of £10,000 and a useful life of five years. Pensive calculates the annual straight-line depreciation for the machine as:

1. Purchase cost of £60,000 – estimated salvage value of £10,000 = Depreciable asset cost of £50,000
2. 1 ÷ 5-year useful life = 20% depreciation rate per year
3. 20% depreciation rate × £50,000 depreciable asset cost = £10,000 annual depreciation

---

Sum-of-the-Years' Digits Method

The sum of the years' digits (SYD) method is more appropriate than straight-line depreciation if the asset depreciates more quickly or has greater production capacity in earlier years than it does as it ages. Use the following formula to calculate it:

$$\text{Depreciation percentage} = \frac{\text{Number of estimated years of life as of beginning of the year}}{\text{Sum of the years' digits}}$$

The following table contains examples of the sum of the years' digits noted in the denominator of the preceding formula:

Total Depreciation Period	Initial Sum of the Years' Digits	Calculation
2 years	3	1 + 2
3 years	6	1 + 2 + 3
4 years	10	1 + 2 + 3 + 4
5 years	15	1 + 2 + 3 + 4 + 5

The concept is most easily illustrated with the following example.

EXAMPLE

Pensive Corporation buys a Procrastinator Elite machine for £100,000. The machine has no estimated salvage value, and a useful life of five years. Pensive calculates the annual sum of the years' digits depreciation for this machine as:

Year	Number of estimated years of life as of beginning of the year	SYD Calculation	Depreciation Percentage	Annual Depreciation
1	5	5/15	33.33%	£33,333
2	4	4/15	26.67%	26,667
3	3	3/15	20.00%	20,000
4	2	2/15	13.33%	13,333
5	1	1/15	6.67%	6,667
Totals	15		100.00%	£100,000

The sum of the years' digits method is clearly more complex than the straight-line method, which tends to limit its use unless software is employed to automatically track the calculations for each asset.

Double-Declining Balance Method

The double declining balance (DDB) method is a form of accelerated depreciation. It may be more appropriate than the straight-line method if an asset experiences an inordinately high level of usage during the first few years of its useful life.

To calculate the double-declining balance depreciation rate, divide the number of years of useful life of an asset into 100 percent, and multiply the result by two. The formula is:

$$(100\% \div \text{Years of useful life}) \times 2$$

The DDB calculation proceeds until the asset's salvage value is reached, after which depreciation ends.

EXAMPLE

Pensive Corporation purchases a machine for £50,000. It has an estimated salvage value of £5,000 and a useful life of five years. The calculation of the double declining balance depreciation rate is:

$$(100\% \div \text{Years of useful life}) \times 2 = 40\%$$

By applying the 40% rate, Pensive arrives at the following table of depreciation charges per year:

Year	Book Value at Beginning of Year	Depreciation Percentage	DDB Depreciation	Book Value Net of Depreciation
1	£50,000	40%	£20,000	£30,000
2	30,000	40%	12,000	18,000
3	18,000	40%	7,200	10,800
4	10,800	40%	4,320	6,480
5	6,480	40%	1,480	5,000
Total			£45,000	

Note that the depreciation in the fifth and final year is only for £1,480, rather than the £3,240 that would be indicated by the 40% depreciation rate. The reason for the smaller charge is that Pensive stops any further depreciation once the remaining book value declines to the amount of the estimated salvage value.

An alternative form of double declining balance depreciation is 150% declining balance depreciation. It is a less aggressive form of depreciation, since it is calculated as 1.5 times the straight-line rate, rather than the 2x multiple that is used for the double declining balance method. The formula is:

$$(100\% \div \text{Years of useful life}) \times 1.5$$

EXAMPLE

[Note: We are repeating the preceding example, but using 150% declining balance depreciation instead of double declining balance depreciation]

Pensive Corporation purchases a machine for £50,000. It has an estimated salvage value of £5,000 and a useful life of five years. The calculation of the 150% declining balance depreciation rate is:

$$(100\% \div \text{Years of useful life}) \times 1.5 = 30\%$$

By applying the 30% rate, Pensive arrives at the following table of depreciation charges per year:

Year	Book Value at Beginning of Year	Depreciation Percentage	150% DB Depreciation	Book Value Net of Depreciation
1	£50,000	30%	£15,000	£35,000
2	35,000	30%	10,500	24,500
3	24,500	30%	7,350	17,150
4	17,150	30%	5,145	12,005
5	12,005	30%	7,005	5,000
Total			£45,000	

In this case, the depreciation expense in the fifth and final year of £3,602 (£12,005 × 30%) results in a net book value that is somewhat higher than the estimated salvage value of £5,000, so Pensive instead records £7,005 of depreciation in order to arrive at a net book value that equals the estimated salvage value.

Depletion Method

Depletion is a periodic charge to expense for the use of natural resources. Thus, it is used in situations where a company has recorded an asset for such items as oil reserves, coal deposits, or gravel pits. The calculation of depletion involves these steps:
1. Compute a depletion base.
2. Compute a unit depletion rate.
3. Charge depletion based on units of usage.

The depletion base is the asset that is to be depleted. It is comprised of the following four types of costs:
- *Acquisition costs.* The cost to either buy or lease property.
- *Exploration costs.* The cost to locate assets that may then be depleted. In most cases, these costs are charged to expense as incurred.
- *Development costs.* The cost to prepare the property for asset extraction, which includes the cost of such items as tunnels and wells.
- *Restoration costs.* The cost to restore property to its original condition after depletion activities have been concluded.

To compute a unit depletion rate, subtract the salvage value of the asset from the depletion base and divide it by the total number of measurement units that are expected to be recovered. The formula for the unit depletion rate is:

$$\text{Unit depletion rate} = \frac{\text{Depletion base} - \text{Salvage value}}{\text{Total units to be recovered}}$$

Then create the depletion charge based on actual units of usage. Thus, if 500 barrels of oil are extracted and the unit depletion rate is £5.00 per barrel, £2,500 can be charged to depletion expense.

The estimated amount of a natural resource that can be recovered will change constantly as assets are gradually extracted from a property. As you revise the estimated remaining amount of extractable natural resource, incorporate these estimates into the unit depletion rate for the remaining amount to be extracted. This is not a retrospective calculation.

EXAMPLE

Pensive Corporation's subsidiary Pensive Oil drills a well with the intention of extracting oil from a known reservoir. It incurs the following costs related to the acquisition of property and development of the site:

Land purchase	£280,000
Road construction	23,000
Drill pad construction	48,000
Drilling fees	192,000
Total	£543,000

In addition, Pensive Oil estimates that it will incur a site restoration cost of £57,000 once extraction is complete, so the total depletion base of the property is £600,000.

Pensive's geologists estimate that the proven oil reserves that are accessed by the well are 400,000 barrels, so the unit depletion charge will be £1.50 per barrel of oil extracted (£600,000 depletion base ÷ 400,000 barrels).

In the first year, Pensive Oil extracts 100,000 barrels of oil from the well, which results in a depletion charge of £150,000 (100,000 barrels × £1.50 unit depletion charge).

At the beginning of the second year of operations, Pensive's geologists issue a revised estimate of the remaining amount of proven reserves, with the new estimate of 280,000 barrels being 20,000 barrels lower than the original estimate (less extractions already completed). This means that the unit depletion charge will increase to £1.61 (£450,000 remaining depletion base ÷ 280,000 barrels).

During the second year, Pensive Oil extracts 80,000 barrels of oil from the well, which results in a depletion charge of £128,800 (80,000 barrels × £1.61 unit depletion charge).

At the end of the second year, there is still a depletion base of £321,200 that must be charged to expense in proportion to the amount of any remaining extractions.

Units of Production Method

Under the units of production method, the amount of depreciation that is charged to expense varies in direct proportion to the amount of asset usage. Thus, more depreciation is charged in periods when there is more asset usage, and less depreciation in periods when there is less asset usage. It is the most accurate method for charging depreciation, since it links closely to the wear and tear on assets. However, it also requires that asset usage is tracked, which means that its use is generally limited to more expensive assets. Also, you need to be able to estimate total usage over the life of the asset.

> **Tip:** Do not use the units of production method if there is not a significant difference in asset usage from period to period. Otherwise, a great deal of time will be spent tracking asset usage, resulting in a depreciation expense that varies little from the results that would have been derived with the straight-line method (which is far easier to calculate).

Follow these steps to calculate depreciation under the units of production method:
1. Estimate the total number of hours of usage of the asset, or the total number of units to be produced by it over its useful life.
2. Subtract any estimated salvage value from the capitalized cost of the asset, and divide the total estimated usage or production from this net depreciable cost. This yields the depreciation cost per hour of usage or unit of production.
3. Multiply the number of hours of usage or units of actual production by the depreciation cost per hour or unit, which results in the total depreciation expense for the accounting period.

If the estimated number of hours of usage or units of production changes over time, incorporate these changes into the calculation of the depreciation cost per hour or unit of production. This will alter the depreciation expense on a go-forward basis.

EXAMPLE

Pensive Corporation's gravel pit operation, Pensive Dirt, builds a conveyor system to extract gravel from a gravel pit at a cost of £400,000. Pensive expects to use the conveyor to extract 1,000,000 tons of gravel, which results in a depreciation rate of £0.40 per ton (1,000,000 tons ÷ £400,000 cost). During the first quarter of activity, Pensive Dirt extracts 10,000 tons of gravel, which results in the following depreciation expense:

£0.40 Depreciation cost per ton × 10,000 Tons of gravel = £4,000 Depreciation expense

Land Depreciation

Nearly all fixed assets have a useful life, after which they no longer contribute to the operations of a company or they stop generating revenue. During this useful life, they are depreciated, which reduces their cost to what they are supposed to be worth at the end of their useful lives. Land, however, has no definitive useful life, so there is no way to depreciate it.

The one exception is when some aspect of the land is actually used up, such as when a mine is emptied of its ore reserves. In this case, depreciate the natural resources in the land using the depletion method, as described earlier in this section.

Land Improvement Depreciation

Land improvements are enhancements to a plot of land to make it more usable. If these improvements have a useful life, depreciate them. If functionality is being added to the land and the expenditures have a useful life, record them in a separate land improvements account. Examples of land improvements are:
- Drainage and irrigation systems
- Fencing
- Landscaping
- Parking lots and walkways

A special item is the ongoing cost of landscaping. This is a period cost, not a fixed asset, and so should be charged to expense as incurred.

EXAMPLE

Pensive Corporation buys a parcel of land for £1,000,000. Since it is a purchase of land, Pensive cannot depreciate the cost. Pensive intends to use the land as a parking lot, so it spends £400,000 to pave the land, and add walkways and fences. It estimates that the parking lot has a useful life of 20 years. It should record this cost in the land improvements account and depreciate it over 20 years.

Depreciation Accounting Entries

The basic depreciation entry is to debit the depreciation expense account (which appears in the income statement) and credit the accumulated depreciation account (which appears in the balance sheet as a contra account that reduces the amount of fixed assets). Over time, the accumulated depreciation balance will continue to increase as more depreciation is added to it, until such time as it equals the original cost of the asset. At that time, stop recording any depreciation expense, since the cost of the asset has now been reduced to zero.

The journal entry for depreciation can be a simple two-line entry designed to accommodate all types of fixed assets, or it may be subdivided into separate entries for each type of fixed asset.

EXAMPLE

Pensive Corporation calculates that it should have £25,000 of depreciation expense in the current month. The entry is:

	Debit	Credit
Depreciation expense	25,000	
Accumulated depreciation		25,000

In the following month, Pensive's controller decides to show a higher level of precision at the expense account level, and instead elects to apportion the £25,000 of depreciation among different expense accounts, so that each class of asset has a separate depreciation charge. The entry is:

	Debit	Credit
Depreciation expense – Automobiles	4,000	
Depreciation expense – Computer equipment	8,000	
Depreciation expense – Furniture and fixtures	6,000	
Depreciation expense – Office equipment	5,000	
Depreciation expense – Software	2,000	
Accumulated depreciation		25,000

EXAMPLE

Pensive Corporate has £1,000,000 of fixed assets, for which it has charged £380,000 of accumulated depreciation. This results in the following presentation on Pensive's balance sheet:

Fixed assets	£1,000,000
Less: Accumulated depreciation	(380,000)
Net fixed assets	£620,000

Pensive then sells a machine for £80,000 that had an original cost of £140,000, and for which it had already recorded accumulated depreciation of £50,000. It records the sale with this journal entry:

	Debit	Credit
Cash	80,000	
Accumulated depreciation	50,000	
Loss on asset sale	10,000	
Fixed assets		140,000

As a result of this entry, Pensive's balance sheet presentation of fixed assets has changed, so that fixed assets before accumulated depreciation have declined to £860,000, and accumulated depreciation has declined to £330,000. The new presentation is:

Fixed assets	£860,000
Less: Accumulated depreciation	(330,000)
Net fixed assets	£530,000

The amount of net fixed assets declined by £90,000 as a result of the asset sale, which is the sum of the £80,000 cash proceeds and the £10,000 loss resulting from the asset sale.

Depreciation is usually charged directly to expense. However, the depreciation associated with the production process can instead be included in factory overhead, which is then allocated to units produced. The net effect is a delay in the recognition of the depreciation, until the units are sold and the related cost of goods sold is recognized.

Derecognition of Property, Plant and Equipment

When management no longer intends to use a fixed asset, the asset should be derecognized. Derecognition refers to the removal of a fixed asset from the accounting records of a business. The lack of intent to use does not necessarily mean that a fixed asset is only derecognized when it is sold or scrapped. An asset may also be derecognized even if it remains on the premises. The key deciding factor when derecognizing a fixed asset is whether the company expects to receive any future economic benefits from its use or disposal. If not, the asset can be derecognized at once.

The date on which disposal occurs is when the recipient obtains control of the asset.

If there is a gain or loss on the derecognition of a fixed asset, the amount is to be recorded in profit or loss. The gain or loss is calculated as the difference between any proceeds from disposal of an asset and its remaining carrying amount. The proceeds received from an asset disposal are to be recorded at fair value. If the buyer defers payment, a portion of the proceeds should be considered interest income.

When a business only infrequently derecognizes fixed assets, any resulting gains are not considered part of the revenue line item in the company's income statement. However, if a company is in the business of routinely buying and selling fixed assets or renting them, the proceeds from sale of these assets are included in revenue.

EXAMPLE

Ambivalence Corporation buys a machine for £100,000 and recognizes £10,000 of depreciation per year over the following ten years. At that time, the machine is not only fully depreciated, but also ready for the scrap heap. Ambivalence gives away the machine for free, and records the following entry.

	Debit	Credit
Accumulated depreciation	100,000	
Machine asset		100,000

EXAMPLE

To use the same example, Ambivalence Corporation gives away the machine after eight years, when it has not yet depreciated £20,000 of the asset's original £100,000 cost. In this case, Ambivalence records the following entry:

	Debit	Credit
Loss on asset disposal	20,000	
Accumulated depreciation	80,000	
Machine asset		100,000

EXAMPLE

Ambivalence Corporation still disposes of its £100,000 machine, but does so after seven years, and sells it for £35,000 in cash. In this case, it has already recorded £70,000 of depreciation expense. The entry is:

	Debit	Credit
Cash	35,000	
Accumulated depreciation	70,000	
Gain on asset disposal		5,000
Machine asset		100,000

What if Ambivalence had sold the machine for £25,000 instead of £35,000? Then there would be a loss of £5,000 on the sale. The entry would be:

	Debit	Credit
Cash	25,000	
Accumulated depreciation	70,000	
Loss on asset disposal	5,000	
Machine asset		100,000

Compensation for Impaired Assets

When a fixed asset is impaired, lost, or given up, and the owner receives compensation from a third party for the asset, the owner recognizes this payment in profit or loss as soon as it is recorded as a receivable.

Decommissioning Liabilities

A business may incur an obligation to dismantle equipment or restore a property to its original condition, once the end of an asset's useful life has been reached. The costs associated with these activities are known as decommissioning liabilities. This obligation may be incurred when an asset is initially constructed or installed, or at some later date during its use.

The following rules apply to possible changes in the amount of this decommissioning liability:

- *Cost model in use*. If an asset is measured using the cost model, any change in the decommissioning liability also offsets the cost of the related asset. If a decrease in the decommissioning liability exceeds the carrying amount of the related asset, recognize the remainder in profit or loss. If an increase in the decommissioning liability increases the cost of the related asset, it may be necessary to test the asset for impairment, to see if an impairment loss should be recognized.

- *Revaluation model in use*. If an asset is measured using the revaluation model, any change in the decommissioning liability alters the revaluation surplus or deficit associated with that asset. A decrease in the decommissioning liability is recognized in other comprehensive income and within the revaluation surplus, though the reversal of a revaluation deficit should be recognized in profit or loss. If the amount of the decrease would exceed the carrying amount of an asset under the cost model, recognize the excess amount in profit or loss. An increase in the decommissioning liability is recognized in profit or loss, though the elimination of any existing revaluation surplus should first be recognized in other comprehensive income.

Under both models, if there are changes in the decommissioning liability after the useful life of an asset has been completed, the changes are to be reflected immediately in profit or loss.

Decommissioning Funds

A business may contribute cash to a fund that is intended to pay for the costs of decommissioning a facility, such as a nuclear plant, or for remediating groundwater pollution, and so forth. A company may set up its own fund for this purpose, or contribute cash to a general fund into which other companies are also required to contribute assets. In the latter case, the funding requirements of contributors may increase if one of the other contributors goes bankrupt. The funds are usually administered by an independent trustee, and the contributors have restricted access to contributed funds.

When a company has an obligation to pay decommissioning costs for a fixed asset, it should separately recognize the amount of the decommissioning liability and the amount of its payments into the fund, which means that these amounts appear in separate liability and asset line items, respectively, in the balance sheet.

If the company has the right to be reimbursed by the fund for any amounts not used for decommissioning, the company should recognize the reimbursement at the lesser of the company's share of the fair value of the net assets in the fund that are attributable to the contributors, or the recognized amount of the decommissioning obligation. If there is a subsequent change in the right to receive reimbursement, other than what is caused by payments to or from the fund, recognize it in profit or loss.

If the company incurs an additional obligation to contribute funds, as may arise from the bankruptcy of a fellow contributor, recognize an additional liability if it is probable that the additional amount must be paid.

Property, Plant and Equipment Disclosures

For each class of fixed assets, disclose the following information in the notes accompanying the financial statements:
- A reconciliation for the period of the carrying amount, showing changes caused by additions, assets held for sale, business combinations, revaluations, impairment losses recognized or reversed, depreciation, exchange rate differences, and other changes
- Depreciation methods and useful lives used
- The basis for measuring the gross carrying amount
- The beginning and ending gross carrying amounts and accumulated depreciation, in aggregate

In addition, disclose the following information:
- Any assets pledged as security for liabilities
- Any changes in accounting estimates related to salvage values, useful lives, depreciation methods, and removal or restoration costs
- Any commitments to acquire fixed assets
- Any title restrictions
- Compensation paid by third parties for fixed assets that were impaired, lost, or given up
- The amount of expenditures capitalized into the carrying amount of assets under construction
- If assets were revalued, note the following:
  - The revaluation date, and whether an independent appraiser was involved
  - By class, the carrying amount that would have been recognized under the cost model
  - The revaluation surplus, any change in the amount for the period, and any restrictions on its distribution to shareholders

If a company is paying cash into a decommissioning fund, disclose the following information:
- The nature of the company's interest in the fund
- Any restrictions on access to assets in the fund
- If potential additional payments must be made, disclose the nature of the liability, estimate the financial effect, indicate any remaining uncertainties, and note the possibility of any later reimbursement

If a company experiences a change in its decommissioning liability and uses the revaluation model, disclose any resulting change in the revaluation surplus that is triggered by the liability change.

In addition, IFRS recommends disclosure of the following items, but does not require it:

- The carrying amount of idle fixed assets
- The carrying amount of retired fixed assets that are not classified as held for sale
- The gross carrying amount of any fixed assets that are fully depreciated and still in use
- If the cost model is used, any material differences between the fair value and carrying amount of fixed assets

Summary

Even a brief perusal of this chapter will make it clear that the accounting for fixed assets is one of the more time-consuming accounting activities, simply because the related accounting records must be monitored (and possibly adjusted) for years. Accordingly, the efficient accountant will do anything possible to charge expenditures to expense at once, rather than recording them as fixed assets. The best options for reducing the number of fixed assets are to maintain a high capitalization limit, and to adopt a skeptical attitude when anyone wants to add subsequent expenditures to a fixed asset. Also, avoid using the revaluation model whenever possible, since it adds unnecessary complexity to the accounting process. The result should be a considerably reduced number of fixed assets.

Chapter 15
Intangible Assets

Introduction

Most fixed assets are tangible assets, such as equipment, furniture, and buildings. However, they can also include intangible assets, such as computer software, licenses, and franchise agreements. Depending on the circumstances, intangible assets can comprise a large part of the asset base of a business, and so deserve detailed attention from the accounting department to ensure that they are properly recognized. In this chapter, we discuss the nature of intangible assets and how to account for them, as well as the related topic of web site costs.

IFRS Source Documents

- IAS 38, *Intangible Assets*
- SIC 32, *Intangible Assets – Web Site Costs*

Overview of Intangible Assets

An intangible asset is one that lacks physical substance, and from which an entity expects to generate economic returns for more than one accounting period. Examples of intangible assets are:

Marketing-related intangible assets:

- Internet domain names
- Newspaper mastheads
- Noncompetition agreements
- Trademarks

Customer-related intangible assets:

- Customer lists
- Customer relationships
- Order backlogs

Artistic-related intangible assets:

- Literary works
- Motion pictures and television programs
- Musical works
- Performance events

- Pictures
- Video recordings

Contract-based intangible assets:

- Broadcast rights
- Employment contracts
- Fishing licenses
- Franchise agreements
- Lease agreements
- Licensing agreements
- Mortgage servicing rights
- Service contracts
- Use rights (such as drilling rights or water rights)

Technology-based intangible assets:

- Computer software
- Patented technology
- Trade secrets (such as secret formulas and recipes)

Intangible assets may be aggregated into classes for accounting treatment. Examples of intangible asset classes are brand names, publishing titles, computer software, licenses and franchises, copyrights and patents, designs and prototypes, and assets under development.

Intangible assets can sometimes be treated as an integral part of a tangible asset. For example, the operating system with which a computer is pre-loaded is rarely accounted for as a separate intangible asset. Instead, its cost is included in the cost of the computer asset.

Accounting for Intangible Assets

An intangible asset can only be accounted for separately when it is clearly identifiable. An asset is considered identifiable when it can be separately sold, licensed, transferred, or exchanged, or it arises from certain contractual rights. In order to recognize an intangible asset, it must be possible to reliably measure the cost of the asset and its probable future economic benefits. These assertions are assumed to be satisfied if a business directly acquires an intangible asset, but must be proven if the assets are to be segregated from a business acquisition.

EXAMPLE

Suture Corporation pays an outside attorney £40,000 to file a patent application for an electronic method for destroying cancer cells, and incurs £35,000 of internal labor costs to provide the documentation needed for the patent application. Suture expects to earn millions in licensing fees from its ownership of the patent. Later, Suture spends £250,000 to defend the patent from a competing claim.

Suture should capitalize the £75,000 associated with the patent application, but must charge the defense cost to expense as incurred.

The initial accounting for an intangible asset is to record the asset at its cost, which should include the following items to the extent that they are incurred to acquire the asset and bring the asset to its working condition:

Costs to prepare the asset for use	Non-refundable purchase taxes	Purchase price
Employee benefits	Professional fees	Testing costs
Import duties		Wages

The cost of an intangible asset should be compiled minus the amounts of any related trade discounts and rebates. Also, the costs of new product introductions, conducting business in a new location, overhead, and administration should not be included in the cost of an intangible asset. Further, if the payment terms to acquire an intangible asset are deferred beyond normal credit terms, the cost to capitalize is the cash price equivalent; any amount above the cash price equivalent should be charged to interest expense.

Costs are accumulated into an intangible asset until the date when the asset has reached the condition required for it to operate in the manner intended by management. Thus, any costs incurred after that date to redeploy an asset should be charged to expense as incurred, rather than being added to its cost.

Once an intangible asset has been recorded, it is amortized over its useful life. If there is no discernible usage pattern, amortization should be on a straight-line basis. If an intangible asset is used in the construction of products or services, it can instead be allocated to inventory.

EXAMPLE

Thimble Clean buys the rights to a patented technology that allows it to manufacture potent detergents in pill form, which are dropped into washing machines. Thimble pays £200,000 for the technology, and decides to amortize this cost through the units of production method, where it will amortize £0.25 for every pill manufactured. Thimble includes this £0.25 cost in the standard cost of the product, which increases the recorded cost of inventory. Thimble then charges this inventory cost to the cost of goods sold whenever it sells a detergent pill.

Intangible Assets Acquired in a Business Combination

Many intangible assets are acquired as part of a business combination, where the acquirer pays a certain amount for an acquiree, and then assigns a portion of the purchase price to specific tangible and intangible assets of the acquiree, with any unassigned residual amount designated as goodwill. Many of these intangible assets are being recognized for the first time; that is, the acquiree may never have recognized them during its years of operation as an independent entity.

An intangible asset acquired through a business combination is recorded at its fair value as of the acquisition date. If there is some uncertainty about the range of possible fair values, it may be necessary to use an average of the various possible valuations, weighted based on their probabilities.

EXAMPLE

Pulsed Laser Drilling Corporation acquires a competitor that has made a significant investment in the development of a high-powered laser for drilling oil wells. At the time of the acquisition, the competitor had signed a contract with a large oil and gas exploration company to use the laser drill for a total fee of £18,000,000. The discounted cash flows associated with this contract are £7,200,000, which is used as a substitute for fair value by Pulsed Laser in estimating the valuation of the project that it should record as an intangible asset.

Here are several additional rules that may apply to the recognition of intangible assets acquired in a business combination:

- *Linked asset*. If an intangible asset is linked to a contract or other specifically identifiable asset or liability, recognize the intangible asset as part of the related item.
- *Research and development projects*. It is allowable to recognize an in-process research and development project of an acquiree as an intangible asset, as long as the project meets the criteria for an intangible asset.
- *Similar assets*. Similar intangible assets can be combined into a single asset, though they must have useful lives of roughly the same duration.

Once a research and development project has been recognized as an intangible asset by the acquirer, the following rules apply to any additional expenditures made in association with that project:

- *Research expenditures*. Expenditures made on research activities are charged to expense as incurred.
- *Development expenditures*. Expenditures made on development activities are charged to expense as incurred, unless they satisfy all of the following capitalization requirements:
  - Future economic benefits are probable
  - Management intends to complete and use the asset, and has the ability to do so
  - Technical feasibility of the product has been demonstrated
  - The amount of the development expenditure can be reliably measured

     o   There are adequate resources to complete the project

Internally Developed Intangible Assets

It is possible under IFRS to recognize internally-generated intangible assets. To do so, split expenditures related to a prospective intangible asset into those incurred during the research and development phases of constructing the asset. All research-related expenditures are to be charged to expense as incurred. Examples of research-related expenditures are:

- Activities designed to acquire new knowledge
- The search for and application of research findings
- The search for and/or formulation of product or process alternatives

Expenditures related to development activities can be capitalized as intangible assets, but only if they meet all of the criteria already noted for acquired development activities, which are reproduced here:

- Future economic benefits are probable
- Management intends to complete and use the asset, and has the ability to do so
- Technical feasibility of the product has been demonstrated
- The amount of the development expenditure can be reliably measured
- There are adequate resources to complete the project

Examples of development-related expenditures are:

- The design and testing for prototypes, or of alternative materials, processes, and so forth
- The design of tools, molds, and related items that involve new technology applications
- The design, construction, and operation of a pilot plant that is not intended for commercial production levels

IFRS does not allow the following internally-generated items or similar items to be recognized as intangible assets:

- Brands
- Customer lists
- Goodwill
- Mastheads
- Publishing titles

EXAMPLE

The Electronic Inference Corporation is developing a new manufacturing process for its electronic calculator line. The company expends £150,000 on the development of this process through the first half of 20X2, and is then able to demonstrate as of July 1 that the process meets the criteria for an intangible asset. The £150,000 expended prior to that date must be charged to expense.

The company estimates that the recoverable amount of knowledge embodied in the new process is £300,000. In the following four months, the company incurs an additional £330,000 of costs, which it capitalizes into an intangible asset. Since the capitalized amount is £30,000 higher than the recoverable amount, the controller writes off the difference as an asset impairment.

A number of items cannot be capitalized into intangible assets, and must instead be charged to expense as incurred. This situation arises because the expenditures do not meet the criteria listed earlier for development activities. Examples of expenditures that are rarely capitalized as intangible assets are those related to training activities, advertising and promotions, relocations, reorganizations, and start-up activities.

Other Forms of Intangible Asset Acquisition

In this section, we describe several additional scenarios under which a business may acquire an intangible asset:

- *Asset exchanges.* A business may acquire an intangible asset through a non-monetary exchange. The cost of the acquired asset is measured at fair value, unless the exchange has no commercial substance. If fair value cannot be derived, the carrying amount of the asset given up is used instead. A transaction is considered to have commercial value when the expected future cash flows (in terms of risk, timing, and/or amount) of a business will change because of the transaction.
- *Government grants.* A government entity may grant an intangible asset, such as airport landing rights, to a business. If so, the recipient has the choice of either recognizing the asset at its fair value, or at some nominal amount plus those expenditures needed to prepare the asset for its intended use.

Subsequent Intangible Asset Recognition

Once an intangible asset has initially been measured, you have a choice of continuing to measure it at cost (the cost model), or of revaluing it on a regular basis (the revaluation model). Both models are addressed in this section.

The Cost Model

Under the cost model, continue to carry the cost of an intangible asset, minus any accumulated amortization and accumulated impairment losses. This is the simplest approach, since the least amount of accounting is required.

When the cost model is selected, it should be applied to an entire class of intangible assets; thus, you cannot shift between the cost and revaluation models for individual items within a class of assets.

The Revaluation Model

If it is possible to measure the fair value of an asset reliably on an active market, there is an option to carry the asset at its revalued amount. There are few active markets for intangible assets, which renders this option unavailable in many situations. Subsequent to revaluation, the amount carried on the books is the fair value, less subsequent accumulated amortization and accumulated impairment losses. Under this approach, continue to revalue intangible assets at sufficiently regular intervals to ensure that the carrying amount does not differ materially from the fair value in any period.

If the revaluation model is initially used and you later find that there is no longer an active market from which to derive a revaluation, subsequently use the last revalued amount as the carrying amount, less any accumulated amortization or accumulated impairment losses for the periods since the last revaluation. It is possible that the termination of an active market indicates that the value of the asset has been impaired, which may call for impairment testing.

The fair values of some intangible assets may be quite volatile, necessitating frequent revaluations. This is not necessary when there is a history of insignificant movements in the fair value of assets.

When an intangible asset is revalued, there are two ways to deal with any amortization that has accumulated since the last revaluation. The choices are:

- Force the carrying amount of the asset to equal its newly-revalued amount by proportionally restating the amount of the accumulated amortization; or
- Eliminate the accumulated amortization against the gross carrying amount of the newly-revalued asset. This method is the simpler of the two alternatives, and is used in the following example.

EXAMPLE

The Red Herring Fish Company owns a fishing license for herring, which it purchased for £100,000. The term of the license is ten years, after which the fisheries department of the federal government will auction it again to the highest bidder. There is an active resale market for fishing licenses, since boat operators are constantly entering and departing the market for herring fishing.

After two years, Red Herring has amortized £20,000 of the carrying amount of the fishing license. At that time, the fisheries department announces that it will begin to reduce the number of licenses sold at auction, with the intent of eventually having 30% fewer fishing licenses outstanding. This prospective restriction in supply triggers an immediate jump in the resale market for the price of fishing licenses, to £130,000. Red Herring revalues its fishing license asset based on this jump in price by eliminating all accumulated amortization associated with the asset and then increasing the carrying amount of the asset. The entries are:

	Debit	Credit
Accumulated amortization	20,000	
Intangible assets - licenses		20,000
To eliminate accumulated depreciation		
Intangible assets - licenses	50,000	
Revaluation reserve		50,000
To match carrying amount to revalued amount		

Red Herring must now amortize the new £130,000 carrying amount of the fishing license over its remaining eight-year term. If the company uses the straight-line method to do so, the annual amortization will be £16,250.

If you elect to use the revaluation model and a revaluation results in an increase in the carrying amount of an intangible asset, recognize the increase in other comprehensive income, as well as accumulate it in equity in an account entitled "revaluation surplus." However, if the increase reverses a revaluation decrease for the same asset that had been previously recognized in profit or loss, recognize the revaluation gain in profit or loss to the extent of the previous loss (thereby erasing the loss).

If a revaluation results in a decrease in the carrying amount of an intangible asset, recognize the decrease in profit or loss. However, if there is a credit balance in the revaluation surplus for that asset, recognize the decrease in other comprehensive income to offset the credit balance. The decrease recognized in other comprehensive income decreases the amount of any revaluation surplus already recorded in equity.

The following table summarizes the proper recognition of revaluation changes just described:

Asset Revaluation Change	Recognition
Value increases	Recognize in other comprehensive income and in the "revaluation surplus" equity account
Value increases, and reverses a prior revaluation decrease	Recognize gain in profit or loss to the extent of the previous loss, with the remainder in other comprehensive income
Value decreases	Recognize in profit or loss
Value decreases, but there is a credit in the revaluation surplus	Recognize in other comprehensive income to the extent of the credit, with the remainder in profit or loss

In essence, IFRS requires the prominent display of any revaluation losses, and gives less reporting stature to revaluation gains.

If a fixed asset is derecognized, transfer any associated revaluation surplus to retained earnings. The amount of this surplus transferred to retained earnings is the difference between the amortization based on the original cost of the asset and the amortization based on the revalued carrying amount of the asset.

When the revaluation model is selected, it should be applied to an entire class of intangible assets; do not shift between the revaluation and cost models for individual items within a class of assets. This rule does not apply when there is no active market for the assets, since it is then impossible to use the revaluation method.

Intangible Asset Derecognition

An intangible asset should be removed from the accounting records (derecognized) when it is disposed of, or when the company no longer expects to derive any additional economic benefits from it. The disposal date is when the recipient obtains control of the asset.

When an intangible asset is derecognized, recognize in profit or loss any gain or loss on the disposal, which is calculated as the difference between the net sale proceeds and the remaining carrying amount of the asset. Any consideration paid to the business in exchange for a sold intangible asset should be recognized at its fair value. If payment is deferred, the difference between the amount eventually paid and the cash price equivalent should be recognized as interest income.

Web Site Costs

A business may incur costs, both internally and from third parties, to develop and maintain a web site on which it promotes and sells its products and services. IFRS considers such a web site to be an internally generated intangible asset. Its development cost can only be capitalized if it complies with all of the following requirements:

- Future economic benefits are probable
- Management intends to complete and use the asset, and has the ability to do so
- Technical feasibility of the product has been demonstrated
- The amount of the development expenditure can be reliably measured
- There are adequate resources to complete the project

If these requirements cannot be met, all expenditures related to the web site should be charged to expense as incurred.

Subject to the preceding requirements, development costs that can be capitalized include obtaining a domain name, acquiring hardware and software, installing applications, designing web pages, preparing and uploading information, and stress testing.

All other costs related to a website must be charged to expense as incurred. These costs include feasibility studies, defining specifications, evaluating alternatives, site hosting, advertising products and services on the site, and site maintenance.

When determining the useful life of a web site for the purpose of amortizing related costs that have been capitalized, IFRS recommends that the useful life be "short."

EXAMPLE

The Close Call Company compiles the cost of its new web site, which is used by customers to place orders for cross-town delivery services. The following table shows which items will be capitalized into an intangible asset and which will be charged to expense, on the assumption that the web site meets the criteria for capitalization as an internally developed intangible asset:

Expenditure Type	Capitalize	Charge to Expense
Planning activities		
Feasibility study		£8,000
Hardware and software requirements specification		12,000
Product evaluation		18,000
Preference selection		5,000
Infrastructure development		
Obtain domain name	£20,000	
Develop operating system and application code	120,000	
Install developed applications	30,000	
Stress testing	15,000	
Graphical design		
Design web page layout	40,000	
Creating graphics files	20,000	
Operating		
Updates to site graphics		35,000
Addition of new site features		60,000
Registering site with search engines		3,000
Backing up data		7,000
Employee training on website usage		11,000
Totals	£245,000	£159,000

Additional Intangible Asset Issues

The following additional topics apply to the accounting for intangible assets:

- *Useful life, indefinite.* An intangible asset may be determined to have an indefinite useful life when there is no foreseeable limit to the span of time over which the asset will continue to generate cash for the business. Such an asset is not amortized. The useful life of each indefinite-life asset should be reviewed in each reporting period; if the circumstances no longer support indefinite life status, assign it a useful life and begin amortizing it. The switch from an indefinite life to a finite life can be an indicator that the carrying amount of an intangible asset is impaired.

- *Useful life, definite.* If there is a limit to the cash-generating abilities of an intangible asset, amortize it. The useful life of an asset should not exceed the duration of any contract from which it arises, unless the contract can be renewed, and without significant cost. A renewal period should be factored into the determination of useful life when there is evidence that a contract will be renewed, that any renewal requirements will be satisfied, and that the cost of renewal is less than the benefits to be derived from the renewal. When determining the useful life of an intangible asset, consider the following factors:
  - o Anticipated competitor actions impacting the asset
  - o Any limits on use of the asset, such as the useful lives of other assets
  - o Any types of obsolescence that may apply to the asset
  - o Changes in market demand for the output of the asset
  - o Expected asset usage
  - o The maintenance cost required to achieve economic benefits from the asset
  - o Typical useful life durations for similar assets used in a similar way

---

EXAMPLE

AMM Corporation (a contraction of Annoying Marketing Materials) buys a customer list from a competitor, and plans to use it for a variety of bulk mailings. The benefit to be obtained from the list will be relatively short-lived, since the useful life only applies to the customers on the list when it was acquired. Accordingly, AMM plans to amortize the carrying amount of the list over a single year.

EXAMPLE

Radiosonde Communications operates a country music radio station. A government agency awards Radiosonde a broadcast license renewal once every five years, based on minimal requirements related to public service announcements and the filing of relevant license renewal documents. Radiosonde plans to pay the minimal renewal fee required for each subsequent renewal, as it has done for the past two license renewals. Though there are alternatives to radio technology, such as Internet radio stations, these options do not yet appear to threaten the radio business model. Based on this information, the broadcast license asset should be considered to have an indefinite life, and so should not be amortized.

Two years later, the incursions of both satellite radio and Internet radio have substantially reduced the market demand for the country music station. Accordingly, Radiosonde not only conducts an impairment analysis of the broadcast license asset, but also decides not to renew the license, and begins amortizing the post-impairment carrying amount of the asset over the remaining years until the license expires.

- *Amortization period*. When an intangible asset has a finite useful life, begin amortizing it when the asset is in the location and condition needed to be capable of operating as intended by management. Amortization should be halted when an asset is classified as held for sale, or when it is derecognized. The amortization method should reflect the usage pattern of the asset; if there is no discernible usage pattern, use the straight-line method of amortization. In some cases, there may be a predominant limiting factor associated with an intangible asset, such as the loss of a radio license after three years, or the loss of a toll road contract after £150 million in toll revenues have been reached. If so, the amortization should be based on the predominant limiting factor.
- *Amortization adjustments*. Both the amortization period and amortization method should be reviewed at least once a year, and adjusted as necessary.
- *Residual value*. Residual value is deducted from the gross carrying amount of an asset to arrive at the amount of the asset that can be amortized. When an intangible asset has a finite useful life, its residual value is assumed to be zero, unless a third party has committed to buy the asset at the end of its useful life, or a residual value can be derived from an active market for the asset. The amount of the residual value should be reviewed at least annually, and adjusted as necessary.

EXAMPLE

Failsafe Containment is awarded a patent on a magnetic fusion power containment system, from which Failsafe expects to obtain licensing fees for at least 10 years. Failsafe initially recognizes the patent using the cost model, at a carrying amount of £200,000. The company has signed a contract with a utility company to acquire the patent for £80,000 after six years have passed.

Failsafe should apply the residual value of £80,000 to the initial carrying amount of £200,000 to arrive at a depreciable amount of £120,000, and depreciate it over six years. If the straight-line method of amortization is used, this will result in annual amortization of £20,000.

- *Impairment testing*. When an intangible asset has an indefinite useful life, test it for impairment at least once a year, as well as when there is an indication of possible impairment. There is impairment if the recoverable amount of an asset is less than its carrying amount.

Intangible Asset Disclosures

Disclose the following information about intangible assets in the notes accompanying the financial statements for each class of assets, and further subdivided by internally-generated intangible assets and other intangible assets:
- *Amortization expense*. Where the amortization expense appears in the statement of comprehensive income.

- *Amortization methods.* The amortization methods used, if the assets have finite useful lives.
- *Gross amounts.* The beginning and ending balances of gross carrying amounts and the combined amount of accumulated amortization and accumulated impairments.
- *Reconciliation.* A reconciliation of the beginning and ending carrying amounts, including additions from internal development, additions from business combinations, additions acquired separately, assets classified as held for sale, revaluation changes, impairment changes, amortization, foreign currency exchange differences, and other items.
- *Useful life determination.* Whether the useful lives are considered finite or indefinite. If the former, disclose the duration of the useful lives.

If any intangible assets are accounted for under the revaluation model, disclose by asset class the effective date of revaluation, the aggregate carrying amount of revalued items, the carrying amount that would have been recognized if the cost model had been used, and a reconciliation of the revaluation surplus (if any), as well as any restrictions on the distribution of the revaluation surplus to shareholders.

In addition, disclose the following more general information as necessary:

- *Committed purchases.* Any amounts contractually committed for the acquisition of intangible assets.
- *Government grants.* If assets were acquired through a government grant and recognized at fair value, disclose their initial fair values, carrying amounts, and whether they are now measured under the cost model or the revaluation model.
- *Indefinite useful lives.* The carrying amounts of assets with indefinite useful lives, and the reasons for assigning them indefinite status.
- *Material changes.* If there have been material changes in accounting estimate, such as useful lives, amortization methods, and/or residual amounts, disclose the nature and amount of these changes.
- *Material items.* The carrying amount, remaining amortization period, and description of any specific intangible assets that are material to the financial statements.
- *Pledged as security.* The carrying amounts of any intangible assets pledged as security for liabilities.
- *Research and development.* The aggregate amount of research and development expense recognized during the period.
- *Restricted title.* The amount and name of any intangible assets with restricted titles.

IFRS also encourages, but does not require, the disclosure of any fully amortized intangible assets that are still in use, as well as a description of any intangible assets that do not meet the criteria for asset recognition, but which the company controls.

Summary

Most intangible assets are acquired. Since there is rarely an active market for intangible assets, this means that most of these items are recorded using the cost model, which requires little ongoing maintenance once the initial cost has been recognized. Consequently, and with the exception of occasional impairment testing, the accounting for intangible assets tends to be relatively easy.

It may be tempting to go through the additional documentation required to recognize an internally generated intangible asset. However, consider that capitalizing a large amount of expenditures may yield financial results that are unusually profitable, and in exchange for the incurrence of a large amount of amortization in later years that will weigh down reported results in those periods. If you insist on capitalizing these assets, at least disclose in the financial statements what the company's results would have been if the capitalization of internal intangible assets had not taken place.

Chapter 16
Investment Property

Introduction

Investment property is a non-monetary asset that is held with the intent of earning a return, either from its rental or appreciation. The accounting for investment property is somewhat different from the accounting for fixed assets. In this chapter, we describe the nature of investment property, the costing methods available for measuring it, and what types of information to disclose about it.

IFRS Source Document

- IAS 40, *Investment Property*

Overview of Investment Property

An owner holds *investment property* with the intent of either earning rental income, gaining from capital appreciation, or both. Because of this investment focus, an investment property is expected to create cash flows that are separate from the other assets that a business may own. This investment approach is different from *owner-occupied property*, where the property is used to house production or administrative activities, but there is no expectation of rental income or appreciation. Examples of investment property are:

- A building being leased under one or more operating leases
- A building held with the intent of being leased under operating leases, even if that is not currently the case
- Land for which a future use has not yet been determined
- Land held in order to benefit from the appreciation of its price over time
- Property under development that is intended to be an investment property

Conversely, the following are *not* considered to be investment properties:

- Property being developed on behalf of another party
- Property being developed for immediate sale, or ready for immediate sale
- Owner-occupied property that is used by the owner or its employees
- Property being leased under a finance lease (see the Leases chapter)

The following additional concepts may apply to the classification of property as investment property:

- *Extra services.* The owner of an investment property may provide additional services to the occupants of the property, such as janitorial services. If so, the property can still be accounted for as an investment property if the services provided are an insignificant part of the entire arrangement. If the services provided are significant, the property is to be accounted for as an owner-occupied property.

- *Leased to related party.* If a business leases space to its corporate parent or a subsidiary, the property cannot be classified in the consolidated financial statements of the group as investment property, since the entity as a whole is leasing from itself. However, the property could be classified as investment property in the financial statements of just the business leasing the property, since it is an investment property from the perspective of that entity.
- *Multiple uses.* In those cases where different portions of a property could be separately classified as investment property and other types of property, they can be accounted for separately if they can be sold separately. If not, the property can only be accounted for as an investment property if an insignificant proportion of it is used for non-investment purposes.

EXAMPLE

The Sojourn Hotel provides a number of services to its guests, including linen changes, room clean up, meals, and an on-site health club. Since the services provided are significant, Sojourn must account for the property as owner-occupied, rather than investment property.

EXAMPLE

The Acme Conglomerate owns the headquarters building in which its corporate staff works. Since it is owner-occupied, it is classified as a fixed asset.

Acme also owns a building which it obtained through a business combination, and which it is currently upgrading with the intent of leasing the facility. This is classified as an investment property.

Accounting for Investment Property

An investment property can only be recognized as an asset when its cost can be reliably measured and its economic benefits will probably flow to the owning entity. This definition has the following implications:

- *Deferred payment.* If the acquirer of an investment property buys it with a deferred payment, capitalize only that portion of the cost that is the cash price equivalent. Recognize any excess amount paid over the cash price equivalent as interest expense.
- *Ongoing expenditures.* Those expenditures required for the day-to-day servicing of a property are charged to expense as incurred. These items generally fall into the category of repairs and maintenance.
- *Replacement.* If portions of an investment property are replaced (such as a roof), that portion of the property being replaced is derecognized and replaced with the expenditure for the replacement item.

- *Start-up costs*. Those start-up expenditures needed to bring an investment property up to the standard envisaged by management can be capitalized. All other start-up costs are to be charged to expense as incurred.
- *Transaction costs*. If there are transaction costs associated with the initial acquisition of an investment property, include them in the initial measurement of the asset. Examples of such fees are legal services and property transfer taxes.
- *Waste*. If abnormal amounts of material, labor, or other items are wasted during the development of an investment property, charge them to expense as incurred.

The following additional scenarios may apply to the accounting for an investment property:

- *Leased asset*. If an investment property is held under a finance lease (see the Leases chapter), recognize the property at the lower of the present value of its minimum lease payments or its fair value.
- *Non-monetary purchase*. If an investment property is acquired through an exchange of non-monetary assets, measure the cost of the investment property at fair value unless the exchange has no commercial substance or the fair values of assets exchanged cannot be determined. There is no commercial substance when the risk, timing, or amount of an entity's cash flows does not change significantly as the result of a transaction. When the fair values of both the asset given up and received are available as the basis for measuring an investment property, the fair value of the asset received is preferred over the fair value of the asset given up. If no fair value is available, measure the property at the carrying amount of the asset given up.

Once an investment property has been initially recognized, the owner can elect to account for it under either the cost model or the fair value model. Also, the owner must consistently apply the same model to *all* of its investment properties.

Under the *fair value model*, an investment property is recognized at its fair value on an ongoing basis, with any change in fair value recognized in profit or loss in the period in which the fair value change occurs. If a business elects to use the fair value model, it must continue to use the model until the property being measured has either been disposed of or reclassified as owner-occupied, even if the number of comparable market transactions used as the basis for fair value measurements subsequently declines.

IFRS encourages use of the fair value model where valuations are compiled by a qualified and certified independent valuation expert.

EXAMPLE

The Acme Conglomerate buys an office tower in London for £75,000,000, with the intention of leasing it. Acme uses the fair value model to measure its value, and hires a reputable local valuation firm to provide a valuation analysis once a year. Over the next five years, these valuations result in the recognition of the following gains and losses by Acme:

Year	Cost	Fair Value	Recognized Gain or Loss
Initial	£75,000,000	£75,000,000	£0
1		77,000,000	2,000,000
2		82,000,000	5,000,000
3		85,000,000	3,000,000
4		72,000,000	-13,000,000

Under the *cost model*, an investment property is recognized at its cost, which is depreciated on an ongoing basis and periodically evaluated for impairment. This is the simpler of the two models and is less expensive to maintain, and so tends to be used more frequently.

EXAMPLE

The Acme Conglomerate buys a warehouse in Eastbourne for £8,000,000 and intends to lease it to a third party. The property manager estimates that the warehouse will have a useful life of 25 years and will then be torn down, so the asset is depreciated at a rate of £320,000 per year. By the end of the 25-year period, the carrying amount of the property on Acme's books will have been reduced to zero. Since the company has not elected to employ the fair value method, changes in fair value are not measured, and so have no impact on the carrying amount of the asset.

The following additional issues may apply to the investment property accounting topic:

- *Asset pools*. An entity may operate a property fund, for which it sells shares to investors. The entity can choose either the fair value or cost models for this fund, and may still elect to use the other valuation method for its remaining investment properties. However, it cannot use a mix of the methods for the properties *within* such a fund. If an asset is shifted from a pool recorded at fair value to a pool recorded at cost, the fair value of the asset on its transfer date becomes its cost.
- *Basis for fair value*. The measurement of fair value under the fair value method should reflect changes in rental income from an investment property being leased to third parties.
- *Included assets*. When deriving the fair value of an investment property where certain assets are integral to the fair value, do not double count these integral assets as fixed assets. Thus, if the fair value of an investment prop-

erty is based in part on its being furnished, do not also recognize the furnishings as separate assets.

- *Inability to measure fair value.* If the market for comparable properties is inactive, there may not be sufficient comparative information to derive fair value information. If this is the case during the construction of an investment property, but it is expected that fair value information will be available by the time the property has been completed, measure it at cost until the fair value information is available. If it is not possible to obtain fair value information on a continuing basis, then measure the property using the cost model. If the cost model is used because no fair value information is available, it is permissible to use the fair value model for the entity's other investment properties.

Owner-occupied property is accounted for as a normal fixed asset. See the Property, Plant, and Equipment chapter for more information.

Investment Property Transfers

It is possible to transfer assets into or out of an investment property. This is only allowed when there is a change in use. Evidence of a change in use is considered to be *only* one of the following four alternatives:

- *Shift from owner use.* The owner elects to stop its own use of a property as owner-occupied and starts treating it as investment property.
- *Shift to owner use.* The owner elects to stop using a property as an investment and starts using it on an owner-occupied basis.
- *Shift to sale.* The owner intends to sell a property, and so commences work to ready it for sale.
- *Shift from sale.* The owner elects to stop attempting to sell a property, and instead enters into an operating lease with a tenant, which means that the property is now treated as an investment property.

When an entity uses the cost model to account for its investment properties, shifting assets between different classifications of assets (as just noted) results in no change in the cost basis of an asset.

When an entity uses the fair value model to account for its investment properties, the cost for subsequent accounting is considered to be the fair value of an asset on the date when its designated use changes.

If an owner-occupied property is transferred into an investment property classification where it is now carried at fair value, the asset is revalued as of the transfer date. See the Property, Plant, and Equipment chapter for a discussion of asset revaluations. In essence, the revaluation concept means:

- In general, if there is a decrease in the carrying amount of an asset, recognize it in profit or loss.

- If there is a decrease in the carrying amount of an asset, but there is a revaluation surplus, the loss is first offset against the surplus, which means that it is recognized in other comprehensive income.
- In general, if there is an increase in the carrying amount of an asset, it is recognized in other comprehensive income and is considered a revaluation surplus.
- If there is an increase in the carrying amount of an asset, but there was a previous impairment loss, the gain is first offset against the loss, which means that it is recognized in profit or loss.

If an owner has property classified as inventory for sale, and which has been measured using the fair value model, and the property is then transferred to the investment property classification, any change in value on the transfer date is to be recognized in profit or loss.

If a business has been constructing an asset and has been measuring it at cost during the construction period, and intends to measure the asset at fair value, it can do so upon the completion of the asset. When completed, any difference between the carrying amount of the asset and its fair value is recognized in profit or loss.

Investment Property Disposals

When an investment property is disposed of or permanently withdrawn from use, it should be removed from the balance sheet, which is known as *derecognition*. Derecognition can occur when a property is sold, or is leased under a finance lease.

When a portion of a property is disposed of and replaced (as is common when constructed assets wear out and must be replaced), the accounting treatment varies depending on the valuation model used. The differences are:

- *Fair value model*. If an asset is already being measured at its fair value, include the cost of the replacement item in the carrying amount of the asset, and then reassess its fair value.
- *Cost model*. If an asset is already being measured at its cost, derecognize the item being replaced and add the cost of the item being added. If it is not possible to determine the cost of the item being replaced, the cost of the replacement can be used to indicate what the cost of the replaced item was when it was new.

When an investment property is sold or otherwise disposed of, recognize the difference between its carrying amount and the net disposal proceeds as a gain or loss. When making this calculation, measure any consideration received for the property at its fair value. If the amount of consideration received is deferred, the difference between the cash price equivalent and the amount actually paid is to be recognized as interest income by the seller.

Investment Property Disclosures – Fair Value Model

If a business uses the fair value model to measure its investment property, it should disclose the following information:

- *Classification criteria*. The criteria used to distinguish between owner-occupied, held for sale, and investment property.
- *Model used*. The type of valuation model used.
- *Obligations*. Any contractual obligations to buy, construct, or repair investment property.
- *Operating lease classification*. The circumstances under which property interests that are held under operating leases are accounted for as investment property.
- *Profit or loss recognition*. The amount of rental income, direct operating expenses related to rental properties, direct operating expenses related to non-rental properties, and the cumulative change in fair value recognized in profit or loss from the transfer of an asset from a cost method pool to a fair value method pool.
- *Reconciliation*. A reconciliation of the beginning and ending carrying amounts of investment property, including additions from acquisitions, additions from subsequent expenditures, additions from business combinations, assets held for sale, fair value adjustments, foreign exchange differences, transfers into or out of the inventory classification, transfers into or out of the owner-occupied classification, and other changes.
- *Restrictions*. Any restrictions on the realizability of investment property, or on related receipt remittances.
- *Valuation experts*. The extent to which valuation experts are used to measure the fair value of investment property. If there has been no valuation by such a person, disclose this fact.

In those investment property cases where the fair value model cannot be used due to a lack of comparable market transactions, the reconciliation should separate the amounts related to these cases. Further, a business should disclose the affected properties, and why the fair value model cannot be used. If possible, also note a range of estimates within which it is highly likely that the fair value lies for these properties. Finally, when these items are disposed of, note that they have been disposed of, the carrying amount on the sale date, and the gain or loss recognized.

Investment Property Disclosures – Cost Model

If a business uses the cost model to measure its investment property, it should disclose the following information:

- *Model used*. The type of valuation model used.
- *Classification criteria*. The criteria used to distinguish between owner-occupied, held for sale, and investment property.

- *Operating lease classification.* The circumstances under which property interests that are held under operating leases are accounted for as investment property.
- *Profit or loss recognition.* The amount of rental income, direct operating expenses related to rental properties, and direct operating expenses related to non-rental properties.
- *Restrictions.* Any restrictions on the realizability of investment property, or on related receipt remittances.
- *Obligations.* Any contractual obligations to buy, construct, or repair investment property.
- *Depreciation.* The depreciation methods applied to the investment property, as well as the related useful lives or depreciation rates.
- *Gross amounts.* The gross carrying amount, as well as the combined accumulated depreciation and accumulated impairment losses for the investment property at the beginning and end of the reporting period.
- *Reconciliation.* A reconciliation of the beginning and ending carrying amounts of investment property, including additions from acquisitions, additions from subsequent expenditures, additions from business combinations, held for sale items, depreciation, impairment losses, reversed impairment losses, foreign exchange differences, transfers to and from the inventory classification, transfers to and from the owner-occupied classification, and other changes.
- *Fair value.* When it is not possible to reliably estimate the fair value of investment property, describe the property, and explain why its fair value cannot be reliably measured. If possible, also note the range of estimates within which it is highly likely that the fair value lies.

Summary

A company may initiate a variety of operational decisions that make it difficult to discern whether a property should be accounted for as owner-occupied or investment property (which has a significant impact on the related accounting). To clarify the situation, create a policy that states the operational characteristics that will result in accounting treatment as one type of property or the other, and consistently adhere to that policy over time. This can be a major issue for a larger company with numerous investment properties, if it were to account for them on an inconsistent basis.

Chapter 17
Impairment of Assets

Introduction

An asset should not be carried in an entity's accounting records at more than its recoverable amount, which is the amount that can be recovered by a business through the ongoing use or sale of the asset. Otherwise, there is a risk of overstating the assets listed in a company's balance sheet, possibly by a large amount. In this chapter, we address how to identify an impairment situation, how to calculate the amount of an impairment, and the circumstances under which an impairment can be reversed.

IFRS Source Document

- IAS 36, *Impairment of Assets*

Overview of Asset Impairment

In essence, asset impairment has occurred when the carrying amount of an asset is greater than its recoverable amount. If this happens, write off the difference in profit or loss as an impairment loss. The following steps show the general process flow for impairment accounting:
1. Assess whether an asset may be impaired.
2. Measure the recoverable amount of the asset.
3. Measure and recognize the impairment loss.

The steps just indicated are described in greater detail in the following sub-sections.

Indications of Impairment

There should be an assessment of impairment indicators at the end of each reporting period. If it appears that asset impairment may have taken place, estimate the recoverable amount of the impairment. The following are examples of impairment indicators:
- *Adverse effects.* There have been, or are about to be, significant changes that adversely affect the operating environment of the business.
- *Damage or obsolescence.* There is evidence of damage to the asset, or of obsolescence.
- *Discount rate change.* Interest rates have increased, and this will materially impact the value in use of an asset, based on a reduction in the discounted present value of its cash flows. This is only the case if changes in market

interest rates will actually alter the discount rate used to calculate the value in use.

EXAMPLE

Rio Shipping acquired a freighter three years ago for £20 million, and routinely conducts an impairment analysis that is based on the discounted cash flows to be expected from the ship over the next ten years. The discount rate that Rio uses for the analysis is 6%, which is based on the current long-term interest rates that a similar company could obtain in the market place.

Short-term interest rates have recently spiked to 9%. If Rio were to use this rate as the discount rate, it would greatly reduce the present value of future cash flows, and likely create an impairment issue. However, since short-term rates fluctuate considerably, and the freighter still has a long useful life, management judges that this is the wrong interest rate to use as a basis for the discount rate, and elects to ignore it. Their decision is bolstered by the fact that long-term interest rates are holding steady at 6%.

- *Economic performance.* The economic performance of an asset has declined, or is expected to decline. This can include higher than expected maintenance costs, actual net cash flows that are worse than the budgeted amount, or a significant decline in net cash flows or operating profits.
- *Market capitalization change.* The carrying amount of all the assets in the company is more than the entity's market capitalization.
- *Market value decline.* An asset's market value declines significantly more than would be indicated by the passage of time or normal use.
- *Usage change.* There have been or are about to be significant changes in the usage of an asset, such as being rendered idle, plans for discontinuance or restructuring, plans for an early asset sale, or assessing an intangible asset from having an indefinite life to having a finite one.

Any of the preceding indicators or other factors may reveal that there is a possibility of asset impairment; if subsequent investigation reveals that there will be no impairment charge, the mere existence of one or more of these indicators may be grounds for adjusting the useful life, depreciation method, or salvage value associated with an asset.

EXAMPLE

Rio Shipping finds that a worldwide glut in the market for supertankers has reduced the usage level of its Rio Sunrise supertanker by 10 percent. This does not translate into a sufficient drop in the cash flows or market value of the ship to warrant an impairment charge. Nonetheless, Rio's management is concerned that the glut could continue for many years to come, and so it alters the depreciation method for the supertanker from the straight-line method to the 150% declining balance method, in order to accelerate depreciation and reduce the carrying amount of the asset more quickly.

Timing of the Impairment Test

IFRS states that one should assess whether there is any indication of impairment at the end of each reporting period, so this is an extremely frequent test.

Even if there is no indication of impairment, test an intangible asset for impairment if the asset has an indefinite useful life or if it is not yet available for use (e.g., intangible assets that are not yet being amortized). Perform this test at least once a year, and do so at the same time each year. If there are multiple intangible assets, test each one at a different time of the year. If an intangible asset was initially recognized during the current fiscal year, test it for impairment by the end of the current fiscal year.

The reason why the standard requires this annual analysis of intangible assets that are not yet available for sale is that there is more uncertainty surrounding the ability of these assets to generate sufficient future economic benefits. Given the higher level of uncertainty, there is more ongoing risk that they will be impaired.

In addition, conduct an impairment test on any goodwill acquired in a business combination at least once a year.

Recoverable Amount

If there is an indication of impairment, determine the recoverable amount of the asset in question. The recoverable amount is defined as the higher of its fair value less costs of disposal and its value in use.

The *fair value less costs of disposal* is one of the two components of the calculation of an asset's recoverable amount. There are several ways to determine the fair value less costs of disposal, as outlined here.

The best source of information for fair value less costs of disposal is a price in a binding sales agreement in an arm's length transaction, which is adjusted for any incremental costs to sell. It can be difficult to find such a situation that dovetails so perfectly with an in-house asset, so expect to use one of the following approaches that do not yield such perfect information (listed in declining order of preference):

1. *Pricing in an active market.* If an asset trades in an active market, assume that its market price is a reasonable representation of its fair value, from which you would then subtract any costs of disposal to arrive at the fair value less costs of disposal. In such a market, assume that the bid price is the market price. If there are no bid prices, use the price of the most recent transaction instead (as long as there has been no significant change in the economic circumstances since the date of the transaction). An active market is considered to be one in which the items being traded are homogenous, there are willing buyers and sellers, and prices are available to the public.

2. *Best information available.* In the absence of an active market or a binding sale agreement, use the best information available to estimate the amount that you could obtain by disposing of the asset in an arm's length transaction between knowledgeable and willing parties. Consider the result of the recent sales of similar assets elsewhere in the industry as "best information."

> **Tip:** The best information used to derive fair value less costs to sell should not include a forced sale, except if management believes that it will be compelled to sell an asset in this manner.

When deriving fair value less costs of disposal, what is involved in "costs of disposal"? Examples are:

- Asset removal costs
- Costs to bring the asset into condition for sale
- Legal costs
- Taxes on the sale transaction

These are only examples of disposal costs; if there are similar types of costs that relate to a sale transaction, consider them to be disposal costs.

Value in use is the other key component of the calculation of an asset's recoverable value (which must be higher than an asset's carrying amount in order to avoid an asset impairment). Value in use is essentially the discounted cash flows associated with an asset or cash-generating unit. Consider the following issues when deriving an asset's value in use:

- Possible variations in the amount or timing of cash flows related to an asset
- The current market risk-free rate of interest
- Such other factors as illiquidity and risk related to holding the asset

If you feel that these considerations warrant a change in the value in use of an asset, build adjustments into either the cash flows or discount rate used to derive the value in use. Adjustments to the cash flows can include a weighted average of all possible cash flow outcomes.

The cash flow estimates used to derive the value in use should be based on the following:

- Management's best estimate of the economic conditions likely to exist over the remaining useful life of the asset. These estimates should be based on reasonable and supportable assumptions, with a greater weighting given to external evidence.
- The most recent budget or forecast that has been approved by management, covering a maximum of five years (unless a longer period can be justified by having already shown the ability to forecast accurately over a longer period). Do not include any changes in cash flows expected to arise from future restructurings or from the presumed future enhancement of an asset's performance.

> **Tip:** Include in a cash flow analysis those changes arising from a future restructuring, once management has committed to the plan. Thus, if you know that cash flows will improve as a result of such a plan, gaining management approval of the plan may be crucial to avoiding an impairment charge.

- Projections beyond the period covered by the most recent budget or forecast that are extrapolations using a steady or declining growth rate for subsequent years (unless an increasing rate can be justified). Do not use a growth rate that exceeds the long-term average growth rate for the product, market, industry, or country where the company operates (unless a higher rate can be justified).

Tip: One of the reasons for using a steady or declining growth rate in projections is that more favorable conditions will attract more competitors, who will keep the cash flow growth rate from increasing. Thus, if you want to use an increasing cash flow growth rate in a forecast, justify what will keep competitors from driving the rate down, such as the existence of significant barriers to entry, or such legal protection as a patent.

Also, ensure that the assumptions on which the cash flow projections are based are consistent with the results the company has experienced in the past, which thereby establishes another evidence trail which supports the veracity of the cash flow projections.

Tip: Inordinately high cash flow projections are frowned upon, so expect to run afoul of the auditors if you attempt to insert unjustifiable cash flow increases in the value in use calculations. Do not try to avoid an impending impairment charge with alterations to cash flows, since this merely pushes off the inevitable until somewhat later in the useful life of the asset, when it is impossible to hide the issue over the few remaining years of the life of the asset.

When constructing the cash flow projections for the value in use analysis, be sure to include these three categories of cash flow:

- *Cash inflows.* This arises from continuing use of the asset.
- *Cash outflows.* This is from the expenditures needed to operate the asset at a level sufficient to generate the projected cash inflows, and should include all expenditures that can be reasonably allocated to the asset. If this figure is derived for a cash-generating unit where some of the assets have shorter useful lives, the replacement of these assets over time should be considered part of the cash outflows.
- *Cash from disposal.* This is the net cash proceeds expected from the eventual sale of the asset following the end of its useful life.

Do not include in the cash flow projections any cash flows related to financing activities or income taxes.

Tip: As just noted, include in the cash flow projections the cash outflows connected to overhead that is applied to an asset. Since a larger amount of overhead application will reduce the value in use of the asset and make an impairment charge more likely, establish an overhead application procedure that justifiably allocates the smallest amount of overhead possible to any assets that are subject to impairment tests. Only include those overhead costs for which there is a direct linkage to the asset.

Once the cash flows related to an asset have been compiled, establish a discount rate for use in deriving the net present value of the cash flows. This discount rate should reflect the current assessment of:

- The time value of money by the market for an investment similar to the asset under analysis. This means that the risk profile, cash flow timing, and cash flow amounts of the asset should be reflected in the investment for which you are using a market-derived interest rate.
- The risks specific to the asset for which you have not already incorporated adjustments into the cash flow projections.

The Impairment Test

An asset is impaired when its carrying amount is greater than its recoverable amount. In some cases, there is no way to determine the fair value of an asset less costs to sell, since there is no active market for the asset. If so, use the value in use as the recoverable amount of an asset.

Tip: If either an asset's fair value less costs of disposal or its value in use is higher than its carrying amount, there is no impairment. Thus, it is not necessary to calculate both figures as part of an impairment test.

When a fixed asset approaches the end of its useful life, it may be sufficient to use the fair value less costs of disposal as the foundation for an impairment test, and ignore its value in use. The reason is that the value of an asset at this point in its life is mostly comprised of any proceeds from its disposal, rather than from future cash flows (which are likely to be minor).

Tip: The instructions in IAS 36 imply that an investigation of fair values and discount rate calculations for cash flows is needed to conduct an impairment test. However, the standard also states that "estimates, averages, and computational short cuts may provide reasonable approximations" of these requirements. Consequently, use short cuts whenever there is a reasonable basis for doing so.

Recognize an impairment loss when the recoverable amount of an asset is less than its carrying amount. The amount of the loss is the difference between the recoverable amount and the carrying amount. This loss should be recognized immediately in profit or loss.

If you have revalued an asset already, recognize the impairment loss in other comprehensive income to the extent of the prior revaluation, with any additional impairment being recognized as a normal expense.

After an impairment loss is recognized, adjust the depreciation on the asset in future periods to account for the reduced carrying amount of the asset.

EXAMPLE

Rio Shipping owns a small coastal freighter with an original cost of £14 million and estimated salvage value of £4 million, and which it has been depreciating on the straight-line basis for five years. The freighter now has a carrying amount of £9 million.

Rio conducts an impairment test of the freighter asset, and concludes that the fair value less cost to sell of the asset is much lower than original estimates, resulting in a recoverable amount of £7 million. Rio takes a £2 million impairment charge to reduce the carrying amount of the freighter from £9 million to £7 million.

The freighter still has five years remaining on its useful life, so Rio revises the straight-line depreciation for the asset to be £600,000 per year. This is calculated as the revised £7 million carrying amount minus the £4 million salvage value, divided by the five remaining years of the freighter's useful life.

The Cash-Generating Unit

An impairment test should be conducted for an individual asset, unless the asset does not generate cash inflows that are mostly independent of those from other assets. If an asset does not generate such cash inflows, conduct the test at the level of the cash-generating unit of which the asset is a part. All subsequent testing of and accounting for an impairment at the level of a cash-generating unit is identical to its treatment as if it had been an individual asset.

A cash-generating unit is the smallest identifiable group of assets that generates cash inflows independently from the cash inflows of other assets. Examples of cash-generating units are product lines, businesses, individual store locations, and operating regions. It is allowable for a cash-generating unit to have all of its cash inflows derive from internal transfer pricing, as long as the unit could sell its output on an active market. Once a group of assets are clustered into a cash-generating unit, continue to define the same assets as being part of the unit for future impairment testing (unless there is a justifiable reason for a change).

An impairment test should remain at the level of the individual asset rather than for a cash-generating unit in either of the following cases:
- The fair value less costs of disposal of the asset is higher than its carrying amount.
- The value in use (i.e., discounted cash flows) of the asset is estimated to be close to its fair value less costs of disposal.

EXAMPLE

Rio Shipping owns a rail line that extends from its private shipping terminal on Baffin Island to a warehousing area two miles inland, where it stores ore shipped to it from several mines further inland. The rail line exists only to support deliveries of ore, and it has no way of creating cash flows independent of Rio's other operations on Baffin Island. Since it is impossible to determine the recoverable amount of the rail line, Rio aggregates it into a cash-generating unit, which is its entire shipping operation on Baffin Island.

EXAMPLE

Rio Shipping enters into a contract with the Port of New York to provide point-to-point ferry service on several routes across the Hudson River. The Port requires service for 18 hours a day on four routes. One of the four routes has minimal passenger traffic, and so is operating at a significant loss. Rio can identify the ferry asset associated with this specific ferry route.

Rio cannot test for impairment at the individual asset level for the ferry operating the loss-generating route, because it does not have the ability to eliminate that route under its contract with the Port. Instead, it must test for impairment at the cash-generating unit level, which is all of the ferry routes together.

Recognize an impairment loss when the recoverable amount of a cash-generating unit is less than its carrying amount. You cannot reduce the carrying amount of the cash-generating unit as a whole, since it is not recorded in the company's records as such – it is recorded as a group of individual assets. To record the loss, allocate it in the following order:
1. Reduce the amount of any goodwill assigned to the cash-generated unit. If there is any loss still remaining, proceed to the next step.
2. Assign the remaining loss to the assets within the cash-generating unit on the basis of the carrying amount of each asset. When doing so, you cannot reduce the carrying amount of an asset below the highest of its:
   - Value in use (i.e., discounted cash flows)
   - Fair value less costs of disposal
   - Zero

   If it is not possible to assign all of the pro rata portion of a loss to an asset based on the preceding rule, allocate it to the other assets in the cash-generated unit based on the carrying amounts of the other assets.

EXAMPLE

Rio Shipping owns Rio Bay, which is a container ship that it acquired as part of an acquisition. Rio Shipping has allocated £2 million of goodwill from the acquisition to the Rio Bay for the purposes of its annual impairment test. The ship is designated as a cash-generating unit that is comprised of three assets, which are:
   - Hull – Carrying amount of £20 million

- Engines – Carrying amount of £7 million
- Crane hoists – Carrying amount of £3 million

Thus, the total carrying amount of the Rio Bay is £32,000,000, including the allocated goodwill.

Rio determines that the recoverable amount of the Rio Bay is £28,000,000, which represents an impairment loss of £4 million. To allocate the loss to the assets comprising the cash-generating unit, the company first allocates the loss to the outstanding amount of goodwill. This eliminates the goodwill, leaving £2 million to be allocated to the three assets comprising the unit. The allocation is conducted using the following table:

Asset	Carrying Amount	Proportion of Carrying Amounts	Impairment Allocation	Revised Carrying Amount
Hull	£20,000,000	67%	£1,340,000	£18,660,000
Engines	7,000,000	23%	460,000	6,540,000
Crane hoists	3,000,000	10%	200,000	2,800,000
Totals	£30,000,000	100%	£2,000,000	£28,000,000

Asset Impairment Reversals

At the end of each reporting period, assess whether any prior impairment loss has declined. The following are all indicators of such an impairment decline:

- *Economic performance.* The economic performance of the asset is better than expected.
- *Entity performance.* There have been significant favorable changes in the company to enhance the asset's performance or restructure the operations of which it is a part.
- *Environment.* The business environment in which the company operates has significantly improved.
- *Interest rates.* Interest rates have declined, which may reduce the discount rate used to calculate discounted cash flows, thereby increasing the recoverable amount of the asset.
- *Market value.* The asset's market value has increased.

If this analysis concludes that the amount of impairment has declined or been eliminated, estimate the new recoverable amount of the asset and increase the carrying amount of the asset to match its recoverable amount. This adjustment is treated as a reversal of the original impairment loss. Also, document what change in estimates caused the impairment recovery.

If an impairment charge is being reversed, only increase the carrying amount of an asset back to where that carrying amount would have been without the prior impairment charge, and net of any amortization or depreciation that would have been recognized in the absence of an impairment charge. Also, once the reversal is recorded, revise the periodic depreciation charge so that it properly reduces the new carrying amount over the remaining life of the asset.

EXAMPLE

Rio Shipping has almost fully automated the operations of its Rio Giorgio container ship, so that it can cruise the oceans with a crew of just three people (one per shift). Rio Shipping has also installed an advanced impeller propulsion system that cuts the ship's fuel requirements in half. These changes vastly reduce the cash outflows normally needed to operate the ship.

Rio had previously recognized a £4 million impairment loss on Rio Giorgio. The new cash flow situation results in a recoverable amount that matches the carrying amount of the ship prior to its original impairment charge. However, there would have been an additional £200,000 of depreciation during the period between the original impairment loss and the reversal of the impairment charge, so Rio Shipping can only reverse £3.8 million of the original impairment amount.

If an impairment charge is reversed for a cash-generating unit, allocate the reversal to all of the assets comprising that unit on a pro rata basis, using the carrying amounts of those assets as the basis for the allocation. This is the same concept already described for the allocation of an impairment loss – only now it is in reverse. When you calculate this allocation back to individual assets, the resulting asset carrying amount cannot go above the lower of:
- The recoverable amount of the asset, or
- The carrying amount of the asset, net of depreciation or amortization, as if the initial impairment had never been recognized.

If there is an allocation limitation caused by either of these items, allocate the remaining impairment reversal among the other assets in the unit.

EXAMPLE

Rio Shipping conducts a re-examination of the recoverable amount of its Rio Bay container ship, which was described in an earlier example for the initial recognition of impairment losses. Various changes to the propulsion system of the ship have reduced its operating costs to the point where Rio Shipping can justifiably increase its estimate of the ship's recoverable amount by £1 million. The revised carrying amounts of the assets comprising the cash-generating unit are carried forward from the prior example, and are noted below:

Asset	Revised Carrying Amount
Hull	£18,660,000
Engines	6,540,000
Crane Hoist	2,800,000
Total	£28,000,000

The following table shows the adjusted carrying amounts of the three assets following the allocation of the impairment reversal back to them.

Asset	Carrying Amount	Proportion of Carrying Amounts	Initial Reversal Allocation	Adjusted Carrying Amount
Hull	£18,660,000	67%	£670,000	£19,330,000
Engines	6,540,000	23%	230,000	6,770,000
Crane Hoist	2,800,000	10%	100,000	2,900,000
Totals	£28,000,000	100%	£1,000,000	£29,000,000

However, to properly allocate the impairment reversal back to these assets, Rio Shipping must determine the carrying amount of each asset, net of depreciation, as if the initial impairment had never occurred. This causes a problem, because the hull and crane hoist both have a longer estimated useful life than the engines, which are expected to be replaced midway through the life of the other assets. Consequently, the engines have been depreciated at a quicker rate than the other assets, and so cannot accept the full amount of the impairment allocation.

This results in the following additional allocation of the impairment reversal, where only a portion of the allocation can go to the engines, while the remaining impairment reversal is allocated among the other two assets.

Asset	Adjusted Carrying Amount	Carrying Amount as if Impairment Never Occurred*	Impairment Reversal Still to Allocate**	Proportion of Adjusted Carrying Amounts	Second Stage Reversal Allocation
Hull	£19,330,000	£20,500,000		87%	£148,000
Engines	6,770,000	6,600,000	£170,000		
Crane Hoist	2,900,000	3,400,000		13%	£22,000
Totals	£29,000,000		£170,000	100%	£170,000

* Calculation not shown here
** Calculated as the adjusted carrying amount of £6,770,000 minus the carrying amount as if the initial impairment had never occurred, of £6,600,000.

You should recognize any impairment reversal in profit and loss as soon as it occurs.

Even if the analysis to reverse an impairment loss does not actually result in an impairment reversal, it may provide sufficient cause to adjust the remaining useful life of the asset, as well as the depreciation method used or its estimated salvage value.

The preceding discussion of how to reverse an impairment loss applies equally to individual assets and cash-generating units.

> **Tip:** IFRS does not allow the reversal of an impairment loss recognized for goodwill, on the grounds that such a reversal would be caused by an increase in internally generated goodwill. IFRS does not allow the recognition of internally generated goodwill.

Other Impairment Topics

Questions may arise about how to deal with corporate assets in the analysis of impairment, as well as whether to allocate goodwill to cash-generating units. These topics are addressed below.

Corporate Assets

Assets that are recognized at the corporate level are ones that do not generate cash inflows independently of other assets, and you cannot fully attribute their carrying amounts to other cash-generating units. An example of a corporate asset is a research facility. It is not usually possible to allocate the cost of these assets to any cash-generating units, unless there is a direct relationship between them.

Goodwill Allocation to Cash-Generating Units

If a company has acquired assets as part of a business combination, allocate the goodwill associated with that combination to any cash-generating units, but only if those units are expected to benefit from the synergies of the combination.

> **Tip:** You can safely ignore this rule in many cases, because the standard also states that the goodwill allocation only extends down to the point at which management monitors goodwill for its own internal purposes. In most cases, goodwill monitoring only extends down to the business unit level; thus, as long as a cash-generating unit is smaller than a business unit, the requirements of this standard do not apply.

If you *do* allocate goodwill to a cash-generating unit and the company then sells that unit, include the allocated goodwill in the carrying amount of the unit; this will impact the amount of any gain or loss recognized on disposal of the unit.

If a company sells assets from a cash-generating unit to which goodwill has been allocated, assign a portion of the goodwill to the assets being sold, based on the relative values of the assets being sold and that portion of the unit being retained.

EXAMPLE

Rio Shipping had previously acquired a container ship unloading dock in the Port of Los Angeles for £50 million, of which £10 million was accounted for as goodwill. Rio accounts for the overhead cranes in the dock as a cash-generating unit, to which it allocates £6 million of the goodwill associated with the acquisition.

Two years later, Rio sells one of the cranes for £5 million. Management estimates that the value of the remainder of the cash-generating unit is £15 million. Based on this information, Rio's accounting staff allocates £1.5 million of the goodwill to the crane, based on the following calculation:

£6 million goodwill × (£5 million crane value ÷ (£5 million crane value
+ £15 million cash-generating unit value))

= £6 million goodwill × 25% of the combined value of the crane asset
and cash-generating unit
= £1.5 million goodwill allocation

Impairment Testing Efficiencies

You are supposed to test any intangible asset that has an indefinite useful life for impairment on an annual basis. To save time in performing this annual test, use the most recent detailed calculation of such an asset's recoverable amount that was made in a preceding period, but only if the situation meets *all* of the following criteria:

- *Related assets and liabilities are unchanged.* The assets and liabilities of the cash-generating unit of which the intangible asset is a part have not changed significantly (if the intangible asset is part of a cash-generating unit at all);
- *Remote likelihood of change.* The events and circumstances since the last calculation indicate only a remote likelihood that the current recoverable amount would be less than the asset's carrying amount; and
- *Substantial difference.* The most recent calculation of the recoverable amount yielded an amount substantially greater than the asset's carrying amount.

Asset Impairment Disclosures

For each class of assets, disclose the following information about asset impairments in the notes accompanying the financial statements:

- *Impairment recognition.* The amounts of impairment losses and impairment loss reversals recognized in profit or loss, and where this information is located in the statement of comprehensive income.
- *Revalued asset impairment recognition.* The amount of impairment losses and impairment loss reversals on revalued assets recognized in profit or loss, and where this information is located in the statement of comprehensive income.

Whenever there is a material impairment loss or impairment loss reversal, disclose the following at the individual asset or cash-generating unit level:

- *Amount.* The amount of the loss or loss reversal recognized or reversed.

- *Asset information.* The nature of the asset, and the reportable segment (if any) in which it is included.
- *Basis of change.* Whether the recoverable amount of the asset or cash-generating unit is based on the value in use or the fair value less costs of disposal. If the former, disclose the discount rate used to make the current estimate, as well as the discount rate used for the previous estimate. If the latter, disclose the basis used to arrive at fair value less costs of disposal.
- *Cash-generating unit information.* The nature of the cash-generating unit, the amount of the impairment loss or impairment loss reversal, the reportable segment (if any) in which it is included, and any changes in the way the assets in the unit have been aggregated (as well as the reason for the change).
- *Circumstances.* The circumstances leading to the loss or loss reversal.

If there are no material impairment losses or reversals to disclose at the individual asset or cash-generating unit level, disclose the following impairment information instead, in aggregate:

- *Circumstances.* The circumstances leading to the loss or loss reversal.
- *Class information.* The primary classes of assets impacted by any impairment losses, and the classes of assets impacted by the reversal of impairment losses.

A business may have recognized a significant amount of goodwill or intangible assets with indefinite useful lives. If so, disclose the following information for each cash-generating unit for which the carrying amount of these items forms a significant proportion of the entity's total carrying amount of the items:

- *Goodwill allocation.* The amount of goodwill allocated to the cash-generated unit.
- *Intangibles allocation.* The amount of intangible assets with indefinite useful lives allocated to the cash-generating unit.
- *Recoverable amount.* The recoverable amount of the cash-generating unit, and how that amount was determined. In addition:
  - If the recoverable amount is based on value in use, disclose the key assumptions for the cash flow projections used and how each assumption was determined, as well as how these assumptions have changed over time. Also note the discount rate applied to the projections, as well as the duration of the projections, and explain the reason for using cash flows for a period of greater than five years (if applicable). Finally, note the growth rate used to extrapolate cash flow projections beyond the budget period, and justify the rate if it is greater than the long-term growth rate in the company's market or country of operation.
  - If the recoverable amount is based on fair value less costs of disposal, disclose the valuation technique used. If the technique is not

based on a quoted price for an identical unit, disclose key assumptions used and how each assumption was determined, the level of the fair value hierarchy in which the measurement method is placed, and any changes in the valuation technique (and the reason for the change). If the measurement is based on discounted cash flow projections, disclose the projection period, the growth rate used to extrapolate cash flows into the future, and the discount rate applied to those projections.

- *Assumption change.* If there is a reasonably possible change in a key assumption that would cause a carrying amount to exceed its recoverable amount, disclose the amount of the possible change and the value assigned to the targeted assumption. Also note the amount by which the value must change in order to match the recoverable amount to the carrying amount.

If the allocation of goodwill and intangible assets with indefinite lives is allocated across a number of cash-generating units, with minor allocations to each unit, disclose this fact, along with the aggregate allocated carrying amount of these items.

If the recoverable amounts of a group of cash-generated units are based on the same key assumptions, and the carrying amount of the goodwill and intangible assets with indefinite lives allocated to this group form a significant proportion of the company's total carrying amount of goodwill and intangible assets with indefinite lives, disclose the following additional information:

- *Assumptions.* All key assumptions used, and how management determines the values assigned to those assumptions.
- *Goodwill.* The aggregate carrying amount of all goodwill assigned to this group of units.
- *Intangible assets.* The aggregate carrying amount of all intangible assets with indefinite lives assigned to this group of units.
- *Assumption change.* If there is a reasonably possible change in a key assumption that would cause the carrying amount of a group to exceed its recoverable amount, disclose the amount by which the recoverable amount of the group currently exceeds its carrying amount. Also note the amount assigned to that key assumption, and the amount by which it must change in order to match the recoverable amount to the carrying amount.

If a business is required to report segment information (see the Operating Segments chapter), disclose for each segment the amount of impairment losses recognized in the period, as well as the amount of impairment loss reversals in the period.

If any goodwill acquired in a business combination has not been allocated to a cash-generating unit, state why the allocation has not taken place, and the amount of unallocated goodwill.

Summary

The review, measurement, and recognition of asset impairments can be quite time-consuming, and requires a certain amount of disclosure in the notes accompanying the financial statements. The situation is aggravated when the basis for an impairment loss changes in a subsequent period, resulting in further labor to measure, recognize, and disclose an impairment reversal. Given these issues, it makes sense to create a company policy for what constitutes a material amount of impairment to recognize. Below the threshold level defined in the policy, no impairment losses or reversals should be recognized. This policy should be discussed with the company's auditors, who can give input regarding the threshold recognition level to incorporate into the policy.

For the reasons just noted, impairment losses and reversals should require several levels of approval before being recognized. It is entirely possible that a lower-level accountant may calculate a need for a large number of small impairment charges and reversals, which a more senior person with a better grasp of the efficiencies involved would be less inclined to approve.

Chapter 18
Assets Held for Sale and
Discontinued Operations

Introduction

From time to time, a business may find that it no longer needs certain assets, and so will put them up for sale or discontinue their use. IFRS mandates that such assets and the results of their operations be segregated in the financial statements, so that readers can discern their impact on the financial results and financial position of a business. In this chapter, we describe the accounting for assets designated as being held for sale, as well as the disclosure of discontinued operations.

IFRS Source Document

- IFRS 5, *Non-Current Assets Held for Sale and Discontinued Operations*

Accounting for Non-Current Assets Held for Sale

An asset or a disposal group (which is a group of assets and liabilities to be disposed of together) is to be classified as held for sale if it is expected that the carrying amount of the asset will be recovered primarily through a sale, rather than through the ongoing use of the asset. The held for sale designation only applies if:
- The asset or disposal group is available for immediate sale in its current condition; and
- It is highly probable that the asset or disposal group will be sold.

The sale of an asset or disposal group is only considered highly probable when all of the following conditions are present:
- Management has committed to a sale plan;
- The search for a buyer is currently being pursued;
- The asset or disposal group is being actively marketed for sale;
- The price being offered is reasonable in relation to its fair value;
- The sale is expected to be completed within one year; and
- Significant changes to the plan or its withdrawal are unlikely.

EXAMPLE

The management of Thurston Enterprises wants to shift its warehouse to a new and more automated facility. To do so, it commits to the sale of the present warehouse and actively markets it at the market price. The real estate agent handling the transaction believes that a buyer can be found within one year.

To make the best use of company resources, the management team intends to continue operating from the existing warehouse until a buyer is found, and while the new facility is being constructed. The company does not plan to close on a sale transaction at least until the new facility has been completed and all automated systems have been properly tested.

Since the seller refuses to complete a sale until the new facility is ready, the existing facility cannot be considered available for immediate sale in its current condition, and so should not be classified as held for sale.

EXAMPLE

Flipped Enterprises specializes in buying business properties, upgrading them, and selling them off within a short period of time at a higher price. Because Flipped does not intend to resell its properties until they have been properly renovated, these assets cannot initially be classified as held for sale, since they are not available for immediate sale.

The following additional scenarios and rules may apply to the held for sale classification:

- *Assets to be abandoned.* If an asset or disposal group is to be abandoned, rather than sold, it cannot be classified as held for sale. A temporarily idled asset is not considered to be abandoned.
- *Assets to be distributed.* If the intent is for an asset or disposal group to be distributed to the owners of the business, they are classified as held for distribution to owners, rather than held for sale.
- *Duration extension.* It is allowable to extend the period over which a sale will occur to more than one year, if the delay is caused by circumstances beyond the control of the entity, and management is still committed to sell the asset or disposal group. An extension of the one-year period is allowed in all of the following circumstances:
  - When the held for sale designation was first applied, it was expected that a third party would impose conditions that would delay the transaction, a firm purchase commitment would probably be obtained within one year, and a response to the imposed conditions could not begin until the purchase commitment was obtained.
  - When a firm purchase commitment is obtained, after which conditions are unexpectedly imposed that will delay the sale, the seller has taken action to respond to the conditions, and a favorable resolution is expected.
  - Conditions formerly considered unlikely arise during the sale period that will extend the sale period, the seller has taken steps to respond to the situation, and the asset is being actively marketed at a reasonable price.

EXAMPLE

The management of the Tesla Power Company has committed to the sale of a coal-fired power generation facility, and believes that a firm purchase commitment can be obtained within one year. Since power generation is a regulated industry, the sale is subject to regulatory approval. Such approval may take time to obtain, since there has been a public outcry over the use of coal for power generation. Thus, Tesla is aware that conditions will be imposed on a sale, but can take no action until it finds a buyer and applies to the regulatory agency to complete the sale. Under these circumstances, Tesla can classify the facility as held for sale.

EXAMPLE

The management of Creekside Industrial commits to a plan to sell its battery production facility, and accordingly classifies the property as held for sale. A buyer is found, who makes a firm commitment to purchase the property. During the due diligence phase of the purchase, the buyer discovers that battery acid has leaked into the ground and is now flowing into the local creek. Creekside is required by the buyer to remediate this problem, which will require more than a year to rectify. Creekside takes immediate steps to remediate the problem, and expects that the situation will be resolved. Under these circumstances, Creekside can continue to classify the facility as held for sale.

EXAMPLE

The management of Excalibur Shaving Company commits to a plan to sell its old razor blade production line, and accordingly classifies it as held for sale. However, the market subsequently declines for premium razor blades, so Excalibur is unable to sell the production line during the next year. The company continues to actively market the equipment, but believes that the market will become more heated, and so does not reduce the offered price to the existing market rate. Since the asset is not being marketed at a reasonable price, it can no longer be classified as held for sale.

- *Intent to resell.* In those instances when a business acquires an asset or disposal group with the intent of reselling it, it can immediately classify the asset as held for sale, but only if it expects to complete a sale within one year, and any other criteria for this classification can be met within a few months of the acquisition date.
- *Late classification.* If an asset or a disposal group meets the criteria for the held for sale classification after the end of a reporting period, but before the financial statements are authorized for issuance, this fact should be disclosed in the notes accompanying the financial statements.
- *Shareholder approval.* In those cases where a sale is contingent upon shareholder approval, only consider the sale of an asset or disposal group to be highly likely if shareholder approval is also highly likely.

An asset that qualifies as being held for sale should be measured at the lower of its carrying amount or its fair value less costs to sell. When this results in recognition at an amount lower than the carrying amount, recognize an impairment loss at once for the difference. If there is a subsequent increase in fair value less costs to sell, it is allowable to recognize the associated gain, capped at the amount of any cumulative impairment loss.

EXAMPLE

Finchley Fireworks designates its Radlett production facility as held for sale. Because of the designation, Finchley must measure the Radlett facility at the lower of its carrying amount or its fair value less costs to sell. The carrying amount of the facility is £650,000, while its fair value less costs to sell is only £425,000. Accordingly, Finchley should recognize an impairment loss of £225,000 in profit or loss, which reduces the carrying amount of the facility to its fair value less costs to sell.

When an asset is classified as held for sale, it should not be depreciated. The same accounting applies to any asset being held for distribution to owners.

The following special accounting considerations may apply to the preceding guidance:

- *Intent to resell.* In those cases where a business acquires an asset or disposal group with the intent of reselling it, the effect of the preceding accounting guidance is that it will be initially measured at the lower of its carrying amount or fair value less costs to sell.
- *Costs to sell.* When a sale is expected to be completed in more than one year, measure the costs to sell (as used in the lesser of the carrying amount or fair value less costs to sell calculation) at their present cost. Any subsequent increase in this cost is to be recognized as a financing cost when the sale is eventually completed.
- *Criteria no longer met.* If an asset or disposal group no longer meets the held for sale criteria, immediately remove it from this classification, and measure it at the lower of either:
  - Its carrying amount prior to being classified as held for sale, less any depreciation that would have been recognized if the asset had never been classified as held for sale; or
  - Its recoverable amount as of the date when the held for sale classification no longer applies. The recoverable amount is the greater of an asset's value in use and its fair value less costs to sell. Value in use is the present value of the cash flows expected from an asset or cash-generating unit.

Any measurement adjustments made to the carrying amount of an asset or asset group after the held for sale designation is removed are to be recognized at once in profit or loss. If only a portion of the assets in a disposal group are no longer classified as held for sale, any other assets and liabilities remaining in the group can still be classified as held for sale, if they continue to meet the criteria for this classification.

Disclosure of Non-Current Assets Held for Sale

When there are non-current assets or disposal groups held for sale, disclose the following information in the financial statements or the accompanying notes:

- *Asset classes.* If there are several classes of assets and liabilities that are being held for sale, disclose them by class, either within the balance sheet or in the accompanying notes. This requirement is waived if a subsidiary that is held for sale was acquired with the intent of selling it.
- *Classification change.* If an asset or disposal group is no longer classified as held for sale, note the circumstances of the decision and its effect on the results of operations for all periods presented.
- *Cumulative income or expense.* If there is any cumulative income or expense associated with an asset or disposal group that is classified as held for sale and which is recognized in other comprehensive income, it must be classified separately in other comprehensive income.
- *Description.* Describe the asset or disposal group, as well as the circumstances of the sale, and the expected timing of the disposal.
- *Gain or loss.* If an impairment gain or loss was recognized on the adjustment of an asset or disposal group to its fair value less costs to sell, state the amount of the gain or loss.
- *Presentation.* An asset or disposal group that qualifies as being held for sale should be presented separately in the balance sheet. Similarly, if there are liabilities in a disposal group, present them separately from other liabilities in the balance sheet. If there are assets and liabilities in a disposal group, they are not to be presented as a net amount in the balance sheet.
- *Segment.* For publicly-held companies, note the segment in which the asset or disposal group is presented.

If assets or disposal groups were classified in the comparative balance sheets for prior periods as being held for sale, do not re-classify them if the classification has changed in the most recent balance sheet.

Disclosure of Discontinued Operations

A discontinued operation is a component of an entity that is either held for sale or which has been disposed of, and which is either:

- A subsidiary acquired with the intent of reselling it;
- Part of a plan to dispose of a major business line or area of activities; or
- A major business line or area of operations.

A *component of an entity* contains operations and cash flows that can be clearly distinguished from the remainder of a business. Thus, a component is considered to be a cash-generating unit of a business.

A company should disclose a sufficient amount of information for users to understand the effects of discontinued operations. This means that a single line item in the income statement be presented that comprises the following:

- The post-tax profit or loss earned by discontinued operations; and
- The post-tax gain or loss from the measurement to fair value less costs to sell or the disposal of the discontinued operations.

In addition, disclose the following information in the financial statements or the notes accompanying them:

- *Adjustments.* If there are adjustments in the current period to the disposal of a discontinued operation in a prior period, classify it separately in the discontinued operations section of the income statement, and disclose its nature. Such changes typically arise from purchase price adjustments, indemnification issues, and the resolution of other uncertainties related to a disposal.
- *Analysis.* A breakdown of the discontinued operations line item into its component parts, including revenue, expenses, pre-tax profit or loss, income tax expense, any gain or loss on measurement or disposal and the associated income tax. This is not required for a subsidiary that was acquired with the intent to resell it.
- *Cash flows.* The net cash flows from the operating, investing, and financing activities of the operation. This is not required for a subsidiary that was acquired with the intent to resell it.
- *Income attributable to owners.* The income from continuing operations and from discontinued operations that is attributable to the owners of the parent entity.

For comparability purposes, the disclosures noted here should be included in the financial statements for all reporting periods presented.

If a component of an entity is no longer classified as held for sale, shift its results of operations from the discontinued operations section to the income from continuing operations section of the income statement. This restatement applies to all comparison periods reported. When this restatement is included in the comparison periods, label the restated amounts as being re-presented from discontinued operations.

EXAMPLE

A sample format for a company's income statement that includes the results of discontinued operations is:

Continuing Operations	
Sales	£1,000,000
Cost of goods sold	425,000
Gross profit	575,000
Selling and administrative expenses	430,000
Profit before tax	145,000
Income tax expense	50,000
Profit from continuing operations	95,000
Discontinued Operations	
Profit from discontinued operations	32,000
Profit for the period	£127,000
Profit attributable to:	
Owners of the parent	
Profit from continuing operations	35,000
Profit from discontinued operations	12,000
Profit attributable to owners of the parent	47,000
Noncontrolling interests	
Profit from continuing operations	60,000
Profit from discontinued operations	20,000
Profit attributable to noncontrolling interests	80,000
Total profit from all sources	£127,000

Summary

Assets to be classified as held for sale must first meet a number of requirements. Consider taking full advantage of this broad set of requirements by allowing very few assets or disposal groups to be classified as held for sale. The held for sale classification requires special reformatting of the financial statements, as well as the exemption of certain assets from depreciation, and further accounting effort if anything is ever reclassified out of the held for sale classification. In short, insist on full compliance with IFRS to avoid the held for sale designation as much as possible.

Chapter 19
Provisions, Contingent Liabilities
and Contingent Assets

Introduction

Most organizations have liabilities of various kinds, about which they do not possess perfect information regarding the timing or amount of payments. Depending on the circumstances, it may be necessary to recognize or at least disclose information about these liabilities. In this chapter, we delve into the definitions of provisions and contingent liabilities, and how to account for them. We also address the accounting for contingent assets.

IFRS Source Document

- IAS 37, *Provisions, Contingent Liabilities and Contingent Assets*
- IFRIC 21, *Levies*

Overview of Provisions

A provision is a liability whose timing or amount is uncertain. Examples of provisions are:
- Decommissioning costs for a facility
- Obligations to clean up environmental damage
- Obligations to pay lawsuit damages
- Warranty obligations for products sold

A provision can be distinguished from other types of liabilities, such as accounts payable, whose amounts are defined on a supplier invoice, and which are due for settlement on a specific date. An accrued liability is not a provision, since this type of liability relates to specific goods or services that have already been received. While it may be necessary to estimate the amount of an accrued liability, a liability is clearly present, and the level of uncertainty tends to be minor.

A provision is recognized when the circumstances meet the following criteria:
- There is a present obligation that arises from a past event;
- Settlement with company resources will probably be required; and
- The amount of the liability can be reliably estimated.

EXAMPLE

Subterranean Access sells well digging equipment. Subterranean has a generous warranty policy, under which it repairs or replaces all damaged or nonfunctioning products within one year of the sale date. Given the uses to which its products are put, Subterranean tends to experience relatively high warranty claims. The company controller reviews the warranty situation to see if a provision should be recognized, and notes the following points:

- The company offers a warranty as part of each product sale, so there is a present obligation that arises from a past event.
- Given the company's historical experience with warranty claims, it is much more likely than not that claims will be presented to the company.
- The company has a long history of settling warranty claims, and so can readily derive an expected settlement amount.

Based on the facts of the situation, Subterranean should recognize a provision for warranty claims.

If it is not possible to meet all three of the preceding conditions, do not record a provision. Instead, continue to review the situation in each succeeding reporting period to see if the conditions have been met, and recognize the provision in whichever period the conditions are met.

The following clarifications apply to the conditions for recognizing a provision:

- A past event is considered to have created an obligation if it is more likely than not that an obligation exists at the end of a reporting period. This decision should be based on all available evidence.
- A past event is considered to have created a current obligation when the obligation can be legally enforced, or when there is a *constructive obligation*, where other parties have a valid expectation that the business will settle the obligation.
- A provision is not recognized for a future event, since a business could take action now to avoid that future event. For example, if there is pending legislation to require enhanced water filtration systems at a chemical plant, a company could avoid the liability by selling off or shutting down the plant.
- There is no obligation that could result in the recognition of a provision, unless a company action that potentially creates the obligation has been communicated to the parties to whom the obligation would be owed.
- A past event may not give rise to a provision until a later date, when the business makes a statement that creates a constructive obligation, or a law is passed that retroactively creates an obligation. It is not sufficient for a law to be proposed; it must be virtually certain of being enacted as drafted before it gives rise to an obligation from which a provision should be recognized.
- If there are a number of similar obligations, consider the entire group of obligations when determining the probability of whether the company will have to make a payment, rather than at the level of each individual obligation. For example, the probability of a single warranty claim on a specific

product sale is quite low, but when warranty claims for all product sales are considered, a certain amount of warranty claims will probably be paid.

EXAMPLE

Elkins Engineering is being sued by a client over a supposedly faulty building design that may be causing air conditioning problems. After consulting with a number of air conditioning experts about the issues raised by the client, the management of Elkins concludes that it is more likely than not that an obligation exists, and so recognizes a provision of £200,000 to cover its expected liability related to the lawsuit.

EXAMPLE

The Hilltop Hog Company has operated a slaughterhouse for many years near the town of Hilltop. During that time, the company has buried the unusable parts of hog carcasses in a nearby field. While completely legal, the buried offal is causing a stench that annoys the local residents. After several years of inaction, Hilltop's management issues a press release, in which it commits to more properly dispose of the remains. This communication creates a constructive obligation, so the company should recognize a provision for the proposed cleanup operation.

EXAMPLE

Omni Consulting is housed in a facility that it owns. The roof of the building is designed to last for 20 years, and the roof has been in existence for 19 years. Omni cannot recognize a provision for replacement of the roof in the following year, because a provision is based on a past obligating event, and replacement of the roof is a future obligation. Omni could even avoid the obligation by moving to a new building.

Accounting for Provisions

The amount of a provision to recognize is a company's best estimate of the amount that would be required for it to rationally settle a liability at the end of the current reporting period. The estimate of this amount could be based on what it would cost to transfer the obligation to a third party. The amount of this estimate can be difficult to discern, and so may require the judgment of management, possibly with input drawn from similar prior situations or the advice of experts. If there are a number of estimated payout amounts that are not closely clustered together, it may be necessary to recognize an expected value, which is based on the probabilities of various payouts being made. If one payout estimate in a range of estimates is no more likely to occur than another, recognize the midpoint of the range as the provision.

EXAMPLE

Green Lawn Care manufactures electric lawn mowers. Based on its past experience with warranty claims, no warranty claims will be received for 90% of its products. A battery replacement will be required for 8% of the products, which will cost £50, and a motor replacement will be required for 2% of the products, which will cost £175. Green sells

100,000 lawn mowers. Based on these probabilities and costs, the warranty provision that the company should recognize is calculated as follows:

$$(75\% \times £0 \times 100,000 \text{ Units}) + (8\% \times £50 \times 100,000 \text{ Units}) + (2\% \times £175 \times 100,000 \text{ Units}) = £750,000 \text{ Provision}$$

The following additional factors may apply to the accounting for a provision:

- *Future operating losses.* It is not acceptable to recognize a provision for a future operating loss, since a future loss is not considered a current liability. However, if a future loss is anticipated, this may be grounds for reviewing company assets for impairment.
- *Impact of future event.* It is possible that a future event will impact the amount of an obligation that will be paid out. If so, adjust the recognized amount of a provision to reflect the future event. For example, the operator of a nuclear power generating facility is aware of new technology that will be helpful in reducing the cleanup cost associated with the environmental damage caused by the facility. An assessment of the cost reductions that may be generated by this technology can be included in the calculation of a provision. However, the reduction of a provision based on the anticipated development of technology that does not yet exist is not allowed.
- *Impact of new legislation.* It may be necessary to recognize a provision when it is virtually certain that new legislation will be enacted, the terms of the legislation are known, and it is certain to be implemented. In most cases, not all of these variables will be known, so it is generally advisable to wait until legislation has been enacted.
- *Onerous contracts.* A company may be party to an onerous contract, where the obligations outweigh the expected benefits. If so, the net obligation under the contract should be recognized as a provision. The amount to recognize is the least net cost of exiting from the contract. "Least net cost" is the lower of the cost of fulfilling a contract and the penalties associated with not fulfilling it. A provision is not needed if such a contract can be cancelled with no penalty to the company.
- *Ongoing provision adjustments.* IFRS requires that provisions be reviewed at the end of each reporting period, and adjusted to match the best estimate of the obligation amount. If management believes it is no longer probable that a payout will be required under a provision, it is permissible to reverse the provision.
- *Present value.* When a payout under a provision is not expected for some time, and the effect of the time value of money on the provision is therefore material, recognize the present value of the provision. When present value is used, the carrying amount of a provision increases in each subsequent reporting period, to incorporate the passage of time. This periodic increase is accounted for as a borrowing cost. If settlement is expected to be in the near future, the effect of the time value of money will be immaterial, and so can

be ignored. Use the market interest rate as the discount rate used to calculate the present value of a provision.

EXAMPLE

Argo Drilling leases property from a government entity for oil exploration and development purposes. Part of the agreement mandates that Argo pay for remediation of the property once all drilling has been completed and any oil extracted. Based on its experience with similar arrangements, the management of Argo realizes that 75% of the eventual restoration cost will be based on the construction of the drilling pad, and 25% on the later extraction of oil.

At the end of the current reporting period, Argo has completed the drilling pad, but has not commenced drilling. At this point, Argo can take action to avoid 25% of the remediation costs by not drilling. Consequently, it should only recognize a provision for that 75% of the remediation costs that are linked to the construction of the drilling pad. If Argo later elects to begin drilling, it must then recognize a provision for the remaining 25% of the remediation cost.

EXAMPLE

Green Lawn Care leases its current headquarters location under a five-year lease. At the end of the fourth year, Green moves to a new location. The terms of the old facility lease do not allow Green to cancel the lease or sublease the facility. Green should recognize a provision in the amount of the remaining unavoidable lease payments.

If the terms of the lease had allowed Green to sublease, the appropriate amount of the provision would be the difference between expected payments received from the sublease agreement and the lease payments to the landlord under the original lease.

The Provision for Restructuring

A restructuring is a plan to materially change either the manner in which a business is conducted or the scope of its business. Examples of restructurings are the termination of a line of business or geographic location, relocating business activities, eliminating a layer of management, and a reorganization that alters the nature and focus of company operations.

It is possible to recognize a provision for a corporate restructuring, as long as all of the preceding requirements for a provision have been met. In addition, management must have a formal plan for the restructuring that identifies that portion of the business and principal locations that will be affected, as well as the function, location, and approximate number of employees who will be terminated, the amount of expenditures related to the restructuring, and when the plan will be implemented. Also, the actions or announcements of management must have raised an expectation among those affected that it will proceed with the restructuring. The following additional factors may apply:

- *Board notification.* In some countries, the decision to restructure ultimately lies with a separate board whose members may not include management. If so, an announcement of management's intentions may be considered to have taken place once it notifies this board of its intention to restructure, since the members of the board may represent those individuals who will be impacted by the plan.
- *Decision as basis for provision.* If management or the board of directors reaches a decision to proceed with a restructuring, this is not by itself sufficient grounds for recognizing a related provision. In order to justify the use of a provision, management would also have to begin implementation of the plan or announce the main features of the plan to those affected by it, and do so by the end of the reporting period.
- *Detail provided.* A simple announcement of a restructuring is not a sufficient method for raising expectations among those affected; instead, the announcement must be in sufficient detail regarding the features of the plan that a valid expectation is raised that the restructuring will take place.
- *Timing.* If a restructuring is announced for a period well in the future, this does not raise a valid expectation that the plan will be implemented. Instead, the start date and implementation time frame should be short enough that management would not have a significant opportunity to modify the plan.

EXAMPLE

At its December 31 board meeting, the board of directors of Argo Drilling decides to adopt a plan to shut down its South American drilling operations. However, the company does not communicate this plan to those affected by the end of the reporting period, so no restructuring provision can be recognized in the current period.

If the board had chosen to announce a layoff associated with the shutdown of drilling operations to the affected employees on the same date as its decision to do so, the company could have recognized a restructuring provision in the current period.

If management begins to implement a restructuring plan or announces its main features to those affected by it after the last day of a reporting period, it should disclose the restructuring if the activity is considered material, and knowledge of it could influence the decisions of those who use the company's financial statements.

It is not permissible under IFRS to include in a restructuring provision any identifiable future operating losses. Instead, these losses are to be recognized only as they are incurred.

Management may be tempted to dump as many expenses as possible into a restructuring provision, thereby clearing the way for the recognition of outsized profits in future reporting periods. IFRS restricts this behavior by only allowing the direct expenditures related to a restructuring to be included in the related provision. Expenditures included in the provision should not be associated with the ongoing activities of the business. Thus, the provision should not include costs related to marketing, new investments, or the relocation or retraining of those employees whose employment will continue with the company after the restructuring.

Accounting for Contingent Liabilities

A contingent liability is not recognized, because it has not yet been confirmed that a business has an obligation, or it is not yet possible to make a reliable estimate of the amount due, or it is not probable that the business has to pay out resources to settle the obligation. Under these circumstances, a contingent liability is disclosed, but not recognized. The only situation in which a contingent liability is not even disclosed is when the possibility of the business having to pay is remote.

There are situations where a business may be jointly and severally liable for an obligation, along with one or more other entities. In this case, that portion of the liability the business assumes will be met by the other parties should be classified as a contingent liability. The remaining portion for which the business expects to be liable, and for which it can estimate a probable payment, is recognized as a provision.

Tip: There may be a number of contingent liabilities hovering in the background of a company's operations, none of which yet have a sufficient probability of payment that recognition as a provision is justified. However, this situation can change, so review contingent liabilities on a regular basis to see if the probability of payout has increased to the point where they should be recognized as provisions.

Accounting for Contingent Assets

There may be a possibility that a business will receive an asset at some point in the future. For example, a company may be pursuing a lawsuit against a business partner, the outcome of which could be a large settlement in the company's favor. Under IFRS, such a contingent asset is not recognized, on the grounds that doing so may result in the recognition of income that will never actually be realized.

Only when the receipt of an asset is virtually certain can a company recognize it. To use the preceding lawsuit example, a jury award to the company would still not result in the virtual certainty of receipt, since the other party may not have the funds available with which to pay the award. Receipt of the asset could be considered virtually certain only when the payment arrived in the company's bank account.

When it appears probable that the receipt of economic benefits will occur, a contingent asset should be disclosed.

Accounting for Reimbursements

There may be cases where a business is reimbursed by a third party for some portion or all of a provision, such as through the use of an insurance policy. The amount of this reimbursement can only be recognized if it is virtually certain that the business will be reimbursed in the event of a settlement of the obligation embodied by a provision. Also, the amount of the reimbursement asset recognized cannot be larger than the amount of the provision with which it is paired.

If recognized, treat the reimbursement as a separate asset, so it is not netted against the amount of the provision. However, it is permissible to net the provision expense and reimbursement amount in the income statement.

EXAMPLE

A cargo ship operated by Silesian Shipping is attacked by pirates in the Indian Ocean and sunk. The value of the ship and its cargo is £20,000,000. The ship and cargo were insured, less a 30% deductible, and the insurer has already stated in writing that it will reimburse the company. Silesian can recognize a reimbursement asset of £14,000,000, which represents the anticipated amount of the reimbursement claim to be paid by the insurer.

Accounting for Levies

A government may impose a levy on an organization. The first indication that a levy may exist is the enactment of legislation allowing a government to impose the levy. The levy should be recognized by the organization as soon as a triggering event occurs. An example of a triggering event for a levy that is based on revenue is the generation of that revenue. For example, if a levy will be imposed at a rate of 0.5% of gross sales, then the entity should recognize the levy at that percentage rate as the revenue is generated. The following additional circumstances may apply:

- *Future periods obligation.* A business is required by the government to continue operating in future periods. This does not mean that the levies associated with those future periods should be recognized now.
- *Levy asset.* If the amount of a levy has been paid in advance, the entity should recognize it as a prepaid asset, which will be charged to expense in later periods.
- *Progressive obligation.* If there is an obligating event that triggers a levy, and that event is spread over a period of time, then the levy should also be recognized over a period of time, rather than all at once. Thus, a levy based on revenues should be recognized in proportion to the amount of revenue generated over time.
- *Threshold attainment.* If a levy is only applied after a certain threshold level has been reached, an organization should not recognize the levy if the entity is currently operating below the designated threshold level.

Disclosure of Provisions and Contingent Items

When a business recognizes a provision, it should disclose the following information in the notes accompanying its financial statements for each class of provision:

- *Carrying amount.* The carrying amount of the provision at the beginning and end of the reporting period.

- *Changes.* The nature and amount of any new provisions made, as well as increases in existing provisions.
- *Present value related.* Any increase in the discounted amount of provisions that were caused by the passage of time or a change in the discount rate used to derive present value.
- *Reversals.* Any unused provision amounts that were reversed in the period.
- *Usage.* The amounts used in the provisions in the period.

It is not necessary to provide comparative information for the preceding disclosures that relate to any earlier reporting periods shown alongside the financial statements for the current reporting period.

In addition, disclose the following information about each class of provision that is reported in the financial statements:

- *Description.* The nature and expected payment timing for the obligations.
- *Reimbursement.* The amounts of any reimbursements related to provisions, including the amount of any reimbursement assets that have been recognized.
- *Uncertainties.* Any uncertainties regarding the timing or amount of the payments to be made.

A provision is reported separately from trade payables and other forms of accounts payable.

If there are any contingent liabilities for which the probability of occurrence is less than remote, disclose by class of contingent liability a description of the liability, an estimate of its financial effect, any payment or timing uncertainties, and whether any reimbursements can be expected. If it is not practicable to disclose this information, state this point.

If there appear to be contingent assets, describe the nature of these assets and (if possible) provide an estimate of their financial effect. If it is not practicable to disclose this information, state this fact. When making these disclosures, avoid misleading the users of this information about the likelihood of income actually being recognized from the contingent assets.

There may be cases where a company is embroiled in a dispute with a third party, and disclosing some of the information required in this section may harm its position in regard to settling the dispute. If so, it is not necessary to disclose any information that would harm the company. Instead, disclose the nature of the dispute, state that certain information is not being disclosed, and why it is not being disclosed.

When aggregating information for the reporting of provisions, be careful to separate clearly disparate types of provisions. For example, all of the various warranties related to company products or services could probably be grouped into a single class, while provisions related to the settlement of lawsuits are clearly different, and so should be aggregated into a separate class.

EXAMPLE

The following are sample disclosures related to provisions:

The company has recognized a provision for expected warranty claims on its drilling products sold during the past 12 months. It is expected that the majority of this expenditure will be incurred in the next three months, and all of the expenditure will be incurred within one year.

The company has recognized a provision of £500,000 related to the decommissioning costs of several drilling pads. These costs are expected to be incurred in no less than five years, and in not more than 15 years. The provision has been estimated at current prices, and using existing technology. The provision is based on the present value of future expenditures, using a 4% discount rate.

The company is engaged in litigation with a competitor who alleged copyright infringement of a drilling process used by the company, and is seeking damages of £25,000,000. The information usually required by IAS 37, *Provisions, Contingent Liabilities and Contingent Assets* is not disclosed on the grounds that it could prejudice the outcome of the litigation. Management is of the opinion that the claim has no merit, and will require no payout of funds.

Summary

The key element to consider when dealing with provisions and contingencies is the concept of materiality. It is not necessary to recognize or disclose an item that is immaterial. In the interests of efficiency, it makes sense to avoid the recognition or disclosure of excessively small matters. By avoiding this burden, the accounting staff can reduce the effort required to monitor and update minor liability issues. In addition, the readers of a company's financial statements are not inundated with a large amount of picayune liability issues that might otherwise give the impression of an organization weighted down by an excessive number of liabilities.

Chapter 20
Revenue from Contracts with Customers

Introduction

Historically, the accounting standards related to the recognition of revenue have built up in a piecemeal manner, with guidance being established separately for certain industries and types of transactions. The result has been an inconsistent set of standards that, while workable, have not resulted in revenue recognition principles that could be applied consistently across many industries.

The accounting for revenue has been streamlined to a considerable extent with the release of IFRS 15. Now, the overall intent of revenue recognition is to do so in a manner that reasonably depicts the transfer of goods or services to customers, for which consideration is paid that reflects the amount to which the seller expects to be entitled. The following sections describe the five-step process of revenue recognition, as well as a number of ancillary topics.

The Nature of a Customer

Revenue recognition only occurs if the third party involved is a customer. A customer is an entity that has contracted to obtain goods or services from the seller's ordinary activities in exchange for payment.

In some situations, it may require a complete examination of the facts and circumstances to determine whether the other party can be classified as a customer. For example, it can be difficult to discern whether there is a customer in collaborative research and development activities between pharmaceutical entities. Another difficult area is payments between oil and gas partners to settle differences between their entitlements to the output from a producing field.

EXAMPLE

The Red Herring Fish Company contracts with Lethal Sushi to co-develop a fish farm off the coast of Iceland, where the two entities share equally in any future profits. Lethal Sushi is primarily in the restaurant business, so developing a fish farm is not one of its ordinary activities. Also, there is no clear consideration being paid to Lethal. Based on the circumstances, Red Herring is not a customer of Lethal Sushi.

Steps in Revenue Recognition

IFRS 15 establishes a series of actions that an entity takes to determine the amount and timing of revenue to be recognized. The main steps are:
1. Link the contract with a specific customer.
2. Note the performance obligations required by the contract.
3. Determine the price of the underlying transaction.
4. Match this price to the performance obligations through an allocation process.
5. Recognize revenue as the various obligations are fulfilled.

We will expand upon each of these steps in the following sections.

Step One: Link Contract to Customer

The contract is used as a central aspect of revenue recognition, because revenue recognition is closely associated with it. In many instances, revenue is recognized at multiple points in time over the duration of a contract, so linking contracts with revenue recognition provides a reasonable framework for establishing the timing and amounts of revenue recognition.

A contract only exists if there is an agreement between the parties that establishes enforceable rights and obligations. It is not necessary for an agreement to be in writing for it to be considered a contract. More specifically, a contract only exists if the following conditions are present:

- *Approval.* All parties to the contract have approved the document and substantially committed to its contents (based on all relevant facts and circumstances). The parties can be considered to be committed to a contract despite occasional lapses, such as not enforcing prompt payment or sometimes shipping late. Approval can be in writing or orally.
- *Rights.* The document clearly identifies the rights of the parties.
- *Payment.* The payment terms are clearly stated. It is acceptable to recognize revenue related to unpriced change orders if the seller expects that the price will be approved and the scope of work has been approved.
- *Substance.* The agreement has commercial substance; that is, the cash flows of the seller will change as a result of the contract, either in terms of their amount, timing, or risk of receipt. Otherwise, organizations could swap goods or services to artificially boost their revenue.
- *Probability.* It is probable that the organization will collect the amount stated in the contract in exchange for the goods or services that it commits to provide to the other party. In this context, "probable" means "likely to occur." This evaluation is based on the customer's ability and intention to pay when due. The evaluation can incorporate a consideration of the past practice of the customer in question, or of the class of customers to which that customer belongs.

If these criteria are not initially met, the seller can continue to evaluate the situation to see if the criteria are met at a later date.

> **Note:** These criteria do not *have* to be re-evaluated at a later date, unless the seller notes a significant change in the relevant facts and circumstances.

EXAMPLE

Prickly Corporation has entered into an arrangement to sell a large quantity of rose thorns to Ambivalence Corporation, which manufactures a number of potions for the amateur witch brewing market. The contract specifies monthly deliveries over the course of the next year.

Prior to the first shipment, Prickly's collections manager learns through her contacts that Ambivalence has just lost its line of credit and has conducted a large layoff. It appears that the customer's ability to pay has deteriorated significantly, which calls into question the probability of collecting the amount stated in the contract. In this case, there may no longer be a contract for the purposes of revenue recognition.

EXAMPLE

Domicilio Corporation, which develops commercial real estate, enters into a contract with Cupertino Beanery to sell a building to Cupertino to be used as a coffee shop. This is Cupertino's first foray into the coffee shop business, having previously only been a distributor of coffee beans to shops within the region. Also, there are a massive number of coffee shops already established in the area.

Domicilio receives a £100,000 deposit from Cupertino when the contract is signed. The contract also states that Cupertino will pay Domicilio an additional £900,000 for the rest of the property over the next three years, with interest. This financing arrangement is nonrecourse, meaning that Domicilio can repossess the building in the event of default, but cannot obtain further cash from Cupertino. Cupertino expects to pay Domicilio from the cash flows to be generated by the coffee shop operation.

Domicilio's management concludes that it is not probable that Cupertino will pay the remaining contractual amount, since its source of funds is a high-risk venture in which Cupertino has no experience. In addition, the loan is nonrecourse, so Cupertino can easily walk away from the arrangement. Accordingly, Domicilio accounts for the initial deposit and future payments as a deposit liability, and continues to recognize the building asset. If it later becomes probable that Cupertino will pay the full contractual amount, Domicilio can then recognize revenue and an offsetting receivable.

Whether a contract exists can depend upon standard industry practice, or vary by legal jurisdiction, or even vary by business segment.

There may be instances in which the preceding criteria are not met, and yet the customer is paying consideration to the seller. If so, revenue can be recognized only when one of the following events has occurred:

- The contract has been terminated and the consideration received by the seller is not refundable; or
- The seller has no remaining obligations to the customer, substantially all of the consideration has been received, and the payment is not refundable.

These alternatives focus on whether the contract has been concluded in all respects. If so, there is little risk that any revenue recognized will be reversed in a later period, and so is a highly conservative approach to recognizing revenue.

If the seller receives consideration from a customer and the preceding conditions do not exist, then the payment is to be recorded as a liability until such time as the sale criteria have been met.

A contract is not considered to exist when each party to the contract has a unilateral right to terminate a contract that has not been performed, and without compensating the other party. An unperformed contract is one in which no goods or services have been transferred to the customer, nor has the seller received any consideration from the customer in exchange for any promised goods or services.

In certain situations, it can make sense to combine several contracts into one for the purposes of revenue recognition. For example, if there is a portfolio of contracts that have similar characteristics, and the entity expects that treating the portfolio as a single unit will have no appreciable impact on the financial statements, it is acceptable to combine the contracts for accounting purposes. This approach may be particularly valuable in industries where there are a large number of similar contracts, and where applying the model to each individual contract could be impractical.

> **Tip:** When accounting for a portfolio of contracts, adjust the accompanying estimates and assumptions to reflect the greater size of the portfolio.

If the seller enters into two or more contracts with a customer at approximately the same time, these contracts can be accounted for as a single contract if any of the following criteria are met:

- *Basis of negotiation.* The contracts were negotiated as a package, with the goal of attaining a single commercial objective.
- *Interlinking consideration.* The consideration that will be paid under the terms of one contract is dependent upon the price or performance noted in the other contract.
- *Performance obligation.* There is essentially one performance obligation inherent in the two contracts.

EXAMPLE

Domicilio Corporation enters into three contracts with Milford Sound to construct a concert arena. These contracts involve construction of the concrete building shell, installation of seating, and the construction of a staging system. The three contracts are all needed in order to arrive at a functioning concert arena. Final payment on all three contracts shall be made once the final customer (a local municipality) approves the entire project.

Domicilio should account for these contracts as a single contract, since they are all directed toward the same commercial goal, payment is dependent on all three contracts being completed, and the performance obligation is essentially the same for all of the contracts.

Step Two: Note Performance Obligations

A performance obligation is essentially the unit of account for the goods or services contractually promised to a customer. The performance obligations in the contract must be clearly identified. This is of considerable importance in recognizing revenue, since revenue is considered to be recognizable when goods or services are transferred to the customer. Examples of goods or services are:

Item Sold	Example of the Seller
Arranging for another party to transfer goods or services	Travel agent selling airline tickets
Asset construction on behalf of a customer	Building construction company
Grant of a license	Software company issuing licenses to use its software
Grant of options to purchase additional goods or services	Airline granting frequent flier points
Manufactured goods	Manufacturer
Performance of contractually-mandated tasks	Consultant
Readiness to provide goods or services as needed	Snow plow operator, alarm system monitoring
Resale of merchandise	Retailer
Resale of rights to goods or services	Selling a priority for a new-model car delivery
Rights to future goods or services that can be resold	Wholesaler gives additional services to retailer buying a particular product

There may also be an implicit promise to deliver goods or services that is not stated in a contract, as implied by the customary business practices of the seller. If there is a valid expectation by the customer to receive these implicitly-promised goods or services, they should be considered a performance obligation. Otherwise, the seller might recognize the entire transaction price as revenue when in fact there are still goods or services yet to be provided.

If there is no performance obligation, then there is no revenue to be recognized. For example, a company could continually build up its inventory through ongoing production activities, but just because it has more sellable assets does not mean that it can report an incremental increase in the revenue in its income statement. If such an activity-based revenue recognition model were allowed, organizations could increase their revenues simply by increasing their rate of activity.

If there is more than one good or service to be transferred under the contract terms, only break it out as a separate performance obligation if it is a distinct obligation or there are a series of transfers to the customer of a distinct good or service. In the latter case, a separate performance obligation is assumed if there is a consistent pattern of transfer to the customer.

The "distinct" label can be applied to a good or service only if it meets both of the following criteria:

- *Capable of being distinct.* The customer can benefit from the good or service as delivered, or in combination with other resources that the customer can readily find; and
- *Distinct within the context of the contract.* The promised delivery of the good or service is separately identified within the contract.

Goods or services are more likely to be considered distinct when:

- The seller does not use the goods or services as a component of an integrated bundle of goods or services.
- The items do not significantly modify any other goods or services listed in the contract.
- The items are not highly interrelated with other goods or services listed in the contract.

The intent of these evaluative factors is to place a focus on how to determine whether goods or services are truly distinct within a contract. There is no need to assess the customer's intended use of any goods or services when making this determination.

EXAMPLE

Aphelion Corporation sells a package of goods and services to Nova Corporation. The goods include a deep field telescope, an observatory to house the telescope, and calibration services for the telescope.

The observatory building can be considered distinct from the telescope and calibration services, because Nova could have the telescope installed in an existing facility instead. However, the telescope and calibration services are linked, since the telescope will not function properly unless it has been properly calibrated. Thus, one performance obligation can be considered the observatory, while the telescope and associated calibration can be stated as a separate obligation.

EXAMPLE

Norrona Software enters into a contract with a Scandinavian clothing manufacturer to transfer a software license for its clothing design software. The contract also states that

Norrona will install the software and provide technical support for a two-year period. The installation process involves adjusting the data entry screens to match the needs of the clothing designers who will use the software. The software can be used without these installation changes. The technical support assistance is intended to provide advice to users regarding advanced features, and is not considered a key requirement for software users.

Since the software is functional without the installation process or the technical support, Norrona concludes that the items are not highly interrelated. Since these goods and services are distinct, the company should identify separate performance obligations for the software license, installation work, and technical support.

In the event that a good or service is not classified as distinct, aggregate it with other goods or services promised in the contract, until such time as a cluster of goods or services have been accumulated that can be considered distinct.

The administrative tasks needed to fulfill a contract are not considered to be performance obligations, since they do not involve the transfer of goods or services to customers. For example, setting up information about a new contract in the seller's contract management software is not considered a performance obligation.

Step Three: Determine Prices

This step involves the determination of the transaction price built into the contract. The transaction price is the amount of consideration to be paid by the customer in exchange for its receipt of goods or services. The transaction price does not include any amounts collected on behalf of third parties.

EXAMPLE

The Twister Vacuum Company sells its vacuum cleaners to individuals through its chain of retail stores. In the most recent period, Twister generated £3,800,000 of receipts, of which £200,000 was sales taxes collected on behalf of local governments. Since the £200,000 was collected on behalf of third parties, it cannot be recognized as revenue.

The transaction price may be difficult to determine, since it involves consideration of the effects noted in the following subsections.

Variable Consideration

The terms of some contracts may result in a price that can vary, depending on the circumstances. For example, there may be discounts, rebates, penalties, or performance bonuses in the contract. Or, the customer may have a reasonable expectation that the seller will offer a price concession, based on the seller's customary business practices, policies, or statements. Another example is when the seller intends to accept lower prices from a new customer in order to develop a strong customer relationship. If so, set the transaction price based on either the most likely amount or the probability-weighted expected value, using whichever method yields that amount of consideration most likely to be paid. In more detail, these methods are:

- *Most likely.* The seller develops a range of possible payment amounts, and selects the amount most likely to be paid. This approach works best when there are only two possible amounts that will be paid.
- *Expected value.* The seller develops a range of possible payment amounts, and assigns a probability to each one. The sum of these probability-weighted amounts is the expected value of the variable consideration. This approach works best when there are a large number of possible payment amounts. However, the outcome may be an expected value that does not exactly align with any amount that could actually be paid.

EXAMPLE

Grissom Granaries operates grain storage facilities along the Danube River. Its accounting staff is reviewing a contract that has just been signed with a major farming co-operative, and concludes that the contract could have four possible outcomes, which are noted in the following expected value table:

Price Scenario	Transaction Price	Probability	Probability-Weighted Price
1	£1,500,000	20%	£300,000
2	1,700,000	35%	595,000
3	2,000,000	40%	800,000
4	2,400,000	5%	120,000
		Expected Value	£1,815,000

The expected value derived from the four possible pricing outcomes is £1,815,000, even though this amount does not match any one of the four pricing outcomes.

Whichever method is chosen, be sure to use it consistently throughout the contract, as well as for similar contracts. However, it is not necessary to use the same measurement method to measure each uncertainty contained within a contract; different methods can be applied to different uncertainties.

Also, review the circumstances of each contract at the end of each reporting period, and update the estimated transaction price to reflect any changes in the circumstances.

EXAMPLE

Cantilever Construction has entered into a contract to tear down and replace five bridges along a major highway. The local government (which owns and maintains this section of the highway) is extremely concerned about how the work will interfere with traffic on the highway. Accordingly, the government includes in the contract a clause that penalizes Cantilever £10,000 for every hour over the budgeted amount that each bridge demolition and construction project shuts down the interstate, and a £15,000 bonus for every hour saved from the budgeted amount.

Cantilever has extensive experience with this type of work, having torn down and replaced 42 other bridges along the highway in the past five years. Based on the company's experience with these other projects and an examination of the budgeted hours allowed for shutting down the interstate, the company concludes that the most likely outcome is £120,000 of variable consideration associated with the project. Cantilever accordingly adds this amount to the transaction price.

Possibility of Reversal

Do not include in the transaction price an estimate of variable consideration if, when the uncertainty associated with the variable amount is settled, it is probable that there will be a significant reversal of cumulative revenue recognized. The assessment of a possible reversal of revenue could include the following factors, all of which might increase the probability of a revenue reversal:

- *Beyond seller's influence.* The amount of consideration paid is strongly influenced by factors outside of the control of the seller. For example, goods sold may be subject to obsolescence (as is common in the technology industry), or weather conditions could impede the availability of goods (as is common in the production of farm products).
- *Historical practice.* The seller has a history of accepting a broad range of price concessions, or of changing the terms of similar contracts.
- *Inherent range of outcomes.* The terms of the contract contain a broad range of possible consideration amounts that might be paid.
- *Limited experience.* The seller does not have much experience with the type of contract in question. Alternatively, the seller's prior experience cannot be translated into a prediction of the amount of consideration paid.
- *Long duration.* A considerable period of time may have to pass before the uncertainty can be resolved.

> **Note:** The probability of a significant reversal of cumulative revenue recognized places a conservative bias on the recognition of revenue, rather than a neutral bias, so there will be a tendency for recognized revenue levels to initially be too low. However, this approach is reasonable when considering that revenue information is more relevant when it is not subject to future reversals.

If management expects that a retroactive discount will be applied to sales transactions, the seller should recognize a refund liability as part of the revenue recognition when each performance obligation is satisfied.

For example, if the seller is currently selling goods for £100 but expects that a 20% volume discount will be retroactively applied at the end of the year, the resulting entry should be:

	Debit	Credit
Accounts receivable	100	
Revenue		80
Refund liability		20

EXAMPLE

Medusa Medical sells a well-known snake oil therapy through a number of retail store customers. In the most recent month, Medusa sells £100,000 of its potent Copperhead Plus combination healing balm and sunscreen lotion. The therapy is most effective within one month of manufacture and then degrades rapidly, so that Medusa must accept increasingly large price concessions in order to ensure that the goods are sold. Historically, this means that the range of price concessions varies from zero (in the first month) to 80% (after four months). Of this range of outcomes, Medusa estimates that the expected value of the transactions is likely to be revenue of £65,000. However, since the risk of obsolescence is so high, Medusa cannot conclude that it is probable that there will not be a significant reversal in the amount of cumulative revenue recognized. Accordingly, management concludes that the price point at which it is probable that there will not be a significant reversal in the cumulative amount of revenue recognized is actually closer to £45,000 (representing a 55% price concession). Based on this conclusion, the controller initially recognizes £45,000 of revenue when the goods are shipped to retailers, and continues to monitor the situation at the end of each reporting period, to see if the recognized amount should be adjusted.

EXAMPLE

Iceland Cod enters into a contract with Lethal Sushi to provide Lethal with 10,000 pounds of cod per year, at €15 per pound. If Lethal purchases more than 10,000 pounds within one calendar year, then a 12% retroactive price reduction will be applied to all of Lethal's purchases for the year.

Iceland has dealt with Lethal for a number of years, and knows that Lethal has never attained the 10,000 pound level of purchases. Accordingly, through the first half of the year, Iceland records its sales to Lethal at their full price, which is €30,000 for 2,000 pounds of cod.

In July, Lethal acquires Wimpy Fish Company, along with its large chain of seafood restaurants. With a much larger need for fish to supply the additional restaurants, Lethal now places several large orders that make it quite clear that passing the 10,000 pound threshold will be no problem at all. Accordingly, Iceland's controller records a cumulative revenue reversal of €3,600 to account for Lethal's probable attainment of the volume purchase discount.

EXAMPLE

Armadillo Industries is a new company that has developed a unique type of ceramic-based body armor that is extremely light. To encourage sales, the company is offering a 90-day money back guarantee. Since the company is new to the industry and cannot predict the level of returns, there is no way of knowing if a sudden influx of returns might trigger a significant reversal in the amount of cumulative revenue recognized. Accordingly, the company must wait for the money back guarantee to expire before it can recognize any revenue.

Time Value of Money

If the transaction price is to be paid over a period of time, this implies that the seller is including a financing component in the contract. If this financing component is a significant financing benefit for the customer and provides financing for more than one year, adjust the transaction price for the time value of money. In cases where there is a financing component to a contract, the seller will earn interest income over the term of the contract.

A contract may contain a financing component, even if there is no explicit reference to it in the contract. When adjusting the transaction price for the time value of money, consider the following factors:

- *Standalone price.* The amount of revenue recognized should reflect the price that a customer would have paid if it had paid in cash.
- *Significance.* In order to be recognized, the financing component should be significant. This means evaluating the amount of the difference between the consideration to be paid and the cash selling price. Also note the combined effect of prevailing interest rates and the time difference between when delivery is made and when the customer pays.

If it is necessary to adjust the compensation paid for the time value of money, use as a discount rate the rate that would be employed in a separate financing transaction between the parties as of the beginning date of the contract. The rate used should reflect the credit characteristics of the customer, including the presence of any collateral provided. This discount rate is not to be updated after the commencement of the contract, irrespective of any changes in the credit markets or in the credit standing of the customer.

EXAMPLE

Hammer Industries sells a large piece of construction equipment to Eskimo Construction, under generous terms that allow Eskimo to pay Hammer the full amount of the £119,990 receivable in 24 months. The cash selling price of the equipment is £105,000. The contract contains an implicit interest rate of 6.9%, which is the interest rate that discounts the purchase price of £119,990 down to the cash selling price over the two year period. The controller examines this rate and concludes that it approximates the rate that Hammer and Eskimo would use if there had been a separate financing transaction between them as of the contract inception date. Consequently, Hammer recognizes interest income during the two-year period prior to the payment due date, using the following calculation:

Year	Beginning Balance	Interest (at 6.9% Rate)	Ending Balance
1	£105,000	£7,245	£112,245
2	112,245	7,745	119,990

As of the shipment date, Hammer records the following entry:

	Debit	Credit
Loan receivable	105,000	
Revenue		105,000

At the end of the first year, Hammer recognizes the interest associated with the transaction for the first year, using the following entry:

	Debit	Credit
Loan receivable	7,245	
Interest income		7,245

At the end of the second year, Hammer recognizes the interest associated with the transaction for the second year, using the following entry:

	Debit	Credit
Loan receivable	7,745	
Interest income		7,745

These entries increase the size of the loan receivable until it reaches the original sale price of £119,990. Eskimo then pays the full amount of the receivable, at which point Hammer records the following final entry:

	Debit	Credit
Cash	119,990	
Loan receivable		119,990

Also, note that the financing concept can be employed in reverse; that is, if a customer makes a deposit that the seller expects to retain for more than one year, the financing component of this arrangement should be recognized by the seller. Doing so properly reflects the economics of the arrangement, where the seller is using the cash of the customer to fund its purchase of materials and equipment for a project; if the seller had not provided the deposit, the seller would instead have needed to obtain financing.

There is assumed *not* to be a significant financing component to a contract in the presence of any of the following factors:

- *Advance payment*. The customer paid in advance, and the customer can specify when goods and services are to be delivered.

- *Variable component.* A large part of the consideration to be paid is variable, and payment timing will vary based on a future event that is not under the control of either party.
- *Non-financing reason.* The reason for the difference between the contractual consideration and the cash selling price exists for a reason other than financing, and the amount of the difference is proportional to the alternative reason.

EXAMPLE

Spinner Maintenance offers global technical support to the owners of rooftop solar power systems in exchange for a €400 fee. The fee pays for service that spans the first five years of the life of the power systems, and is purchased as part of the package of solar panels and initial installation work. This maintenance is intended to provide phone support to homeowners who are researching why their power systems are malfunctioning. The support does not include any replacement of solar panels for hail damage.

The support period is quite extensive, but Spinner concludes that there is no financing component to these sales, for the following reasons:
- The administrative cost of a monthly billing would be prohibitive, since the amount billed on a monthly basis would be paltry.
- Those more technologically proficient customers would be less likely to renew if they could pay on a more frequent basis, leaving Spinner with the highest-maintenance customers who require the most support.
- Customers are more likely to make use of the service if they are reminded of it by the arrival of monthly invoices.

In short, Spinner has several excellent reasons for structuring the payment plan to require an advance payment, all of which are centered on maintaining a reasonable level of profitability. The intent is not to provide financing to customers.

EXAMPLE

Glow Atomic sells a nuclear power plant to a French provincial government. The certification process for the plant is extensive, spanning a six-month test period. Accordingly, the local government builds into the contract a provision to withhold 20% of the contract price until completion of the test period. The rest of the payments are made on a milestone schedule, as the construction work progresses. Based on the circumstances and the amount of the withholding, the arrangement is considered to be non-financing, so Glow Atomic does not break out a financing component from the total consideration paid.

Noncash Consideration

If the customer will be paying with some form of noncash consideration, measure the consideration at its fair value. If it is not possible to measure the payment at its fair value, instead use the standalone selling price of the goods or services to be delivered to the customer. This approach also applies to payments made with equity instruments. In rare cases, the customer may supply the seller with goods or services that are intended to assist the seller in its fulfillment of the related contract. If the seller gains control of these assets or services, it should consider them to be noncash consideration paid by the customer.

EXAMPLE

Industrial Landscaping is hired by Pensive Corporation to mow the lawns and trim shrubbery at Pensive's corporate headquarters on a weekly basis throughout the year. Essentially the same service is provided each week. Pensive is a startup company with little excess cash, so it promises to pay Industrial with 25 shares of Pensive stock at the end of each week.

Industrial considers itself to have satisfied its performance obligation at the end of each week. Industrial should determine the transaction price as being the fair value of the shares at the end of each week, and recognizes this amount as revenue. There is no subsequent change in the amount of revenue recognized, irrespective of any changes in the fair value of the shares.

Payments to Customers

The contract may require the seller to pay consideration to the customer, perhaps in the form of credits or coupons that the customer can apply against the amounts it owes to the seller. This may also involve payments to third parties that have purchased the seller's goods or services from the original customer. If so, treat this consideration as a reduction of the transaction price. The following special situations may apply:

- *Customer supplies a good or service.* The customer may provide the seller with a distinct good or service; if so, the seller treats the payment as it would a payment to any supplier.
- *Supplier payment exceeds customer delivery.* If the customer provides a good or service to the seller, but the amount paid by the seller to the customer exceeds the fair value of the goods or services it receives in exchange, the excess of the payment is considered a reduction of the transaction price. If the fair value of the goods or services cannot be determined, then consider the entire amount paid by the seller to the customer to be a reduction of the transaction price.

If it is necessary to account for consideration paid to the customer as a reduction of the transaction price, do so when the later of the following two events have occurred:

- When the seller recognizes revenue related to its provision of goods or services to the customer; or
- When the seller either pays or promises to pay the consideration to the customer. The timing of this event could be derived from the customary business practices of the seller.

EXAMPLE

Dillinger Designs manufactures many types of hunting rifles. Dillinger enters into a one-year contract with Backwoods Survival, which has not previously engaged in rifle sales. Backwoods commits to purchase at least £240,000 of rifles from Dillinger during the contract period. Also, due to the considerable government-mandated safety requirements associated with the sale of rifles, Dillinger commits to pay £60,000 to Backwoods at the inception of the contract; these funds are intended to pay for a locking gun safe to be kept at each Backwoods store, as per firearms laws pertaining to retailers.

Dillinger determines that the £60,000 payment is to be treated as a reduction of the £240,000 sale price. Consequently, whenever Dillinger fulfills a performance obligation by shipping goods under the contract, it reduces the amount of revenue it would otherwise recognize by 25%, which reflects the proportion of the £60,000 payment related to locking gun safes of the £240,000 that Dillinger will be paid by Backwoods.

Refund Liabilities

In some situations, a seller may receive consideration from a customer, with the likelihood that the payment will be refunded. If so, the seller records a refund liability in the amount that the seller expects to refund back to the customer. The seller should review the amount of this liability at the end of each reporting period, to see if the amount should be altered.

Step Four: Allocate Prices to Obligations

Once the performance obligations and transaction prices associated with a contract have been identified, the next step is to allocate the transaction prices to the obligations. The basic rule is to allocate that price to a performance obligation that best reflects that amount of consideration to which the seller expects to be entitled when it satisfies each performance obligation. To determine this allocation, it is first necessary to estimate the standalone selling price of those distinct goods or services as of the inception date of the contract. If it is not possible to derive a standalone selling price, the seller must estimate it. This estimation should involve all relevant information that is reasonably available, such as:
- Competitive pressure on prices
- Costs incurred to manufacture or provide the item
- Item profit margins
- Pricing of other items in the same contract
- Standalone selling price of the item
- Supply and demand for the items in the market
- The seller's pricing strategy and practices
- The type of customer, distribution channel, or geographic region
- Third-party pricing

The following three approaches are acceptable ways in which to estimate a standalone selling price:

- *Adjusted market assessment.* This involves reviewing the market to estimate the price at which a customer in that market would be willing to pay for the goods and services in question. This can involve an examination of the prices of competitors for similar items and adjusting them to incorporate the seller's costs and margins.
- *Expected cost plus a margin.* This requires the seller to estimate the costs required to fulfill a performance obligation, and then add a margin to it to derive the estimated price.
- *Residual approach.* This involves subtracting all of the observable standalone selling prices from the total transaction price to arrive at the residual price remaining for allocation to any non-observable selling prices. This method can only be used if one of the following situations applies:
  - The seller sells the good or service to other customers for a wide range of prices; or
  - No price has yet been established for that item, and it has not yet been sold on a standalone basis.

The residual approach can be difficult to use when there are several goods or services with uncertain standalone selling prices. If so, it may be necessary to use a combination of methods to derive standalone selling prices, which should be used in the following order:

1. Estimate the aggregate amount of the standalone selling prices for all items having uncertain standalone selling prices, using the residual method.
2. Use another method to develop standalone selling prices for each item in this group, to allocate the aggregate amount of the standalone selling prices.

Once all standalone selling prices have been determined, allocate the transaction price amongst these distinct goods or services based on their relative standalone selling prices.

Tip: Appropriate evidence of a standalone selling price is the observable price of a good or service when the seller sells it to a similar customer under similar circumstances.

Once the seller derives an approach for estimating a standalone selling price, it should consistently apply that method to the derivation of the standalone selling prices for other goods or services with similar characteristics.

EXAMPLE

Luminescence Corporation manufactures a wide range of light bulbs, and mostly sells into the wholesaler market. The company receives an order from the federal government for two million fluorescent bulbs, as well as for 100,000 units of a new bulb that operates outdoors at very low temperatures. Luminescence has not yet sold these new bulbs to anyone. The total price of the order is €7,000,000. Luminescence assigns €6,000,000 of the total price to the fluorescent bulbs, based on its own sales of comparable orders. This leaves €1,000,000 of the total price that is allocable to the low temperature bulbs. Since Luminescence has not yet established a price for these bulbs and has not sold them on a standalone basis, it is acceptable to allocate €1,000,000 to the low temperature bulbs under the residual approach.

If there is a subsequent change in the transaction price, allocate that change amongst the distinct goods or services based on the original allocation that was used at the inception of the contract. If this subsequent allocation is to a performance obligation that has already been completed and for which revenue has already been recognized, the result can be an increase or reduction in the amount of revenue recognized. This change in recognition should occur as soon as the subsequent change in the transaction price occurs.

Allocation of Price Discounts

It is assumed that a customer has received a discount on a bundled purchase of goods or services when the sum of the standalone prices for these items is greater than the consideration to be paid under the terms of a contract. The discount can be allocated to a specific item within the bundled purchase, if there is observable evidence that the discount was intended for that item. In order to do so, all of the following criteria must apply:

1. Each distinct item in the bundle is regularly sold on a standalone basis;
2. A bundle of some of these distinct items is regularly sold at a discount to their standalone selling prices; and
3. The discount noted in the second point is essentially the same as the discount in the contract, and there is observable evidence linking the entire contract discount to that bundle of distinct items.

If this allocation system is used, the seller must employ it before using the residual approach noted earlier in this section. Doing so ensures that the discount is not applied to the other performance obligations in the contract to which prices have not yet been allocated.

In all other cases, the discount is to be allocated amongst all of the items in the bundle. In this latter situation, the allocation is to be made based on the standalone selling prices of all of the performance obligations in the contract.

EXAMPLE

The Hegemony Toy Company sells board games that re-enact famous battles. Hegemony regularly sells the following three board games:

Product	Standalone Selling Price
Hastings Battle Game	€120
Stalingrad Battle Game	100
Waterloo Battle Game	80
Total	€300

Hegemony routinely sells the Stalingrad and Waterloo products as a bundle for €120.

Hegemony enters into a contract with the War Games International website to sell War Games the set of three games for €240, which is a 20% discount from the standard price. Deliveries of these games to War Games will be at different times, so the related performance obligations will be settled on different dates.

The €60 discount would normally be apportioned among all three products based on their standalone selling prices. However, because Hegemony routinely sells the Stalingrad/Waterloo bundle for a €60 discount, it is evident that the entire discount should be allocated to these two products.

If Hegemony later delivers the Stalingrad and Waterloo games to War Games on different dates, it should allocate the €60 discount between the two products based on their standalone selling prices. Thus, €33.33 should be allocated to the Stalingrad game and €26.67 to the Waterloo game. The allocation calculation is:

Game	Allocation
Stalingrad	(€100 individual game price ÷ €180 combined price) × €60 discount = €33.33
Waterloo	(€80 individual game price ÷ €180 combined price) × €60 discount = €26.67

If the two games are instead delivered at the same time, there is no need to conduct the preceding allocation. Instead, the discount can be assigned to them both as part of a single performance obligation.

Allocation of Variable Consideration

There may be a variable amount of consideration associated with a contract. This consideration may apply to the contract as a whole, or to just a portion of it. For example, a bonus payment may be tied to the completion of a specific performance obligation. It is allowable to allocate variable consideration to a specific performance obligation or a distinct good or service within a contract when the variable payment terms are specifically tied to the seller's efforts to satisfy the performance obligation.

EXAMPLE

Nova Corporation contracts with the Deep Field Scanning Authority to construct two three-meter telescopes that will operate in tandem in the low-humidity Atacama Desert in Chile. The terms of the contract include a provision that can increase the allowable price charged, if the commodity cost of the titanium required to build the telescope frames increases. Based on the prices stated in forward contracts at the contract inception date, it is likely that this variable cost element will increase the transaction price by £250,000. The variable component of the price is allocated to each of the telescopes equally.

Subsequent Price Changes

There are a number of reasons why the transaction price could change after a contract has begun, such as the resolution of uncertain events that were in need of clarification at the contract inception date. When there is a price change, the amount of the change is to be allocated to the performance obligations on the same basis used for the original price allocation at the inception of the contract. This has the following ramifications:

- Do not re-allocate prices based on subsequent changes in the standalone selling prices of goods or services.
- When there is a price change and that price is allocated, the result may be the recognition of additional or reduced revenue that is to be recognized in the period when the transaction price changes.
- When there has been a contract modification prior to a price change, the price allocation is conducted in two steps. First, allocate the price change to those performance obligations identified prior to the modification if the price change is associated with variable consideration promised before modification. In all other cases, allocate the price change to those performance obligations still remaining to be settled as of the modification date.

The result should be a reported level of cumulative revenue that matches the amount of revenue an organization would have recognized if it had the most recent information at the inception date of the contract.

Step Five: Recognize Revenue

Revenue is to be recognized as goods or services are transferred to the customer. This transference is considered to occur when the customer gains control over the good or service. Indicators of this date include the following:

- When the seller has the right to receive payment.
- When the customer has legal title to the transferred asset. This can still be the case even when the seller retains title to protect it against the customer's failure to pay.
- When physical possession of the asset has been transferred by the seller. Possession can be inferred even when goods are held elsewhere on con-

signment, or by the seller under a bill-and-hold arrangement. Under a bill-and-hold arrangement, the seller retains goods on behalf of the customer, but still recognizes revenue.

- When the customer has taken on the significant risks and rewards of ownership related to the asset transferred by the seller. For example, the customer can now sell, pledge, or exchange the asset.
- When the customer accepts the asset.
- When the customer can prevent other entities from using or obtaining benefits from the asset.

It is possible that a performance obligation will be transferred over time, rather than as of a specific point in time. If so, revenue recognition occurs when any one of the following criteria are met:

- *Immediate use*. The customer both receives and consumes the benefit provided by the seller as performance occurs. This situation arises if another entity would not need to re-perform work completed to date if the other entity were to take over the remaining performance obligation. Routine and recurring services typically fall into this classification.

EXAMPLE

Long-Haul Freight contracts to deliver a load of goods from Paris to Berlin. This service should be considered a performance obligation that is transferred over time, despite the fact that the customer only benefits from the goods once they are delivered. The reason for the designation as a transference over time is that, if a different trucking firm were to take over partway through the journey, the replacement firm would not have to re-perform the freight hauling that has already been completed to date.

EXAMPLE

Maid Marian is a nationwide home cleaning service run by friars within the Franciscan Order. Its customers both receive and simultaneously consume the cleaning services provided by its staff. Consequently, the services provided by Maid Marian are considered to be performance obligations satisfied over time.

- *Immediate enhancement*. The seller creates or enhances an asset controlled by the customer as performance occurs. This asset can be tangible or intangible.
- *No alternative use*. The seller's performance does not create an asset for which there is an alternative use to the seller (such as selling it to a different customer). In addition, the contract gives the seller an enforceable right to payment for the performance that has been completed to date. A lack of alternative use happens when a contract restricts the seller from directing the asset to another use, or when there are practical limitations on doing so, such as the incurrence of significant economic losses to direct the asset else-

where. The determination of whether an asset has an alternative use is made at the inception of the contract, and cannot be subsequently altered unless both parties to the contract approve a modification that results in a substantive change in the performance obligation.

Construction contracts are likely to be designated as being performance obligations that are transferred over time. Under this approach, they can use the percentage-of-completion method to recognize revenue, rather than the completed contract method. This means that they can recognize revenue as a construction project progresses, rather than waiting until the end of the project to recognize any revenue.

EXAMPLE

Oberlin Acoustics is contractually obligated to deliver a highly-customized version of its Rhino brand electric guitar to a diva-grade European rock star. The contract clearly states that this customized version can only be delivered to the designated customer, and it is likely that this individual would pursue legal action if Oberlin were to attempt to sell it elsewhere (such as to the lead guitarist of a rival band). Also, Oberlin might have to incur significant costs to reconfigure the guitar for sale to a different customer. In this situation, there is no alternative use.

However, if Oberlin had instead contracted to deliver one of its standard Rhino brand guitars, the company could easily transfer the asset to a different customer, since the products are essentially interchangeable. In this case, there would be a clear alternative use.

EXAMPLE

Tesla Power Company is hired by a local government to construct one of its new, compact fusion power plants in the remote hinterlands of Malawi. There is clearly no alternative use for the power plant, since Tesla would have to incur major costs to dismantle the facility and truck it out of the remote area before it could be sold to a different customer. However, the contract states that 50% of the price will be paid at the end of the contract period, and there is no enforceable right to any payment; this means that Tesla must consider its performance obligation to be satisfied as of a point in time, rather than over time.

EXAMPLE

Hassle Corporation is in talks with a potential acquirer. The acquirer insists that Hassle have soil tests conducted in the area around its main production facility, to see if there has been any leakage of pollutants. Hassle engages Wilson Environmental to conduct these tests, which is a three-month process. The contract includes a clause that Wilson will be paid for its costs plus a 20% profit if Hassle cancels the contract. The acquisition talks break off after two months, so Hassle notifies Wilson that it no longer needs the environmental report. Since Wilson cannot possibly sell the information it has collected to a different customer, there is no alternative use. Also, since Wilson has an enforceable right to payment for all work completed to date, the company can recognize revenue over time by measuring its progress toward satisfying the performance obligation.

Measurement of Progress Completion

When a performance obligation is being completed over a period of time, the seller recognizes revenue through the application of a progress completion method. The goal of this method is to determine the progress of the seller in achieving complete satisfaction of its performance obligation. This method is to be consistently applied over time, and shall be re-measured at the end of each reporting period.

> **Note:** The method used to measure progress should be applied consistently for a particular performance obligation, as well as across multiple contracts that have obligations with similar characteristics. Otherwise, reported revenue will not be comparable across different reporting periods.

Both output methods and input methods are considered acceptable for determining progress completion. The method chosen should incorporate due consideration of the nature of the goods or services being provided to the customer. The following sub-sections address the use of output and input methods.

Output Methods

An output method recognizes revenue based on a comparison of the value to the customer of goods and services transferred to date to the remaining goods and services not yet transferred. There are numerous ways to measure output, including:

- Surveys of performance to date
- Milestones reached
- The passage of time
- The number of units delivered
- The number of units produced

Another output method that may be acceptable is the amount of consideration that the seller has the right to invoice, such as billable hours. This approach works when the seller has a right to invoice an amount that matches the amount of performance completed to date.

The number of units delivered or produced may not be an appropriate output method in situations where there is a large amount of work-in-process, since the value associated with unfinished goods may be so substantial that revenue could be materially under-reported.

The method picked should closely adhere to the concept of matching the seller's progress toward satisfying the performance obligation. It is not always possible to use an output method, since the cost of collecting the necessary information can be prohibitive, or progress may not be directly observable.

EXAMPLE

Viking Fitness operates a regional chain of fitness clubs that are oriented toward younger, very athletic people. Members pay a €1,200 annual fee, which gives them access to all of the clubs in the chain during all operating hours. In effect, Viking's performance obligation is to keep its facilities open for use by members, irrespective of whether they actually use the facilities. Clearly, this situation calls for measurement of progress completion based on the passage of time. Accordingly, Viking recognizes revenue from its annual customer payments at the rate of €100 per member per month.

Input Methods

An input method derives the amount of revenue to be recognized based on the to-date effort required by the seller to satisfy a performance obligation relative to the total estimated amount of effort required. Examples of possible inputs are costs incurred, labor hours expended, and machine hours used. If there are situations where the effort expended does not directly relate to the transfer of goods or services to a customer, do not use that input. The following are situations where the input used could lead to incorrect revenue recognition:

- The costs incurred are higher than expected, due to seller inefficiencies. For example, the seller may have wasted a higher-than-expected amount of raw materials in the performance of its obligations under a contract.
- The costs incurred are not in proportion to the progress of the seller toward satisfying the performance obligation. For example, the seller might purchase a large amount of materials at the inception of a contract, which comprise a significant part of the total price.

Tip: If the effort expended to satisfy performance obligations occur evenly through the performance period, consider recognizing revenue on the straight-line basis through the performance period.

EXAMPLE

Eskimo Construction is hired to build a weather observatory in Svalbard, which is estimated to be a six-month project. Utilities are a major concern, especially since the facility is too far away from the local town of Longyearbyen for a power line to be run out to it. Accordingly, a large part of the construction cost is a diesel-powered turbine generator. The total cost that Eskimo intends to incur for the project is:

Turbine cost	€1,250,000
All other costs	2,750,000
Total costs	€4,000,000

The turbine is to be delivered and paid for at the beginning of the construction project, but will not be incorporated into the facility until late summer, when the building is scheduled to be nearly complete.

Eskimo intends to use an input method to derive the amount of revenue, using costs incurred. However, this approach runs afoul of the turbine cost, since the immediate expenditure for the turbine gives the appearance of the project being 31.25% complete before work has even begun. Accordingly, Eskimo excludes the cost of the turbine from its input method calculations, only using the other costs as the basis for deriving revenue.

The situation described in the preceding example is quite common, since materials are typically procured at the inception of a contract, rather than being purchased in equal quantities over the duration of the contract. Consequently, the accountant should be particularly mindful of this issue and incorporate it into any revenue recognition calculations based on an input method.

A method based on output is preferred, since it most faithfully depicts the performance of the seller under the terms of a contract. However, an input-based method is certainly allowable if using it would be less costly for the seller, while still providing a reasonable proxy for the ongoing measurement of progress.

Change in Estimate

Whichever method is used, be sure to update it over time to reflect changes in the seller's performance to date. If there is a change in the measurement of progress, treat the change as a change in accounting estimate.

A change in accounting estimate occurs when there is an adjustment to the carrying amount of an asset or liability, or the subsequent accounting for it. Changes in accounting estimate occur relatively frequently, and so would require a considerable amount of effort to make an ongoing series of retroactive changes to prior financial statements. Instead, IFRS only requires that changes in accounting estimate be accounted for in the period of change and thereafter. Thus, no retrospective change is required or allowed.

Progress Measurement

It is only possible to recognize the revenue associated with progress completion if it is possible for the seller to measure the seller's progress. If the seller lacks reliable progress information, it will not be possible to recognize the revenue associated with a contract over time. There may be cases where the measurement of progress completion is more difficult during the early stages of a contract. If so, it is allowable for the seller to instead recognize just enough revenue to recover its costs in satisfying its performance obligations, thereby deferring the recognition of other revenue until such time as the measurement system yields more accurate results.

Right of Return

A common right granted to customers is to allow them to return goods to the seller within a certain period of time following the customer's receipt of the goods. This return may take the form of a refund of any amounts paid, a general credit that can be applied against other billings from the seller, or an exchange for a different unit. The proper accounting for this right of return involves three components, which are:

1. Recognize the net amount of revenue to which the seller expects to be entitled after all product returns have been factored into the sale.
2. A refund liability that encompasses the number of units that the seller expects to have returned to it.
3. An asset based on the right to recover products from customers who have demanded refunds. This asset represents a reduction in the cost of goods sold. The amount is initially based on the former carrying amount of the inventory, less recovery costs and expected reductions in the value of the returned products.

This accounting requires the seller to update its assessment of future product returns at the end of each reporting period, both for the refund liability and the recovery asset. This update may result in a change in the amount of revenue recognized.

> **Note:** When a customer exchanges one product for another product with the same characteristics (such as an exchange of one size shirt for another), this is not considered a return.

EXAMPLE

Ninja Cutlery sells high-end ceramic knife sets through its on-line store and through select retailers. All customers pay up-front in cash. In the most recent month, Ninja sold 5,000 knife sets, which sold for an average price of €250 each (€1,250,000 in total). The unit cost is €150. Based on the history of actual returns over the preceding 12-month period, Ninja can expect that 200 of the sets (4% of the total) will be returned under the company's returns policy. Recovery costs are immaterial, and Ninja expects to be able to repackage and sell all returned products for a profit. Based on this information, Ninja records the following transactions when the knife sets are originally delivered:

	Debit	Credit
Cash	1,250,000	
Revenue		1,200,000
Refund liability		50,000

	Debit	Credit
Cost of goods sold	720,000	
Recovery asset	30,000	
Inventory		750,000

In these entries, the refund liability is calculated as the 200 units expected to be returned, multiplied by the average price of €250 each. The recovery asset is calculated as the 200 units expected to be returned, multiplied by the unit cost of €150.

Consistency

The preceding five steps must be applied consistently to all customer contracts that have similar characteristics, and under similar circumstances. The intent is to create a system of revenue recognition that can be relied upon to yield consistent results.

Contract Modifications

A contract modification occurs when there is a scope or price change to the contract, and the change is approved by both signatories to the contract. Other terms may be used for a contract modification, such as a change order. It is possible that a contract modification exists, despite the presence of a dispute between the parties concerning scope or price. All of the relevant facts and circumstances must be considered when determining whether there is an enforceable contract modification that can impact revenue recognition.

If a change in contract scope has already been approved, but the corresponding change in price to reflect the scope change is still under discussion, the seller must estimate the change in price. This estimate is based on the criteria used to determine variable consideration.

Treatment as Separate Contract

There are circumstances under which a contract modification might be accounted for as a separate contract. For this to be the case, the following two conditions must both be present:

- *Distinct change.* The scope has increased, to encompass new goods or services that are distinct from those offered in the original contract.
- *Price change.* The price has increased enough to encompass the standalone prices of the additional goods and services, adjusted for the circumstances related to that specific contract.

When these circumstances are met, there is an economic difference between a modified contract for the additional goods or services and a situation where an entirely new contract has been created.

EXAMPLE

Blitz Communications is buying one million cell phone batteries from Creekside Industrial. The parties decide to alter the contract to add the purchase of 200,000 battery chargers for a price increase of £2.8 million. The associated price increase includes a 30% discount, which Creekside was already offering to Blitz under the terms of the original contract. This contract change reflects a distinct change that adds new goods to the contract, and includes an associated price change that has been adjusted for the discount terms of the contract. This contract modification can be accounted for as a separate contract.

Treatment as Continuing Contract

It may not be possible to treat a contract modification as a separate contract. If so, there are likely to be goods or services not yet transferred to the customer as of the modification date. The seller can account for these residual deliveries using one of the following methods:

- *Remainder is distinct.* If the remaining goods or services to be delivered are distinct from those already delivered under the contract, account for the modification as a cancellation of the old contract and creation of a new one. In this case, the consideration that should be allocated to the remaining performance obligations is the sum total of:
    - The original consideration promised by the customer but not yet received; and
    - The new consideration associated with the modification.

EXAMPLE

Grizzly Golf Carts, maker of sturdy golf carts for overweight golfers, contracts with a local suburban golf course to deliver two golf carts for a total price of €12,000. The carts are different models, but have the same standalone price, so Grizzly allocates €6,000 of the transaction price to each cart. One cart is delivered immediately, so Grizzly recognizes €6,000 of revenue. Before the second cart can be delivered, the golf course customer requests that a third cart be added to the contract; this is a heftier cart that has a built-in barbecue grill. The contract price is increased by €8,000, which is less than the €10,000 standalone price of this model.

Since the second and third carts are distinct from the first cart model, there is a distinct change in the contract, which necessitates treating the change as a new contract. Accordingly, the second and third carts are treated as though they are part of a new contract, with the remaining €14,000 of the transaction price totally allocated to the new contract.

EXAMPLE

As noted in an earlier example, Nova Corporation contracted with the Deep Field Scanning Authority to construct two three-meter telescopes. The terms of the contract included a provision that could increase the allowable price charged by £250,000, with this price being apportioned equally between the two telescopes. One month into the contract period, Deep Field completely alters the configuration of the second telescope, from a reflector to a catadioptric model. The change is so significant that this telescope can now be considered a separate contract. However, since the variable price was already apportioned at the inception of the original contract, the £125,000 allocated to each telescope will continue. This is because the variable consideration was promised prior to the contract modification.

- *Remainder is not distinct.* If the remaining goods or services to be delivered are not distinct from those already delivered under the contract, account for the modification as part of the existing contract. This results in an adjustment to the recognized amount of revenue (up or down) as of the modification date. Thus, the adjustment involves calculating a change in the amount of revenue recognized on a cumulative catch-up basis.

EXAMPLE

Domicilio Corporation enters into a contract to construct the world headquarters building of the International Mushroom Farmers' Cooperative. Mushroom requires its architects to be true to the name of the organization, with the result being a design for a squat, dark building with no windows, high humidity, and a unique waste recycling system. Domicilio has not encountered such a design before, and so incorporates a cautious stance into its assumptions regarding the contract terms.

The contract terms state that Domicilio will be paid a total of €12,000,000, broken into a number of milestone payments. There is also a €100,000 on-time completion bonus. At the inception of the contract, Domicilio expects the following financial results:

Transaction price	€12,000,000
Expected costs	9,000,000
Expected profit (25%)	€3,000,000

The project manager anticipates trouble with several parts of the construction project, and advises strongly against including any part of the completion bonus in the transaction price.

At the end of seven months, the project manager is surprised to find that Domicilio is on target to complete the work on time. Also, the company has completed 65% of its performance obligation, based on the €5,850,000 of costs incurred to date relative to the total amount of expected costs. Through this point, the company has recognized the following revenues and costs:

Revenue	€7,800,000
Costs	5,850,000
Gross profit	€1,950,000

The project manager is still uncomfortable with recognizing any part of the completion bonus.

With one month to go on the project, the project manager finally allows that Domicilio will likely complete the project one week early, though he has completely lost all interest in eating mushrooms. At this point, the company has completed 92.5% of its performance obligation (based on costs incurred), so the controller recognizes an additional €92,500 for that portion of the €100,000 on-time completion bonus that has already been earned.

- *Mix of elements.* If the remaining goods or services to be delivered are comprised of a mix of distinct and not-distinct elements, separately identify the different elements and account for them as per the dictates of the preceding two methods.

226

Entitlement to Payment

At all points over the duration of a contract, the seller should have the right to payment for the performance completed to date, if the customer were to cancel the contract for reasons other than the seller's failure to perform. The amount of this payment should approximate the selling price of the goods or services transferred to the customer to date; this means that costs are recovered, plus a reasonable profit margin. This reasonable profit margin should be one of the following:

- A reasonable proportion of the expected profit margin, based on the extent of the total performance completed prior to contract termination; or
- A reasonable return on the cost of capital that the seller has experienced on its cost of capital for similar contracts, if the margin on this particular contract is higher than the return the seller typically generates from this type of contract.

An entitlement to payment depends on contractual factors, such as only being paid when certain milestones are reached or when the customer is completely satisfied with a deliverable. There may not be an entitlement to payment if one of these contractual factors is present. Further, there may be legal precedents or legislation that may interfere with or bolster an entitlement to payment. For example:

- There may be a legal precedent that gives the seller the right to payment for all performance to date, even though this right is not clarified within the contract terms.
- Legal precedent may reveal that other sellers having similar rights to payment in their contracts have not succeeded in obtaining payment.
- The seller may not have attempted to enforce its right to payment in the past, which may have rendered its rights legally unenforceable.

Conversely, the terms of a contract may not legally allow a customer to terminate a contract. If so, and the customer still attempts to terminate the contract, the seller may be entitled to continue to provide goods or services to the customer, and require the customer to pay the amounts stated in the contract. In this type of situation, the seller has an enforceable right to payment.

An enforceable right to payment may not match the payment schedule stated in a contract. The payment schedule does not necessarily sync with the seller's right to payment for performance. For example, the customer could have insisted upon delayed payment dates in the payment schedule in order to more closely match its ability to make payments to the seller.

EXAMPLE

A customer of Hodgson Industrial Design pays a £50,000 nonrefundable upfront payment to Hodgson at the inception of a contract to overhaul the design of the customer's main product. The customer does not like Hodgson's initial set of design prototypes, and cancels the contract. On the cancellation date, Hodgson's billable hours on the project sum to £65,000.

Hodgson has an enforceable right to retain the £50,000 it has already been paid. The right to be paid for the remaining £15,000 depends on the contract terms and legal precedents.

Bill-and-Hold Arrangements

There is a bill-and-hold arrangement between a seller and customer when the seller bills the customer, but initially retains physical possession of the goods that were sold; the goods are transferred to the customer at a later date. This situation may arise if a customer does not initially have the storage space available for the goods it has ordered.

In a bill-and-hold arrangement, the seller must determine when the customer gains control of the goods, since this point in time indicates when the seller can recognize revenue. Customer control can be difficult to discern when the goods are still located on the premises of the seller. The following are indicators of customer control:

- The customer can direct the use of the goods, no matter where they are located
- The customer can obtain substantially all of the remaining benefits of the goods

Further, the following conditions must all be present for the seller to recognize revenue under a bill-and-hold arrangement:

- *Adequate reason.* There must be a substantive reason why the seller is continuing to store the goods, such as at the direct request of the customer.
- *Alternate use.* The seller must not be able to redirect the goods, either to other customers or for internal use.
- *Complete.* The product must be complete in all respects and ready for transfer to the customer.
- *Identification.* The goods must have been identified specifically as belonging to the customer.

Under a bill-and-hold arrangement, the seller may have a performance obligation to act as the custodian for the goods being held at its facility. If so, the seller may need to allocate a portion of the transaction price to the custodial function, and recognize this revenue over the course of the custodial period.

EXAMPLE

Micron Metallic operates stamping machines that produce parts for washing machines. Micron's general manager has recently decided to implement the just-in-time philosophy throughout the company, which includes sourcing goods with suppliers who are located as close to Micron as possible. One of these suppliers is Horton Corporation, which designs and builds stamping machines for Micron. In a recent contract, Micron buys a customized stamping machine and a set of spare parts intended for that machine. Since Micron is implementing just-in-time concepts, it does not want to store the spare parts on its premises, and instead asks Horton to store the parts in its facility, which is just down the street from the Micron factory.

Micron's receiving staff travels to the Horton facility to inspect the parts and formally accepts them. Horton also sets them aside in a separate storage area, and flags them as belonging to Micron. Since the parts are customized, they cannot be used to fulfill any other customer orders. Under the just-in-time system, Horton commits to having the parts ready for delivery to Micron within ten minutes of receiving a shipping order.

The arrangement can clearly be defined as a bill-and-hold situation. Consequently, Horton should apportion the transaction price between the stamping machine, the spare parts, and the custodial service involved in storing the parts on behalf of Micron. The revenue associated with the machine and parts can be recognized at once, while the revenue associated with the custodial service can be recognized with the passage of time.

Consideration Received from a Supplier

A supplier may pay consideration to its customer, which may be in the form of cash, credits, coupons, and so forth. The customer can then apply this consideration to payments that it owes to the supplier, thereby reducing its net accounts payable.

The proper accounting for this type of consideration is to reduce the purchase price of the goods or services that the customer is acquiring from the supplier in the amount of the consideration received. If the consideration received relates to the customer attaining a certain amount of purchasing volume with the supplier (i.e., a volume discount), recognize the consideration as a reduction of the purchase price of the underlying transactions. This recognition can be made if attainment of the consideration is both probable and can be reasonably estimated. If these criteria cannot be met, then wait for the triggering milestones, and recognize them as the milestones are reached. Factors that can make it more difficult to determine whether this type of consideration is probable or reasonably estimated include:

- *Duration.* The relationship between the consideration to be received and purchase amounts spans a long period of time.
- *Experience.* The customer has no historical experience with similar products, or cannot apply its experience to changing circumstances.
- *External factors.* External factors can influence the underlying activity, such as changes in demand.
- *Prior adjustments.* It has been necessary to make significant adjustments to similar types of expected consideration in the past.

EXAMPLE

Puller Corporation manufactures plastic door knobs. Its primary raw material is polymer resin, which it purchases in pellet form from a regional chemical facility. Puller will receive a 2% volume discount if it purchases at least €500,000 of pellets from the supplier by the end of the calendar year. Puller has a long-term relationship with this supplier, has routinely earned the discount for the last five years, and plans to place orders in this year that will comfortably exceed the €500,000 mark. Accordingly, Puller accrues the 2% discount as a reduction of the purchase price of its pellet purchases throughout the year.

EXAMPLE

Puller has just entered into a new relationship with another supplier that will deliver black dye to the factory for inclusion in all of the company's black door knob products. This supplier offers a 5% discount if purchases exceed €50,000 for the calendar year. Puller has not sold this color of door knob before and so has no idea of what customer demand may be. Given the high level of uncertainty regarding the probability of being awarded the discount, Puller elects to record all purchases at their full price, and will re-evaluate the probability of attaining the discount as the year progresses.

The only exceptions to this accounting are:
- When the customer specifically transfers an asset to the supplier in exchange. If so, the customer treats the transaction as it would any sale to one of its customers in the normal course of business. If the amount paid by the supplier is higher than the standalone selling price of the item transferred to the supplier, the customer should account for the excess amount as a reduction of the purchase price of any goods or services received from the supplier.
- The supplier is reimbursing the customer for selling costs that the customer incurred to sell the supplier's products to third parties. If so, the amount of cash received is used to reduce the indicated selling costs. If the amount paid by the supplier is greater than the amount for which the customer applied for reimbursement, record the excess as a reduction of the cost of sales.
- The consideration is related to sales incentives offered by manufacturers who are selling through a reseller. When the reseller is receiving compensation in exchange for honoring incentives related to the manufacturer's products, the reseller records the amount received as a reduction of its cost of sales. This situation only arises when all of the following conditions apply:
  - The customer can tender the incentive to any reseller as part of its payment for the product;
  - The reseller receives reimbursement from the manufacturer based on the face amount of the incentive;
  - The reimbursement terms to the reseller are only determined from the incentive terms offered to consumers; they are not negotiated between the manufacturer and reseller; and
  - The reseller is an agent of the manufacturer in regard to the sales incentive transaction.

If only a few or none of these criteria are met for a sales incentive offered by a manufacturer, account for the transaction as a reduction of the purchase price of the goods or services that the reseller acquired from the manufacturer. If all of the criteria *are* met, consider the transaction to be a revenue-generating activity for the reseller.

Customer Acceptance

A customer may include an acceptance clause in a contract with a seller. An acceptance clause states that the customer has the right to inspect goods and reject them or demand proper remedial efforts before formal acceptance. Normally, customer control over goods occurs as soon as this acceptance step has been completed.

There are situations in which the seller can determine that control has passed to a customer, even if a formal acceptance review has not yet taken place. This typically occurs when customer acceptance is based upon a delivery meeting very specific qualifications, such as certain dimension or weight requirements. If the seller can determine in advance that these criteria have been met, it can recognize revenue prior to formal customer acceptance. If the seller cannot determine in advance that a customer will accept the delivered goods, it must wait for formal acceptance before it can confirm that the customer had taken control of the delivery, which then triggers revenue recognition.

EXAMPLE

Stout Tanks, Inc. manufactures scuba tanks, which it sells in bulk to a large customer in Bonaire, Drive-Thru Scuba. Drive-Thru insists upon a complete hydrostatic test of each tank before accepting delivery, since an exploding air tank is a decidedly terminal experience for a diver wearing the tank. Stout decides to conducts its own hydrostatic test of every tank leaving its factory. Since Stout is conducting the same test as Drive-Thru, Stout can reasonably establish that customer acceptance has occurred as soon as the scuba tanks leave its factory. As such, Stout can recognize revenue on the delivery date, and not wait for Drive-Thru to conduct its test.

Even if a customer recognizes revenue in advance of formal customer acceptance, it may still be necessary to determine whether there are any remaining performance obligations to which a portion of the transaction price should be allocated. For example, a seller may have an obligation to not only manufacture production equipment, but also to install it at the customer site. This later step could be considered a separate performance obligation.

A variation on the customer acceptance concept is when a seller delivers goods to a customer for evaluation purposes. In this case, the customer has no obligation to accept or pay for the goods until the end of a trial period, so control cannot be said to have passed to the customer until such time as the customer accepts the goods or the trial period ends.

Customer Options for Additional Purchases

A seller may offer customers a number of ways in which to obtain additional goods or services at reduced rates or even for free. For example, the seller may offer a discount on a contract renewal, award points to frequent buyers, host periodic sales events, and so on.

When a contract grants a customer the right to acquire additional goods or services at a discount, this can be considered a performance obligation if the amount is material and the customer is essentially paying in advance for future goods or services. In this case, the seller recognizes revenue associated with the customer option when:

- The option expires; or
- The future goods or services are transferred to the customer.

If revenue is to be recognized for such an option, allocate the transaction price to the option based on the relative standalone price of the option. In the likely event that the standalone selling price of the option is not directly observable, use an estimate of its price. The derivation of this estimate should include the discount that the customer would obtain by exercising the option, adjusted for the following two items:

- Reduced by the amount of any discount that the customer could have received without the option, such as a standard ongoing discount offered to all customers; and
- The probability that the customer will not exercise the option.

A material right to additional purchases of goods or services is not considered to have been passed to a customer if the option is at a price that reflects the standalone selling price of a good or service. In this case, there is no particular advantage being granted to the customer, since it could just as easily purchase the goods or services at the same price, even in the absence of the option.

EXAMPLE

Twister Vacuum Company sells its top-of-the-line F5 vacuum cleaner to 50 customers for €800 each. As part of each sale, Twister gives each customer a discount code that, if used, gives the customer a 50% discount on the purchase of Twister's F1 hand-held vacuum cleaner, which normally sells for €100. The discount expires in 60 days.

In order to determine the standalone selling price of the discount code, Twister estimates (based on past experience) that 30% of all customers will use the code to purchase the F1 model. This means that the standalone selling price of the discount code is €15, which is calculated as follows:

€100 F1 standalone price × 50% discount × 30% probability of code usage = €15

The combined standalone selling prices of the F5 vacuum and the discount code sum to €815. Twister uses this information to allocate the €800 transaction price between the product and the discount code, using the following calculation:

Performance Obligation	Allocated Price	Calculation
F5 vacuum cleaner	€785.28	(€800 ÷ €815) × €800
Discount code	14.72	(€15 ÷ €815) × €800
Total	€800.00	

This allocation means that Twister can recognize €785.28 of revenue whenever it completes a performance obligation related to the sale of the F5 units to the 50 customers. Twister also allocates €14.72 to the discount code and recognizes the revenue associated with this item either when it is redeemed by a customer in the purchase of an F1 vacuum cleaner, or when the code expires.

EXAMPLE

Sojourn Hotel has a customer loyalty program that grants customers one loyalty point for each night that they stay in a Sojourn-affiliated hotel. Each loyalty point can be redeemed to reduce another stay at a Sojourn hotel by €5. If not used, the points expire after 24 months. During the most recent reporting period, customers earn 60,000 loyalty points on €2,000,000 of customer purchases. Based on past experience, Sojourn expects 60% of the points to be redeemed. Based on the likelihood of redemption, each point is worth €3 (calculated as €5 redemption value × 60% probability of redemption), so all of the points awarded are worth €180,000 (calculated as €3/ point × 60,000 points issued).

The loyalty points program gives a material right to customers that they would not otherwise have had if they had not stayed at a Sojourn hotel (i.e., entered into a contract with Sojourn). Thus, Sojourn concludes that the issued points constitute a performance obligation. Sojourn then allocates the €2,000,000 of customer purchases for hotel rooms to the hotel room product and the points awarded based on their standalone selling prices, based on the following calculations:

Performance Obligation	Allocated Price	Calculation
Hotel rooms	€1,834,862	(€2,000,000 ÷ €2,180,000) × €2,000,000
Loyalty points	165,138	(€180,000 ÷ €2,180,000) × €2,000,000
Total	€2,000,000	

The €165,138 allocated to loyalty points is initially recorded as a contract liability. The €1,834,862 allocated to hotel rooms is recognized as revenue, since Sojourn has completed its performance obligation related to these overnight stays.

As of the end of the next quarterly period, Sojourn finds that 8,000 of the loyalty points have been redeemed, so it recognizes revenue related to the loyalty points of €22,018 (calculated as 8,000 points ÷ 60,000 points × €165,138).

Licensing

A seller may offer a license to use intellectual property owned by the seller. Examples of licensing arrangements are:

- Licensing to use software
- Licensing to listen to music
- Licensing to view a movie
- Franchising the name and processes of a restaurant
- Licensing of a book copyright to republish the book
- Licensing to use a patent within a product

If a contract contains both a licensing agreement and a provision to provide goods or services to the customer, the seller must identify each performance obligation within the contract and allocate the transaction price to each one.

If the licensing agreement can be separated from the other elements of a contract, the seller must decide whether the license is being transferred to the customer over a period of time, or as of a point in time. A key point in making this determination is whether the license is intended to give the customer access to the intellectual property of the seller only as of the point in time when the license is granted, or over the duration of the license period. The first case would indicate that the revenue associated with the license is recognized as of a point in time, while the second case would indicate that the revenue is recognized over a period of time.

A license is more likely to have been granted as of a point in time when a customer can direct the use of a license and obtain substantially all of the remaining benefits from the license on the date when the license is granted to it. This will not be the case if the intellectual property to which the customer has rights continues to change throughout the license period, which occurs when the seller continues to engage in activities that significantly affect its intellectual property.

The intent of the seller of a license is to provide the customer with the right to access its intellectual property when the seller commits to update the property, the customer will be exposed to the effects of those updates, and the updates do not result in the transfer of a good or service to the customer. These conditions may not be stated in a contract, but could be inferred from the seller's customary business practices. For example, if the customer pays the seller a royalty based on its sales of products derived from intellectual property provided by the seller, this implies that the seller will be updating the underlying intellectual property. If these conditions are present, the associated revenue should be recognized over time, rather than as of a point in time.

If the facts and circumstances of a contract indicate that the revenue associated with a contract should be recognized as of a point in time, this does not mean that the revenue can be recognized prior to the point in time when the customer can use and benefit from the license. This date may be later than the commencement date of the underlying contract. For example, the license to use intellectual property may be granted, but the actual property may not yet have been delivered to the customer or activated.

If it is not possible to separate the licensing agreement from the other components of a contract, account for them as a single performance obligation. An example of when this situation arises is when a license is integrated into a tangible product to such an extent that the product cannot be used without the license.

> **Note:** A guarantee by the seller that it will defend a patent from unauthorized use is not considered a performance obligation.

A contract under which there is a right to use a license may include the payment of a royalty to the seller. This arrangement may occur, for example, when the customer is acting as a distributor to re-sell the licensed intellectual property to other parties. In this situation, the seller may only recognize the royalty as revenue as of the later of these two events:

- The subsequent sale to or usage by the third party has occurred; or
- The underlying performance obligation associated with the royalty has been satisfied.

EXAMPLE

Territorial Lease Corporation (TLC) has spent years accumulating a massive database of oil and gas leases throughout Scandinavia. It sells this information to oil and gas exploration companies, which use it to derive the prices at which they are willing to bid for oil and gas leases. TLC sells the information in three ways, which are:

- It sells a CD that contains lease information that is current as of the ship date. TLC does not issue any further updates to customers. Since TLC does not update the intellectual property, the associated revenue recognition can be considered to occur as of a point in time, which is the delivery date of the CD.
- The company also sells subscriptions to an on-line database of lease information, which it updates every day. Since TLC is continually upgrading the database, the recognition of revenue is considered to take place over time. Accordingly, TLC recognizes revenue over the term of the subscriptions it sells.
- TLC sells its lease information to another company, Enviro Consultants, which repurposes the information for the environmental remediation industry. The information is billed to the customers of Enviro, and Enviro pays TLC a 50% royalty once Enviro receives payment from its customers. Since the subsequent sale of the information has occurred by the time TLC receives royalty payments, it can recognize the payments as revenue upon receipt.

Nonrefundable Upfront Fees

In some types of contracts, it is customary for the seller to charge a customer a nonrefundable upfront fee. Examples of these fees are:

- Health club member ship fee
- Phone service activation fee
- Long-term contract setup fee

There may be a performance obligation associated with these fees. In some cases, it could actually relate to an activity that the seller completes at the beginning of a contract. However, this activity rarely relates to the fulfillment of a performance obligation by the seller, and simply represents an expenditure. Consequently, the most appropriate treatment of this fee is to recognize it as revenue when the goods or services stated in the contract are provided to the customer. Several additional issues to consider are:

- *Recognition period*. If the seller grants the customer a material option to renew the contract, the revenue recognition period associated with the up-front fee is extended over the additional contract term.
- *Setup costs*. It is possible that the costs incurred to set up a contract are an asset, which should be charged to expense over the course of the contract.

EXAMPLE

Providence Alarm Systems offers its customers a home monitoring system that includes a £200 setup fee and a monthly £35 charge to monitor their homes through an alarm system, for a minimum one-year period. Providence does not charge the setup fee again if a customer chooses to renew.

The setup activities that Providence engages in do not transfer a good or service to customers, and so do not create a performance obligation. Thus, the upfront fee can be considered an advance payment relating to the company's monthly monitoring activities. Providence should recognize the £200 fee over the initial one-year monitoring period, as services are provided.

Principal versus Agent

There are situations where the party providing goods or services to a customer is actually arranging to have another party provide the goods and services. In this case, the party is an agent, not the principal party acting as seller. Use the following rules to differentiate between the two concepts of principal and agent:

Criterion	Principal	Agent
Controls the good or service before transfer to customer	Yes	No
Obtains legal title just prior to transfer to seller	Either	Either
Hires a subcontractor to fulfill some performance obligations	Yes	No
Arranges for the provision of goods or services by another party	No	Yes
Does not have inventory risk before or after the customer orders goods, including the absence of risk related to product returns	No	Yes
Does not have discretion in establishing prices	No	Yes
The consideration paid to the selling entity is in the form of a commission	No	Yes
There is no exposure to credit risk that the customer will not pay	No	Yes

The differentiation between principal and agent is of some importance, for a principal recognizes the gross amount of a sale, while an agent only recognizes the fee or commission it earns in exchange for its participation in the transaction. This fee or commission may be the net amount remaining after the agent has paid the principal the amount billed for its goods or services provided to the customer.

In a situation where the seller is initially the principal in a transaction but then hands off the performance obligation to a third party, the seller should not recognize the revenue associated with the performance obligation. Instead, the seller may have assumed the role of an agent.

EXAMPLE

High Country Vacations operates a website that puts prospective vacationers in touch with resorts located in ski towns around the world. When a vacationer purchases a hotel room on the website, High Country takes a 15% commission from the resort where the hotel room is located. The resort sets the prices for hotel rooms. High Country is not responsible for the actual provision of hotel rooms to vacationers.

Since High Country does not control the hotel rooms being provided, is arranging for the provision of services by a third party, does not maintain an inventory of rooms, cannot establish prices, and is paid a commission, the company is clearly an agent in these transactions. Consequently, High Country should only recognize revenue in the amount of the commissions paid to it, not the amount paid by vacationers for their hotel rooms.

EXAMPLE

Dirt Cheap Tickets sells discounted tickets for cruises with several prominent cruise lines. The company purchases tickets in bulk from cruise lines and must pay for them, irrespective of its ability to re-sell the tickets to the public. Dirt Cheap can alter the prices of the tickets that it purchases, which typically means that the company gradually lowers prices as cruise dates approach, in order to ensure that its excess inventory of tickets is sold. There is no credit risk, since tickets are paid for at the point of purchase. If customers have issues with the cruise lines, Dirt Cheap will intercede on their behalf, but generally encourages them to go directly to the cruise lines with their complaints.

Based on its business model, Dirt Cheap is acting as the principal. It controls the goods being sold, has inventory risk, and actively alters prices. Consequently, Dirt Cheap can recognize revenue in the gross amount of the tickets sold.

Repurchase Agreements

A repurchase agreement is a contract in which the seller agrees to sell an asset and either promises or has the option to repurchase the asset. The asset that the seller repurchases can be the original asset sold, a substantially similar asset, or an asset of which the original unit is a part.

There are three variations on the repurchase agreement:
- *Forward.* The seller has an obligation to repurchase the asset.
- *Call option.* The seller has the right to repurchase the asset.
- *Put option.* The seller has an obligation to repurchase the asset if required to by the customer.

If the contract is essentially a forward or call option, the customer never gains control of the asset, since the seller can or will take it back. Given the circumstances, revenue recognition can vary as follows:
- *Reduced repurchase price.* If the seller either can or must repurchase the asset for an amount less than the original selling price (considering the time value of money), the seller accounts for the transaction as a lease.
- *Same or higher repurchase price.* If the seller either can or must repurchase the asset for an amount equal to or greater than the original selling price (considering the time value of money), the seller accounts for the transaction as a financing arrangement.
- *Sale-leaseback.* If the transaction is a sale-leaseback arrangement, the seller accounts for the transaction as a financing arrangement.

When a customer has a put option, the proper accounting depends upon the market price of the asset and the existence of a sale-leaseback arrangement. The alternatives are:
- *Incentive to exercise option.* If the customer has a significant economic incentive to exercise the option, the seller accounts for the transaction as a lease. Such an incentive would exist, for example, when the repurchase price exceeds the expected market value of an asset through the period when the put option can be exercised (considering the time value of money).
- *No incentive to exercise option.* If the customer does not have an economic incentive to exercise a put option, the seller accounts for the agreement as a sale of a product with a right of return.
- *Sale-leaseback.* Even if the seller has a significant economic incentive, as noted in the last bullet point, if the arrangement is a sale-leaseback arrangement, the seller accounts for it as a financing arrangement.
- *Higher repurchase price.* If the repurchase price is equal to or higher than the selling price and is more than the asset's expected market value (considering the time value of money), the seller accounts for it as a financing arrangement.
- *Higher repurchase price with no incentive.* In the rare case where the repurchase price is equal to or higher than the original purchase price, but is less than or equal to the expected market value of the asset (considering the time value of money), this indicates that the customer has no economic incentive to exercise the option. In this case, the seller accounts for the transaction as a sale of a product with a right of return.

When the seller accounts for a transaction as a financing arrangement, the seller continues to recognize the asset, as well as a liability for any consideration it has received from the customer. The difference between the amount of consideration paid by and due to the customer is to be recognized as interest and processing (or related) costs.

If a call option or put option expires without being exercised, the seller can derecognize the repurchase liability and recognize revenue instead.

EXAMPLE

Domicilio Corporation sells a commercial property to Mole Industries for €3,000,000 on March 1, but retains the right to repurchase the property for €3,050,000 on or before December 31 of the same year. This transaction is a call option.

Control over the property does not pass to Mole Industries until after the December 31 termination date of the call option, since Domicilio can repurchase the asset. In the meantime, Domicilio accounts for the arrangement as a financing transaction, since the exercise price exceeds the amount of Mole's purchase price. This means that Domicilio retains the asset in its accounting records, records the €3,000,000 of cash received as a liability, and recognizes interest expense of €50,000 over the intervening months, which gradually increases the amount of the liability to €3,050,000.

On December 31, Domicilio lets the call option lapse; it can now derecognize the liability and recognize €3,050,000 of revenue.

EXAMPLE

Assume the same transaction, except that the option is a requirement for Domicilio to repurchase the property for €2,900,000 at the behest of the customer, Mole Industries. This is a put option. The market value by the end of the year is expected to be lower than €2,900,000.

At the inception of the contract, it is apparent that Mole will have an economic incentive to exercise the put option, since it can earn more from exercising the option than from retaining the property. This means that control over the property does not really pass to Mole. In essence, then, the transaction is to be considered a lease.

Unexercised Rights of Customers

A customer may prepay for goods or services to be delivered at a later date, which the seller initially records as a liability, and later as revenue when the goods or services are delivered. However, what if the customer does not exercise all of its rights to have goods or services delivered? The unexercised amount of this prepayment may be referred to as *breakage*.

The amount of breakage associated with a customer prepayment should be recognized as revenue. The question is, when should the recognition occur? There are two possible scenarios:

- *Existing pattern.* If there is a historical pattern of how a customer exercises the rights associated with its prepayments, the seller can estimate the amount of breakage likely to occur, and recognize it in proportion to the pattern of rights exercised by the customer.
- *No expectation.* If there is no expectation that the seller will be entitled to any breakage, the seller recognizes revenue associated with breakage only when there is a remote likelihood that the customer will exercise any remaining rights.

No revenue related to breakage should be recognized if it is probable that such recognition will result in a significant revenue reversal at a later date.

In a situation where there are unclaimed property laws, the seller is legally required to remit breakage to the applicable government entity. In this case, the breakage is recorded as a liability (rather than revenue), which is cleared from the seller's books when the funds are remitted to the government.

EXAMPLE

Clyde Shotguns receives a €10,000 deposit from a customer, to be used for the construction of a custom-made shotgun. Clyde completes the weapon and delivers it to the customer, recognizing €9,800 of revenue based on the number of billable hours expended. Clyde notifies the customer of the residual deposit amount, but the customer does not respond, despite repeated attempts at communication. Under the escheatment laws of the local state government, Clyde is required to remit these residual funds to the state if they have not been claimed within three years. Accordingly, Clyde initially records the €200 as an escheatment liability, and pays over the funds to the government once three years have passed.

Warranties

A warranty is a guarantee related to the performance of delivered goods or services. If related to a product, the seller typically guarantees the replacement or repair of the delivered goods. If related to a service, the warranty may involve replacement services, or a full or partial refund.

If a customer has the option to separately purchase a warranty, this is to be considered a distinct service to be provided by the seller. As such, the warranty is to be considered a separate performance obligation, with a portion of the transaction price allocated to it. If there is no option for the customer to separately purchase a warranty, the warranty is instead considered an obligation of the seller, in which case the following accounting applies:

- Accrue a reserve for product warranty claims based on the prior experience of the business. In the absence of such experience, the company can instead rely upon the experience of other entities in the same industry. If there is considerable uncertainty in regard to the amount of projected product warranties, it may not be possible to record a product sale until the warranty period has expired or more experience has been gained with customer claims.

- Adjust the reserve over time to reflect changes in prior and expected experience with warranty claims. This can involve a credit to earnings if the amount of the reserve is too large, and should be reduced.
- If there is a history of minimal warranty expenditures, there is no need to accrue a reserve for product warranty claims.

A warranty may provide a customer with a service, as well as a guarantee that provided goods or services will function as claimed. Consider the following items when determining whether a service exists:

- *Duration.* The time period needed to discover whether goods or services are faulty is relatively short, so a long warranty period is indicative of an additional service being offered.
- *Legal requirement.* There is a legal requirement to provide a warranty, in which case the seller is more likely to just be offering the mandated warranty without an additional service.
- *Tasks.* If the warranty requires the seller to perform specific tasks that are identifiable with the remediation of faulty goods or services, there is unlikely to be any additional identifiable service being offered.

If an additional service is being offered through a warranty, consider this service to be a performance obligation, and allocate a portion of the transaction price to that service. If the seller cannot reasonably account for this service separately, instead account for both the assurance and service aspects of the warranty as a bundled performance obligation.

There may be a legal obligation for the seller to compensate its customers if its goods or services cause harm. If so, this is not considered a performance obligation. Instead, this legal obligation is considered a loss contingency. A loss contingency arises when there is a situation for which the outcome is uncertain, and which should be resolved in the future, possibly creating a loss. For example, there may be injuries caused by a company's products when it is discovered that lead-based paint has been used on toys sold by the business.

When deciding whether to account for a loss contingency, the basic concept is that you should only record a loss that is probable, and for which the amount of the loss can be reasonably estimated. If the best estimate of the amount of the loss is within a range, accrue whichever amount appears to be a better estimate than the other estimates in the range. If there is no "better estimate" in the range, accrue a loss for the minimum amount in the range.

If it is not possible to arrive at a reasonable estimate of the loss associated with an event, only disclose the existence of the contingency in the notes accompanying the financial statements. Or, if it is not probable that a loss will be incurred, even if it is possible to estimate the amount of a loss, only disclose the circumstances of the contingency without accruing a loss.

If the conditions for recording a loss contingency are initially not met, but then *are* met during a later accounting period, the loss should be accrued in the later period. Do not make a retroactive adjustment to an earlier period to record a loss contingency.

Contract-Related Costs

Thus far, the discussion has centered on the recognition of revenue – but what about the costs that an organization incurs to fulfill a contract? In this section, we separately address the accounting for the costs incurred to initially obtain a contract, costs incurred during a contract, and how these costs are to be charged to expense.

Costs to Obtain a Contract

An organization may incur certain costs to obtain a contract. If so, it is allowable to record these costs as an asset, and amortize them over the life of the contract. The following conditions apply:

- The costs must be incremental; that is, they would not have been incurred if the organization had not obtained the contract.
- If the amortization period will be one year or some lesser period, it is allowable to simply charge these costs to expense as incurred.
- There is an expectation that the costs will be recovered.

An example of a contract-related cost that could be recorded as an asset and amortized is the sales commission associated with a sale, though as a practical expedient it is usually charged to expense as incurred.

EXAMPLE

A water engineering firm bids on a contract to investigate the level of silt accumulation in the Charlottenburg Canal in Germany, and wins the bid. The firm incurs the following costs as part of its bidding process.

Staff time to prepare proposal	€18,000
Printing fees	2,500
Travel costs	5,000
Commissions paid to sales staff	15,000
	€40,500

The firm must charge the staff time, printing fees, and travel costs to expense as incurred, since it would have incurred these expenses even if the bid had failed. Only the commissions paid to the sales staff can be considered a contract asset, since that cost should be recovered through its future billings for consulting services.

Costs to Fulfill a Contract

In general, any costs required to fulfill a contract should be recognized as assets, as long as they meet all of these criteria:
- The costs are tied to a specific contract;
- The costs will be used to satisfy future performance obligations; and
- There is an expectation that the costs will be recovered.

Costs that are considered to relate directly to a contract include the following:
- *Direct labor.* Includes the wages of those employees directly engaged in providing services to the customer.
- *Direct materials.* Includes the supplies consumed in the provision of services to the customer.
- *Cost allocations.* Includes those costs that relate directly to the contract, such as the cost of managing the contract, project supervision, and depreciation of the equipment used to fulfill the contract.
- *Chargeable costs.* Includes those costs that the contract explicitly states can be charged to the customer.
- *Other costs.* Includes costs that would only be incurred because the seller entered into the contract, such as payments to subcontractors providing services to the customer.

Other costs are to be charged to expense as incurred, rather than being classified as contract assets. These costs include:
- *Administration.* General and administrative costs, unless the contract terms explicitly state that they can be charged to the contract.
- *Indistinguishable.* Costs for which it is not possible to determine whether they relate to unsatisfied or satisfied performance obligations. In this case, the default assumption is that they relate to satisfied performance obligations.
- *Past performance costs.* Any costs incurred that relate to performance obligations that have already been fulfilled.
- *Waste.* The costs of resources wasted in the contract fulfillment process, which were not included in the contract price.

EXAMPLE

Tele-Service International enters into a contract to take over the phone customer service function of Artisan's Delight, a manufacturer of hand-woven wool shopping bags. Tele-Service incurs a cost of €50,000 to construct an interface between the inventory and customer service systems of Artisan's Delight and its own call database. This cost relates to activities needed to fulfill the requirements of the contract, but does not result in the provision of any services to Artisan's Delight. This cost should be amortized over the term of the contract.

Tele-Service assigns four of its employees on a full-time basis to handle incoming customer calls from Artisan's customers. Though this group is providing services to the customer, it is not generating or enhancing the resources of Tele-Service, and so its cost cannot be recognized as an asset. Instead, the cost of these employees is charged to expense as incurred.

Amortization of Costs

When contract-related costs have been recognized as assets, they should be amortized on a systematic basis that reflects the timing of the transfer of related goods and services to the customer. If there is a change in the anticipated timing of the transfer of goods and services to the customer, update the amortization to reflect this change. This is considered a change in accounting estimate.

Impairment of Costs

The seller should recognize an impairment loss in the current period when the carrying amount of an asset associated with a contract is greater than the remaining payments to be received from the customer. The calculation is:

Remaining consideration to be received – Costs not yet recognized as expenses
= Impairment amount (if result is a negative figure)

Note: When calculating possible impairment, adjust the amount of the remaining consideration to be received for the effects of the customer's credit risk.

At a later date, if the conditions causing the original impairment have improved or no longer exist, it is allowable to reverse some or all of the impairment loss. The amount of this impairment loss reversal cannot exceed the amount of the original impairment, net of any subsequent amortization.

Exclusions

The revenue recognition rules contained within IFRS 15 do not apply to the following areas, for which more specific recognition standards apply:
- Lease contracts
- Insurance contracts
- Financial instruments involving receivables, investments, liabilities, debt, derivatives, hedging, or transfers and servicing
- Guarantees, not including product or service warranties
- Nonmonetary exchanges between entities in the same line of business, where the intent is to facilitate sales transactions to existing or potential customers

---

EXAMPLE

Two distributors of heating oil swap stocks of different grades of heating oil, so that they can better meet the forecasted demand of their customers. No revenue recognition occurs in this situation, since the two parties are in the same line of business and the intent of the transaction is to facilitate sales to potential customers.

Since IFRS 15 only applies to contracts with customers, there are a number of transactions that do not incorporate these elements, and so are not covered by the provisions of this Topic. Consequently, the following transactions and events are not covered:

- Dividends received
- Non-exchange transactions, such as donations received
- Changes in regulatory assets and liabilities caused by alternative revenue programs for rate-regulated entities

Revenue Disclosures

There are a number of disclosures related to revenue. As a general overview, the intent of the disclosures is to reveal enough information so that readers will understand the nature of the revenue, the amount being recognized, the timing associated with its recognition, and the uncertainty of the related cash flows. More specifically, disclosures are required in the following three areas for both annual and interim financial statements:

- *Contracts.* Disclose the amount of revenue recognized, any revenue impairments, the disaggregation of revenue, performance obligations, contract balances, and the amount of the transaction price allocated to the remaining performance obligations. Contract balances should include beginning and ending balances of receivables, contract assets, and contract liabilities. In particular:
  - *Revenue.* Separately disclose the revenue recognized from contracts with customers.
  - *Impairment losses.* Separately disclose any impairment losses on receivables or contract assets that arose from contracts with customers. These disclosures must be separated from the disclosure of losses from other types of contracts.
  - *Disaggregation.* Disaggregate the reported amount of revenue recognized into categories that reflect the nature, amount, timing, and uncertainty of cash flows and revenue. Examples are:
    - By contract type (such as by cost-plus versus fixed-price contract)
    - By country or region
    - By customer type (such as by retail versus government customer)

- By duration of contract
- By major product line
- By market
- By sales channels (such as by Internet store, retail chain, or wholesaler)
- By transfer timing (such as sales as of a point in time versus over time)

The nature of this disaggregation may be derived from how the organization discloses information about revenue in other venues, such as within annual reports, in presentations to investors, or when being evaluated for financial performance or resource allocation judgments. If the entity is publicly-held and therefore reports segment information, consider how the reporting of disaggregated revenue information might relate to the revenue information reported for segments of the business. It is also allowable for certain non-public entities to *not* disaggregate revenue information, but only if this disclosure is replaced by the disclosure of revenue by the timing of transfers to customers, and with a discussion of how economic factors (such as contract types or customer types) impact the nature, amount, timing, and uncertainty of cash flows and revenue.

EXAMPLE

Lowry Locomotion operates a number of business segments generally related to different types of trains. It compiles the following information for its disaggregation disclosure:

(000s) Segments	Freight Trains	Passenger Trains	Railbus	Total
Primary Geographical Markets				
Europe	€53,000	€41,000	€14,000	€108,000
North America	91,000	190,000	---	281,000
	€144,000	€231,000	€14,000	€389,000
Major Product Lines				
Diesel	€106,000	€---	€---	€106,000
Electric	38,000	190,000	14,000	242,000
Trolleys	---	41,000	---	41,000
	€144,000	€231,000	€14,000	€389,000
Timing of Revenue Recognition				
Goods transferred at a point in time	€129,000	€189,000	€11,000	€329,000
Services transferred over time	15,000	42,000	3,000	60,000
	€144,000	€231,000	€14,000	€389,000

o *Contract-related.* The disclosure of contract balances for all entities shall include the opening and closing balances of receivables, contract assets, and contract liabilities. Publicly-held and certain other entities must provide considerably more information. This includes:

- Revenue recognized in the period that was included in the contract liability at the beginning of the period, and revenue recognized in the period from performance obligations at least partially satisfied in previous periods (such as from changes in transaction prices).
- How the timing of the completion of performance obligations relates to the timing of payments from customers and the impact this has on the balances of contract assets and contract liabilities.
- Explain significant changes in the balances of contract assets and contract liabilities in the period. Possible causes to discuss might include changes caused by business combinations, impairments, or cumulative catch-up adjustments.

- o *Performance obligations.* Describe the performance obligations related to contracts with customers, which should include the timing of when these obligations are typically satisfied (such as upon delivery), significant payment terms, the presence of any significant financing components, whether consideration is variable, and whether the consideration may be constrained. Also note the nature of the goods or services being transferred, and describe any obligations to have a third party transfer goods or services to customers (as is the case in an agent relationship). Finally, describe any obligations related to returns, refunds, and warranties.
- o *Price allocations.* If there are remaining performance obligations to which transaction prices are to be allocated, disclose the aggregate transaction price allocated to those unsatisfied obligations. Also note when this remaining revenue is likely to be recognized, either in a qualitative discussion or by breaking down the amounts to be recognized by time band. None of these disclosures are needed if the original expected duration of a contract's performance obligation is for less than one year. Also, certain non-public entities can elect to not disclose any of this information.

EXAMPLE

Franklin Oilfield Support provides gas field maintenance to gas exploration companies in Africa. Franklin discloses the following information related to the allocation of transaction prices to remaining performance obligations:

Franklin provides gas field maintenance services to several of the larger gas exploration firms in the Jubilee field in Ghana. The company typically enters into two-year maintenance service agreements. Currently, the remaining performance obligations are for €77,485,000, which are expected to be satisfied within the next

24 months. These obligations are noted in the following table, which also states the year in which revenue recognition is expected:

(000s)	20X1	20X2	Totals
Revenue expected to be recognized:			
Gates contract	€14,250	€7,090	€21,340
Hollander contract	23,825	17,900	41,725
Ives contract	9,070	5,350	14,420
Totals	€47,145	€30,340	€77,485

- *Judgments*. Note the timing associated with when performance obligations are satisfied, as well as how the transaction price was determined and how it was allocated to the various performance obligations. In particular:
    - *Recognition methods*. When performance obligations are to be satisfied over time, describe the methods used to recognize revenue, and explain why these methods constitute a faithful depiction of the transfer of goods or services to customers.
    - *Transfer of control*. When performance obligations are satisfied as of a point in time, disclose the judgments made to determine when a customer gains control of the goods or services promised under contracts.
    - *Methods, inputs and assumptions*. Disclose sufficient information about the methods, inputs, and assumptions used to determine transaction prices, the constraints on any variable consideration, allocation of transaction prices, and measurement of obligations for returns, refunds, and so forth. The discussion of transaction prices should include how variable consideration is estimated, how non-cash consideration is measured, and how the time value of money is used to adjust prices.
    - *Disclosure avoidance*. Certain non-public entities can elect not to disclose information about the following items pertaining to judgments:
        - Why revenue recognition methods constitute a faithful depiction of the transfer of goods or services to customers.
        - The judgments made to determine when a customer gains control of the goods or services promised under contracts.
        - All methods, inputs, and assumptions used, though this information must still be supplied in regard to the determination of whether variable consideration is constrained.
- *Asset recognition*. Note the recognized assets associated with obtaining or completing the terms of the contract. This shall include the closing balances of contract-related assets by main category of asset, such as for setup costs and the costs to obtain contracts. The disclosure should also include the

amount of amortization expenses and impairment losses recognized in the period. Also describe:

- *Judgments.* The judgments involved in determining the amount of costs incurred to obtain or fulfill a customer contract.
- *Amortization.* The amortization method used to charge contract-related costs to expense in each reporting period.

A non-public entity can elect not to make the disclosures just noted for asset recognition.

It may be necessary to aggregate or disaggregate these disclosures to clarify the information presented. In particular, do not obscure information by adding large amounts of insignificant detail, or by combining items whose characteristics are substantially different.

There may be a change in estimate related to the measurement of progress toward completion of a performance obligation. If the change in estimate will affect several future periods, disclose the effect on income from continuing operations, net income, and any related per-share amounts (if the entity is publicly held). This disclosure is only required if the change is material. If there is not an immediate material effect, but a material effect is expected in later periods, provide a description of the change in estimate.

Summary

A key benefit of IFRS 15 is that the recognition of revenue from contracts with customers will now be quite consistent across a number of contract types and industries. Previously, industry-specific standards did not always treat essentially the same types of transactions in a similar manner. This may mean that some industries may experience significant recognition changes, since they were previously governed by highly specific recognition rules. Some entities, irrespective of their industry, may find that their recognition accounting will also change to a considerable extent if they had previously been using an interpretation of the existing standards that is no longer valid. For many industries, however, especially those involving retail transactions, the net effect of this standard is minimal.

Chapter 21
Employee Benefits and Retirement Plans

Introduction

There are a number of benefit plan arrangements that can be extended to employees, such as short-term benefits that are consumed in the current period, specific types of benefits issued after employee retirement, and the returns and principal on funds invested on behalf of employees. In this chapter, we address how to account for and disclose each of these variations on employee benefits and retirement plans.

IFRS Source Documents

- IAS 19, *Employee Benefits*
- IAS 26, *Accounting and Reporting by Retirement Benefit Plans*
- IFRIC 14, *The Limit on a Defined Benefit Asset, Minimum Funding Requirements and their Interaction*

Short-term Employee Benefits

Short-term employee benefits are those for which there is an expectation of settlement within the next 12 months. Examples of these benefits are:

Automobile lease	Holiday pay	Parking
Bonuses	Housing	Profit sharing pay
Car allowance	Medical care	Sick leave pay

If there is a subsequent change in the expectation for when short-term benefits will be disbursed, it may be necessary to reclassify the benefits as long-term benefits.

When an employee renders services for which there are associated short-term benefits, the employer should recognize an accrued liability, and does not have to incorporate discounted present value calculations into this liability. If the employer has already paid for benefits that will not be earned by employees for multiple periods, the unearned portion of these payments should be recorded in the prepaid expenses account, and charged to expense as earned. The basic accounting for a prepaid expense follows these steps:

1. Upon the initial recordation of a supplier invoice in the accounting system, verify that the item meets the employer's criteria for a prepaid expense.
2. If the item meets the employer's criteria, charge it to the prepaid expenses account. If not, charge the invoice to expense in the current period.

3. Record the amount of the expenditure in the prepaid expenses reconciliation spreadsheet.
4. At the end of the accounting period, establish the number of periods over which the item will be amortized, and enter this information in the reconciliation spreadsheet.
5. At the end of the accounting period, create an adjusting entry to amortize a portion of the cost to the most relevant expense account.
6. Once all amortizations have been completed, verify that the total in the spreadsheet for the current accounting period matches the total balance in the prepaid expenses account. If not, reconcile the two and adjust as necessary.

Tip: When there is a small expenditure for a short-term benefit, charge it to expense as incurred, even if it relates to a future period. This approach reduces the number of reconciling items to track.

EXAMPLE

Hammer Industries pays the £120,000 disability insurance for its entire workforce at the beginning of the year, and intends to ratably charge it to expense over the year. Its initial entry is:

	Debit	Credit
Prepaid expenses	120,000	
Accounts payable		120,000

At the end of each subsequent accounting period throughout the year, Hammer amortizes the prepaid expenses account with the following journal entry, which will result in the charging of the entire amount of prepaid insurance to expense by the end of the year:

	Debit	Credit
Insurance expense	10,000	
Prepaid expenses		10,000

The following additional accounting issues may apply to the accounting by an employer for short-term employee benefits:

- *Overhead allocation.* In some cases, it may be permissible to include short-term employee benefits in the cost pools that are then assigned to manufactured goods. See the Inventories chapter for more information.
- *Paid absences.* When an employer allows its employees to accumulate paid absence time (such as accrued vacation pay), it recognizes expense when employees provide the services that earn them the paid absence time. In those cases where the right to paid absences does not accumulate, the cost of paid time off is charged to expense as incurred. Common examples of paid absences for which the right does not accumulate are jury duty, bereavement pay, maternity leave, and military service.

EXAMPLE

There is already an existing accrued balance of 40 hours of unused vacation time for Fred Smith on the books of Kelvin Corporation. In the most recent month that has just ended, Fred accrued an additional five hours of vacation time (since he is entitled to 60 hours of accrued vacation time per year, and $60 \div 12 =$ five hours per month). He also used three hours of vacation time during the month. This means that, as of the end of the month, Kelvin should have accrued a total of 42 hours of vacation time for him (40 hours existing balance + 5 hours additional accrual - 3 hours used).

Fred is paid £30 per hour, so his total vacation accrual should be £1,260 (42 hours × £30/hour). The beginning balance for him is £1,200 (40 hours × £30/hour), so Kelvin accrues an additional £60 of vacation liability.

EXAMPLE

Martha Smith gives birth, so Kelvin Corporation grants her maternity leave for one month, at the amount of her normal full pay. Since this is not an accumulating benefit, Kelvin did not accrue the expected amount of maternity leave in advance. Instead, it charges this cost to expense as incurred.

- *Profit sharing and bonus plans.* Do not recognize the expected payout cost of a profit sharing or bonus plan, unless a past event causes an obligation and this amount can be reliably measured. There is *only* an obligation when there is no realistic alternative for a business, other than to pay the indicated amounts. Grounds for reliable estimation are only considered to be present when there is a formula for calculating the amount of payment, or past practice clearly shows the amount of the obligation, or management determines the amount to be paid before the financial statements are authorized for issuance.

EXAMPLE

Kelvin Corporation operates a profit sharing plan, under which it pays a 10% share of annual profits to those of its employees who have been with the company for the entire year. Though there is employee turnover, the terms of the plan state that the full 10% will be paid to qualifying employees. Thus, the company accrues an expense for the full 10% of profits.

Alternatively, if the profit sharing plan had stated that 10% of profits were to be paid out to those working for the company at the beginning of the year, but only if they were still working for the company at the end of the year, this effectively means that some lesser amount than 10% will actually be paid out, assuming a certain amount of employee turnover. In this case, historical experience could be used to arrive at a profit sharing accrual that is less than the 10% figure.

Post-Employment Benefits

Post-employment benefits, as the name implies, relate to those benefits received by employees after they have retired from their employer. Examples of post-employment benefits are lump sum payments, pensions, life insurance, medical care, and long-term disability benefits. It also includes termination benefits, since they are issued after an employee has left the employer. Depending on the terms of the underlying plans, post-employment benefits may be issued to the beneficiaries of employees, such as their surviving family members. Post-employment benefit plans fall into two classifications, which are:

- *Defined benefit plans*. This is a benefit plan under which the employer is responsible for the amount of benefits paid out from the plan; the amount of funds it pays into the plan is predicated on the estimated future cost of benefit payouts. In these plans, the risk that benefits will be less than expected falls on the employer.
- *Defined contribution plans*. This is a benefit plan under which the employer is only responsible for the amount of funds it pays into the plan, not the amount of benefits that are eventually paid out from the plan. The amount eventually received by former employees is based on a combination of the funds paid into the plan and any subsequent investment returns. In these plans, the risk that benefits will be less than expected falls on former employees.

Employers may sometimes band together to offer a defined benefit plan or defined contribution plan to their employees. In such a plan (known as a *multi-employer plan*), an individual employer accounts for its share of payments into the plan in exactly the same manner as if the plan were designed solely for the use of that employer. If a multi-employer plan is a defined benefit plan and there is not sufficient information available for an employer to account for the plan as a defined benefit plan, it can instead account for the plan as a defined contribution plan.

There may be a method in place among the employers in a multi-employer plan to distribute any plan surplus among the members, or to fund a deficit. When an employer uses the accounting for a defined contribution plan and such surpluses or deficits are allocated out, the employer should recognize the asset or liability in profit or loss.

When the members of a multi-employer plan are under common control, such as a parent and its subsidiaries, this is not considered a multi-employer plan. Participation in such a plan is considered a related party transaction.

A local government may mandate that all employers in its region enroll in a government-managed benefit plan. If so, account for payments into such a plan in the same manner as for a multi-employer plan. This type of plan may be considered a defined benefit or defined contribution plan, but if the method of payment into it is on a pay-as-you-go basis with no obligation to pay future benefits, it is typically treated as a defined contribution plan.

An employer may purchase an insurance contract that requires an insurer to provide post-employment benefits. This type of contract is considered a defined contribution plan for accounting purposes. The contract is instead considered a defined benefit plan if the employer has an obligation to pay benefits directly when due, or to pay additional benefits that the insurer does not pay.

Defined Contribution Plans

The accounting for a defined contribution plan is far simpler than for a defined benefit plan. Under a defined contribution arrangement, the employer charges to expense the contributions made into the plan. If there is an overpayment, this is classified as a prepaid expense. In those rare cases where the employer does not plan to make payments into a defined contribution plan for at least 12 months, it should record the associated liability on a discounted basis.

EXAMPLE

Kelvin Corporation has a defined contribution plan, under which it matches the first 5% of employee gross pay that employees choose to have deducted from their wages and placed in a retirement account. In the most recent period, the matching amount was £28,000. Kelvin accrues this amount as an expense, though it does not plan to settle the liability until the beginning of the following reporting period.

Defined Benefit Plans

A defined benefit plan is one in which the employer guarantees the benefits that will be paid. The accounting for defined benefit plans is immensely more complex than for a defined contribution plan, because the employer is responsible for the cost of benefits that may not be paid out for a number of years. The basic accounting steps are:

1. *Calculate the funding deficit or surplus.* Use the *projected unit credit method* (discussed later) to determine the cost of a benefit earned by employees in exchange for current and prior period service. This involves a number of estimates, such as employee turnover, employee mortality, future changes in medical costs, and future changes in salaries. The amount of this benefit is then discounted to its present value, after which the fair value of all existing plan assets are deducted from it.

2. *Calculate net defined benefit.* Adjust the balance from the first step for the effect of limiting any net defined benefit asset at the asset ceiling. The *asset ceiling* is the present value of any economic benefits available as plan refunds or reductions in future contributions to a benefit plan. This economic benefit is available if it can be realized at some point during the life of the plan, and is measured as the surplus at the end of the reporting period, less any associated costs, such as taxes. A plan refund is only available when the employer has an absolute right to the refund. The economic benefit from a

reduction in future contributions is calculated as the future service cost for each period over the lesser of the expected life of the plan and the expected life of the entity.

3. *Recognize items in profit or loss.* Determine the amounts of current service costs, past service cost, gain or loss on settlement, or net interest in the net defined benefit that can be recognized in profit or loss.

4. *Remeasure the net defined benefit.* Determine the remeasurement of the net defined benefit to be recognized in other comprehensive income. This re-measurement includes the following items:

    -   Actuarial gains and losses
    -   The return on plan assets, less the amounts included in the net inter-est on the net defined benefit
    -   The change in the effect of the asset ceiling, not including those amounts incorporated into the net interest on the net defined benefit

---

Tip: IFRS suggests that a qualified actuary be used to measure defined benefit obligations. Given the obvious complexity of the associated accounting, it is nearly mandatory to do so, especially if the actuary can provide the related accounting entries and supporting detail.

If a business only chooses to employ an actuary at long intervals to measure its benefit liability, it should adjust the current liability balance for any material transactions or circumstances in the interim, such as variations in interest rates.

Tip: IFRS allows for the use of computational shortcuts in some cases, if they provide a reliable approximation of what the normal computation process would yield.

The following additional accounting issues can apply to a defined benefit plan:

-   *Constructive obligation.* There may be a constructive obligation to pay benefits, even in the absence of a legal obligation. This situation arises when altering an informal practice would cause unacceptable damage to employee relations.

-   *Presentation.* If an employer has a net defined benefit liability or asset, it should present the amount in the balance sheet.

-   *Surplus.* If there is a surplus in a defined benefit plan, the employer measures the net amount of this asset as the lower of the surplus or the asset ceiling. The asset ceiling is the present value of any economic benefits available as plan refunds or reductions in future contributions to a benefit plan. An asset surplus typically arises when a benefit plan is overfunded, or when there are actuarial gains.

EXAMPLE

Kelvin Corporation has a long-standing practice of funding a defined benefit pension plan. There is no legal obligation for Kelvin to do so, but it has been engaged in this practice for many years. Not receiving this benefit would likely increase employee turnover significantly, since they rely upon it to supplement their other retirement income. Given the circumstances, Kelvin has a constructive obligation to account for the benefits issued.

Projected Unit Credit Method

The projected unit credit method is used to calculate the present value of a defined benefit obligation, as well as any related current service cost and past service cost. In essence, the method adds a unit of benefits to which employees are entitled. It then measures each of these units separately in order to arrive at the final benefit obligation.

EXAMPLE

Hodgson Industrial Design has a defined benefit plan. The plan states that a lump sum will be paid to each employee upon retirement, which equates to 2% of their final compensation for each year of service to Hodgson. The aggregate amount of compensation paid to employees in the current year is £10,000,000. Management expects this rate of pay to increase by 4%, compounded, in each future year. The discount rate that Hodgson employs is 10%. The following table shows how the company's benefit obligation increases over time, with no changes in actuarial assumptions. Realistically, the calculated results in the table would likely be lower if any employees were to terminate their employment prior to retirement.

(000,000s)

Year	1	2	3	4	5
Assumed compensation	£10	£10.4	£10.8	£11.2	£11.7
Benefit attributed to:					
- Prior years	0	117	234	351	468
- Current year	117	117	117	117	117
Current + prior years	117	234	351	468	585
Beginning obligation	--	79.9	175.8	290.1	425.5
Interest at 10%	--	8.0	17.6	29.0	42.5
Current service cost	79.9	87.9	96.7	106.4	**117.0**
Closing obligation	79.9	175.8	290.1	425.5	585.0

Note: The Year 1 obligation is the present value of the benefit attributed to prior years. The current service cost is the present value of the benefit that is attributed to the current year.

Attribution of Benefits to Periods of Service

The present value of defined benefit obligations and current service costs should be attributed to periods of service as defined under the corporate benefit formula. However, use the following straight-line attribution when employee service in later years will result in a materially higher benefit level than in earlier years:

+	The date when additional employee service leads to no material additional benefits, other than from compensation increases
-	The date when employee service first results in benefits under the plan
=	Amortization period

EXAMPLE

Micron Metallic provides its employees with a monthly pension of ¼% of their final compensation for each year of service with the company. The pension is payable once employees are 68 years old.

The benefit provided equals the present value of each monthly pension as of the applicable person's retirement date, through the expected date of death. The present value of the defined benefit obligation is calculated as:

	Present value of monthly pension payments of ¼% of final compensation level
×	Number of years of service through the end of the reporting period
=	Present value of defined benefit obligation

The benefits under a defined benefit plan are conditional, since they are based on ongoing future employment. If an employee leaves an employer prior to the vesting date, then that person will not receive any benefits. Thus, measuring the defined benefit obligation requires the accountant to estimate what proportion of employees will not become vested.

A defined benefit obligation will continue to increase until such time as any additional employee service time does not lead to a material amount of additional benefits. If there is such a date, attribute benefits to the reporting periods prior to that date, as per the plan formula. Otherwise, benefits would be mistakenly attributed to later periods, when they have actually already been earned. Conversely, if employee service in later years will trigger a materially higher benefit level, amortize the benefit on a straight-line basis until the date when no material additional benefits accrue.

EXAMPLE

Micron Metallic has a post-retirement benefit plan, the terms of which mandate that Micron will pay out a £10,000 retirement payment to all employees who have worked for the company at least 25 years, but before they reach age 60. Since service beyond the age of 60 does not lead to a material increase in the amount of the payout, the company should attribute the £10,000 benefit to each year from age 35 to 60, with an adjustment to incorporate the probability that employees may not complete the service period.

Micron also maintains a post-employment medical plan, under which retired employees are reimbursed for 25% of their medical costs if they work for the company for at least 10 years, and which increases the reimbursement to 60% if their service period is at least 25 years. The 25-year vesting period results in a substantially higher benefit level. To account for these variations in its medical plan, Micron uses the following calculations:

- None of the expected medical costs are attributed to employees not expected to reach 10 years of service.
- 2.5% of the present value of expected medical costs (25% reimbursement ÷ 10-year service period) is attributed to each year of service for those employees expected to reach 10 years of service but not 25 years of service.
- 2.4% of the present value of expected medical costs (60% reimbursement ÷ 25-year service period) is attributed to each year of service for those employees expected to reach 25 years of service.

Actuarial Assumptions

Actuarial assumptions are a company's best estimates regarding the variables that go into the calculation of post-employment benefit costs. There are a number of these assumptions that can impact benefit costs, including:

- *Demographic assumptions.* Includes estimates for employee mortality, turnover rates, disability, early retirement, and dependents who will be benefit-eligible.
- *Financial assumptions.* Includes the discount rate used, benefit levels, future salary levels, and the proportion of benefit costs to be paid by employees. Additional comments are:
  - *General.* Financial assumptions should be based on market expectations for the period over which obligation settlement is expected.
  - *Benefit limits.* Should incorporate any limitations or caps placed on the employer's share of benefit costs.
  - *Discount rate.* Should be based on market yields on high quality corporate bonds. If the market for such bonds is thin in a country, use the yield on government bonds instead. This rate is used to discount post-employment benefit obligations.
  - *Salaries.* Should include the estimated future amount of compensation increases that impact benefits, which requires consideration of inflation, seniority levels, promotions, and supply and demand in the labor market.

- *State benefits.* Incorporates any future changes in the amount of state benefits that impact benefit plan payments. This is necessary when the changes were enacted in the current reporting period, or evidence suggests that state benefits will change in a predictable manner.

The number of assumptions multiplies when the effects of a medical benefits plan are thrown into the mix. In this case, assumptions can address the frequency and cost of future claims, which in turn are comprised of assumptions about changes in the health of employees, technology changes, changes in the method of delivering health care, and so forth.

In general, the actuarial assumptions used to develop benefit liabilities should be both unbiased and mutually compatible. Assumptions are considered to not be biased when they are not imprudently optimistic, nor too conservative. A key issue is the compatibility of assumptions, so that (for example) the estimated rate of inflation is in accord with the rate at which compensation will be increased over time. If assumptions are not compatible, the results of a benefit formula will be difficult to justify.

Past Service Cost

Past service cost is any change in the present value of a defined benefit obligation that is caused by a plan amendment or curtailment. In other words, a retroactive change impacts the cost of benefits that employees already earned from their service in prior periods.

Before calculating a past service cost, remeasure the net defined benefit using the current fair value of plan assets before applying the plan amendment or curtailment. Then determine the existence of any past service cost on this new baseline. If there is a cost, recognize it on the earlier of the plan amendment or curtailment date, or when the business recognizes any related restructuring costs or termination benefits.

EXAMPLE

Hassle Corporation offers a pension plan that provides a pension of 0.5% of the final salary of every qualifying employee for each year of service, following a 15-year vesting period. The board of directors of Hassle decides to increase the amount of the plan to 0.8%. On the date when this change is approved, the present value of the increased benefit is:

Employees with ≥ 15years of service	£257,000
Employees with < 15 years of service	162,000
	£419,000

Hassle should recognize the £257,000 portion of the pension increase at once, since it relates to employees who are already vested.

The average remaining vesting period for the remaining employees is seven years, so Hassle should amortize the remaining £162,000 portion of the pension increase over the next seven years.

Gains and Losses on Settlement

Settlement occurs when there is a termination of any further obligations by the employer under a defined benefit plan. The gain or loss on settlement is calculated as the difference between the present value of the obligation being settled and the actual settlement price. The full amount of the gain or loss is recognized when the settlement occurs.

If an employer buys an insurance policy to take over its obligations under a defined benefit plan, this only constitutes a settlement when the employer no longer has any legal or constructive obligation to pay additional amounts if the insurance policy does not pay out all of the benefits mandated by the defined benefit plan.

Measurement of Plan Assets

An employer has a plan deficit when the fair value of plan assets is less than the present value of its defined benefit obligations, or a plan surplus when the fair value of plan assets exceeds the present value of its defined benefit obligations. The key element in this calculation is the fair value of plan assets, which is not always readily determinable. If not, use the discounted expected future cash flows associated with the assets as a substitute for fair value.

An employer may occasionally be reimbursed for its expenditures under a defined benefit plan. It should recognize these reimbursements only when their receipt is virtually certain, and should classify such an incoming reimbursement as a separate asset.

Defined Benefit Costs

IFRS requires that a business recognize the following three components of defined benefit cost:

- *Service cost.* This is a combination of current service cost, past service cost, and gains or losses on settlement, and is recognized in profit or loss.
- *Net interest on the net defined benefit liability.* This is calculated by multiplying the net defined benefit liability or asset by the discount rate, and is recognized in profit or loss.
- *Remeasurements of the net defined benefit.* Remeasurement of the benefit includes actuarial gains and losses, the return on plan assets, and changes in the effect of the asset ceiling. It is recognized in other comprehensive income. It is never subsequently reclassified to profit or loss, but can be transferred within equity.

Termination Benefits

A termination benefit arises from the decision to terminate the employment of an employee. These benefits most commonly are paid out in a lump sum, but can also be a step-up in the amount of post-employment benefits paid.

The accounting for a termination benefit depends upon the existence of a clause to provide additional services in exchange for the benefit. For example, if no additional services are required of an employee, the act of termination triggers the immediate recognition of the associated termination benefits. However, if a benefit is only paid if an employee provides additional future services, it should be recognized over the future service period. More specifically, IFRS mandates that termination benefits be recognized on the earlier of the date when the employer can no longer withdraw the benefit offer, or when it recognizes costs for a restructuring. When the employer can no longer withdraw its offer of benefits is considered to be the earlier of when an employee accepts the termination benefits or when any kind of restriction on the employer's ability to withdraw the offer takes effect.

EXAMPLE

The management of Giro Cabinetry decides to shut down its Durham facility in three months and to terminate the employment of all 100 employees who work at the facility at that time. The company announces a retention bonus of £24,000 that will be paid to any of the employees who continue to work for the company until the shutdown date. This bonus is in exchange for services to be provided over the next three months, so Giro should charge £800,000 to expense in each of the next three months to account for the retention bonus (adjusted for subsequent employee turnover).

Defined Contribution Plan Disclosures

In each period, an employer operating a defined contribution plan should disclose the contribution amount recognized as an expense.

When financial statements are prepared for a defined contribution plan, it should include a statement of net assets available for benefits, which should contain the following information:

- The asset balance at the end of the period
- The basis of asset valuation
- Details about any investment greater than 5% of net assets or 5% of any class of security
- Details of any investment in the employer
- Any liabilities other than the actuarial present value of promised retirement benefits

The following disclosures should accompany the statement of net assets for a defined contribution plan:

- *Policies.* The funding policy and investment policies.

- *Activities*. Significant activities during the period, the effects of any plan changes, membership changes, and changes in its terms and conditions.
- *Statements*. Separate statements on which are disclosed the transactions and investment performance during the period, and its financial position at the end of the period.
- *Fair value*. If plan assets are not carried at fair value, disclose why fair value is not used.

The report of a retirement benefit plan could contain such information as the name of the employer, the employee groups covered, the number of participants receiving benefits, the type of plan, whether participants contribute to the plan, a description of promised benefits, any plan termination terms, and any changes in this information during the reporting period.

Defined Benefit Plan Disclosures

There are a number of disclosures related to defined benefit plans that focus on their characteristics, risks, amounts, and impact on cash flows. The following information should be included in the notes that accompany the financial statements:

Plan characteristics:

- *Overall*. The nature of the benefits provided.
- *Changes*. A description of any amendments, curtailments and settlements.
- *Governance*. A description of the governance responsibilities for the plan.
- *Regulatory framework*. A description of the regulatory framework for which the plan is designed.
- *Risks*. The risks to which the plan exposes the employer.

Plan amounts:

- *Reconciliation*. A reconciliation of changes during the period in plan assets, the present value of the defined benefit obligation, the effect of the asset ceiling, and reimbursement rights. The reconciliation should include (if applicable) the current service cost, interest income or expense, return on plan assets, actuarial gains and losses from demographic assumptions, actuarial gains and losses from financial assumptions, changes from limiting a benefit asset to the asset ceiling, past service cost gains and losses from settlements, effects of exchange rates, employer contributions, participant contributions, payments from the plan, and the effects of disposals and business combinations.
- *Asset classes*. Separate the fair value of plan assets into classes, where classes are based on the nature and risk of the assets. There should be a further subdivision between those asset classes for which there is a quoted market price in an active market, and those for which this information is not available. Possible asset classes include cash and cash equivalents, equity

instruments, debt instruments, real estate, derivatives, and asset-backed securities.

- *Own instruments*. The amounts of the company's own financial instruments that are held as plan assets, at their fair value.
- *Own property*. The amounts of company-occupied property that are held as plan assets, at their fair value.
- *Assumptions*. The significant actuarial assumptions employed in the determination of the present value of the defined benefit obligation.

Also, it may be useful to disclose the basis used to determine the amount of economic benefit available, which is used in the determination of the asset ceiling, which in turn factors into the calculation of the net defined benefit asset.

Cash flows:

- *Contributions*. The expected amount of contributions to the plan in the next fiscal year.
- *Funding*. The employer's funding arrangements and policies that may affect future contributions to the plan.
- *Matching strategies*. The use of any strategies to match assets to liabilities, in order to manage risk.
- *Maturity profile*. A description of the maturity profile of the defined benefit obligation, including the weighted average duration of the obligation. Consider a discussion of the timing of benefit payments.
- *Sensitivity analysis*. For each significant actuarial assumption, a sensitivity analysis that shows how the defined benefit obligation would have been altered by changes in the assumption, as well as the methods used to prepare these analyses and any changes in these methods from the previous period.

Multi-employer plans:

- *Allocations*. How deficits or surpluses are to be allocated to the participating employers in the event of a withdrawal from the plan or the plan's termination.
- *Funding*. The plan's minimum and normal funding arrangements, as well as how contributions are calculated.
- *Liabilities*. The extent to which the employer can be liable for the obligations of other employers in the plan.
- *Alternative treatment*. If the employer accounts for the plan as a defined contribution plan, disclose the fact that the plan is actually a defined benefit plan, why there is not enough information to account for it as such, expected contributions to the plan in the next fiscal year, information about any plan surplus or deficit that may impact future contributions, and the level of the employer's participation in the plan when compared to the other plan participants.

Risk sharing between plans (where plans are under common control):

- *Charging policy.* The contractual agreement or policy for charging the net defined benefit cost. If there is no agreement or policy, state this fact.
- *Contribution policy.* The policy for calculating the contribution to be made by the employer.

Additionally, it may be necessary to provide some of the preceding information on a disaggregated basis. For example, disclosures could be made for different geographic locations, regulatory environments, or reporting segments of a business.

Finally, do not offset the assets of one plan against the liabilities of another plan, unless there is a legal right to use the assets of one plan to reduce the liabilities of the other plan, or the company intends to realize the surplus in one plan and use it to settle obligations under the other plan.

Defined Benefit Plan Financial Statements

When financial statements are prepared for a defined benefit plan, it should use either of the following statements:

- The net assets available for benefits, the actuarial present value of promised retirement benefits, and the resulting excess or deficit amount; or
- A statement of net assets available for benefits, and a statement of changes in net assets available for benefits, plus footnote disclosure of the actuarial present value of promised retirement benefits. Alternatively, the actuarial information can be provided in an accompanying actuarial report.

A statement of net assets available for benefits should include the following information:

- The asset balance at the end of the period
- The basis of asset valuation
- Details about any investment greater than 5% of net assets or 5% of any class of security
- Details of any investment in the employer
- Any liabilities other than the actuarial present value of promised retirement benefits

A statement of changes in net assets available for benefits should include the following information:

- Employer contributions
- Employee contributions
- Investment income
- Other income
- Benefits paid or payable
- Administrative expenses

- Other expenses
- Income taxes
- Profits and losses on the disposal of investments or changes in their value
- Transfers to and from other plans

Also disclose for the separate financial statements of a defined benefit plan the following items:

- *Activities*. Any significant activities in the period, the effect of any changes relating to the plan, changes in its membership, or changes in its terms and conditions.
- *Actuarial changes*. The effect of actuarial changes in actuarial assumptions that impacted the actuarial present value of promised retirement benefits.
- *Actuarial information*. Actuarial information, provided either with the financial statements or via a separate report. Note whether the present value of expected payments are based on current or projected salaries.
- *Assumptions*. Significant actuarial assumptions made, and the method used to derive the actuarial present value of promised retirement benefits.
- *Fair value*. If plan assets are not carried at fair value, disclose why fair value is not used.
- *Funding adequacy*. Describe the adequacy of planned future funding.
- *Policies*. The policy for funding promised benefits, and any investment policies.
- *Relationships*. State the relationship between the actuarial present value of promised retirement benefits and the net assets available for benefits.
- *Statements*. Separate statements on which are disclosed the transactions and investment performance during the period, and its financial position at the end of the period.
- *Valuation date*. The date of the last actuarial valuation.

The report of a retirement benefit plan could contain such information as the name of the employer, the employee groups covered, the number of participants receiving benefits, the type of plan, whether participants contribute to the plan, a description of promised benefits, any plan termination terms, and any changes in this information during the reporting period.

Summary

A defined benefit plan is startlingly more complex to account for than a defined contribution plan. The level of complexity nearly demands the use of an outside actuarial expert to routinely provide an employer with the information needed to properly account for its benefit plan. Conversely, the defined contribution plan is simple to measure and recognize. In addition, the defined benefit plan places all of the risk of changes in the cost of benefits on the employer, which can severely impact profits in many future periods. For these reasons, we strongly advocate the sole use of defined contribution plans. While the accounting staff is rarely at the center of the decision to use a defined benefit plan, it should at least present its views regarding the complexity and added cost of such plans to the management team.

Chapter 22
Share-based Payment

Introduction

Many organizations issue payments to their employees that are derived in some manner from the price of company stock. These payments may ultimately be paid in cash or shares. Similarly, though less commonly, share-based payments may be made to people or entities outside of the business, such as when legal services are paid for with company shares. The accounting for these payments varies, depending upon how they are calculated and paid. In this chapter, we address the various scenarios under which different types of accounting for share-based payments are applied.

IFRS Source Document

- IFRS 2, *Share-based Payment*

Overview of Share-based Payments

There are a number of possible ways in which a company could issue shares as a form of payment, perhaps through the outright issuance of shares, or share options, or warrants. No matter which method of payment is employed, the overriding goal of the accounting for these payments is to charge their effects to expense or an asset. More specifically, the accounting can fall into one of the following two areas:

- *Equity-settled, share-based payment.* If the company only pays with its shares, it records an increase in equity, with an offsetting debit to the relevant asset or expense account to which the payment relates.
- *Cash-settled, share-based payment.* If the company pays an amount in cash that is calculated from a certain number of shares, it records a liability, with an offsetting debit to the relevant asset or expense account to which the payment relates.

We will explore these issues further in the following sections.

Share-based Payments Settled with Equity

As noted in the last section, equity-settled, share-based transactions are recorded as an increase in equity, with an offsetting debit to the relevant asset or expense account to which the payment relates. This measurement should be based on the fair value of the goods or services received. If it is not possible to measure their fair value, measure the transaction at the fair value of the equity instruments that are used to settle the liability. The following additional issues may apply:

- *Payments to employees.* When services are rendered by employees or others providing similar services, it is usually not possible to measure the transaction at the fair value of the services received. Accordingly, measure these transactions at the fair value of the equity instruments granted, as of the grant date. This is a significant issue, since it applies to share options granted to employees.

- *Payments to parties other than employees.* When share-based payments are made to parties other than employees, it is assumed that the fair value of the goods or services received can be estimated in a reliable manner. The fair value of these items should be measured at the date when the company receives the goods or the services are rendered. If it is not possible to measure the fair values of the goods or services received, use the fair value of the equity instruments paid as of the date when the company receives the goods or the services are rendered.

EXAMPLE

Snyder Corporation orders specially-designed GPS chips from a supplier, for inclusion in its next GPS satellite. As an inducement to deliver the chips by August 31, Snyder offers 5,000 shares to the supplier. The GPS chips are custom-designed for Snyder, so it is not possible to directly determine their fair value. As an alternative, Snyder values the inducement transaction using the market price of its shares on the August 31 delivery date, which is £10 per share. This results in the recognition of a £50,000 expense on the delivery date.

- *Unidentifiable goods or services.* If the fair value of the goods or services to be received is less than the fair value of the equity consideration paid, this may mean that additional unidentifiable goods or services are yet to be received. If so, measure the unidentifiable items as the difference between the fair values of the identifiable items and the equity consideration as of the grant date.

- *Vesting.* There is not usually a vesting period associated with equity paid in exchange for goods or services. If there is no vesting, recognize the asset or expense associated with an equity payment at once. If there is a vesting period, it is assumed that the related services will be rendered during the vesting period, which means that the related expense is recognized over the vesting period. Also, if equity instruments do not vest because a vesting condition was not satisfied, do not recognize any asset or expense related to the transaction.

- *Market conditions.* A market condition may be included in a vesting arrangement, such as requiring that a company's share price reach a certain point before an option can be exercised. When estimating fair value, take the existence of market conditions into account. However, once fair value has been established, the related amounts of goods or services are to be recognized, even if it is found by the end of the vesting period that the market condition has not been met.

- *Reload feature.* A share option may contain a reload feature, where an employee is automatically granted additional options if he or she exercises existing options and uses shares to satisfy the exercise price. When there is a reload feature, do not include it in the estimation of the fair value of options granted. If a reload feature is triggered, account for it as an entirely new option grant.

- *Subsequent measurement.* Once a share-based payment has been measured and equity has been increased by the amount measured, there is no subsequent adjustment to equity. For example:
  - o   An expense is recognized for options granted in exchange for services, but the option recipient later forfeits the options. The issuing company cannot reverse its expense recognition.
  - o   An employee never exercises vested options, so they lapse. The issuing company cannot reverse the amount of compensation expense related to the options.

EXAMPLE

Luminescence Corporation issues 10,000 share options to a key employee, with a four-year vesting period. The shares have a fair value of £80,000 as of the grant date, so the company recognizes compensation expense related to the options of £20,000 in each of the next four years.

Luminescence issues 5,000 share options to another employee, which will vest when the development of a product has been completed and it is launched. The estimated amount of time required to develop the project is an additional 12 months. On the grant date, the options are valued at £36,000. Accordingly, the company recognizes compensation expense related to the options of £3,000 per month. If the estimated duration of the development process changes, the company should adjust its recognition period to match the revised estimate.

Luminescence issues 12,000 share options (valued at £80,000) to the supplier of the company's computer support services, which shall vest over the next year in proportion to the number of service requests resolved within one hour. Based on historical results, the company controller ratably accrues an expense of £60,000 to reflect the estimated issuance of 75% of the options. Once the year is complete, it is apparent that the supplier has been worse than usual at responding to service calls, and so is only entitled to 62% of the original option grant, which is £49,600. Accordingly, the controller adjusts the expense to £49,600 for the year.

Luminescence issues 4,000 share options to an attorney who handles the company's trademark litigation. The options are contingent upon the price of the company's stock exceeding £15 within the next 12 months. The attorney is expected to meet all other service conditions associated with the grant. Accordingly, the company recognizes the fair value of the grant over the 12-month period, irrespective of whether the market condition feature is met.

Luminescence grants 200,000 restricted stock units to its chief engineer, which vest on the grant date. The fair value of the grant is £500,000, which is triple his compensation for the past year. Under the terms of the arrangement, the RSUs will only be transferred to the engineer ratably over the next five years if he complies with the terms of the non-compete agreement. Since the RSUs are essentially linked to the non-compete agreement, and the amount of the future payouts are quite large, it is evident that the arrangement is really intended to be compensation for future services yet to be rendered to the company. Consequently, the appropriate accounting treatment is not to recognize the expense at once, but rather to recognize it ratably over the remaining term of the non-compete agreement.

When it is not possible to measure the fair value of goods or services received, the alternate valuation technique is to use the fair value of the equity instruments granted. This fair value should be based on available market prices, adjusted for any special terms and conditions associated with the equity instruments granted. If it is not possible to derive a market price for the equity instruments, the alternative is to use an accepted valuation methodology for pricing financial instruments. Models that are commonly used to derive fair value are the Black-Scholes-Merton formula and the lattice model. Key characteristics of these models are:

- *Black-Scholes-Merton formula.* Assumes that options are exercised at the end of the arrangement period, and that price volatility, dividends, and interest rates are constant through the term of the option being measured.
- *Lattice model.* Can incorporate ongoing changes in price volatility and dividends over successive time periods in the term of an option. The model assumes that at least two price movements are possible in each measured time period.

A key component of the value of a company's stock is its volatility, which is the range over which the price varies over time, or is expected to vary. Since an employee holding a stock option can wait for the highest possible stock price before exercising the option, that person will presumably wait for the stock price to peak before exercising the option. Therefore, a stock that has a history or expectation of high volatility is worth more from the perspective of an option holder than one that has little volatility. The result is that a company with high stock price volatility will likely charge more employee compensation to expense for a given number of shares than a company whose stock experiences low volatility.

Stock price volatility is partially driven by the amount of leverage that a company employs in its financing. Thus, if a business uses a large amount of debt to fund its operations, its profit will fluctuate in a wider range than a business that uses less debt, since the extra debt can be used to generate more sales, but the associated interest expense will reduce net profits if revenues decline.

EXAMPLE

Armadillo Industries grants an option on £25 stock that will expire in 12 months. The exercise price of the option matches the £25 stock price. Management believes there is a 40% chance that the stock price will increase by 25% during the upcoming year, a 40% chance that the price will decline by 10%, and a 20% chance that the price will decline by 50%. The risk-free interest rate is 5%. The steps required to develop a fair value for the stock option using the lattice model are:

1. Chart the estimated stock price variations.
2. Convert the price variations into the future value of options.
3. Discount the options to their present values.

The following lattice model shows the range and probability of stock prices for the upcoming year:

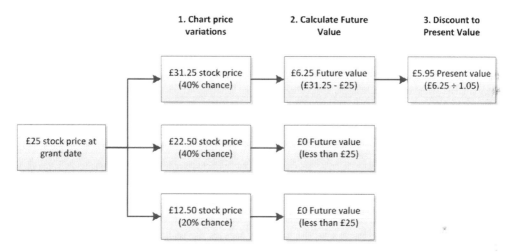

In short, the option will expire unexercised unless the stock price increases. Since there is only a 40% chance of the stock price increasing, the present value of the stock option associated with that scenario can be assigned the following expected present value for purposes of assigning a fair value to the option at the grant date:

£5.95 Option present value × 40% Probability = £2.38 Option value at grant date

EXAMPLE

Armadillo Industries issues stock options with 10-year terms to its employees. All of these options vest at the end of four years (known as *cliff vesting*). The company uses a lattice-based valuation model to arrive at an option fair value of £15. The company grants 100,000 stock options. On the grant date, it assumes that 10% of the options will be forfeited. The exercise price of the options is £25.

Given this information, Armadillo charges £28,125 to expense in each month. The calculation of this compensation expense accrual is:

$$(£15 \text{ Option fair value} \times 100,000 \text{ Options} \times 90\% \text{ Exercise probability}) \div 48 \text{ Months} = £28,125$$

It is possible that the fair value of the equity instruments granted cannot be determined. If so, measure these items based on their *intrinsic value*, which is the difference between their fair value and the amount the recipient must pay to acquire the shares. This amount is to be measured at the end of each reporting period, through the final settlement, exercise, or forfeiture date, with all changes being recognized in profit or loss. The final amount recognized is only based on the final number of shares that vest or are exercised. Only in this case is it permissible to reverse an expense accrual for an expense that was previously recognized in relation to shares that do not vest or options that are not exercised. The following two additional scenarios may apply to the intrinsic value measurement methodology:

- If settlement of a share-based payment occurs during a vesting period, treat the early settlement as accelerated vesting, which means that all remaining expenses that would have been recognized in a later period are recognized in the settlement period.
- When an option holder pays the issuer on the settlement date, treat this payment as a deduction from equity. However, in the unlikely case that the payment from the option holder is greater than the intrinsic value of the equity instruments being bought, recognize the difference as an expense.

EXAMPLE

Underwater Anomalies, which conducts shipwreck searches, has not uncovered a profitable wreck for some time, and so is reduced to paying for services with share options. Each option has an exercise price of £2 and a fair value of £10. The intrinsic value of each option is therefore £8, which is the difference between the fair value and exercise price.

It is not uncommon for a business to alter the terms under which equity instruments were issued. For example, it may have originally issued share options at an exercise price that is now well above the market price of the company's shares, and so institutes a modification to reduce the exercise price. The following accounting applies to these modifications for equity instruments issued to both employees and outside parties:

- *Minimum recognition.* The minimum amount to recognize is the fair value of the equity instruments granted, unless the instruments do not vest. This minimum level of recognition applies, even if there are subsequent modifications to the terms under which an instrument was granted, and even if the instrument is subsequently cancelled.

- *Additional recognition.* If terms modifications are favorable to the recipient of an equity instrument (that is, the fair value is increased), recognize the incremental increase in value.
- *Cancellation or settlement.* If an equity issuance is cancelled or settled (but not forfeited), account for the event as though the vesting period has been accelerated. This means that the remaining expense that would have been recognized over subsequent periods is recognized entirely in the current period. If any payment is made to the recipient of a grant when the grant is cancelled or settled, account for it as though the equity instrument had been repurchased, which is a reduction of equity. If this payment exceeds the fair value of the grant, recognize the difference as an expense.
- *Replacement.* If an equity instrument is essentially cancelled and replaced by a new equity instrument, the minimum accounting is to recognize the fair value of the equity instruments originally granted, plus any increase in the compensation paid to the recipient through the new issuance. This incremental change in fair value is the fair value of the replacement instruments, less the net fair value of the cancelled instruments. Net fair value is the fair value of the cancelled instruments just prior to their cancellation, minus the amount of any payment made to the recipient that is considered a deduction from equity.

EXAMPLE

The board of directors of Armadillo Industries initially grants 5,000 stock options to the engineering manager, with a vesting period of four years. The shares are worth £100,000 at the grant date, so the controller plans to recognize £25,000 of compensation expense in each of the next four years. After two years, the board is so pleased with the performance of the engineering manager that they accelerate the vesting schedule to the current date. The controller must therefore accelerate the remaining £50,000 of compensation expense that had not yet been recognized to the current date.

EXAMPLE

Armadillo Industries issues 10,000 stock options to various employees in 20X1. The designated exercise price of the options is £25, and the vesting period is four years. The total fair value of these options is £20,000, which the company charges to expense ratably over four years, which is £5,000 per year.

One year later, the market price of the stock has declined to £15, so the board of directors decides to modify the options to have an exercise price of £15.

Armadillo incurs additional compensation expense of £30,000 for the amount by which the fair value of the modified options exceeds the fair value of the original options as of the date of the modification. The accounting department adds this additional expense to the remaining £15,000 of compensation expense associated with the original stock options, which is a total unrecognized compensation expense of £45,000. The company recognizes this amount ratably over the remaining three years of vesting, which is £15,000 per year.

Share-based Payments Settled with Cash

As noted earlier, cash-settled, share-based payments are recorded as a liability, with an offsetting debit to the relevant asset or expense account to which the payment relates. The amount of this liability is measured at the fair value of the goods or services acquired, and is continually remeasured in each reporting period until the liability is settled. If the fair value changes during this measurement period, the change is recognized at once in profit or loss.

A common application of the cash settlement concept is when employees are granted share appreciation rights, under which they are paid cash if the underlying company shares increase in value. Assuming that there is indeed a run-up in the price of the company's stock, the value of the stock appreciation rights increase over time, which results in an increase in the associated recognition of compensation expense.

When share appreciation rights are granted, it is assumed that the corresponding service period has already been completed (unless there is evidence to the contrary), which means that the full amount of associated cost for the goods or services provided are recognized as expense on the grant date. Conversely, if the rights apply to a service period that has not yet occurred, the expense is recognized over that period.

EXAMPLE

Uncanny Corporation grants 20,000 share appreciation rights (SARs) to its chief executive officer (CEO). Each SAR entitles the CEO to receive a cash payment that equates to the increase in value of one share of company stock above a baseline value of £25. The award cliff vests after two years. The fair value of each SAR is calculated to be £11.50 as of the grant date. The entry to record the associated amount of compensation expense for the first year is:

	Debit	Credit
Compensation expense	115,000	
Share-based compensation liability		115,000

At the end of the first year of vesting, the fair value of each SAR has increased to £12.75, so an additional entry is needed to adjust the vested amount of compensation expense for the £12,500 incremental increase in the value of the award over the first year (calculated as £1.25 increase in SAR fair value × 20,000 SARs × 0.5 service period).

At the end of the vesting period, the fair value of each SAR has increased again, to £13.00, which increases the total two-year vested compensation expense for the CEO to £260,000. Since £127,500 of compensation expense has already been recognized at the end of the first year, the company must recognize an additional £132,500 of compensation expense.

Share-based Payments with Cash Alternatives

Some share-based payment instruments allow either the issuer or the recipient of an equity payment to select settlement in cash or equity. In these cases, the issuer should account for the transaction as though it were a cash-settled share-based transaction, if there is a liability to settle in cash. Otherwise, the transaction is treated as a payment that is settled with equity. These transactions are handled differently, depending upon whether the counterparty or the issuing entity can select the form of payment. The following subsections address the alternative treatments.

Counterparty Has Choice of Settlement

When the issuer of an equity instrument has granted the recipient the right to choose cash or equity as payment, this is essentially a compound financial instrument that contains debt (i.e., the right to receive cash) and equity components. The accounting for this situation is:

- *Parties other than employees.* When such a compound financial instrument is issued to an entity other than an employee, and when the fair value of the goods or services provided can be measured directly, the proper measurement is to subtract the fair value of the debt component from the fair value of the goods or services received, to arrive at the value of the equity component.
- *Transactions with employees.* When such a compound financial instrument is issued to an employee, separately measure the fair values of the debt component and the equity component. The fair value of the instrument is the combined fair values of these two elements.

When the instrument is eventually settled, the liability portion of the compound financial instrument is to be remeasured to its fair value. The accounting then varies, depending on the manner of payment:

- *Paid with equity.* If the transaction results in only equity instruments being issued to the recipient, the liability is then shifted into equity, and is considered to be the consideration paid for the equity instruments issued.
- *Paid with cash.* If the transaction results in only cash being paid in settlement, the cash payment settles the full amount of the liability. If there was an equity component to the transaction that had already been recognized in equity, there is no change to its previous recognition.

EXAMPLE

Subterranean Access buys drilling equipment for £300,000 on March 31. The supplier has the option of being paid with either 50,000 Subterranean shares on December 31 or a cash payment in one month that will equal the market price on that date of 40,000 shares. The company's controller estimates that the end-of-year option has a fair value of £375,000 and the one-month option has a fair value of £275,000.

When Subterranean receives the drilling equipment, the controller should debit the fixed asset account for £300,000, credit a liability account for £275,000 (which represents the cash option) and credit equity for £25,000. The £25,000 portion of the entry represents the difference between the price of the drilling equipment and the fair value of the associated liability.

Issuer Has Choice of Settlement

If the issuing entity can choose whether to pay in stock or cash, it must decide whether there is a current obligation to pay in cash. This is the case when the use of equity instruments is impossible (such as when there is no authorization to issue additional shares), there is a corporate policy to pay in cash, past practice has been to always settle in cash, or to settle in cash when requested to by the counterparty. If there is a current obligation to pay in cash, account for the transaction as a cash-settled share-based payment. When a cash payment is made, treat it as a deduction from equity.

If there is no obligation to pay in cash, account for the transaction as an equity-settled share-based payment. When an equity payment is made, no further accounting is required, beyond the initial recognition of the payment on the date of grant.

When the issuing entity can choose between modes of payment, the usual alternative is to pick the choice having the lower fair value. If the entity instead elects to pay using the choice that has the higher fair value, charge the difference in the fair values of the choices to expense as of the settlement date.

Share-based Payment Disclosures

When a business is involved in share-based payment arrangements, it should disclose the following information in the notes accompanying its financial statements:

- *Descriptions.* Describe each type of share-based payment arrangement in use during the period, including their terms, vesting requirements, maximum option term, and whether settlement is in cash or equity. This information can be aggregated for similar types of arrangements.
- *Option information.* Describe the number and weighted average exercise prices for options outstanding at the beginning of the reporting period, as well as separately for those options granted, forfeited, exercised, and expired during the period, and separately for those options outstanding at the end of the period, and exercisable at the end of the period.
- *Exercised options.* If options were exercised during the period, disclose the weighted average share price on the exercise date. This information can instead be a weighted average share price during the period, if options were exercised several times during the period.

- *Options outstanding.* For those options remaining outstanding at the end of the period, note the range of exercise prices and the weighted average contractual life remaining.

In those cases where the entity derived the fair value of goods or services received, or of equity instruments issued, provide the following information about fair values:
- *Share options.* If share options were granted, disclose the weighted average fair value of these options as of the measurement date, plus the option pricing model used and the inputs to that model, how expected volatility was determined and the extent to which it was based on historical volatility information, and how other option features were incorporated into the fair value measurement.
- *Other equity instruments.* If equity instruments other than share options were granted during the period, disclose the number and weighted average fair value of these items as of the measurement date, how fair value was determined, how expected dividends were incorporated into the fair value calculation, and how other instrument features were incorporated into the fair value measurement.
- *Modified arrangements.* If a share-based payment was modified during the period, explain the modifications, note the incremental change in fair value resulting from the modifications, and disclose how the incremental change in fair value was determined.

It may also be necessary to disclose the following information:
- *Fair value measurement.* If the fair values of goods or services received were used to value share-based payments, disclose how the fair values were determined. If it was not possible to derive the fair values of goods or services, state this point and why it was not possible to do so.
- *Expenses.* Disclose the total expense derived from share-based payment transactions in which the goods or services received were immediately charged to expense. Separately disclose that part of the expense arising from equity-settled share-based payments.
- *Liabilities.* Note the total carrying amount of liabilities derived from share-based payment transactions at the end of the period, as well as the total end-of-period intrinsic value of those liabilities for which the counterparty's rights have vested.

Summary

The accounting for share-based payments does not have to be especially difficult, as long as each one is properly documented and follows a standard payment approach, such as always paying with shares and never allowing the option for a cash payment. However, if the terms of each share-based payment differ, it can represent an accounting nightmare, where the accounting staff has to research the proper accounting for each individual transaction and then track them all separately.

Consequently, it is best to adopt just one or two standard forms of share-based payment, and apply them consistently to all such arrangements. Ideally, there should be no more than one share-based arrangement for payments made to employees, and one for payments made to outsiders.

Chapter 23
Income Taxes

Introduction

The accounting for income taxes can be among the more complex accounting topics, since it deals with both the current and future tax consequences of converting existing assets into cash, and the eventual settlement of existing liabilities. Depending on these expected outcomes, a business may need to recognize either a deferred tax liability or asset. Since the expectations for the values at which assets and liabilities will eventually be converted to cash or settled are always changing, this means that the estimated amounts of future taxes will also likely change on an ongoing basis.

Most of the discussion in this chapter focuses on the proper accounting treatment of current and deferred tax liabilities and assets, though we also address income tax presentation and disclosure topics.

IFRS Source Documents

- IAS 12, *Income Taxes*
- SIC 25, *Income Taxes – Changes in the Tax Status of an Entity or its Shareholders*

The Tax Base Concept

A central concept of income tax accounting is the *tax base*. This is the amount attributed to an asset or liability for tax purposes, and which will be deductible for tax purposes against any revenues generated from use of the asset or liability.

EXAMPLE

Nova Corporation acquired a grinding machine several years ago for £80,000. For tax purposes, Nova has already charged £20,000 of this cost to depreciation. The tax base of the machine is therefore £60,000. The telescope mirrors that will be produced with the grinding machine will generate taxable revenue. This tax base will continue to decline over time as Nova continues to depreciate the machine, and charge the depreciation expense against future revenue.

EXAMPLE

Finchley Fireworks recognizes accrued expenses of £12,000. Since Finchley reports its taxable results using the cash basis of accounting, the accrued expenses have no tax base. If

Finchley were to instead report its taxable results using the accrual basis of accounting, the accrued expenses would have a tax base of £12,000.

Here are several variations on the tax base concept:
- *Customer prepayments.* If revenue is received in advance, it is initially recorded as a liability. The tax base of this liability is its carrying amount, minus any revenue that will not be taxable in later periods.
- *Not recognized.* Depending on the tax jurisdiction, some assets and liabilities have a tax base, but are not recognized under IFRS as being assets or liabilities. For example, a jurisdiction may require that research and development costs be recognized as an asset for tax purposes, but are charged to expense as incurred under IFRS. This delay in the recognition of expense for tax purposes is considered a deferred tax asset.

Differences between the tax base and carrying amount of assets and liabilities are set by tax law, and usually only apply to a relatively small number of balance sheet line items. In all other cases, the tax base and carrying amount of an asset or liability should be identical.

Current Tax Liabilities and Assets

When there is a tax liability due in the current period, a business must charge it to expense and either record an offsetting liability or pay the amount of the liability. If the business pays an amount that exceeds its current tax liability, it recognizes the overage as an asset.

When there is a benefit related to a tax loss in the current period, and that amount can be carried back to recover a tax already recognized in a previous period, a business should recognize the benefit as an asset.

Deferred Tax Liabilities and Assets

There are many cases in which a business may incur a tax obligation that will not be paid until a later period, or a potential reduction of a tax obligation that also cannot be utilized until a later period. These situations result in deferred tax liabilities and deferred tax assets, respectively. The following general principles apply to deferred tax liabilities and assets:
- *Tax rates.* A deferred tax asset or liability is measured at the tax rates expected to apply to the business in the period when they are eventually used, based on tax rates that have already been enacted or announced.
- *Discounting.* Despite the fact that deferred tax liabilities and assets may persist over many years, they are not to be discounted to their present values. The reason for not doing so is that it would be very difficult to determine when these items will actually be used or settled, which increases the risk of deriving an incorrect present value.

- *Review*. The carrying amounts of all deferred tax assets must be reviewed at the end of each reporting period, and reduced to the extent that it is no longer probable that sufficient taxable profit will be available to offset them. These reductions can be reversed at a later date if the expected amount of taxable income increases again.

Taxable Temporary Differences

A taxable temporary difference is a difference between the tax base and carrying amount of an asset or liability that will result in taxable amounts in future periods. Eventually, the difference between the tax base and carrying amount will disappear as the related asset or liability is consumed; hence the concept that these taxable differences are "temporary." In short, the passage of time eventually eliminates all taxable temporary differences. Examples of situations in which taxable temporary differences arise are:

- A tax jurisdiction allows interest income to be recognized when the related cash amount is received. Since the cash amount is always received after month-end, and the affected business always accrues the income in advance of receipt, there is a deferred tax liability associated with the late recognition of interest income.

- Many tax jurisdictions allow companies to use accelerated depreciation methods for tax reporting purposes. If these companies use a less aggressive depreciation approach for their internal record keeping, such as the straight-line method, this delays the recognition of taxable income, which is a deferred tax liability.

- Certain aspects of IFRS allow a business to revalue its assets to their fair values. Tax jurisdictions may not allow this revaluation to carry over for tax reporting purposes, which results in a temporary difference that may be a deferred tax asset or deferred tax liability, depending upon whether an asset is revalued upward or downward.

- Under the equity method of accounting, the carrying amount of a parent company's investment in another entity will vary over time, while the tax base for that investment may not change. The result is a temporary difference that may be a deferred tax asset or deferred tax liability, depending upon changes in the recorded value of the investment.

- When an acquirer takes over another business, the acquirer can generally record the acquired assets and liabilities at their fair values. However, the applicable tax jurisdiction may require that the tax base of the previous owner be carried forward for these assets, resulting in a tax difference.

- An acquirer may record a goodwill asset in relation to a business combination, in an amount matching the difference between the compensation paid and the fair value of all assets and liabilities acquired. Many tax jurisdictions do not allow the recognition of any reduction in goodwill as a tax-deductible expense, even though such reductions will reduce accounting profits. In these jurisdictions, then, goodwill has a mandatory tax base of zero, which will yield a temporary difference for as long as the acquirer maintains the goodwill asset in its accounting records.

The general rule for taxable temporary differences is to recognize a deferred tax liability for the tax that must be paid in future periods, except when the liability comes from the initial recognition of:

- Goodwill; or
- A transaction that is not a business combination and does not affect accounting or taxable profit.

EXAMPLE

Nova Corporation's tax advisor points out that it is permissible to use accelerated depreciation for tax purposes on a new vacuum deposition machine for its mirror operations. The company elects to use straight-line depreciation in order to calculate its accounting profit in each period. The difference in depreciation methods results in a taxable temporary difference, which will disappear when the asset has been fully depreciated.

EXAMPLE

Finchley Fireworks reports its taxable results using the cash basis of accounting. For tax purposes, the company deducts the monthly rent on its headquarters building from revenues as soon as it pays the rent. Since the rent is paid in advance, the company records this payment as a prepaid expense for its own internal record keeping. Given these two differences in treating the transaction, a taxable temporary difference arises, which will disappear once Finchley charges the rent to expense on its own books.

EXAMPLE

Hammer Industries acquires a small regional competitor, and recognizes £2,000,000 of goodwill as a result of the transaction. The tax jurisdiction in which Hammer is located permits the amortization of goodwill over a 20-year period on a straight-line basis. This means that the tax basis of the goodwill asset declines by 5% per year, which is £100,000. After one year, and assuming no goodwill impairment, this means there is a taxable temporary difference of £100,000, for which Hammer can recognize a deferred tax liability.

EXAMPLE

The Subterranean Access drilling company has a drilling rig that originally cost £200,000, and which now has a carrying amount of £120,000, due to £80,000 of straight-line depreciation that has been recorded since the asset was acquired.

Thus far, the company has used accelerated depreciation to record taxable depreciation on the drilling rig of £160,000, leaving a tax base of £40,000.

The company's income tax rate is 35%. The difference between the £120,000 carrying amount and the £40,000 tax base is a taxable temporary difference of £80,000. Based on this difference and the tax rate, Subterranean Access recognizes a deferred tax liability of

£28,000 (calculated as £80,000 taxable temporary difference × 35% tax rate). The deferred tax liability is the delayed amount of income taxes that the company must eventually recognize over the remaining depreciable life of the drilling rig.

EXAMPLE

Nova Corporation revalues a class of its fixed assets, resulting in an increase in their values of £500,000, from a carrying amount of £20,000,000 to a new amount of £20,500,000. The tax base of these assets is £18,500,000. Nova's tax rate is 35%. There had been a deferred tax liability of £525,000 prior to the revaluation (calculated as the £1,500,000 difference between the tax base and the old carrying amount, multiplied by the 35% tax rate). This amount now increases by £175,000 to reflect the £500,000 increase in carrying amount, multiplied by the 35% tax rate.

Deductible Temporary Differences

A deductible temporary difference is a difference between the tax base and carrying amount of an asset or liability that will result in deductible amounts in future periods. For example, a deductible temporary difference arises when the tax base of an asset is greater than its carrying amount, which means that a larger tax benefit exists than would otherwise be indicated by the carrying amount. Eventually, the difference between the tax base and carrying amount will disappear as the related asset or liability is consumed. Thus, the passage of time will result in the elimination of all deductible temporary differences. Examples of situations in which deductible temporary differences arise are:

- A company may charge pension costs to expense as employees complete the service periods mandated by vesting requirements. However, tax jurisdictions may not allow these expenses until the pension benefits are actually paid out to employees, which may not be until many years have passed. During the intervening period, the company has a deferred tax asset.
- A company may charge research costs to expense as incurred, but a tax jurisdiction may require that these costs be capitalized and then amortized over time. If so, the company has a deferred tax asset until the amortization period is complete.
- An acquirer may buy another business and record the assets and liabilities of that business at their fair values. If the fair value of an asset is lower than its existing tax base, the difference is a deferred tax asset.
- Certain aspects of IFRS allow a business to revalue its assets to their fair values. Tax jurisdictions may not allow this revaluation to carry over for tax reporting purposes, which results in a temporary difference that may be a deferred tax asset or deferred tax liability, depending upon whether an asset is revalued upward or downward.

The general rule for deductible temporary differences is to recognize a deferred tax asset to the extent that it is probable that the difference can be utilized against taxable profits. Thus, if there is no probability of having taxable profits, deductible temporary differences should not be recognized. However, it is possible to recognize a deferred tax asset to the extent there will be sufficient offsetting taxable profit relating to the same tax jurisdiction and the same taxable entity. A deferred tax asset can also be recognized to the extent that the company can use tax planning opportunities to create taxable profits in the future. A *tax planning opportunity* is an action that a business can take to increase its taxable income in order to take advantage of a tax loss or tax credit carryforward that would otherwise expire. For example, a company could sell an investment in a municipal bond (for which there is no taxable income) and use the proceeds to buy a corporate bond (for which the interest income is taxable).

EXAMPLE

The standard accounting policy for Nova Corporation is to recognize a warranty expense with each of the telescopes that it ships, which is primarily related to the possible failure of the mechanical components of its motor drives. However, the tax jurisdiction in which Nova resides does not allow the warranty cost to be charged to expense until actual warranty claims are paid out. In the most recent reporting period, Nova recognizes a warranty expense of £20,000, for which there is a tax base of zero. The difference is a deductible temporary difference. Assuming a 35% tax rate, Nova should recognize a deductible temporary tax of £7,000, though only if it is probable that the company will earn a sufficient amount of taxable profits in later periods to offset this tax asset.

EXAMPLE

In the current period, Nova Corporation reports an accounting profit of £150,000. In addition, it has £20,000 of taxable temporary differences and £12,000 of deductible temporary differences. Its taxable income is calculated as:

Accounting profit	+	£150,000
Taxable temporary differences	-	20,000
Deductible temporary differences	+	12,000
Taxable profit	=	£142,000

EXAMPLE

At the end of its most recent reporting period, Hammer Industries has the following asset and liability balances in its accounting and tax records:

(000s)	Carrying Amount	Tax Base	Temporary Difference
Cash	£1,900	£1,900	£0
Accounts receivable	6,700	7,000	-300
Inventory	4,800	5,000	-200
Fixed assets	14,700	7,700	7,000
Accounts payable	3,400	3,400	0
	£31,500	£25,000	£6,500

The differences in the table for accounts receivable and inventory are caused by the recognition by Hammer of a £300,000 bad debt reserve against accounts receivable and an inventory obsolescence reserve of £200,000, neither of which are allowed for tax purposes. The £7,000,000 difference between the carrying amount and the tax base of the fixed assets is caused by the company's use of accelerated depreciation for tax purposes and straight-line depreciation for the calculation of its accounting profit.

Given the company's 35% tax rate, Hammer records a deferred tax provision of £2,275,000 (calculated as the total temporary difference of £6,500,000 × 35% tax rate).

Unused Tax Losses and Tax Credits

A deferred tax asset related to unused tax losses and unused tax credits is only recognized to the extent that sufficient future taxable income will be generated to offset the tax asset. Since the existence of unused tax losses strongly implies recent company losses, it is quite possible that there is not a near-term expectation for future taxable income, so it may not be possible to recognize this type of deferred tax asset at all. The existence of convincing evidence of future taxable income is sufficient evidence to recognize a deferred tax asset, though the nature of the evidence must be disclosed in a company's financial statements.

When determining whether there will be sufficient future taxable income available to warrant the recognition of a deferred tax asset, consider the following points:

- The probability of generating taxable profits prior to the expiration of the tax asset
- The sufficiency of taxable temporary differences related to the same tax jurisdiction
- Whether tax planning opportunities are available
- Whether the prior tax losses were caused by issues that are unlikely to arise again

Reassessment of Unrecognized Deferred Tax Assets

In each reporting period, reassess all deferred tax assets that have not yet been recognized. It is allowable to recognize these deferred tax assets to the extent that it now appears probable that future taxable profits will offset them. However, once an unrecognized tax asset expires, it is withdrawn from consideration for recognition in a future period.

Investments in Other Entities

When a business initially records an investment in subsidiaries, branches, associates, or joint arrangements, the entry is usually at cost, which will also be the initial tax base. Over time, the carrying amount of this investment may change, due to the business' share of any undistributed profits, or a write-down in the carrying amount of an investment to its recoverable amount. Also, when there is a foreign subsidiary, exchange rate changes can result in a difference between the carrying amount and tax base of an investment.

When there is a difference between the carrying amount and tax base of these types of investments, an entity should recognize a deferred tax liability, unless the entity can control the timing of when the temporary difference is reversed, and it is not probable that the difference will reverse in the foreseeable future.

A deferred tax asset should only be recognized on the difference between the carrying amount and tax base of these types of investments when it is probable that the underlying temporary differences will reverse in the foreseeable future, and there will be a sufficient amount of taxable profit against which the temporary difference can be offset.

Tax Rates

A business may be subject to a graduated income tax rate, and generates a sufficient amount of income to be subject to several levels of this tax structure. For example, a tax jurisdiction may charge a 10% income tax on the first £1,000,000 of profits, and a 30% tax on all additional profits. In this situation, a business should derive an expected average tax rate, and use it to derive the amount of deferred tax assets and liabilities.

In some tax jurisdictions, the income tax rate may change if some portion of earnings is paid out to shareholders in the form of dividends. In this situation, the amount at which deferred tax assets and liabilities are recognized is based on the tax rate that applies to undistributed profits.

EXAMPLE

The government of Azorbistan encourages companies located within its boundaries to distribute their profits to shareholders by taxing undistributed earnings at a 60% tax rate. The tax rate on distributed profits is only 20%. In its year-end financial statements, Azor Mining Corporation makes no mention of dividends declared, and recognizes 100,000 Azorbian pounds in profits. Accordingly, the company recognizes a current tax liability and tax expense of 60,000 pounds.

At the next board meeting in the following year, the board of directors of Azor declares an 80,000 pound dividend, which allows the company to declare a 32,000 pound reduction of its income tax expense, along with a current tax asset in the same amount. The 32,000 pound income tax reversal is calculated as:

$$\text{(60\% Tax on undistributed earnings} - \text{20\% Tax on distributed earnings)}$$
$$\times \text{80,000 Pound dividend}$$
$$= \text{32,000 Pounds}$$

When an asset is sold or a liability is settled, the local tax jurisdiction may apply a different income tax rate to the transaction, depending upon the type of transaction. For example, selling an asset may trigger an asset sale tax that varies from the standard income tax rate. When this is the case, measure deferred tax assets and liabilities at the tax rates that you currently expect to apply when the underlying assets are recovered or the liabilities are settled.

EXAMPLE

Sharper Designs owns a ceramic extruder that it uses to create high-end ceramic knives for professional chefs. The extruder currently has a carrying amount of £150,000 and a tax base of £90,000. Sharper Designs will incur a tax rate of 15% if it sells the extruder. The company is currently charged an incremental tax rate of 35% on its operating income.

Given the differing tax rates, the company has two choices. It can:
- Sell the extruder now and recognize a deferred tax liability of £9,000 (calculated as £60,000 differential ×15% tax rate)
- Continue to use the extruder and recognize a deferred tax liability of £21,000 (calculated as £60,000 differential × 35% tax rate)

Current and Deferred Tax Recognition

The general rule for the recognition of income taxes is that both current and deferred taxes are recognized in profit or loss for the current period, except to the extent that the tax is caused by a business combination, or the underlying event appears in other comprehensive income or directly in equity. To be more specific about the exceptions:
- *Other comprehensive income items.* Income taxes appear in other comprehensive income if the underlying transaction also appears in other comprehensive income. For example, a fixed asset revaluation or foreign exchange differences due to the translation of financial statements both appear in other comprehensive income, along with their tax effects.
- *Equity items.* IFRS allows the effects of a small number of items to be charged directly to equity, such as retrospective changes to accounting policies. When this happens, the related tax effect is also recorded in equity.
- *Business combination.* When there is a business combination, some elements of the transaction may include tax issues such as those just noted for other comprehensive income or equity items, and which therefore call for recognition outside of profit or loss.

Additional tax recognition issues are:
- *Acquired deferred tax assets.* An acquirer may obtain tax loss carryforwards or other types of deferred tax assets from an acquiree. The circumstances may not dictate that these assets be recognized separately as part of the business combination. However, if new information about the facts and circumstances that existed at the acquisition date causes these assets to be recognized, use them to reduce the amount of goodwill generated by the

acquisition. If there is no goodwill, recognize these tax assets in profit or loss.

- *Dividend withholding.* Depending on the tax jurisdiction, a business may be required to pay a portion of the dividends issued to shareholders to the tax authorities, which is considered a withholding on behalf of the shareholders. The business acts as the agent of the tax authorities when it remits the withheld amount. The company should charge the amount of the withholding to equity, as a part of the dividends paid.

- *Share-based payments.* A business may issue share-based payments to its employees. The business may recognize the expense associated with the employee services received in exchange for these payments, though some tax jurisdictions only allow a tax deduction when the related share options are exercised. This timing difference in recognition of the expense for tax purposes creates a deferred tax asset. If the tax jurisdiction only permits a deduction based on a future share price at which an option will be exercised, estimate the deduction based on the company's share price at the end of the reporting period.

- *Tax asset recoverability.* If there is a subsequent judgment that a tax asset is not as recoverable as previously expected (since there may be no offsetting future profits), it will be necessary to derecognize the asset. When these types of changes occur, they are recognized in profit or loss. This situation can arise as part of a business combination, when the combined results of the merged entities may alter expected future profits to a sufficient extent to trigger the recognition or derecognition of a tax asset.

- *Tax rate changes.* A deferred tax asset or liability may have initially been established based on the existence of a certain tax rate. If that rate changes, so too must the related tax asset or liability.

Changes in Tax Status

There may be an alteration in the tax status of a business, perhaps because its legal form of incorporation has changed, or it is now publicly held, or because the parent entity has moved to a different country. When these types of changes occur, it may result in a change in the taxes applied to the business; tax rates may change, or perhaps the business will no longer qualify for tax incentives, or maybe it will qualify for new tax incentives.

When there is a change in tax status, both the current and deferred tax consequences of the change should be recognized in profit or loss in the period when the change occurs. If the tax status change relates to items that are recognized in equity, recognize the associated tax effects in equity. If the tax status change relates to items that are recognized in other comprehensive income, recognize the associated tax effects in other comprehensive income.

Income Tax Presentation

Consider the following points when presenting information about income taxes in the financial statements:

- *Current tax offsets.* It is only allowable to offset current tax assets and liabilities when a business has a legal right to actually set off the recognized amounts, and intends to either settle the amounts on a net basis or realize the asset and settle the liability simultaneously. A legal right to set off tax assets and liabilities usually only arises when both relate to taxes levied by the same tax jurisdiction.
- *Deferred tax offsets.* It is only allowable to offset deferred tax assets and liabilities when a business has a legal right to actually set off the recognized amounts, and the deferred items relate to taxes levied by the same tax jurisdiction on either the same entity, or on different entities that plan to settle the amounts on a net basis or realize the asset and settle the liability simultaneously in those periods when they come due.

In addition, the tax expense related to the profit or loss from ordinary activities is to be presented as part of profit or loss.

Income Tax Disclosures

There are a number of disclosures required for income taxes, which are as follows:

- *General.* The major elements of tax expense must be disclosed separately. The elements requiring separate disclosure include:
    - The current tax expense
    - Tax adjustments recognized in the period for the current tax of prior periods
    - The amount of deferred tax expense related to the creation or reversal of temporary differences
    - The amount of deferred tax expense related to changes in tax rates or new taxes
    - The benefit from a previously unrecognized tax loss, credit, or temporary difference in a prior period that offsets a current tax expense, or separately to reduce a deferred tax expense
    - A deferred tax expense caused by the write-down of a deferred tax asset or the reversal of its write-down
    - The amount of tax expense associated with changes in accounting policies or accounting errors that are not accounted for retrospectively
- *Equity-related.* The aggregate amount of all current and deferred taxes relating to items that were charged directly to equity.
- *OCI-related.* The amount of income tax related to each component of other comprehensive income.

- *Reconciliation.* A discussion of the relationship between income taxes and accounting profit. This can be in the form of a reconciliation of the tax expense to the accounting profit multiplied by the applicable tax rate, or a reconciliation of the average effective tax rate and the applicable tax rate. In either case, describe the basis on which the applicable tax rate is computed. The average effective tax rate is the tax expense divided by the accounting profit.
- *Rate change.* The reasons for any changes in the applicable tax rate from the previous reporting period.
- *Deductible temporary differences.* The amount of any deductible temporary differences, unused tax losses, and unused tax credits for which there is no recognition of a deferred tax asset, as well as any expiration dates.
- *Temporary differences.* The aggregate amount of any temporary differences related to investments in subsidiaries, associates, and joint arrangements, where deferred tax liabilities have not been recognized.
- *Balance sheet presentation.* The amount of deferred tax assets and liabilities for each type of temporary difference, unused tax loss, and unused tax credit that appears in the balance sheet.
- *Income statement presentation.* The amount of deferred income taxes recognized in profit or loss for each type of temporary difference, unused tax loss, and unused tax credit that is recognized in the income statement.
- *Discontinued operations.* The tax expense related to the gain or loss on discontinued operations, and the tax expense related to the ordinary activities of these operations.
- *Dividend consequences.* The amount of income tax consequences related to any dividends that were declared prior to financial statement issuance, but for which there is no liability in the financial statements.
- *Pre-acquisition asset change.* The amount of any change in a pre-acquisition deferred tax asset that is caused by a business combination.
- *Post-acquisition asset change.* If deferred tax benefits are not recognized as part of a business combination, but are recognized at a later date, describe what caused the benefits to be recognized.
- *Unusual tax asset recognition.* The amount of any deferred tax asset and the reason for its recognition when using it is dependent on unusually large future taxable profits, and the entity has recognized a loss in the current or preceding period.
- *Dividend consequences.* The income tax consequences resulting from the payment of dividends to shareholders, where doing so alters the income tax rate paid. Note the tax consequences that are practicably determinable, and whether there are any tax consequences that are not practicably determinable.

EXAMPLE

Selected sample disclosures are:

Major components of tax expense (000s)

Current tax expense	£1,820
Deferred tax expense relating to the origination and reversal of temporary differences	170
Deferred tax expense resulting from reduction in tax rate	360
Tax expense	£2,350

Income tax relating to other comprehensive income (000s)

Deferred tax relating to revaluation of fixed assets	£490

Explanation of relationship between tax expense and accounting profit (000s)

Accounting profit	£6,170
Tax at the 35% applicable rate	£2,160
Tax effect of expenses that are not deductible in calculating taxable profit:	
Government fines	620
Charitable giving	170
Tax expense	£2,950

Summary

From the perspective of efficient accounting, it is generally best to avoid recognizing deferred tax assets if there is even a reasonable chance that the offsetting amount of taxable profits will not be generated in the near future. This choice will be particularly easy to make when there is a history of minimal profits, or profits that swing in such a random manner that they are essentially impossible to predict.

The typical accountant usually remembers to recognize income taxes at the end of each reporting period. What is not so readily remembered is that there may also be tax effects associated with transactions that are recognized in other comprehensive income or directly in equity, and for which tax effects must also be recognized. It is useful to include this point in the closing procedures for each reporting period.

Chapter 24
Business Combinations

Introduction

When one entity purchases another entity, it is referred to as a business combination. In a business combination, the acquirer must integrate the financial statements of the acquiree into its own financial statements, which can be a complex process. IFRS contains specific rules for doing so, with the intent of bringing some standardization to the process. In this chapter, we address the accounting for and disclosure of a business combination.

IFRS Source Document

- IFRS 3, *Business Combinations*

The Acquisition Method

When a business combination is completed, the acquirer must ensure that it properly identifies, measures, and recognizes all of the assets and liabilities of the acquiree, as well as any non-controlling interest in the acquiree, and any goodwill arising from the acquisition. This process, which is called the *acquisition method*, can be a complex process. Accordingly, we break it down in the following sub-sections to address each aspect of the method separately. The sub-sections are stated in the approximate order of the work flow that one would follow to account for a business combination.

Identification of a Business Combination

Before accounting for a business combination, it is first necessary to determine if a business combination has occurred. A business combination has only occurred if a business has been acquired. If not, a transaction is instead accounted for as a purchase of assets.

In essence, a business is defined as an entity that uses its own processes to transform inputs into outputs. Thus, the acquisition of a group of machines from another company is probably not a business combination, since none of these elements are present. The acquisition of a startup company can be more difficult to classify as a business combination, for it may not yet contain many processes, and not yet have any outputs. In marginal situations where it is not clear that a business is being acquired, look for the following signs that indicate business operations:
- The entity has at least begun planning its primary activities
- The entity has employees and/or intellectual property that could be used to transform inputs

- The entity is implementing a plan to generate outputs
- The entity can access customers capable of purchasing its outputs

Usually, the presence of a business is clear; the most difficult recognition situations arise when a business is so new at the point of acquisition that it has not yet begun those activities normally found in a business operation.

Identify the Acquirer

The entity that gains control of the other entity is considered the acquirer. This is not always clear, especially in reverse acquisition situations where a privately-held business is rolling itself into a publicly-held shell company. Indicators of the acquirer are:

- The acquirer is transferring away cash or accepting liabilities as part of the transaction
- The acquirer issues its equity to the owners of the other party
- The acquirer may be significantly larger than the other entity
- The acquirer pays a premium for the equity interests of the other entity
- The management team of the acquirer dominates the management of the combined entity
- The owners of the acquirer can appoint or remove a majority of the board of directors
- The owners of the acquirer retain the largest share of voting rights

If a new entity is formed as part of a business combination, as arises in a triangular merger, the new entity may not be the acquirer; the acquirer may instead be one of the original entities.

Determine the Acquisition Date

A business combination should be accounted for as of the acquisition date, which is the date on which the acquirer obtains control of the acquiree. This is normally the closing date, which is when the acquirer formally transfers payment to the owners of the acquiree, and takes on the assets and liabilities of the acquiree. However, a separate agreement could initiate control on a different date, so consider all facts to ensure that the correct date is chosen.

Recognize Assets, Liabilities, and Non-controlling Interests

In essence, the key principle underlying the accounting for a business combination is for the acquirer to recognize all assets, liabilities, and non-controlling interests in the acquiree, as of the acquisition date. All assets and liabilities recognized should be at their fair values on the acquisition date. The valuation assigned to non-controlling interests should be at either their values or their proportionate share of the acquiree's recognized net assets.

When a business is acquired, the acquirer essentially starts with a large asset known as goodwill, which represents the net purchase price, and which it wants to whittle down by shifting as much of the asset to individually recognized assets and liabilities as possible. These assets and liabilities are eventually depreciated, amortized, or settled in some other manner, and so are eliminated from the acquirer's balance sheet. Eventually, only goodwill remains on the balance sheet; the acquirer must monitor the goodwill balance over time and possibly write it off as a loss if the underlying acquired business has lost value.

The following points outline the key elements of how the recognition of assets and liabilities is to be achieved:

- *Recognition criteria*. Only assets and liabilities that would normally be recognized under IFRS can be recognized in a business combination.
- *New assets and liabilities*. It is permissible for the acquirer to recognize assets and liabilities that the acquiree had not recognized in the past. For example, the acquirer may recognize a number of intangible assets, such as customer lists and brand names. These situations arise because the acquiree was not allowed under IFRS rules to recognize internally-developed assets. Intangible items are recognized if they can be separated from the acquiree and sold, licensed, or exchanged. Even if an intangible item cannot be transferred away in this manner, it may still qualify as a recognizable intangible item if it exists under a contractual relationship. Examples of intangible assets are:

Broadcast rights	Internet domain names	Noncompetition agreements
Computer software	Lease agreements	Order backlog
Customer lists	Licensing agreements	Patented technology
Customer relationships	Literary works	Pictures
Employment contracts	Motion pictures	Service contracts
Franchise agreements	Musical works	Trademarks

EXAMPLE

Hubble Corporation acquires Aphelion Enterprises. Aphelion sells large telescopes to high-end amateurs throughout the world. Normally, Hubble would classify Aphelion's customer list as a valuable intangible asset, since it could theoretically be sold to a third party. However, Aphelion has signed confidentiality agreements with its clients that prevent it from selling or leasing their contact information. Since there is a restriction on use of the list, Hubble cannot recognize the customer list as an intangible asset.

The Aphelion brand name has been heavily promoted for years, and could potentially be sold to a competing telescope firm. Since the brand is transferable, Hubble could recognize the brand as an intangible asset.

- *Assembled workforce.* Many business combinations involve the acquisition of an assembled workforce, which may appear to be an obvious intangible asset. However, recognition of an assembled workforce is specifically prohibited under IFRS, since it is presumed to be part of the goodwill asset.
- *Contingent liabilities.* If an acquiree has a contingent liability, the acquirer recognizes the liability even if it is not probable that an outflow of resources will be required to settle the liability.
- *Contracts being negotiated.* If contracts with customers are still in the process of being negotiated on the acquisition date, these contracts cannot yet be considered assets, and so cannot be recognized as such by the acquirer. Do not subsequently record these contracts as assets if they are finalized after the acquisition date.
- *Indemnification asset.* The seller may take on the obligation to indemnify the acquirer, based on the outcome of a contingency that was not resolved as of the acquisition date, thereby guaranteeing that the acquirer will not suffer a loss, or that its loss will be capped. The acquirer should recognize an indemnification asset at the same time that it recognizes a loss on an item that is to be indemnified.
- *Operating leases.* Determine whether each operating lease is favorable or unfavorable in relation to current market terms. If the terms of the lease are favorable, recognize an intangible asset. If the terms are unfavorable, recognize a liability.

EXAMPLE

New Centurion Corporation, translator of Latin texts, is acquired by Gaelic Textbooks. New Centurion has been leasing a facility for the past 20 years in a rent-controlled district. The rent agreement cannot be transferred. The rent paid is now seriously below the market rate. Despite the non-transferal clause, Gaelic can recognize the difference between the rent paid and the market rate as an intangible asset, since the asset exists under a contractual relationship.

- *Reacquired rights.* As part of a business combination, an acquirer may reacquire a right that it had previously granted to an acquiree, such as a distribution license or a technology licensing arrangement. A reacquired right is considered a separately-identifiable intangible item. If there is a difference between the terms of the reacquired right and current market transactions, recognize it as a settlement gain or loss.

EXAMPLE

Amblin' Ale acquires Belgium Bottlers, to which Amblin' had formerly granted an exclusive distribution arrangement within Belgium. Amblin' therefore reacquires the distribution rights, which it can recognize as an intangible asset. Amblin' plans to amortize the asset over the remaining term of the original arrangement.

Recognize Goodwill or a Bargain Purchase Gain

After all assets and liabilities have been measured, as just described, the acquirer either recognizes a goodwill asset or a bargain purchase gain. Goodwill is measured as follows:

+	Fair value of consideration paid as of the acquisition date
+	Non-controlling interest in the acquiree
+	Fair value of any prior equity interest in the acquiree held by the acquirer, as of the acquisition date
-	Identifiable assets acquired
+	Identifiable liabilities assumed
=	Goodwill

EXAMPLE

Jefferson Industrial acquires Pathmark Manufacturing for £6,500,000. Jefferson's accounting staff identifies tangible Pathmark assets with a fair value of £5,800,000, intangible assets that it values at £4,000,000, and liabilities of £3,700,000. The goodwill associated with the transaction is therefore derived as follows:

+	Fair value of consideration paid	£6,500,000
+	Liabilities assumed	3,700,000
-	Tangible assets acquired	-5,800,000
-	Intangible assets acquired	-4,000,000
=	Goodwill	£400,000

The amount of consideration paid to the sellers of the acquiree is measured at its fair value on the acquisition date. This fair value measurement applies to all assets paid, liabilities assumed, and equity interests issued by the acquirer. This guidance can potentially apply to many types of consideration paid, such as:

- A business owned by the acquirer
- Cash
- Debt or convertible debt
- The transfer of intellectual property
- Warrants

The fair value of the consideration paid may vary from its carrying amount on the books of the acquirer. If there is a difference, and the consideration is being paid to the owners of the acquiree, the acquirer recognizes a gain or loss in the amount of the difference. However, if the consideration is instead paid to the acquiree entity, and the acquirer then gains control over the acquiree, the acquirer must continue to recognize the consideration paid at its carrying amount; otherwise, the acquirer would be adjusting the basis of its assets by shifting assets internally.

The acquirer may offer contingent consideration to the owners of the acquiree, such as a payment that is based on the subsequent profitability of the acquiree. If so, the acquirer should recognize its best estimate of the fair value of this additional consideration as of the acquisition date. The amount of this consideration may change over time, based on changes arising after the acquisition date. If so, the accounting treatment depends upon the nature of the consideration, as follows:

- *Equity consideration.* If the contingent consideration is paid in equity, the amount of this consideration is not to be remeasured.
- *Other consideration.* If the contingent consideration is paid with some form of asset, remeasure the consideration at each reporting date, and recognize any changes in the fair value of the contingent consideration in profit or loss.

EXAMPLE

EuroDesigns buys Danforth Engineering. Part of the purchase agreement contains a clause under which EuroDesigns will pay Danforth's former owners 50% of the profits of Danforth that are in excess of £200,000 in each of the next three years. Management's best estimate of the total amount of these payments is £800,000, which it recognizes as contingent consideration as of the acquisition date.

The recognition of goodwill is the most common state of affairs. However, it is also possible that an acquirer will pay an amount that is less than the fair values of the assets acquired and liabilities assumed, perhaps due to the seller's need to rush the sale transaction. This is known as a *bargain purchase*. If there is a bargain purchase, the acquirer recognizes a gain in profit or loss as of the acquisition date that is based on the net difference between the consideration paid and the assets and liabilities acquired.

EXAMPLE

The owners of Failsafe Containment have to rush the sale of the business in order to obtain funds for estate taxes, and so agree to a below-market sale to Armadillo Industries for £5,000,000 in cash of a 75% interest in Failsafe. Armadillo hires a valuation firm to analyze the assets and liabilities of Failsafe, and concludes that the fair value of its net assets is £7,000,000 (of which £8,000,000 is assets and £1,000,000 is liabilities), and the fair value of the 25% of Failsafe still retained by its original owners has a fair value of £1,500,000.

Since the fair value of the net assets of Failsafe exceeds the consideration paid and the fair value of the noncontrolling interest in the company, Armadillo must recognize a gain in earnings, which is calculated as follows:

£7,000,000 Net assets - £5,000,000 Consideration - £1,500,000 Noncontrolling interest
= £500,000 Gain on bargain purchase

Armadillo records the transaction with the following entry:

	Debit	Credit
Assets acquired	8,000,000	
Cash		5,000,000
Liabilities assumed		1,000,000
Gain on bargain purchase		500,000
Equity – noncontrolling interest in Failsafe		1,500,000

Additional Acquisition Issues

An acquirer may elect to gain control over an acquiree in stages, by acquiring an initial non-controlling stake and then increasing the percentage over time. This is called a *step acquisition*. The accounting for a step acquisition is to re-measure at fair value the equity interest already held on the date when the acquirer finally gains control over the acquiree. If this measurement results in a change from the existing carrying amount of the investment, the acquirer should recognize the resulting gain or loss. If the acquirer had previously been recognizing changes in the value of its (at that time) non-controlling interest in other comprehensive income, the amount of these changes should be recognized when control is achieved, as though the acquirer had disposed of its prior non-controlling interest.

It is entirely possible that the measurement of an acquisition will not be complete on the acquisition date, since some issues will not be resolved, possibly for a number of months. If so, the acquirer should record provisional amounts as of the acquisition date, and then retrospectively adjust those provisional amounts for any new information obtained about the facts and circumstances in existence on the acquisition date. This may result in the recognition of entirely new assets and liabilities. The offset to changes in provisional amounts is an increase or reduction in the goodwill balance. The period over which these retrospective changes can be made is limited to one year from the acquisition date. Realistically, most applicable information should be available within a few months of the acquisition date.

EXAMPLE

Armadillo Industries acquires Cleveland Container on December 31, 20X3. Armadillo hires an independent appraiser to value Cleveland, but does not expect a valuation report for three months. In the meantime, Armadillo issues its December 31 financial statements with a provisional fair value of £4,500,000 for the acquisition. Three months later, the appraiser reports a valuation of £4,750,000 as of the acquisition date, based on an unexpectedly high valuation for a number of fixed assets.

In Armadillo's March 31 financial statements, it retrospectively adjusts the prior-year information to increase the carrying amount of fixed assets by £250,000, as well as to reduce the amount of goodwill by the same amount.

The participants in a business combination may have been business partners prior to the acquisition. If so, there may be a number of pre-existing arrangements between the parties as of the acquisition date. These arrangements should be kept separate from the acquisition transaction. Doing so can reduce the number of assets and liabilities incorporated into the acquisition transaction.

The acquirer may incur a number of costs as part of an acquisition, such as advisory fees, accounting services, legal advice, valuation services, finder's fees, and the costs of running an acquisitions department. These costs are to be charged to expense as incurred. However, if there are costs associated with issuing debt or equity instruments as part of a business combination, these costs are to be dealt with as described in the Financial Instruments chapter.

Reverse Acquisitions

A reverse acquisition occurs when the legal acquirer is actually the acquiree for accounting purposes. The reverse acquisition concept is most commonly used when a privately-held business buys a public shell company for the purposes of rolling itself into the shell and thereby becoming a publicly-held company. This approach is used to avoid the expense of engaging in an initial public offering.

To conduct a reverse acquisition, the legal acquirer issues its shares to the owners of the legal acquiree (which is the accounting acquirer). The fair value of this consideration is derived from the fair value amount of equity the legal acquiree would have had to issue to the legal acquirer to give the owners of the legal acquirer an equivalent percentage ownership in the combined entity.

When a reverse acquisition occurs, the legal acquiree may have owners who do not choose to exchange their shares in the legal acquiree for shares in the legal acquirer. These owners are considered a noncontrolling interest in the consolidated financial statements of the legal acquirer. The carrying amount of this noncontrolling interest is based on the proportionate interest of the noncontrolling shareholders in the net asset carrying amounts of the legal acquiree prior to the business combination.

EXAMPLE

The management of High Noon Armaments wants to take their company public through a reverse acquisition transaction with a public shell company, Peaceful Pottery. The transaction is completed on January 1, 20X4.

The balance sheets of the two entities on the acquisition date are as follows:

	Peaceful (Legal Acquirer, Accounting Acquiree)	High Noon (Legal Subsidiary, Accounting Acquirer)
Total assets	£100	£8,000
Total liabilities	£0	£4,500
Shareholders' equity		
Retained earnings	10	3,000
Common stock		
100 shares	90	
1,000 shares		500
Total shareholders' equity	100	3,500
Total liabilities and shareholders' equity	£100	£8,000

On January 1, Peaceful issues 0.5 shares in exchange for each share of High Noon. All of High Noon's shareholders exchange their holdings in High Noon for the new Peaceful shares. Thus, Peaceful issues 500 shares in exchange for all of the outstanding shares in High Noon.

The quoted market price of Peaceful shares on January 1 is £10, while the fair value of each common share of High Noon shares is £20. The fair values of Peaceful's few assets and liabilities on January 1 are the same as their carrying amounts.

As a result of the stock issuance to High Noon investors, those investors now own 5/6ths of Peaceful shares, or 83.3% of the total number of shares. To arrive at the same ratio, High Noon would have had to issue 200 shares to the shareholders of Peaceful. Thus, the fair value of the consideration transferred is £4,000 (calculated as 200 shares × £20 fair value per share).

Goodwill for the acquisition is the excess of the consideration transferred over the amount of Peaceful's assets and liabilities, which is £3,900 (calculated as £4,000 consideration - £100 of Peaceful net assets).

Based on the preceding information, the consolidated balance sheet of the two companies immediately following the acquisition transaction is:

	Peaceful	High Noon	Adjustments	Consolidated
Total assets	£100	£8,000	£3,900	£12,000
Total liabilities	£0	£4,500	£--	£4,500
Shareholders' equity				
Retained earnings	10	3,000	-10	3,000
Common stock				
100 shares	90		-90	--
1,000 shares		500		500
600 shares			4,000	4,000
Total shareholders' equity	100	3,500	3,900	7,500
Total liabilities and shareholders' equity	£100	£8,000	£3,900	£12,000

Subsequent Measurement

Once a business combination has been initially recorded, the assets and liabilities are to be accounted for in the normal manner, as required by IFRS for the relevant classifications of items. However, the following exceptions apply:

- *Contingent consideration.* The amount of contingent consideration to be paid may change after the acquisition date, based on events occurring after that date. The obvious example is when an acquiree achieves an earnings target that entitles its former owners to an additional payment. In this situation, the accounting depends upon the type of consideration paid, which is:
  - *Equity payment.* If the consideration is paid in some form of equity, no further accounting is necessary.
  - *Other payment.* If the consideration is not in equity (a cash payment or a change in the amount of debt payable is typical), record the change at its fair value, which triggers the recognition of a gain or loss.
- *Indemnification assets.* If an indemnification asset is recorded, management should evaluate it in each reporting period to see if it is still collectible, and adjust its recorded amount accordingly.
- *Reacquired rights.* When an acquirer reacquires a legal right that it had previously granted to the acquiree when it was an independent entity, the amount of this asset is to be amortized over the remaining term of the original contract with the acquiree. If the acquirer then sells the reacquired right to a third party, the remaining carrying amount of the asset is used as the basis for determining any gain or loss on the sale.

Business Combination Disclosures

When an acquirer completes a business combination, it should disclose sufficient information for users to evaluate the nature and financial effect of a transaction. This applies if the combination occurred either within the reporting period or before the financial statements were authorized for issuance. The following is considered sufficient disclosure:

- *Acquisition costs.* The amount of acquisition costs, the amount charged to expense, and where these items are located in the financial statements. Also note any of these costs not charged to expense, and how they were recognized.
- *Assets and liabilities.* The amounts of each major class of asset acquired and liability assumed.
- *Bargain purchase.* If there was a bargain purchase, note the amount of any gain recognized, and where the gain is located in the financial statements. Also note the reasons why the combination resulted in a gain.
- *Combination in stages.* If a combination was completed in stages, note the fair value on the acquisition date of the interest held in the acquiree immediately prior to the combination, as well as any gain or loss resulting from the remeasurement to fair value, and where this information is located in the financial statements.

EXAMPLE

On June 30, 20X1, Armadillo acquired 20% of the outstanding common stock of High Pressure Designs ("High Pressure"). On March 31, 20X3, Armadillo acquired 45% of the outstanding common stock of High Pressure. The fair value of Armadillo's equity holdings in High Pressure was £3,500,000 at the acquisition date, which represented a £200,000 gain. The gain is recorded in other income in the company's income statement for the quarter ended March 31, 20X3.

- *Consideration.* The total fair value of the consideration paid, as well as by class of consideration, such as cash, liabilities incurred, and equity interests paid. If there is contingent consideration, state the amount recognized, describe the arrangement, and estimate the range of possible payments; if the range cannot be estimated or is unlimited, disclose these points.

EXAMPLE

The contingent consideration arrangement contained within the purchase agreement for Darnley Enterprises is to pay Darnley's former owners 25% of the profits of Darnley that are in excess of £500,000 for the next three years. There is no upper limit on the amount that can be paid. Management estimates that the range of payments will be from £0 to £2,000,000 in each of the three years.

- *Contingent liabilities*. Describe the nature of each obligation and when it may be paid, as well as related uncertainties, and any expected reimbursement. If it is not possible to measure the fair value of a contingent liability, disclose why the measurement cannot be made, and (if possible) an estimate of its financial effect, related uncertainties, and any possible reimbursement.

EXAMPLE

The company has recognized a contingent liability of £150,000 for expected warranty claims on products sold by Darnley in the past 12 months. The bulk of this expenditure is expected to occur in the next three months, and all of it by the end of the fiscal year. No reimbursement of these funds by a third party is expected.

- *Date*. The date of the acquisition.
- *Description*. The name of the acquiree, a description of it, the reasons for the combination, and how the acquirer gained control of it.

EXAMPLE

On February 15, 20X4, Peacock acquired 100% of the outstanding ordinary shares of Green Plumage ("Green") with an all-cash purchase, and obtained control of Green at that time. Green is a provider of exotic animals to zoos throughout the world. As a result of the acquisition, Peacock expects to be the leading provider of leased exotic animals in all markets outside of Asia, and expects to enact a small increase in its leasing rates.

- *Equity interest*. The percent of the acquiree's voting equity acquired.
- *Financial results*. The revenue and profit or loss of the acquiree following the acquisition date that have been included in the statement of comprehensive income, as well as the revenue and profit or loss of the combined entity as though the acquisition had taken place at the beginning of the fiscal year.

EXAMPLE

The revenue included in the consolidated statement of comprehensive income since February 15, 20X4 contributed by Green Plumage ("Green") was £16,300,000. Green also contributed £1,900,000 of profits during the same period. If Green had been consolidated from January 1, 20X4, the consolidated statement of comprehensive income would have included revenue of £17,800,000 and profit of £2,200,000.

- *Goodwill tax deduction*. The amount of goodwill expected to be tax deductible.

- *Goodwill.* The factors that comprise the recognized amount of goodwill, such as planned synergies and assets that do not qualify for separate recognition.

EXAMPLE

The goodwill of £5,000,000 arising from the acquisition of Arbuthnot Distillery consists primarily of the synergies and economies of scale expected from combining the purchasing contracts and distribution operations of the two companies.

- *Non-controlling interest.* If there is a non-controlling interest in the acquiree, disclose the amount of this interest and how it was measured. Also note the valuation method and inputs used to measure each of these interests.

EXAMPLE

The fair value of the non-controlling interest in Darnley Enterprises was estimated by applying a market approach. The fair value measurements are based on significant inputs for similar items, and so represent a fair value measurement categorized within Level 2 of the fair value hierarchy. Key assumptions used in determining the valuation were an adjustment for lack of control of Darnley by the non-controlling interest, and financial multiples of entities considered similar to Darnley.

- *Receivables.* If receivables are being acquired, state their fair value, the gross contractual amount, and the estimated amount of these cash flows that will not be collected. This information should be separated by class of receivable.

EXAMPLE

The fair value of the financial assets acquired includes credit card receivables with a fair value of £3,200,000. The gross amount of these receivables due is £3,650,000, of which £450,000 is expected to be uncollectible.

- *Separate transactions.* A description of any transactions with the acquiree that are reported separately from the business combination, as well as how they were accounted for, the amounts recognized, and where the information is located in the financial statements. If these transactions essentially settle a pre-existing relationship, state how the settlement amount was determined.

If the effect of a business combination is immaterial, but the cumulative effect of several combinations in the same period is material, disclose all of the preceding information in aggregate for the group of business combinations.

If a material business combination is completed after the reporting period but before the financial statements have been authorized for issuance, provide the complete set of disclosures just noted. However, this is not necessary if (as is frequently the case) the accounting for the business combination is not yet complete; if so, note which disclosures could not be made, and why.

If adjustments were recognized in the current period that relate to business combinations that were initially recognized in prior periods, provide sufficient disclosures to evaluate the financial effects of the adjustments. These disclosures shall include:

- *Contingent consideration.* Continue to report changes in the recognized amounts of contingent assets and liabilities, until they are settled. Also note changes in the range of possible outcomes and the reasons for these changes, as well as the valuation methods and inputs used to measure these contingent items.

EXAMPLE

As of year-end, the amount originally recognized for the contingent consideration arrangement with the former owners of Darnley Enterprises had not changed. Management now estimates that the expected upper end of the range of possible contingent payments has declined from £2,000,000 in each of the next three years to no more than £1,200,000 in each of the next three years.

- *Contingent liabilities.* Continue to report changes in the provisions for contingent liabilities until they are settled, including changes in their carrying amounts, provisions added or reversed, expected reimbursements, and a description of the nature of these items, the expected timing of payouts, and the level of uncertainty regarding their timing or amounts.

EXAMPLE

As of year-end, the amount of expected warranty claims has increased by £30,000, for which an additional reserve has been recognized. With four months remaining in the warranty period to which these claims apply, the range of future warranty-related payments is estimated to be between £140,000 and £200,000.

- *Gains and losses.* The amount and nature of any gains or losses recognized that relate to assets or liabilities acquired in a prior business combination, if they are material enough to impact a reader's understanding of the financial statements.

- *Goodwill reconciliation.* Reconcile the beginning and ending carrying amounts of goodwill and accumulated impairment losses, including additional goodwill recognized, adjustments related to the recognition of deferred tax assets, goodwill included in assets designated as held for sale, impairment losses, foreign exchange rate differences, and other changes.
- *Incomplete accounting.* For business combinations where the accounting is incomplete, state the reasons why, the items for which accounting is incomplete, and the nature and amount of any adjustments made in the reporting period.

If the effect of the adjustments for a single business combination is immaterial, but the cumulative effect of the adjustments for several combinations in the same period is material, disclose all of the preceding information for adjustments in aggregate.

Summary

One of the more burdensome aspects of acquisition accounting is the requirement to retrospectively adjust the provisional amounts that were initially recorded as part of a business combination. Retrospective adjustment is to be avoided, since it involves modifying the financial statements of prior periods. To avoid this issue, set a high threshold for materiality when deciding if a retrospective change should be made. Also, delay the reporting of the accounting period in which an acquisition takes place for as long as possible, so that adjustments can be made before the financial statements have been issued.

The accounting for a reverse acquisition is particularly difficult, since it is encountered rarely and involves adjustments that are not usually found in a business combination. It is best to engage the services of a reverse acquisition accounting specialist, to ensure that this transaction is recorded correctly. Otherwise, the consolidated information reported by the public company that arises from such a transaction may require subsequent adjustment, which will be plainly visible to the investment community through the company's public filings of financial information.

Chapter 25
Financial Instruments

Introduction

The discussion of financial instruments occupies more space within IFRS than any other topic, including how financial instruments are to be measured, recognized, presented, and disclosed within the financial statements. Though IFRS professes to limit itself to providing general principles upon which to construct accounting transactions, the treatment of financial instruments verges most closely upon the rules-based guidance used in Generally Accepted Accounting Principles. Accordingly, the discussion of financial instruments in the following sections will appear unusually dense when compared to other IFRS topics.

IFRS Source Documents

- IFRS 7, *Financial Instruments: Disclosures*
- IFRS 9, *Financial Instruments*
- IAS 32, *Financial Instruments: Presentation*
- IAS 39, *Financial Instruments: Recognition and Measurement*

Measurement of Financial Assets and Liabilities

This section covers how to initially measure financial assets and liabilities, as well as how to treat later reclassifications of these items. There is an additional discussion of the measurement of derivatives that are incorporated into other financial instruments.

Initial Measurement

A financial asset or liability is to initially be measured at its fair value, plus or minus any transaction costs associated with the related asset acquisition or liability issuance. The basis of measurement may subsequently change, but the initial measurement is at fair value.

It is also possible to designate an asset as being measured at fair value through profit or loss, which means that all subsequent changes in the fair value of an item are immediately recognized in profit or loss. This option is available if doing so reduces an inconsistency in how an asset is measured, and in certain other circumstances. Once the option is taken, future measurements must also be made at fair value.

Alternatively, a financial asset may be measured at fair value through other comprehensive income, which means that changes in the value of the asset are stated in other comprehensive income, rather than profit or loss. Once the asset is sold, the gain or loss in other comprehensive income is shifted to profit or loss. Such treatment is possible only when the following two conditions are present:

- The related business objective is to hold the asset in order to collect contractual cash flows and to sell the asset; and
- The asset's terms trigger cash flows on certain dates that are comprised of principal and interest.

EXAMPLE

The Close Call Company acquires 1,000 shares of Global Industrial for £50,000 and classifies the shares as at fair value through profit or loss. After one year, the quoted price of the shares declines, reducing their value to £40,000. After an additional year, Close Call sells the shares for £62,000. The related entries are:

	Debit	Credit
Assets at fair value through profit or loss	50,000	
Cash		50,000
To record initial stock purchase		

	Debit	Credit
Loss on decline in asset value	10,000	
Assets at fair value through profit or loss		10,000
To record decline in value after one year		

	Debit	Credit
Cash	62,000	
Assets at fair value through profit or loss		40,000
Gain on sale of assets		22,000
To record sale of stock		

A financial instrument may also be classified as an equity instrument. This is only the case if the instrument contains no obligation to deliver a financial asset to another entity, or to exchange financial assets or liabilities under potentially unfavorable conditions. Also, if the instrument will be settled in the entity's own equity instruments, it either does not require the issuance of a variable amount of the entity's equity instruments, or involves the exchange of a fixed payment for a fixed amount of the entity's equity instruments.

If an investment is in an equity instrument, an entity can make an irrevocable election to present changes in the fair value of that instrument in other comprehensive income. This election is not available if the equity instrument is classified as held for trading. Dividends received on such investments are to be recognized in profit or loss.

The following bullet points denote the rules under which certain financial instruments should be classified:

- *Preference shares.* A preference share would normally be considered an equity instrument. However, if its terms require the issuer to redeem it for a fixed amount, classify it instead as a financial liability.
- *Puttable instruments.* A puttable instrument gives the holder the option to demand payment from the issuer. In most cases, the issuer should classify a puttable instrument as a liability.
- *Derivative with settlement choices.* If the holder of a derivative instrument can choose the form of settlement, the derivative is classified as either a financial asset or liability, unless all settlement choices result in classification as an equity instrument.
- *Compound financial instruments.* If a financial instrument contains elements of both a liability and equity instrument, classify and measure each part separately. This situation is most likely to arise when an instrument creates a financial liability and grants the holder the option to convert the liability into an equity instrument of the issuer (as is the case with a convertible bond). In this case, determine the fair value of the liability component first, and then assign any remaining residual value to the equity instrument.

EXAMPLE

The Close Call Company issues 1,000 convertible bonds that mature in four years, and which have a face value of £1,000 each. The total proceeds garnered by Close Call are therefore £1,000,000. The prevailing market interest rate on the issuance date is 8%.

Close Call measures the liability and equity components of this compound instrument by measuring the liability component first, and assigning the residual amount to the equity component. The present value of the £1,000,000 of bond principal due in four years is £735,030, using the 8% discount rate. Therefore, the equity component of the instrument is assigned the residual value of £264,970.

Subsequent Measurement

Once a financial asset has initially been measured, it must subsequently be measured either at its fair value or amortized cost. This decision is based on a combination of the cash flow characteristics of the asset and the related business model for managing this type of asset. Measurement should be at amortized cost when the company's business model is to hold the asset in order to obtain principal and interest payments. In all other circumstances, a financial asset is measured at its fair value.

EXAMPLE

Capitalist Lending is in the business of acquiring portfolios of loans from banks, and collecting the principal and interest payments on those loans until they have been paid off. Capitalist should measure these loan portfolios at their amortized cost, since it intends to hold the loans until their maturity.

Capitalist Lending also has a division that acquires bundles of home mortgages from lenders and repackages them into securities, which it sells. In this case, Capitalist intends to sell off the mortgages through the securitization vehicle, and so should measure the mortgages at their fair values.

All financial liabilities should be subsequently measured at their amortized cost, with the following exceptions:

- Financial liabilities that are being measured at fair value through profit or loss, such as derivatives.
- Financial liabilities arising from a financial asset transfer that does not qualify for derecognition, because the entity continues to retain the risks and rewards of ownership.
- Financial guarantee contracts, which are measured at the greater of the loss allowance and the amount initially recognized less the cumulative amount of income recognized. The same measurement applies to commitments to provide a loan at a below-market rate.
- Contingent consideration payable by the acquirer in a business combination. Subsequent changes in the fair value of this consideration are recognized in profit or loss.

When measuring financial assets at their amortized cost, the standard measurement technique is the effective interest method (which is described in the following example).

EXAMPLE

Currency Bank purchases a loan that had been issued by another bank, at a stated principal amount of £100,000, which the debtor will repay in three years, with three annual interest payments of £5,000 and a balloon payment of £100,000 upon the maturity date of the loan.

Currency acquired the loan for £90,000, which is a discount of £10,000 from the principal amount of the loan. Based on this information, Currency calculates an effective interest rate of 8.95%, which is shown in the following amortization table:

Year	(A) Beginning Amortized Cost	(B) Interest and Principal Payments	(C) Interest Income (A × 8.95%)	(D) Debt Discount Amortization (C – B)	Ending Amortized Cost (A + D)
1	£90,000	£5,000	£8,055	£3,055	£93,055
2	93,055	5,000	8,328	3,328	96,383
3	96,383	105,000	8,617	3,617	100,000

When the cash flows associated with a financial asset have been modified (perhaps through renegotiation), recalculate the gross carrying amount of the asset, which is considered the present value of the revised cash flows, using the asset's original effective interest rate. This revision will result in the recognition of either a modification gain or loss in profit or loss.

Expected Credit Losses

An organization may anticipate that credit losses related to its financial assets will occur in the future. If so, it should recognize a loss allowance for these expected losses. The amount of this allowance is recognized in other comprehensive income. On each subsequent reporting date, if the credit risk on a financial instrument has not changed significantly, the loss allowance for that item should equal the 12-month expected credit loss. However, if the credit risk has increased significantly, the loss allowance shall instead equate to the lifetime expected credit loss. When there is an adjustment to the amount of expected credit losses, the change is recognized in profit or loss; this is classified as an impairment gain or loss.

The treatment of expected credit losses is somewhat different for trade receivables. As long as the receivables do not contain a significant financing component, the loss allowance should always equate to the lifetime expected credit loss. This approach may still be used when there is a financing component, if mandated by the entity's accounting policy. This approach may also be applied to lease receivables, if mandated by the entity's accounting policy.

The measurement of expected credit losses should involve a probability-weighted analysis of a range of possible outcomes, as well as the time value of money.

Impairment

If there is no reasonable expectation for recovering a financial asset, write off all or a portion of the carrying amount of the asset.

If financial assets are recorded at their amortized costs, periodically assess whether there is objective evidence that these amortized costs are impaired. Objective evidence is considered to be an event or several events in combination that will have a negative impact on the future cash flows associated with a financial asset, and which can be reliably estimated. Objective evidence can arise from any of the following items:

- A borrower will probably have to reorganize or enter bankruptcy. However, a credit rating downgrade is not considered direct evidence of impairment, though it may be when combined with additional information.
- A breach of contract.
- A lender grants a concession to a borrower, due to the financial difficulties of the borrower.
- Financial difficulties are experienced by the parties to a contract.
- There is a measurable decrease in cash flows from a group of financial assets which cannot yet be ascribed to a specific asset within a group, with the change caused by a decline in the payment status of borrowers or a regional economic decline that correlates with defaults on assets.
- There is no longer an active market for a financial asset, due to financial difficulties. Impairment has not necessarily occurred just because the financial instruments issued by a company are no longer publicly traded.

EXAMPLE

There has been an increase in the unemployment rate in the region served by Capitalist Lending, which in turn has driven down property prices on the homes for which Capitalist has issued mortgages. This has resulted in a measurable decrease in the estimated future cash flows from those mortgages. These conditions are objective evidence that the mortgages issued by Capitalist Lending are impaired.

If there is objective evidence of impairment, measure the amount of the impairment as the difference between the carrying amount of an asset and the present value of its future estimated cash flows, using as the discount rate the effective interest rate that was used at the initial recognition of the asset. The impairment can be recorded as either a direct deduction from the account in which the financial asset is recorded, or as an addition to an offsetting allowance account, with the loss recognized in profit or loss.

EXAMPLE

Armadillo Industries invests £100,000 in the bonds of Reliable Corporation. In the next month, Reliable issues its financial results, which indicate that it is experiencing exceptional financial difficulties. These financial statements constitute evidence that Reliable will not be able to pay off the full amount of the debt.

Accordingly, Armadillo records an impairment loss in the amount of its best estimate of what Reliable will not be able to pay back, which is £30,000. The entry to directly reduce the investments account is:

	Debit	Credit
Impairment loss	30,000	
Investments		30,000

If there is no objective evidence of impairment for an individual financial asset, include it in a group of assets having similar credit risk characteristics, and review the entire group to see if there is evidence of impairment. If so, apply the preceding process to calculate the amount of the impairment, and apply it to the group of assets.

If there is a subsequent decline in the amount of an impairment loss, it is allowable to reverse the loss that was recognized in a prior period. The amount of this reversal is limited to what the amortized cost of the asset would have been if the original impairment had not taken place. The entire amount of such reversals should be recognized in profit or loss.

It is also possible to subsequently measure a financial asset at its fair value, with all changes in fair value being recognized at once in profit or loss.

Reclassification

If a financial asset is reclassified, doing so is only as of the reclassification date. There is no prior period restatement of gains, losses, or interest that may have been recognized in a prior period. Reclassifications can be treated in multiple ways, as noted in the following points:

- *From cost basis to fair value through other comprehensive income.* If a reclassification involves beginning to measure a financial asset at its fair value through other comprehensive income that had been measured at its amortized cost, the gain or loss caused by the difference between the amortized cost and the fair value is recognized in other comprehensive income.
- *From cost basis to fair value through profit or loss.* If a reclassification involves beginning to measure a financial asset at its fair value through profit or loss, any gain or loss on the difference between the existing carrying amount of the asset and its fair value is recognized in profit or loss at the reclassification date.
- *From fair value through comprehensive income to cost basis.* If a reclassification involves beginning to measure a financial asset at its amortized cost that had been measured at its fair value through comprehensive income, the existing fair value on the reclassification date becomes the carrying amount of the asset. Any cumulative gain or loss already recognized in other comprehensive income is removed from equity and is netted against the fair value of the asset at the reclassification date.

- ***From*** *fair value through comprehensive income* ***to*** *fair value through profit or loss.* When the reclassification is from fair value through comprehensive income to the fair value through profit or loss, continue to measure the asset at its fair value. In addition, reclassify any cumulative gain or loss in other comprehensive income to profit or loss.
- ***From*** *fair value through profit or loss* ***to*** *cost basis.* If a reclassification involves beginning to measure a financial asset at its amortized cost that had been measured at its fair value through profit or loss, the existing fair value on the reclassification date becomes the carrying amount of the asset.
- ***From*** *value through profit or loss* ***to*** *fair value through comprehensive income.* When the reclassification is from the valuation through profit or loss to the fair value through comprehensive income, continue to measure the asset at its fair value.

Financial liabilities are not to be reclassified.

Embedded Derivatives

An embedded derivative is a combination of a derivative and a non-derivative instrument. The derivative element triggers cash flow changes that may be based on such factors as changes in interest rates, commodity prices, foreign exchange rates, and so forth. A derivative that can be transferred away from a financial instrument is considered to be a separate financial instrument, rather than an embedded derivative. When a derivative is embedded in a financial instrument, apply the usual initial measurement criteria to the combined instrument.

If a derivative is embedded within a contract and the contract is not an asset, it is acceptable to separately account for the derivative if the characteristics of the derivative differ from those of the contract, and the entire contract is not measured at fair value through profit or loss.

EXAMPLE

Capitalist Lending issues a debt instrument to a farming enterprise, in which the interest rate is indexed to changes in the price of a corn index. This arrangement is made because the farm's income is closely tied to the price of corn, and it is better able to pay interest when the price of corn is high. Capitalist should account for the debt and derivative elements of the instrument separately, since the risk inherent in the loan and the embedded derivative are dissimilar.

Gains and Losses

The treatment of gains and losses on financial assets and liabilities depends upon whether they are being recorded at their fair value or carrying amounts. The differences are:

- *Measured at fair value through profit or loss.* A gain or loss on a financial asset or liability that is measured at its fair value through profit or loss is recognized in profit or loss, unless it is part of a hedging transaction.
- *Measured at fair value through other comprehensive income.* When a financial asset is measured at fair value through other comprehensive income, gains and losses are recognized in other comprehensive income. Once the asset is derecognized, this cumulative gain or loss is moved from equity to profit or loss. If the asset is instead reclassified, see the preceding Reclassification sub-section for a description of how to handle any associated gains or losses.
- *Measured at carrying amount.* A gain or loss on a financial asset or liability that is measured at its carrying amount is only recognized in profit or loss when the item is derecognized, or reclassified to be measured at its fair value. Gains or losses are also recognized through the ongoing amortization of these items. A loss on a financial asset may also be recognized if it is impaired.

In addition, if a financial liability is being measured at fair value through profit or loss, any portion of a change in fair value that is associated with a change in credit risk is to be recorded within other comprehensive income, while the remaining portion is presented in profit or loss. If this splitting of recognition would expand an accounting mismatch in profit or loss, ignore the separate treatment of credit risk and instead record the entire amount of the gain or loss in profit or loss.

All gains and losses on loan commitments and financial guarantee contracts that are designated as being at fair value through profit or loss are always presented in profit or loss.

Dividends and Interest

Any interest income and expense associated with financial instruments is to be recorded within profit or loss in the period earned.

Dividends received are to be recorded within profit or loss, but only if there is a right to receive payment, the amount of the payment can be reliably measured, and it is probable that the economic benefits linked to the dividends will flow to the receiving entity.

A dividend distribution is to be offset directly against equity, net of any applicable income tax effect. However, if an equity instrument is classified as a liability, any associated dividend payments are instead classified as interest expense.

If there is a transaction cost associated with an equity transaction (such as registration or legal fees), record it as a deduction from equity, net of any applicable income tax effect. If an equity issuance transaction is abandoned, these transaction costs are instead recognized as expenses. If these costs are associated with a compound instrument that is comprised of equity and other elements, the costs are allocated to the various components of the instrument in a rational and consistent manner, and then accounted for in accordance with the type of instrument to which they are allocated.

Hedging

When an adverse change in the fair value or cash flows of an asset or liability is anticipated, a business may pair a hedging instrument with the underlying asset or liability. The hedging instrument is expected to experience changes in its fair value or cash flows that offset the changes in the underlying asset or liability. Such a pairing establishes a hedging relationship, for which the accounting differs from what would be the case if the two instruments were not linked together as a designated hedge.

EXAMPLE

The Close Call Company has acquired a financial asset for £45,000. Close Call anticipates some variability in the value of the asset, and decides to hedge it to mitigate possible future losses. Accordingly, the CFO enters into a derivative contract and designates it as a hedge of the financial asset. Three months later, Close Call experiences a gain of £6,000 on the financial asset and a loss of £5,000 on the derivative. When combined, these gains and losses sum to a £1,000 gain, which Close Call recognizes in profit or loss.

Hedging Instruments

The following rules apply to the use of hedging instruments in a hedging relationship:

- *External parties.* A hedging instrument must involve an external party. If a hedge were to be set up with an instrument that involves a fellow subsidiary entity, the hedge would be eliminated upon consolidation, and therefore would not qualify for hedge accounting within the consolidated financial statements of the entire group. If a subsidiary is only reporting its own results, such a hedge might still be reportable, as long as the counterparty is not consolidated into the subsidiary.
- *Multiple instruments.* Several derivatives can be combined and treated as a hedging instrument.
- *Derivatives.* A derivative that is measured at fair value through profit or loss can be designated as a hedging instrument, with a few exceptions.
- *Non-derivatives.* A non-derivative financial asset or liability can be designated as a hedging instrument, with a few exceptions.

- *Proportion of hedge*. If only a portion of a hedging instrument is designated as a hedge of a financial asset or liability, hedge accounting applies only to the designated portion.

Hedged Items

Quite an array of items can be hedged. The most common items to be hedged are recognized financial assets and liabilities, though other possibilities are the net amount of an investment in a foreign operation, a highly probable forecast transaction, and an unrecognized firm commitment.

Items can be hedged individually or in groups. Grouped hedging only applies when the items included in a group are managed together on a group basis for risk management purposes.

It is acceptable to hedge only a portion of a financial asset or liability. For example, there may be risks associated with only a portion of the cash flows of a financial asset. However, hedge accounting can only be applied to a portion of a hedged item when the effectiveness of the hedge can be measured.

When there is a grouping of financial assets and financial liabilities, hedge accounting does not apply when the net amount of the group is to be hedged. Hedge accounting can only be applied to a group of financial assets *or* a group of financial liabilities.

Accounting for Hedges

The underlying principle of hedge accounting is to recognize the offsetting effects of changes in the value of a hedging instrument and the hedged item with which it is paired by recognizing the changes at the same time, thereby presenting a reduced net impact in any given reporting period.

A hedging relationship only exists for hedge accounting purposes when all of the following conditions are present:

- *Documentation*. There is a formal, documented designation of a hedging relationship at the inception of the hedge, which includes the risk management objective and the strategy for attaining it, as well as how hedge effectiveness will be measured.
- *Cash flow probability*. For a cash flow hedge (as discussed later) that is a forecast transaction, the transaction must be highly probable and have an exposure to cash flow variations that could impact profit or loss.
- *Measurement reliability*. It is possible to reliably measure the effectiveness of both the hedging instrument and the hedged item.
- *Effectiveness*. The hedge is expected to be highly effective in offsetting the changes in fair value or cash flows associated with the hedged item for all periods for which the hedge is designated. The actual results of the hedge should be within the range of 80% to 125% effectiveness.

EXAMPLE

Capitalist Lending designates a hedging relationship, which results in an actual gain on the hedging instrument of £78,000 and a loss on the related financial asset of £100,000. The offset is 78% (measured as £78,000 gain ÷ £100,000 loss). Since the 78% figure is below the minimum threshold for a highly effective lease, the hedging relationship is considered to *not* be highly effective.

In addition, a hedge must be reviewed on a regular basis, and judged to have been highly effective throughout the hedging period. Hedge accounting should stop when the hedging relationship no longer meets the qualifying criteria.

There are three types of hedging scenarios, each of which requires different accounting. The preceding list of hedging conditions applies to all of them. They are listed as follows.

Fair Value Hedge

This is a hedge against changes in the fair value of a hedged item that can be attributed to a specific risk. The accounting for a fair value hedge is:

- If the hedged item is measured at fair value through profit or loss, recognize the gain or loss on the hedging instrument in profit or loss.
- If the hedged item is measured at fair value through other comprehensive income, recognize the gain or loss on the hedging instrument in profit or loss. However, if the hedged item is an equity instrument, then recognize the gain or loss on the hedging instrument in other comprehensive income.
- If the hedged item is measured at cost, adjust its carrying amount with the gain or loss on the hedging instrument, and recognize the change in profit or loss. If the effective interest method is used to measure the hedged item, the adjustment to the carrying amount of the hedged item shall be amortized based on a recalculated effective interest rate. The amortization must be completed by the maturity date of the financial instrument being hedged.

Fair value hedge accounting shall be terminated if the hedge accounting criteria are no longer met, the company revokes the hedging designation, or the hedging instrument expires or is otherwise terminated or exercised.

EXAMPLE

Armadillo Industries buys bonds having a cumulative face value of £80,000, and which pays interest of 6%. The interest rate paid matches the current market interest rate. Armadillo's CFO anticipates that interest rates will increase, which will reduce the market value of the bonds. Accordingly, the CFO engages in an interest rate swap with Currency Bank, under which Armadillo swaps its fixed bond payments for floating interest payments from Currency.

A few months later, interest rates have indeed increased, which reduces the market value of the bonds by £7,000. The swap has increased in value by £6,500, since Armadillo will now receive an increased amount of interest payments from Currency. The related journal entries are:

	Debit	Credit
Hedging loss (hedged item)	7,000	
Investments		7,000
To record decline in value of bonds		

	Debit	Credit
Swap asset	6,500	
Hedging gain (hedging instrument)		6,500
To record increase in value of interest rate swap		

Cash Flow Hedge

This is a hedge against changes in the cash flows associated with a hedged item, which can be attributed to a specific risk. The accounting for a cash flow hedge is:

- Recognize that portion of any gain or loss on an effective hedge in other comprehensive income. The following additional factors may apply:
  - If the hedge is for a forecasted transaction, this amount is shifted to profit or loss when the transaction later results in the recognition of a financial asset or liability that impacts profit or loss. If you expect that any portion of a loss recorded in other comprehensive income will not be recovered in later periods, reclassify it into profit or loss at once.
  - If the hedge is for a forecasted transaction that will result in the recognition of a *non*-financial asset or liability, the accounting treatment is to move the gains and losses recorded in other comprehensive income into the carrying amount of the asset or liability.
- Recognize in profit or loss that portion of any gain or loss on a hedge that is not considered effective.

In all other cases that do not fall under the preceding guidance for a cash flow hedge, the rule is to shift any gains and losses initially recorded in other comprehensive income into profit and loss when the hedged cash flows affect profit or loss.

Cash flow hedge accounting should be discontinued under any of the following circumstances:

- The hedging instrument expires or is otherwise terminated or sold, in which case the gain or loss recorded in other comprehensive income should be shifted to profit or loss only when the forecast transaction occurs.
- The hedging instrument no longer meets the hedge accounting criteria, in which case the gain or loss recorded in other comprehensive income should be shifted to profit or loss only when the forecast transaction occurs.

- The forecast transaction will not occur, in which case the gain or loss recorded in other comprehensive income shall be shifted to profit or loss at once.
- The business revokes the hedging designation. If the hedged transaction is still expected to occur, shift the gain or loss recorded in other comprehensive income to profit or loss only when the forecast transaction occurs. If the hedged transaction is not expected to occur, shift the gain or loss recorded in other comprehensive income to profit or loss at once.

EXAMPLE

Entwhistle Electric orders an automated battery production line from a supplier in the United States for $450,000, for delivery to its London facility in 180 days. Entwhistle's functional currency is the pound. On the date when the contract is signed, Entwhistle expects to pay £375,000, based on the current exchange rate between the U.S. dollar and the pound. The CFO of Entwhistle wants to guard against any weakening of the pound against the dollar over the next 180 days, which would require a larger payment by Entwhistle.

To avoid this risk, the CFO enters into a forward contract to purchase $450,000 in 180 days for £375,000, and designates the forward contract as a hedge against future increases in the price of the dollar as it applies to the production line contract.

90 days later, the pound has indeed declined in value in comparison to the dollar, so that the $450,000 payment will now require a payment of £400,000, which equates to a £25,000 increase in the value of the forward contract. There are no further changes in the exchange rate, so Entwhistle is paid £25,000 when the forward contract is settled. On the contracted delivery date, Entwhistle pays £400,000 for the production line, and reduces the carrying amount of the fixed asset by netting it against the gain on the forward contract. The related entries are:

	Debit	Credit
Forward contract	25,000	
Equity		25,000
To record gain on forward contract to purchase $450,000		

	Debit	Credit
Cash	25,000	
Forward contract		25,000
To settle forward contract		

	Debit	Credit
Fixed asset – production equipment	400,000	
Cash		400,000
To purchase production line equipment		

	Debit	Credit
Equity	25,000	
Fixed asset – production equipment		25,000
To net hedging gain against fixed asset		

Net Investment Hedge in a Foreign Operation

This is a hedge against changes in the amount of an entity's interest in the net assets of a foreign operation. The accounting for a net investment hedge is similar to what was just described for a cash flow hedge. The following rules apply:

- Recognize that portion of any gain or loss on an effective hedge in other comprehensive income. This amount shall be shifted to profit or loss when the net investment in the foreign operation is disposed of.
- Recognize that portion of any gain or loss on a hedge that is not considered effective in profit or loss.

EXAMPLE

Franklin Drilling invests in an oil refinery in Brazil, which it plans to sell in four years. To hedge the investment for the next four years, Franklin borrows 150 million Brazilian reals and designates the loan as a hedge of the net investment in the oil refinery.

Over the next four years, there is a 20 million Brazilian real foreign currency gain on the loan. Franklin defers the gain in equity, and uses it at the end of four years, when it sells the refinery and incurs an offsetting foreign exchange loss.

Other Topics

There are several variations on the preceding hedging topics, which are noted in the following bullet points:

- *Firm commitment foreign currency risk.* When there is a hedge of the foreign currency risk associated with a firm commitment, it can be accounted for as either a fair value hedge or a cash flow hedge.
- *Unrecognized firm commitment.* When there is a hedge of an unrecognized firm commitment, recognize subsequent changes in its fair value as a gain or loss. The fair value changes in the hedging instrument are also recognized in profit or loss.

Financial Asset and Liability Derecognition

This section deals with the measurement of and accounting for various aspects of the derecognition of financial assets and liabilities, as well as several related matters.

Financial Asset Derecognition

A business should derecognize a financial asset under the following circumstances:

- When its contractual right to any cash flows associated with the financial asset expires, or
- When it transfers the financial asset to a third party, where it also transfers the right to receive cash flows or retains this right but assumes an obligation

to pay the cash flows to other parties. If there is an obligation to pay third parties, the transaction is only considered a transfer when:

- o There is no payment obligation unless an equivalent amount is received from the financial instrument; and
- o The business cannot sell or pledge the financial asset; and
- o The business is not allowed a material delay in its payment of the cash flows to the recipients.

In the event of a financial asset transfer, review any retention of risks and rewards, and apply the following rules as applicable:

- If essentially all risks and rewards of ownership have been transferred, derecognize the financial asset, and recognize new assets and liabilities for any rights or obligations created under the transfer agreement.
- If essentially all risks and rewards are retained, continue to recognize the financial asset.
- If the business has not retained control over the financial asset but still retains some risks and rewards, derecognize the financial asset and recognize new assets and liabilities for any rights or obligations created under the transfer agreement.
- If the business has retained control over the financial asset, continue to recognize the financial instrument in the amount of the company's continuing involvement in the asset.

EXAMPLE

Close Call Company sells a financial asset under an agreement where Close Call agrees to repurchase the instrument at a fixed price. Close Call should not derecognize the asset, because the company has retained the risks and rewards of ownership.

Close Call sells another financial asset. This time, it retains a right of first refusal, so that it can repurchase the asset at fair value if the transferee later elects to sell it. In this case, the risks and rewards of ownership have shifted to the transferee, so Close Call should derecognize the asset.

Close Call sells yet another financial asset, this time with a put option attached that allows the transferee the option to sell the asset back to Close Call. The option is currently in the money. In this case, the presence of a put option that will likely be exercised means that Close Call has retained the risks and rewards of ownership, and so should not derecognize the asset.

The transfer of risks and rewards is evaluated based on the change in a business' exposure to the cash flows associated with a financial asset before and after a transfer has been completed. This change can be computed as the before-and-after present value of the cash flows to which a business is exposed.

If a business retains the risks and rewards of ownership, despite having accepted consideration for a financial asset, it should continue to recognize the transferred asset, as well as an offsetting liability in the amount of the consideration received for the asset. If an asset and offsetting liability must be recognized for a transferred asset, the net carrying amount recorded should either match the fair value or the amortized cost of the retained rights and obligations, depending upon whether the entity measures these items at their fair value or amortized cost, respectively. In any following periods, the entity should continue to recognize any income related to the transferred asset, as well as any expenses related to the liability for the consideration received. Further, these income and expense amounts should not be offset against each other.

If there are both rights and obligations associated with a transferred asset that are being recorded, do not net these items together for reporting purposes; they should be reported separately.

The presence or absence of control over a financial asset is the key element in determining how to account for a transferred financial instrument. A business is not considered to have retained control if the transferee has the ability to unilaterally sell the financial asset to an unrelated third party.

When a financial asset is entirely derecognized, there are two possible approaches to accounting for it, which are:

- *Asset not part of larger asset.* Recognize in profit or loss the difference between the consideration received for the asset and its carrying amount.
- *Asset is part of larger asset.* Allocate the carrying amount of the larger financial asset between the portion being derecognized and the portion being retained, based on their relative fair values. Then recognize in profit or loss the difference between the consideration received for the asset and its carrying amount. For this purpose, the recent prices of actual transactions are the best indicator of fair value. When such information does not exist, estimate fair value based on the difference between the fair value of the larger financial asset (in total) and the consideration received from the transferee for the derecognized component.

The following additional situations may apply to a financial asset that has been transferred, where a business should continue to recognize a transferred asset to the extent of its continuing involvement:

- *Guarantee.* If a business has guaranteed a transferred asset, the level of involvement is the lesser of the maximum amount of consideration that it could be required to repay, or the amount of the asset.
- *Option.* If there is an option on the asset, the level of involvement is the amount of the asset that the business may have to repurchase under the terms of the option. If the option is measured at fair value, the level of involvement is the lesser of the option exercise price or the fair value of the asset.

Financial Liability Derecognition

It is only acceptable to derecognize a financial liability when all obligations associated with the liability have been cancelled or discharged, or the liability expires. Several variations on this concept are:

- *Exchange of instruments.* When there is an exchange of debt instruments with substantially different terms, derecognize the old liability and recognize the new liability.
- *Terms change.* If there is a substantial change in the terms of a financial liability, derecognize the old liability and recognize the new liability.

When a financial liability is extinguished or transferred and there is a difference between the consideration paid and the carrying amount of the liability, recognize the difference in profit or loss.

Servicing Assets and Liabilities

When a business transfers a financial instrument, but retains the right to service that instrument for a fee, it should recognize a servicing asset or liability, based on these criteria:

- *Servicing asset.* If the payments under the servicing contract are expected to exceed adequate compensation for the servicing activity, recognize as a servicing asset an allocation of the carrying amount of the original financial instrument.
- *Servicing liability.* If the payments under the servicing contract are not expected to be adequate, the business should recognize a servicing liability at its fair value.

Valuation of Replacement Financial Asset

If the outbound transfer of a financial asset results in a business also recognizing a new financial asset, or assuming a new servicing or other liability, recognize the replacement asset or liability at its fair value.

Collateral

There may be situations where the transferring entity provides non-cash collateral to the recipient of a financial asset. If so, the accounting for the collateral depends upon the terms associated with the underlying contract. The following bullets note the possible variations:

Transferring entity:

- *Right to sell.* If the transferee has the right to sell or repledge the collateral, the transferring entity must classify the collateral separately from its other assets in its balance sheet.

- *Default*. If the transferring entity defaults, it should derecognize the collateral.

Transferee:

- *Sale of collateral*. If the transferee sells the collateral, it must recognize both the proceeds from sale of the collateral and a liability in the amount of the collateral that represents its obligation to return the collateral.
- *Default*. If the transferring entity defaults, the transferee should recognize the collateral at its fair value. If the transferee has already sold the collateral, it should derecognize its obligation to return the collateral.

Financial Instrument Presentation

When a company buys back its shares (known as treasury stock), present the amount of these buybacks as a deduction from equity. No gain or loss is to be recognized on treasury stock transactions. Any amounts paid for treasury stock only appear within the equity section of the balance sheet; they do not appear in the income statement.

It is only allowable to offset financial assets and liabilities and present just the net amount in the balance sheet when there is a legal right to actually offset the assets and liabilities, and when the entity intends to settle with the counterparty on a net basis, or to settle the assets and liabilities simultaneously. Since this situation is exceedingly rare, most businesses will not offset their financial assets and liabilities.

When there are dividends, interest, gains or losses associated with a financial instrument, recognize them in profit or loss. If there is a distribution to the holders of a company's equity instruments, recognize the distributions in equity, not the income statement.

Any transaction cost of an equity transaction is to be deducted directly from equity. These transactions typically include registration fees, printing and legal costs, and advisory fees. However, if these fees are associated with an equity transaction that is abandoned, the fees are to be charged to expense, instead of equity.

Financial Instrument Disclosures

In general, disclosures for financial instruments should enable the users of a company's financial statements to evaluate the impact of financial instruments on the results and financial position of the business.

The following disclosures are required for all financial instruments, except interests in subsidiaries and similar arrangements, employee benefit plans, insurance contracts, share-based payments, and instruments that must be classified as equity instruments.

Balance sheet disclosures:

- *Carrying amounts.* Disclose the aggregate carrying amount of each of the following classes of financial instrument:
    - Assets measured at fair value through profit or loss that were designated as such when initially recognized
    - Assets measured at fair value through profit or loss that must be measured in this manner under IFRS
    - Assets measured at amortized cost
    - Assets measured at fair value through other comprehensive income
    - Liabilities measured at fair value through profit or loss that were designated as such when initially recognized
    - Liabilities measured at fair value through profit or loss that must be measured in this manner under IFRS
    - Liabilities measured at amortized cost
- *Asset measurements at fair value through profit or loss.* If an asset that would normally be measured at its amortized cost is instead measured at fair value through profit or loss, disclose the following:
    - The maximum amount of credit risk exposure
    - The amount of credit risk reduction caused by credit derivatives
    - The cumulative and period-specific change in fair value caused by changes in credit risk (that is not caused by market risk)
    - The cumulative and period-specific change in fair value of any related credit derivatives
- *Liability measurements at fair value through profit or loss.* If a liability is measured at fair value through profit or loss and presents changes in the related credit risk in other comprehensive income, disclose the following:
    - The cumulative change in fair value caused by related changes in credit risk
    - The difference between the amount due at maturity and the current carrying amount of the liability
    - Any transfers in the period within equity of the cumulative gain or loss, as well as the reason for these changes
    - The amount in other comprehensive income that was recognized as the result of a liability derecognition
- *Measurement method.* The method used to derive the fair value of financial assets and liabilities, and why the method is appropriate. If you do not believe the preceding fair value disclosures faithfully represent fair value changes related to credit risk, note the reasons for this position. If reporting changes in credit risk for a liability in other comprehensive income would cause or expand an accounting mismatch in profit or loss, describe how this determination was made.
- *Asset measurements at fair value through other comprehensive income.* If changes in the fair value of investments in equity instruments are to be reported in other comprehensive income, describe which investments have

been so designated, the reasons for using this form of presentation, the ending fair values of these investments, any transfers of cumulative gain or loss within equity and the reasons for these transfers, dividends recognized that relate to derecognized investments, and dividends recognized that relate to investments held. If such an investment is derecognized, note the reason for disposal, its fair value on the derecognition date, and the associated cumulative gain or loss.

- *Reclassifications*. The business may have reclassified a financial asset during the reporting period. If so, disclose the date of reclassification, the amount reclassified, the related change in the business model that triggered the reclassification, and describe the effects on the financial statements. If a reclassified asset is now measured at amortized cost, report the effective interest rate on the date of reclassification and the recognized amount of interest income or expense, and continue to do so until derecognition. Also note for these assets now measured at amortized cost their fair value at the end of the reporting period, as well as the gain or loss on changes in fair value that would have been recognized if reclassification had not occurred.

- *Offsets*. Disclose the effect of netting arrangements on the company's financial position. To do so, note in tabular format the gross amount of those assets and liabilities that can be offset, the amounts that are offset, the net amounts presented in the balance sheet, the amounts subject to a master netting arrangement, and the net amount after deducting the master netting arrangement line item just noted. Also describe the offsetting rights associated with any master netting arrangements.

- *Collateral*. The carrying amount of any financial assets that have been pledged as collateral, and the terms related to the pledge. Conversely, if the entity holds collateral that is the property of another party, and can sell or repledge the collateral even if there is no default by the other party, disclose the fair value of the collateral, the fair value of any collateral that has been sold or repledged and whether there is an obligation to return the collateral, and the terms under which the entity can use the collateral.

- *Credit losses allowance*. When financial assets are carried at fair value through other comprehensive income, no loss allowance is used to reduce the reported amount of these assets, nor is such an allowance to be reported in the balance sheet as a reduction of the carrying amounts of these assets. A loss allowance may be described in the notes to the financial statements.

- *Compound instruments*. Describe the existence of any financial instruments that contain liability and equity components, and which have multiple embedded derivatives whose values are interdependent. An example is callable convertible debt.

- *Defaults and other breaches*. If there are loans payable at the end of a reporting period, disclose any loan defaults and the carrying amount of the defaulted loans. Also state whether a default was remedied or loan terms renegotiated. Also note any other breaches that allow the lender to accelerate loan payment.

- *Transaction costs.* If there are transaction costs associated with the procurement of equity investments in the company, disclose the amount of these costs.

Income statement disclosures:

- *Net gains or losses.* Note all net gains or losses on financial assets or liabilities measured at fair value through profit or loss, and at amortized cost, and financial assets measured at fair value through other comprehensive income.
- *Interest.* Using the effective interest method, disclose the total interest income and total interest expense related to financial assets measured at amortized cost. Do the same for any financial liabilities not measured at fair value through profit or loss.
- *Fees.* Disclose the income and expense for fees generated by financial assets and liabilities not measured at fair value through profit or loss, as well as for fiduciary activities.
- *Derecognition analysis.* Provide an analysis of any gains or losses related to the derecognition of financial assets measured at amortized cost, including the reasons for derecognition.

Other disclosures:

- *Hedging, general.* State the risk management strategy of the entity and how it is used to manage risk. Note how the hedging activities could impact the amount, timing, and uncertainty of the entity's future cash flows. Further, note the effects that hedge accounting have had on the financial statements.
- *Hedging, strategy.* For each category of risk exposure, describe the risk management strategy. The description should be sufficient for users to evaluate how risks occur, how each risk is managed, and the extent of risk exposures. Topics of discussion may include the hedging instruments used, how hedge effectiveness is determined, how the hedge ratio is established, and the sources of hedge ineffectiveness. Finally, for each hedged item, describe how the risk component was determined, and how this component relates to the hedged item in its entirety.
- *Hedging, future cash flows.* For each risk category, note how the terms and conditions of hedging instruments affect the timing, amount, and uncertainty of future cash flows. This should include the timing of the nominal amount of each hedging instrument, and (where applicable) the average price of the hedging instrument. When there are frequent hedging resets, describe the strategy for these hedging relationships and the frequency of the resets. Also disclose the sources of hedge ineffectiveness that will affect hedging relationships.
- *Hedging, effects on financial position and performance.* In a tabular format, note by risk category for each type of hedge the following information:

- ○ *General.* The carrying amount of the hedging instruments, the balance sheet line item that includes the instruments, the hedge fair value change used to determine hedge ineffectiveness, and the nominal amounts of the instruments.
- ○ *Fair value hedges.* The carrying amount of the hedged item, the accumulated amount of fair value hedge adjustments on the hedged item, where the hedged item is located in the statement of financial position, the change in hedge value used to recognize hedge ineffectiveness, and the accumulated amount of fair value hedge adjustments remaining for any hedged items that are no longer being adjusted for hedging gains or losses. Also note the amount of hedge ineffectiveness recognized in profit or loss, and the line item in the statement of comprehensive income where this amount is located.
- ○ *Cash flow hedges and hedges of net investments in a foreign operations.* The change in value of the hedged item that triggered the recognition of hedge ineffectiveness, the balances in the cash flow hedge reserve and foreign currency translation reserve for continuing hedges, and the balances remaining in these reserves for any hedging relationships that no longer have hedge accounting applied to them. Also note by separate risk category the hedging gains or losses recognized in other comprehensive income, any hedge ineffectiveness recognized in profit or loss (and where this is stated in the statement of comprehensive income), and any reclassification adjustments from the cash flow hedge reserve or foreign currency translation reserve (and where this reclassification is located in the statement of comprehensive income).

- • *Fair value.* Disclose the fair value of each class of financial assets and liabilities in comparison to its carrying amount. If a fair value is not available for a financial asset or liability, disclose for each class of items the accounting policy for recognizing the difference between initial fair value and the transaction price, the reason why transaction price is not the best evidence of fair value, and a reconciliation of the difference yet to be recognized as of the beginning and end of the reporting period. These disclosures are not needed when the carrying amount approximates fair value (such as for trade payables).

EXAMPLE

The Close Call Company presents the following table in its financial statement disclosures to clarify those differences between fair value and transaction price that have not yet been recognized in profit or loss:

(000s)	20X1	20X0
Balance at beginning of year	£21.0	£15.3
New transactions	0.7	7.0
Amounts recognized in profit or loss during the year	-5.7	-0.5
Other increases	0.5	--
Other decreases	-0.4	-0.8
Balance at end of year	£16.1	£21.0

Financial instrument risks:

- *Risk, general.* A sufficient disclosure should be made to inform financial statement users about the types and amounts of risks to which a business is exposed from financial instruments. For each type of risk disclosed, note the exposure to risk, how it arises, the policies and processes for managing and measuring the risk, and any changes in these items from the preceding period.

- *Credit risk, strategy.* Note the entity's credit risk management practices and how they relate to the recognition of expected credit losses, as well as significant credit risk concentrations.

- *Credit risk, practices.* Disclose how significant changes in the credit risk of financial instruments are determined, how default is defined, how financial instruments were grouped for collective measurement, how credit impairment is determined, the write-off policy, and similar matters.

- *Credit risk, expected credit losses.* Provide an explanation of changes in the credit loss allowance, provide in a tabular format a reconciliation for the period that shows the changes in the loss allowance for 12-month expected credit losses, the loss allowance at lifetime expected credit losses, and financial assets that were credit-impaired when purchased or originated. Also note the total amount of undiscounted expected credit losses initially recognized in the period. Finally, explain how significant changes in the gross carrying amount of the instruments in the period altered the loss allowance.

- *Credit risk, collateral.* By class of financial instrument, note the maximum exposure to credit risk without reference to any associated collateral, as well as the nature and quality of collateral held. Note any changes in the quality of the collateral resulting from changes in the collateral policy in the period. When a loss allowance has not been recognized due to collateral, provide information about the associated financial instruments. Quantify the extent of the collateral held for credit-impaired financial assets.

- *Credit risk, subject to enforcement*. Note the contractual amount remaining on any assets that were written off in the period, and for which there is on-going enforcement activity.
- *Credit risk, exposure*. Disclose the gross carrying amount of financial assets, by credit risk rating grades, as well as the exposure to credit risk on loan commitments and financial guarantee contracts.
- *Collateral*. When the entity takes possession of collateral during the period, describe the collateral and its carrying amount. If the collateral is not readily convertible into cash, note the policy for disposing of or using collateral assets.
- *Liquidity risk*. Present an analysis of non-derivative financial liabilities that reveals remaining contractual maturities, and separately for derivative financial liabilities. Also describe how the company manages these liquidity risks.
- *Market risk*. Present a sensitivity analysis for each type of market risk to which the business is exposed, showing the impact on profits of reasonably possible changes in risk variables, as well as the methods used to prepare the analysis, and any changes in these methods from the preceding period. If this analysis does not fully represent the risk associated with a financial instrument, disclose the issue.

EXAMPLE

The Close Call Company discloses the following sensitivity analysis related to the impact of changes in interest rates on its profitability:

At year end, if interest rates had been 25 basis points lower, with no changes to other variables, the after-tax profit for the year would have been £700,000 higher, due to lower interest expense on the company's variable-rate debt. If interest rates had been 25 basis points higher, with no changes in other variables, the after-tax profit for the year would have been £420,000 lower, due to higher interest expense on the company's variable-rate debt. The company's profit is more sensitive to interest rate decreases than increases, because the amount of interest rate increases is capped in its debt agreements.

Financial asset transfers:

- *Transfers, general*. A sufficient amount of information should be disclosed to enable the users of a company's financial statements to comprehend the relationship between transferred financial assets that are not fully derecognized and related liabilities, as well as to understand the ongoing involvement in these assets and any associated risks.
- *Transfers where assets not fully derecognized*. When transferred financial assets have not been completely transferred to a third party, disclose by class the nature of the partially transferred items, the remaining risks and rewards

of ownership to which the company is exposed, and any relationship between the transferred assets and associated liabilities. If there are associated liabilities where the counterparty only has recourse to transferred assets, state the fair values of the transferred assets and related liabilities, and the net position. If the company continues to recognize the full amount of transferred assets, disclose the carrying amounts of these assets and any related liabilities. If the company only recognizes the assets to the extent of its continuing involvement in them, disclose the total original carrying amount, the amount still recognized, and the carrying amount of any related liabilities.

EXAMPLE

Capitalist Lending discloses the following information in tabular form regarding the disposition of its financial assets that have been transferred, but not entirely derecognized:

(millions)	Financial Assets at Fair Value through Profit or Loss		Financial Assets at Amortized Cost		Financial Assets at Fair Value through Other Comprehensive Income
	Trading Assets	Derivatives	Mortgages	Consumer Loans	Equity Investments
Carrying amount of assets	£4.3	£1.7	£143.7	£100.4	£10.8
Carrying amount of associated liabilities	-0.9	-0.4	-14.1	-21.5	-3.0
For liabilities with recourse only to transferred assets:					
Fair value of assets	£1.0	£0.4	£16.0	£18.0	£5.5
Fair value of associated liabilities	-0.9	-0.2	-14.1	-21.5	-2.9
Net position	£0.1	£0.2	£1.9	-£3.5	£2.6

- *Transfers where assets are fully derecognized.* When a business completely derecognizes financial assets but continues to be involved in them, it should disclose the carrying amount of the related assets and liabilities and where these items are recognized in the balance sheet, as well as their fair values, the maximum exposure caused by its continuing involvement and how this amount was determined, the undiscounted cash payments that may be needed to repurchase derecognized assets and any remaining contractual maturities for these payments, and any discussions needed to support these disclosures. If there is continuing involvement in financial assets, disclose the gain or loss recognized when the assets were transferred, and any income or expense from the company's continuing involvement. Also, if the proceeds from transfer activity are concentrated within the last few days of a reporting period, disclose when the bulk of the transfer activity took place, the gains or losses recognized within that period, and the total proceeds from transfers within that period.

EXAMPLE

Capitalist Lending discloses the following information in tabular form regarding its financial assets that have been completely derecognized:

(millions) Type of Ongoing Involvement	Carrying Amount of Continuing Involvement in Balance Sheet			Fair Value of Continuing Involvement		Maximum Exposure to Loss
	Financial Assets at Fair Value through Profit or Loss	Financial Assets at Fair Value through OCI*	Financial Liabilities at Fair Value through Profit or Loss	Assets	Liabilities	
Written put options			-£0.5		-£4.9	£16.3
Purchased call options	£7.3			£6.3		11.1
Securities lending			-9.0	2.6	-0.8	24.7
Totals	£7.3		-£9.5	£8.9	-£5.7	£52.1

* OCI – Other Comprehensive Income

Summary

Despite the comparatively large amount of discussion given to financial instruments within IFRS, it is entirely possible that a business will have few of these items to measure or report; this topic tends to be of more interest to the financial institutions that deal with financial instruments on a daily basis, and those larger organizations that use derivatives to hedge certain activities and financial positions.

The paperwork related to hedge accounting is particularly onerous. By complying with it, a business does a better job of matching reported short-term gains and losses between hedged items and hedging instruments. However, many of these short-term gains and losses have no impact on cash flows until the underlying instruments have been settled, in which case the accounting department is essentially engaging in a large amount of compliance paperwork to smooth out its reported profit or loss. If such smoothing is of little importance to management, it is more efficient to simply engage in those hedging transactions that make sense, without attempting to comply with the hedging documentation required by IFRS.

Chapter 26
Fair Value Measurement

Introduction

Historically, much of the information in the financial statements has been derived from the original costs at which assets were purchased and liabilities incurred. Over time, this information tends to become more inaccurate as the fair values of the underlying assets and liabilities vary from the values at which they were recorded. Consequently, many aspects of IFRS are designed to force companies to periodically revise certain aspects of their accounting records to reflect fair values, rather than historical costs. In other cases, IFRS presents users with the option of revaluing items to their fair values. When these requirements are stated elsewhere in IFRS, users should consult this chapter to determine how fair value is to be measured and disclosed.

IFRS Source Document

- IFRS 13, *Fair Value Measurement*

Overview of Fair Value

This section describes the fair value concept, how fair value is measured, and the valuation methods used to develop fair value estimates.

General Concepts

The general intent of the fair value concept is to derive the price at which an asset is sold or a liability transferred on the open market. Obtaining this price involves the following concepts:

- An *orderly transaction*, where transactions are of a usual and customary nature. In other words, a sales transaction is not forced, as would be the case in a bankruptcy sale.
- There are *market participants*, who are independent of each other, are knowledgeable about the items being bought and sold, have the ability to enter into transactions, and are not being forced to enter into transactions.
- The transaction takes place in the *principal market* for the item, which is the market having the highest level of activity and volume for that item. If the principal market is not available, then the next most advantageous market is assumed, where the price paid is maximized, net of transaction and transport costs. The market in which a business normally enters into a transaction is considered the principal market.

When deriving fair value from the market price in the principal market, do not adjust the market price for transaction costs. However, if it is necessary to transport goods to or from a principal market, it is acceptable to include transport costs in the derivation of fair value.

If it is not possible to arrive at a fair value, it is possible to estimate fair value using a different valuation technique. When selecting an alternative technique, the overriding issue is to maximize the use of *observable inputs*, which are types of information that are developed from market data that reflect the assumptions used by market participants when setting prices. The selection should also minimize the use of *unobservable inputs*, which are types of information for which market data are not available. This is of some importance, since the fair value concept is based on the presence of market data that market participants would use in deriving prices.

Measurement Issues

When measuring an asset or liability at its fair value, the intent is to conduct the measurement at the level of the individual asset or liability. Doing so means that you should incorporate into the valuation those characteristics of an item that may influence its price. Examples of such characteristics are:

- The condition of an asset, such as an unusual amount of damage or wear
- The location of an asset, such as a distant location that will require unusually high transport costs to retrieve
- Restrictions on the sale of an asset, such as a lien that must be cleared before the sale can proceed
- Restrictions on the use of an asset, such as zoning restrictions on a building

At times, it may be necessary to measure groups of assets or liabilities, rather than single items. This concept is most commonly applied when you want to aggregate items into a *cash-generating unit*, which is a group of assets and liabilities whose cash inflows are mostly independent of the cash inflows of other assets. This means that a fair value could be assigned to an entire business unit.

Initial Recognition

When an asset is acquired or a liability assumed, the price at that point is either the amount paid to acquire the asset or assume the liability. This is not the same as fair value, which is actually the reverse – the price at which the company could sell an asset, or which it would pay to transfer a liability to a third party. This can be a crucial difference, for a business may not buy an asset or incur a liability at their fair values. If IFRS permits the initial recognition of an asset or liability at its fair value for a specific asset or liability, rather than the initial price, recognize a gain or loss on the difference between the transaction price and fair value.

There are a number of situations in which the transaction price could differ from the fair value. For example, a transaction may be between related parties, or one party to a transaction may be forced to sell under duress, or there are unstated rights included in a transaction, or a transaction takes places in a different market from the one in which the fair value was determined.

Measurement of Non-Financial Assets

The fair value concept may be applied to the valuation of non-financial assets. If so, fair value is assumed to be based on the *highest and best use* of an asset. This means that fair value is based on the maximized value of an asset, even if the item is not actually used in that manner. The highest and best use concept is limited by the condition of an asset and any applicable legal restrictions (such as zoning). The use to which an asset is already being put is assumed to be its highest and best use, unless other factors indicate that a different use would achieve a higher valuation.

EXAMPLE

Snyder Corporation acquires a key patent from a defunct rival, and plans to use it in a defensive manner, denying licensing rights to competitors. This defensive approach is not the highest and best use of the patent, since it could be used to earn licensing revenue from rivals. Despite its current use, Snyder should assign a fair value to the patent under the highest and best use concept, as though the company were licensing the patent.

EXAMPLE

Pianoforte International acquires a plot of land as part of its purchase of the assets of a bankrupt rival. The zoning for the land currently designates it as being for industrial use only. An adjacent site was recently re-zoned to accommodate high-density residential apartments. Based on this information, Pianoforte needs to determine the value of the land under the current zoning and under high-density residential zoning, taking into account all necessary conversion costs to the alternative zoning arrangement. Doing so may indicate that the alternative arrangement is the highest and best use of the property, which may alter its fair value.

It is possible that the highest and best use of an asset may require its presumed inclusion in a group of assets and liabilities. If so, value the other assets and liabilities in that group under the same assumption.

Measurement of Liabilities and Equity

The fair value concept assumes that both financial and non-financial liabilities, as well as equity instruments, are sold to a third party on the measurement date, and would not be settled on that date. The formulation of fair value uses the following decision tree, in declining order of preference:
1. Use the quoted price in an active market for an identical item.
2. If the preceding option is not available, use the quoted price in a less active market for an identical item, or other observable inputs.
3. If the preceding two options are not available, use an alternative valuation technique. One option is the *income approach*, which is based on the present

value of future cash flows associated with the item being valued. Another option is the *market approach*, which derives a valuation from similar liabilities or equity instruments.

It is permissible to adjust the quoted price of a liability or equity item only if there are factors specific to the liability or equity item being measured that are not found in the comparable items from which fair value is being derived. For example:

- A liability is compared to a debt instrument issued by another entity whose credit rating differs from that of the company.
- An equity instrument is compared to an equity instrument issued by another company, which contains a super voting privilege not found in the company's equity instrument.

EXAMPLE

The Close Call Company issues 1,000,000 shares to an individual, as payment for the purchase of her company. The shares carry a restriction from resale feature that will automatically terminate in six months. The fair value of these shares is measured based on the quoted price for the company's unrestricted shares, less an adjustment to reflect the increased risk to investors of not being able to trade the shares for the next six months.

The following additional factors may apply to the derivation of fair value for liability or equity items:

- *Credit risk.* When deriving the fair value of a liability, factor in the effect of the company's own credit risk – that is, the risk that the company will not settle the liability. The importance of this factor can vary, depending upon whether a liability is to be settled in cash or goods; if the latter, it may not be physically possible to obtain or produce the goods required by the designated settlement date.
- *Guarantees.* If a third party is providing a guarantee that the company will settle a liability, and the company accounts for this guarantee separately, determine the fair value of the liability without including the effect of the guarantee.

It can be difficult to discern a fair value for liabilities and equity items, especially if they contain transfer restrictions or other unusual features. Nonetheless, there may be an observable market for similar items, from which a fair value can be estimated. As is the case with all fair value measurements, the goal is to derive a value that maximizes observable inputs and minimizes unobservable inputs.

Measurement of a Group of Financial Assets and Liabilities

When a group of financial assets and liabilities are being managed based on their net exposure to market or credit risks, it is permissible to measure the fair value of the group based on the price received to sell an asset for a certain risk exposure, or paid to transfer a liability for a certain risk exposure. Thus, the fair value of the group is measured based on its risk exposure as priced by the market. This type of fair value measurement only applies if a company:

- Manages the group of financial assets and liabilities based on risk exposure, based on a documented strategy;
- Informs key management personnel about the risk information related to the group of financial assets and liabilities; and
- Measures these items at their fair values at the end of each reporting period.

The following additional guidance applies to this topic:

- *Consistent risk durations.* The durations of the risks to which a group of assets and liabilities are exposed should be substantially the same.
- *Consistent risk types.* The market risks to which a group of assets and liabilities are exposed should be the same, rather than having a mix of exposures to such factors as interest rate risk and commodity price risk.
- *Counterparty exposure.* If the financial assets and liabilities in a group relate to a particular counterparty, include in the fair value assessment the effect of the company's net exposure to the credit risk of the counterparty, including the effect of a master netting agreement between the parties (where the obligations of the two parties can be offset against each other).
- *Most applicable price.* Apply that price within the bid-ask spread that best represents fair value under the circumstances.

Valuation Methods

There are a number of methods available for deriving fair value. Among the more popular are:

- *Cost method.* The cost method develops a fair value based on what it would cost to acquire a substitute asset, adjusted for the obsolescence of the existing asset.
- *Income method.* The income method arrives at a fair value through the use of discounted cash flows analysis. A probability-weighted average of several different cash flow scenarios may be required. If options are involved, this can require the use of an option pricing model, such as a lattice model or the Black–Scholes-Merton formula.

EXAMPLE

Vertical Drop Corporation has assumed the decommissioning liability for a ski lift, which will have to be removed from its installation points on the side of a mountain in five years, using Vertical Drop's heavy-lift helicopters. The cost associated with this liability may vary considerably, based on the level of government oversight of the process. Accordingly, Vertical Drop develops a set of possible cash flows, resulting in a £975,000 weighted average cash flow scenario that is calculated as follows:

Cash Flow Estimates		Probability		Expected Cash Flows
£750,000	×	20%	=	£150,000
900,000	×	45%	=	405,000
1,200,000	×	35%	=	420,000
				£975,000

- *Market method.* The market method develops a fair value based on sale transactions for similar assets and liabilities. For example, the sale price of several businesses could be compared to their revenues, and this multiple could then be used to derive the possible value of a business, based on its own sales.

The method selected to derive a valuation should be based on maximum use of observable inputs, while minimizing the use of unobservable inputs.

If there is an active market for identical assets and liabilities, it is probably acceptable to derive a fair value from a single valuation method, since the basis for the valuation is entirely from observable inputs. If the amount of observable information is less apparent, it may be necessary to use multiple valuation methods. If so, evaluate the reasonableness of the results, and select as the designated fair value that amount within the range of valuations that is most representative of fair value.

EXAMPLE

Oberlin Acoustics acquires production equipment through a business combination. The equipment was originally purchased as a standard model, after which it underwent a modest amount of customization. Oberlin considers its current usage to be its highest and best use. The company decides that the cost and market methods can be used to derive the fair value of the equipment, but not the income method, since separately-identifiable cash flows cannot be derived for it.

Oberlin finds quoted prices for similar machines in similar condition and adjusts them to account for the customized nature of the equipment, yielding a fair value range of £80,000 to £88,000 from the market method. The industrial engineering staff estimates the cost required to build substitute equipment that has comparable utility, which indicates a fair value range of £82,000 to £95,000 from the cost method.

The company decides that the lower end of the indicated fair value ranges is most indicative of the fair value of the equipment, because fewer subjective adjustments needed to be made to the information used for the market method.

If the level of equipment customization had been greater, it may not have been possible to use the market approach, in which case Oberlin may have had to rely exclusively upon the results of a cost method analysis.

The valuation methods used should be applied consistently across multiple reporting periods. However, a change is allowed if doing so results in a more representative fair value. Such a situation may arise when new information becomes available, market conditions change, information previously used is no longer available, and so forth. If there is a change in valuation method, treat it as a change in accounting estimate (see the Accounting Policies, Estimate Changes and Errors chapter).

When measuring an asset or liability, and there is a bid price and an ask price, the preferred price to use for valuation purposes is that price within the bid-ask spread that best represents fair value under the circumstances. It is also permissible to use the bid price for asset valuations and the ask price for liability valuations.

IFRS uses a fair value hierarchy to designate three levels of information that can be used as inputs to a valuation method. These levels are:

- *Level 1*. These are quoted prices from active markets in which identical assets or liabilities are sold, which are available on the measurement date. These prices should be used without adjustment whenever possible. This type of information is available for many financial instruments that are traded on stock exchanges.
- *Level 2*. These are inputs other than quoted prices that can be observed for an asset or liability, such as quoted prices for similar items in active markets, and quoted prices for identical items in non-active markets. These prices may be adjusted based on asset location or condition, the comparability of comparison items, market activity, and similar factors.
- *Level 3*. These are inputs that cannot be observed for an asset or liability, such as the entity's own information. These inputs can and should be adjusted for any other available information that incorporates the assumptions of market participants.

Information derived from Level 1 of the hierarchy is always preferred for use in a valuation method, while information derived from Level 3 is the least preferred. If information from a lower level of the hierarchy is used to adjust information in a higher level (such as adjusting a market price with an unobservable input from Level 3), the resulting information is considered to have originated in the lower level.

Any valuation method can be applied to the information originating from any of the levels of the fair value hierarchy.

Fair Value Disclosures

A business should disclose the following information about fair value in the notes accompanying its financial statements, preferably in a tabular format:

- *Valuation techniques*. By asset and liability class, the valuation techniques and inputs used for those assets and liabilities measured at fair value after initial recognition. The following additional information should be provided:
    - o The fair value measurement at the end of the reporting period.
    - o The reason for measurement, for any non-recurring fair value measurements.

- o The level of the fair value hierarchy from which the fair value measurement information is derived.
- o The amounts of any transfers between levels of the fair value hierarchy, the reasons for the transfers, and how the entity decides when a transfer has occurred
- o For measurements derived from Levels 2 or 3 of the fair value hierarchy, the techniques and inputs used, as well as any changes in valuation method and the reason for the change.
- o A reconciliation of beginning and ending Level 3 measurements for recurring fair value measurements, noting total gains or losses recognized in profit or loss (and where they are included in the income statement), total gains or losses recognized in other comprehensive income (and where they are included in the income statement), purchases, sales, issues, settlements, and any transfers into or out of Level 3, along with the reasons for the transfers and the company policy for deciding when a transfer has occurred.
- o The total amount of Level 3 gains and losses included in profit or loss that are attributable to unrealized gains and losses for related assets and liabilities, and where this information appears in the income statement.
- o The valuation processes used for fair value measurements within Level 3.
- o A narrative description of the sensitivity of recurring Level 3 fair value measurements to changes in unobservable inputs, where such changes can trigger significantly different fair value measurements. Also note any interrelationships between the various inputs and how these interrelationships can alter the effects of fair value changes.
- o A disclosure of how changes in unobservable inputs to recurring Level 3 measurements can cause significant fair value changes in financial assets and liabilities, as well as how the changes were calculated.
- o Why the highest and best use of an asset is not being followed, and why this is the case.
- *Effects*. The effect on profit or loss or other comprehensive income of recurring fair value measurements using Level 3 inputs.
- *Fair value not measured*. In those cases where the fair value of assets and liabilities are not measured at fair value, but fair value information is disclosed, note the level of fair value hierarchy information used, the valuation techniques used if Levels 2 or 3 were employed, and any variances from the highest and best use of assets, as well as why this is the case.
- *Group valuation*. If a group of financial assets and liabilities are being managed based on their net exposure and its fair value is based on risk exposure, disclose this fact.

- *Credit enhancements.* If a liability has an attached third-party credit enhancement (such as a guarantee), disclose this fact and whether the enhancement is included in the fair value of the liability.

The classes of assets and liabilities within which these disclosures are made should be based on the nature and risks of the underlying items, as well as the level of the fair value hierarchy from which the related fair value measurements are derived. It may be necessary to aggregate information into several classes for Level 3 information, since Level 3 information tends to be more uncertain.

EXAMPLE

Medusa Medical discloses its recurring fair value measurements in the following tabular format:

		Fair Values Measured at end of Reporting Period		
		Level 1	**Level 2** Significant Other	**Level 3** Significant
(millions)	Totals	Quoted Prices for Identical Assets	Observable Inputs	Unobservable Inputs
Trading equity securities:				
Aerospace industry	£12	£12		
Construction industry	21	17	£4	
Retail industry	8	8		
Total trading equity securities	£41	£37	£4	
Debt securities:				
Commercial paper	£31	£31		
Mortgage-backed securities	18		£11	£7
Treasury bills	29	29		
Total debt securities	£78	£60	£11	£7

Summary

The use of fair values is worthwhile when a business has so little turnover in its balance sheet that the values in some line items vary significantly from their current market values. From this perspective, the imposition of fair value principles is certainly a laudable goal. However, the accountant may have a different perspective on the situation, since he or she must derive fair values on a regular basis, document the reasons for fair value changes, and defend these findings against the inquiries of auditors. Thus, from an efficiency perspective, fair value is an unmitigated pain. From the viewpoint of the accountant, then, the use of fair value is to be avoided, especially when the differences between historical cost and fair value are minor.

Chapter 27
Effects of Changes in Foreign Exchange Rates

Introduction

A large number of businesses routinely engage in foreign currency transactions with their business partners, in which case they probably deal with foreign currencies. Others have subsidiaries located in foreign countries, and need to convert the financial statements of these entities into the currency used by the parent for consolidation purposes. We deal with the accounting for and disclosure of these two situations in the following sections.

IFRS Source Document

- IAS 21, *The Effects of Changes in Foreign Exchange Rates*

Foreign Exchange Transactions

A business may enter into a transaction where it is scheduled to receive a payment from a customer that is denominated in a foreign currency, or to make a payment to a supplier in a foreign currency.

EXAMPLE

Blitz Communications creates enterprise-level telephone systems. Its purchases of circuit boards from South Korea are denominated in the South Korean won, while its purchases of cables from Australia are denominated in the Australian dollar. Since both transactions are settled in currencies other than Blitz's functional currency, they are classified as foreign exchange transactions.

On the date of recognition of each such transaction, record it in the functional currency of the reporting entity, based on the spot exchange rate in effect on that date. It may not be possible to determine the spot exchange rate on the date of recognition of a transaction. If so, it is acceptable to use an average rate for all transactions occurring within a period. An average rate is not an acceptable substitute when the rate fluctuates significantly. If two currencies cannot currently be exchanged, use the exchange rate on the first subsequent date on which an exchange can be made.

If there is a change in the expected exchange rate between the functional currency of the entity and the currency in which a transaction is denominated, record a gain or loss in earnings in the period when the exchange rate changes. This can result in the recognition of a series of gains or losses over a number of accounting periods, if the settlement date of a transaction is sufficiently far in the future. This also means that the stated balances of the related receivables and payables will reflect the current exchange rate as of each subsequent balance sheet date.

EXAMPLE

Armadillo Industries sells goods to a company in the United Kingdom, to be paid in pounds having a value at the booking date of $100,000. Armadillo records this transaction with the following entry:

	Debit	Credit
Accounts receivable	100,000	
Sales		100,000

Later, when the customer pays Armadillo, the exchange rate has changed, resulting in a payment in pounds that translates to a $95,000 sale. Thus, the foreign exchange rate change related to the transaction has created a $5,000 loss for Armadillo, which it records with the following entry:

	Debit	Credit
Cash	95,000	
Foreign currency exchange loss	5,000	
Accounts receivable		100,000

The following table shows the impact of transaction exposure on different scenarios.

Risk When Transactions Denominated in Foreign Currency

	Import Goods	Export Goods
Home currency weakens	Loss	Gain
Home currency strengthens	Gain	Loss

Financial Statement Translation

A company may have subsidiaries located in other countries, and creates financial statements for those subsidiaries that are denominated in the local currency, which is known as the *functional currency*. If so, the parent company will need to translate the financial statements of these subsidiaries into the currency used by the parent company when it creates consolidated financial statements for the entire entity (called the *presentation currency*). The steps in this process are as follows:
1. Determine the functional currency of the foreign entity.
2. Remeasure the financial statements of the foreign entity into the presentation currency of the parent company.
3. Record gains and losses on the translation of currencies.

Determination of Functional Currency

The financial results and financial position of a company should be measured using its functional currency, which is the currency that the company uses in the majority of its business transactions.

If a foreign business entity operates primarily within one country and is not dependent upon the parent company, its functional currency is the currency of the country in which its operations are located. However, there are other foreign operations that are more closely tied to the operations of the parent company, and whose financing is mostly supplied by the parent. In this latter case, the functional currency of the foreign operation is probably the currency used by the parent entity. These two examples anchor the ends of a continuum on which the currency status of most foreign operations will be found. Unless an operation is clearly associated with one of the two examples provided, it is likely that you must make a determination of functional currency based on the unique circumstances pertaining to each entity. For example, the functional currency may be difficult to determine if a business conducts an equal amount of business in two different countries. An examination of the following factors can assist in determining a functional currency:

Indicators	Indicates Use of Foreign Currency as Functional Currency	Indicates use of Presentation Currency as Functional Currency
Cash flow	The cash flows relating to an entity's assets and liabilities are primarily in the foreign currency, and have no direct impact on the cash flows of the parent	The cash flows relating to an entity's assets and liabilities directly affect the cash flows of the parent and are available for remittance to it
Expenses	The labor, material, and other costs of the entity are primarily obtained locally	The labor, material, and other costs of the entity are primarily obtained from the parent's country
Financing	Any financing obtained is primarily denominated in a foreign currency, and locally-generated funds should be able to service the entity's existing and expected debts	Financing is obtained from the parent or is denominated in the currency of the parent; the parent may have to supply more cash to support the subsidiary
Independence	There is a significant amount of autonomy, as evidenced by the local accumulation of cash, expense incurrence, and borrowings in the local currency	The activities of the entity are essentially an extension of the activities of the parent
Intra-entity transactions	There are few intra-entity transactions, and operations are not tightly integrated with those of the parent	There are many intra-entity transactions, and operations are more likely to be tightly integrated with those of the parent
Sales price	Sales prices are mostly based on local competition and regulations, rather than on exchange rate changes	Sales prices are mostly based on exchange rate changes, which can be driven by international price competition

The functional currency in which a business reports its financial results should rarely change. A shift to a different functional currency should be used only when there is a significant change in the economic facts and circumstances. If there is a change in functional currency, do not restate previously-issued financial statements into the new currency. The effects of the change should only be reported on a prospective basis, using the exchange rate between the old and new functional currencies on the date of the change.

EXAMPLE

Armadillo Industries has a subsidiary in Australia, to which it ships its body armor products for sale to local police forces. The Australian subsidiary sells these products and then remits payments back to corporate headquarters. Armadillo should consider U.S. dollars to be the functional currency of this subsidiary.

Armadillo also owns a subsidiary in Russia, which manufactures its own body armor for local consumption, accumulates cash reserves, and borrows funds locally. This subsidiary rarely remits funds back to the parent company. In this case, the functional currency should be the Russian ruble.

Translation of Financial Statements

When translating the financial statements of an entity for consolidation purposes into the reporting currency of a business, translate the financial statements using the following rules:

- *Foreign currency monetary items.* Translate using the closing exchange rate for the reporting period. If there is a difference in the exchange rate from the rate at which a monetary item was translated in the preceding reporting period, record the difference in profit or loss.
- *Non-monetary items measured at historical cost in a foreign currency.* Translate using the exchange rate on the transaction date. If there is a difference in the exchange rate from the rate at which a non-monetary item was translated in the preceding reporting period, record the difference in other comprehensive income. If a gain or loss on a non-monetary item was recognized in profit or loss during the period, any associated exchange component of that transaction should be recognized in profit or loss at the same time.
- *Non-monetary items measured at fair value in a foreign currency.* Translate using the exchange rate on the fair value measurement date. If there is a difference in the exchange rate from the rate at which a non-monetary item was translated in the preceding reporting period, record the difference in other comprehensive income.
- *Net investment.* If a parent entity has a net investment in a foreign entity that is a monetary item, and there is a difference in the exchange rate from the rate at which the investment was translated in the preceding reporting period, record the difference in the consolidated financial statements within

other comprehensive income. This amount is shifted to profit or loss once the parent has disposed of its net investment in the foreign entity.

- *Different balance sheet date.* If the foreign entity being consolidated has a different balance sheet date than that of the reporting entity, use the exchange rate in effect as of the foreign entity's balance sheet date. If there are significant changes in the exchange rate up to the end of the reporting period, adjust for these changes.

If there are translation adjustments resulting from the implementation of these rules, record the adjustments in the equity section of the parent company's consolidated balance sheet.

EXAMPLE

The backhoe operation of Grubstake Brothers has accounts receivable of £1,000,000, a cash dividend payable of £150,000, and a required value added tax remittance of £80,000. Since these items are all settled in cash, they are considered monetary items.

Grubstake also has £170,000 of backhoe parts in stock, £2,000,000 of goodwill, and £8,500,000 of production equipment. Since these items are not settled in cash, they are considered non-monetary items.

EXAMPLE

Grubstake Brothers buys a $500,000 stamping machine from an American supplier in November, when the exchange rate is £1:$1.6, and records the machine as a £312,500 fixed asset. The payable has not yet been settled at the end of the year, when the exchange rate is £1:$1.5. Since Grubstake's functional currency is the British pound, the payable must be translated at year-end using the exchange rate on that date, which results in a payable of £333,333, which is £20,833 higher than the amount at which the fixed asset was recorded. Grubstake records the £20,833 difference in profit or loss as a foreign exchange loss.

EXAMPLE

Armadillo Industries has a subsidiary located in England, which has its net assets denominated in pounds. The functional currency of Armadillo is U.S. dollars. At year-end, when the parent company consolidates the financial statements of its subsidiaries, the U.S. dollar has depreciated in comparison to the pound, resulting in a decline in the value of the subsidiary's net assets.

The following table shows the impact of translation exposure on different scenarios.

Risk When Net Assets Denominated in Foreign Currency

	Assets	Liabilities
Reporting currency weakens	Gain	Loss
Reporting currency strengthens	Loss	Gain

If the process of converting the financial statements of a foreign entity into the reporting currency of the parent company results in a translation adjustment, report the related profit or loss in other comprehensive income.

EXAMPLE

A subsidiary of Armadillo Industries is located in Argentina, and its functional currency is the Argentine peso. The relevant peso exchange rates are:
- 0.20 to the dollar at the beginning of the year
- 0.24 to the dollar at the end of the year (closing rate)
- 0.22 to the dollar for the full-year weighted average rate

The subsidiary had no retained earnings at the beginning of the year. Based on this information, the financial statement conversion is as follows:

(000s)	Argentine Pesos	Exchange Rate	U.S. Dollars
Assets			
Cash	89,000	0.24	21,360
Accounts receivable	267,000	0.24	64,080
Inventory	412,000	0.24	98,880
Fixed assets, net	608,000	0.24	145,920
Total assets	1,376,000		330,240
Liabilities and Equity			
Accounts payable	320,000	0.24	76,800
Notes payable	500,000	0.24	120,000
Common stock	10,000	0.20	2,400
Additional paid-in capital	545,000	0.20	130,800
Retained earnings	1,000	(*)	220
Translation adjustments	0	--	20
Total liabilities and equity	1,376,000		330,240

* Reference from the following income statement

(000s)	Argentine Pesos	Exchange Rate	U.S. Dollars
Revenue	1,500,000	0.22	330,000
Expenses	1,499,000	0.22	329,780
Net income	1,000		220
Beginning retained earnings	0		0
Add: Net income	1,000	0.22	220
Ending retained earnings	1,000		220

A business can opt to present its financial statements in any currency. If it does so, and the functional currency is different from the presentation currency, the following rules apply:

- *Assets and liabilities.* Translate using the closing exchange rate at the balance sheet date for assets and liabilities.
- *Income statement items.* Translate revenues, expenses, gains, and losses using the exchange rate as of the dates when those items were originally recognized. An average rate for the period can be applied to this requirement, unless there is significant fluctuation in the exchange rate.
- *Exchange differences.* Record all resulting exchange differences in other comprehensive income. If the differences relate to a subsidiary that is not wholly-owned, allocate a portion of the differences to the non-controlling interests in the consolidated balance sheet.

If a business is located in a hyperinflationary economy and is translating its financial statements into a different presentation currency, translate all amounts using the closing exchange rate on the balance sheet date.

Hyperinflationary Effects

An entity may find itself operating in a hyperinflationary environment. If so, it must restate its financial statements in accordance with the mandates of IFRS, which are described in the Financial Reporting in Hyperinflationary Economies chapter.

Derecognition of a Foreign Entity Investment

When a company sells or liquidates its investment in a foreign entity, complete the following steps to account for the situation:

1. Remove the translation adjustment recorded in equity and other comprehensive income for the investment
2. Report a gain or loss in the period in which the sale or liquidation occurs

If a company only sells a portion of its investment in a foreign entity, recognize in profit or loss only a proportionate share of the accumulated translation adjustment recognized in other comprehensive income.

Foreign Currency Disclosures

Disclose the following information related to changes in foreign exchange rates:

- *Exchange differences.* The aggregate amount of exchange differences in profit or loss, other than those arising from financial instruments measured at fair value through profit or loss.
- *Exchange differences reconciliation.* A reconciliation of the net exchange differences recognized in other comprehensive income, from the beginning to the end of the period.
- *Different presentation currency.* The fact that a different presentation currency than the functional currency is used, if this is the case, and the reason for the difference.
- *Change in functional currency.* The fact that there has been a change in functional currency, if this is the case, and the reason for the change.
- *Different currency used for presentation.* If the financial statements are presented in a currency that is not the presentation or functional currency and the mandated translation adjustments have not been made, state that the information is supplemental, note the currency being used, the entity's functional currency, and the translation method used to create the supplemental information.

Summary

The key factor to consider when translating financial statements into the reporting currency is the use of average exchange rates. Consider creating a standard procedure for calculating the weighted average exchange rate for each relevant currency for each reporting period and then retain the calculation to justify the exchange rate(s) for audit purposes. Using a weighted average is much more efficient from an accounting perspective than translating specific transactions at the associated exchange rate on a daily basis.

Chapter 28
Borrowing Costs

Introduction

The borrowing costs topic essentially addresses a single issue, which is the capitalization of borrowing costs when those costs are associated with the construction or acquisition of a fixed asset. The capitalization of borrowing costs is not a common issue to be concerned about, unless a business is spending multiple months constructing a fixed asset, and has incurred debt to build the asset. In most other cases, borrowing cost capitalization can be ignored.

In this chapter, we describe the mechanics of borrowing cost capitalization, as well as the relevant accounting and disclosures associated with this topic.

IFRS Source Document

- IAS 23, *Borrowing Costs*

Overview of Borrowing Costs

Borrowing is a cost of doing business, and if a company incurs a borrowing cost that is directly related to a fixed asset, it is reasonable to capitalize this cost, since it provides a truer picture of the total investment in the asset. Since a business would not otherwise have incurred the borrowing cost if it had not acquired the asset, this cost is essentially a direct cost of owning the asset.

Conversely, if a business did not capitalize this borrowing cost and instead charged it to expense, it would be unreasonably reducing the amount of reported earnings during the period when the company incurred the expense, and increasing earnings during later periods, when it would otherwise have been charging the capitalized borrowing cost to expense through depreciation.

According to IFRS, when a business incurs borrowing costs that are directly attributable to the acquisition, production, or construction of qualifying assets, it should capitalize those costs and include them in the cost of the qualifying assets. All other borrowing costs should be charged to expense as incurred. A business is not required to capitalize borrowing costs when the borrowing is associated with an asset that is measured at fair value, or with inventories that are being manufactured on a repetitive basis.

EXAMPLE

Milford Sound builds a new corporate headquarters. The company hires a contractor to perform the work, and makes regular progress payments to the contractor. Milford should capitalize the interest expense related to this project.

Milford Sound creates a subsidiary, Milford Public Sound, which builds custom-designed outdoor sound staging for concerts and theatre activities. These projects require many months to complete, and are accounted for as discrete projects. Milford should capitalize the interest cost related to each of these projects.

Tip: If the amount of borrowing cost that may be applied to a fixed asset is minor, try to avoid capitalizing it. Otherwise, extra time will be spent documenting the capitalization, and the auditors will spend time investigating it – which may translate into higher audit fees.

A borrowing cost is considered to be eligible for capitalization if it would have been avoided if expenditures for a qualifying asset had not been made. For example, a borrowing cost that should be capitalized arises when a business takes on debt specifically to fund the construction of a building.

Considerable judgment can be required to ascertain the correct amount of borrowing costs to capitalize under any of the following circumstances:

- When funds are acquired through a central location, such as the corporate headquarters of the parent company
- When funds are obtained from multiple debt instruments, having varying interest rates
- When funds are denominated in foreign currencies and there are exchange rate fluctuations
- When the entity operates in a highly inflationary environment

When an entity borrows funds for the entire business and allocates the required amount of these funds to qualifying assets, calculate the amount of borrowing costs that can be capitalized using the following formula:

Capitalization rate × Expenditures on qualifying asset = Borrowing costs to capitalize

Further points regarding the contents of this formula are:

- The capitalization rate is the weighted average amount of those borrowing costs of the entity during the period, not including those borrowing costs incurred specifically to acquire a qualifying asset. Depending on the circumstances, it may be more appropriate to use the weighted average of all borrowings for just a single subsidiary, or for a consolidated business.
- The expenditures on a qualifying asset can be considered the average carrying amount of the asset during the measurement period, including those borrowing costs that were capitalized in prior periods.

EXAMPLE

Milford Public Sound incurs an average expenditure over the construction period of an outdoor arena complex of £15,000,000. It has taken out a short-term loan of £12,000,000 at 9% interest specifically to cover the cost of this project. Milford can capitalize the borrowing cost of the entire amount of the £12,000,000 loan at 9% interest, but it still has £3,000,000 of average expenditures that exceed the amount of this project-specific loan.

Milford has two bonds outstanding at the time of the project, in the following amounts:

Bond Description	Principal Outstanding	Interest
8% Bond	£18,000,000	£1,440,000
10% Bond	12,000,000	1,200,000
Totals	£30,000,000	£2,640,000

The weighted-average interest rate on these two bond issuances is 8.8% (£2,640,000 interest ÷ £30,000,000 principal), which is the interest rate that Milford should use when capitalizing the remaining £3,000,000 of average expenditures.

Follow these steps to calculate the amount of interest to be capitalized for a specific project:

1. Construct a table itemizing the amounts of expenditures made and the dates on which the expenditures were made.
2. Determine the date on which borrowing cost capitalization ends.
3. Calculate the capitalization period for each expenditure, which is the number of days between the specific expenditure and the end of the interest capitalization period.
4. Divide each capitalization period by the total number of days elapsed between the date of the first expenditure and the end of the borrowing cost capitalization period to arrive at the capitalization multiplier for each line item.
5. Multiply each expenditure amount by its capitalization multiplier to arrive at the average expenditure for each line item over the capitalization measurement period.
6. Add up the average expenditures at the line item level to arrive at a grand total average expenditure.
7. If there is project-specific debt, multiply the grand total of the average expenditures by the interest rate on that debt to arrive at the capitalized borrowing cost related to that debt.
8. If the grand total of the average expenditures exceeds the amount of the project-specific debt, multiply the excess expenditure amount by the weighted average of the company's other outstanding debt to arrive at the remaining amount of borrowing cost to be capitalized.
9. Add together both capitalized borrowing cost calculations. If the combined total is more than the total borrowing cost incurred by the company during

the calculation period, reduce the amount of borrowing cost to be capitalized to the total borrowing cost incurred by the company during the calculation period.

10. Record the borrowing cost capitalization with a debit to the project's fixed asset account and a credit to the interest expense account.

EXAMPLE

Milford Public Sound is building a concert arena. Milford makes payments related to the project of £10,000,000 and £14,000,000 to a contractor on January 1 and July 1, respectively. The arena is completed on December 31.

For the 12-month period of construction, Milford can capitalize all of the borrowing cost on the £10,000,000 payment, since it was outstanding during the full period of construction. Milford can capitalize the borrowing cost on the £14,000,000 payment for half of the construction period, since it was outstanding during only the second half of the construction period. The average expenditure for which the borrowing cost can be capitalized is calculated in the following table:

Date of Payment	Expenditure Amount	Capitalization Period*	Capitalization Multiplier	Average Expenditure
January 1	£10,000,000	12 months	12/12 months = 100%	£10,000,000
July 1	14,000,000	6 months	6/12 months = 50%	7,000,000
				£17,000,000

* In the table, the capitalization period is defined as the number of months that elapse between the expenditure payment date and the end of the interest capitalization period.

The only debt that Milford has outstanding during this period is a line of credit, on which the interest rate is 8%. The maximum amount of interest that Milford can capitalize into the cost of this arena project is £1,360,000, which is calculated as:

8% Interest rate × £17,000,000 Average expenditure = £1,360,000

Milford records the following journal entry:

	Debit	Credit
Fixed assets – Arena	1,360,000	
Interest expense		1,360,000

Tip: There may be an inordinate number of expenditures related to a larger project, which could result in a large and unwieldy calculation of average expenditures. To reduce the workload, consider aggregating these expenses by month, and then assume that each expenditure was made in the middle of the month, thereby reducing all of the expenditures for each month to a single line item.

The following additional rules may apply to the amount of borrowing costs capitalized in association with a qualifying asset:

- *Start of capitalization.* Begin capitalizing borrowing costs on the commencement date of the qualifying asset. This date is when expenditures are first incurred, borrowing costs are incurred, *and* activities are undertaken to prepare the asset for its intended use.
- *Suspension of capitalization.* Stop capitalizing borrowing costs during extended time periods when the development of a qualifying asset has been suspended. This does not include periods when there is other ongoing technical or administrative work, or when a temporary delay is a necessary part of the asset completion process.
- *Termination of capitalization.* All further capitalization of borrowing costs should cease when substantially all of the tasks needed to prepare a qualifying asset for its intended use have been completed. Minor modifications or routine administrative work should not interfere with the termination of borrowing cost capitalization. If a portion of a qualifying asset is complete and can be used, stop capitalizing the borrowing costs attributable to that portion, even if the remainder of the asset has not yet been completed. Conversely, if a portion of a qualifying asset is complete but cannot be used without the completion of the remainder of the asset, do not stop capitalizing the borrowing costs attributable to that portion of the asset.

EXAMPLE

Milford Public Sound is building three arenas, all under different circumstances. They are:

1. *Arena A.* This is an entertainment complex, including a stage area, movie theatre, and restaurants. Milford should stop capitalizing borrowing costs on each component of the project as soon as it is substantially complete and ready for use, since each part of the complex can operate without the other parts being complete.
2. *Arena B.* This is a single outdoor stage with integrated multi-level parking garage. Even though the garage is completed first, Milford should continue to capitalize borrowing costs for it, since the garage is only intended to service patrons of the arena, and so will not be operational until the arena is complete.
3. *Arena C.* This is an entertainment complex for which Milford is also constructing a highway off-ramp and road that leads to the complex. Since the complex is unusable until patrons can reach the complex, Milford should continue to capitalize borrowing costs until the off-ramp and road are complete.

- *Invested funds.* The amount of borrowing costs incurred that can be capitalized must be reduced by the amount of any interest income earned from the temporary investment of borrowed funds before they are spent on a qualifying asset.
- *Maximum amount permitted.* An entity is not permitted to capitalize borrowing costs that exceed the amount of the actual borrowing costs in-

curred by the business during a reporting period. Instead, the amount capitalized is capped at the amount of the actual borrowings incurred.

- *Recoverable amount.* When the carrying amount of a qualifying asset (including capitalized borrowing costs) exceeds its recoverable amount, write the carrying amount down to the recoverable amount.

EXAMPLE

Milford Public Sound issues a one-year note for £20,000,000 at 6% interest to pay for the construction of a new arena. At the end of the one-year period, Milford has incurred £1,200,000 in interest costs, but has also earned £250,000 on interest income from the temporary investment of funds received from the note. Thus, the maximum amount of interest expense that Milford can capitalize is £950,000 (£1,200,000 interest cost - £250,000 interest income).

Borrowing Cost Disclosures

If a company has capitalized any of its borrowing costs, disclose the amount of borrowing cost capitalized in the period, as well as the capitalization rate used to derive the amount of capitalized borrowing costs.

EXAMPLE

Suture Corporation discloses the following information about the borrowing costs it has capitalized as part of the construction of a laboratory facility:

> The company incurred borrowing costs of £800,000 during the year. Of that amount, it charged £650,000 to expense and included the remaining £150,000 in the capitalized cost of its Dumont laboratory facility. The capitalized borrowing costs were derived from a capitalization rate of 7.8%.

Summary

The key issue with borrowing cost capitalization is whether to use it at all. It requires a certain amount of administrative effort to compile, and so is not recommended for lower-value fixed assets. Instead, reserve its use for larger projects where including borrowing costs in an asset will improve the quality of the financial information reported by a business. If you choose to capitalize borrowing costs, adopt a procedure for determining the amount to be capitalized and closely adhere to it, with appropriate documentation of the results. This will result in a standardized calculation methodology that auditors can more easily review.

Chapter 29
Leases

Introduction

IFRS allows for the recognition of either finance leases or operating leases by both parties in a leasing arrangement. This chapter describes the accounting and disclosures related to these types of leases from the perspectives of both lessees and lessors, as well as several other issues related to leases.

IFRS Source Documents

- IAS 17, *Leases*
- IFRIC 4, *Determining whether an Arrangement Contains a Lease*
- SIC 15, *Operating Leases – Incentives*
- SIC 27, *Evaluating the Substance of Transactions Involving the Legal Form of a Lease*

Types of Leases

A lease is an arrangement under which the entity owning an asset (the lessor) conveys the right to use the asset to another party (the lessee) in exchange for one or more payments. Under IFRS, the classification of a lease depends upon whether the risks and rewards of ownership pass to the lessee. Examples of these risks and rewards are:
- Loss from idle capacity
- Loss from technological obsolescence
- Loss from changing economic conditions
- Gain from appreciation in value of a leased asset
- Gain from realization of the residual value of a leased asset

If a lease transfers substantially all risks and rewards of ownership to the lessee, it is classified as a *finance lease*. Otherwise, a lease is classified as an *operating lease*. Circumstances under which a lease is usually classified as a finance lease include:
- Ownership of the asset is shifted to the lessee by the end of the lease term.
- The lessee has the option to purchase the asset at price low enough to make it reasonably certain that the option will be exercised.
- Even if title to the asset is not transferred to the lessee, the lease term covers most of the economic life of the asset.
- The present value of minimum lease payments equates to substantially all of the fair value of the asset.

- The asset is so specialized that only the lessee can use it without major modifications.

EXAMPLE

Twill Machinery enters into a lease agreement with Currency Leasing to lease an asset for seven years. The underlying asset's economic life is expected to be eight years. The fair value of the leased asset is £220,000, and the present value of the future minimum lease payments required under the lease agreement is £210,000.

The lease arrangement should be classified as a finance lease, because nearly all of the economic life of the asset (88%) is covered by the lease term; also, the present value of future minimum lease payments comprises nearly all (95%) of the fair value of the asset.

It is possible that the lessee and lessor in a lease transaction will have differing interpretations of how to classify a lease. This situation can arise, for example, when a third party guarantees the residual value on a lease.

The classification of a lease as an operating or finance lease is made at the inception of the lease. A subsequent change in estimates or circumstances is not a valid basis for changing the classification of a lease. However, if the lessor and lessee agree to change the terms of a lease, the revised lease version can be reclassified.

It may be necessary to split a lease that contains land and building elements, and classify each element differently. The following issues may apply to the classification of such a lease:

- *Land life span.* When determining the classification of the land portion of the lease, the land portion is usually considered to have an indefinite life.
- *Payment allocation.* When allocating lease payments between the two elements, do so using the relative fair values of both assets at the beginning of the lease. If it is not possible to allocate lease payments between these elements, classify the entire lease as a finance lease, unless both elements are clearly operating leases.
- *Materiality of land component.* If the land element of the arrangement is immaterial, it is not necessary to split the elements of the lease for accounting purposes. In this case, the economic life of the building is considered the same as the economic life of all assets in the lease.

EXAMPLE

Nuance Corporation enters into a lease agreement that includes a warehouse and the land on which it sits. Under the terms of the lease, Nuance will obtain title to the warehouse in five years, but not title to the land. The fair value of the building is £3,000,000 and the fair value of the land is £1,000,000. The fair value of the minimum lease payments associated with the building is £2,900,000, while the amount associated with the land is £500,000.

Nuance recognizes the building portion of the lease as a financing lease, since title to the warehouse passes to Nuance, and the net present value of lease payments nearly equals its fair value. The company should classify the land portion of the lease as an operating lease, since it does not take title to the land, and the present value of lease payments is only half of its fair value.

Lease Accounting by the Lessee

A lessee is the entity that makes payments to a lessor for the use of an asset owned by the lessor. In this section, we discuss the accounting by the lessee for finance leases and operating leases.

Finance Leases

If a lessee recognizes a lease as a finance lease, the lessee should recognize at lease inception an asset and liability in its financial statements at the lower of the fair value of the leased property or the present value of minimum lease payments. When calculating the present value of minimum lease payments, use as a discount rate the interest rate implicit in the lease. If this interest rate is not readily discernible, use the lessee's incremental borrowing rate. Also, if there are any initial costs associated with the lease, add them to the amount recognized as an asset.

The liability that offsets a recognized lease asset is the amount of future lease payments. IFRS does not allow for the presentation of this liability as a deduction from the leased asset line item in the balance sheet. Instead, the lease liability is split into its current and long-term components and presented within the liabilities section of the balance sheet.

On an ongoing basis, any minimum lease payments made are apportioned between interest expense and a reduction of the lease liability. The calculation of interest expense should result in a constant periodic rate of interest on the remaining balance in the lease payments liability account. If a contingent rent payment is layered on top of a minimum lease payment, charge the entire amount of the contingent payment to expense as incurred.

When an asset is recognized under a finance lease, the asset should be depreciated. The depreciation calculation employed should be consistent with the depreciation calculation used for other fixed assets owned by the lessee. If the lessee does not retain ownership of the asset at the end of the lease term, the depreciation period should be the lesser of the useful life of the asset or the lease term.

EXAMPLE

Mole Industries leases production equipment that has a fair value of £400,000. The lease term is five years, and requires a single payment at the end of each year of £102,837. No residual value is assumed. The implied interest rate associated with the lease is 9%, and the present value of the minimum lease payments is £400,000 (£102,837 annual payment × 3.88965 present value factor for an ordinary annuity of 1 per period).

The basis for Mole's recognition of this arrangement is based on the following table:

Payment	Balance Due	Payment	Interest Expense	Balance Paydown
Year 1	£400,000	£102,837	£36,000	£66,837
Year 2	333,163	102,837	29,985	72,852
Year 3	260,311	102,837	23,428	79,409
Year 4	180,902	102,837	16,281	86,556
Year 5	94,346	102,837	8,491	94,346
	0			

Mole records the initial acquisition of the production equipment with the following entry:

	Debit	Credit
Production equipment	400,000	
Lease obligation		400,000

Mole's first recordation of the first annual lease payment is as follows:

	Debit	Credit
Lease obligation	66,837	
Interest expense	36,000	
Cash		102,837

Mole also depreciates the production equipment over the five-year term of the lease under the straight-line method, using the following annual depreciation entry:

	Debit	Credit
Depreciation expense	80,000	
Accumulated depreciation		80,000

Operating Leases

When a lessee enters into an operating lease, it recognizes lease payments as expense on a straight-line basis through the term of the lease, unless another pattern of recognition more closely adheres to the time pattern over which the lessee benefits from the leasing arrangement. This pattern of recognition applies, even if the actual payments made do not follow the same pattern.

Lease Accounting by the Lessor

A lessor is the entity that leases its assets to another entity, the lessee, in exchange for payments. In this section, we discuss the accounting by the lessee for finance leases and operating leases.

Financing Leases

When a lessor has entered into a lease agreement that is classified as a financing lease, the asset is presumed to be owned by the lessee. Therefore, the lessor reports a receivable in its balance sheet in the amount of its net investment in the lease. Each lease payment made by the lessee is considered a repayment of principal, plus interest income.

If the lessor incurs any up-front costs associated with a lease, such as legal fees or commissions, include these costs in the receivable that the lessee is repaying through its ongoing lease payments. This inclusion will reduce the amount of interest income recognized by the lessor. When a manufacturer or dealer lessor incurs these up-front costs, it should charge them to expense when the related selling profit is recognized, rather than including them in the receivable.

The selling profit for a financing lease is usually recognized by a manufacturer or dealer lessor when the lease term begins, to match the policy of such an entity for outright sales transactions. The revenue recognized when the lease term begins is the lesser of the fair value of the asset leased or the present value of minimum lease payments, discounted at the market interest rate. The offsetting cost of goods sold to be recognized is the carrying amount of the leased property, minus the present value of any unguaranteed residual value.

If a manufacturer or dealer lessor quotes a lessee an artificially low interest rate on a financing lease, the amount of selling profit recognized shall be limited to the profit that would have been recognized if the market interest rate had been charged. Though a selling profit may be recognized when the lease term begins, any interest income associated with the lease is recognized over the term of the lease.

On an ongoing basis, lease payments made by the lessee to the lessor are apportioned by the lessor between interest income and a reduction of the receivable balance. The calculation of interest income should result in a constant periodic rate of interest on the lessor's remaining net investment in the lease.

In any reporting period, if there has been a reduction in the estimated amount of the unguaranteed residual value of a lease, revise the income allocation over the remaining lease term.

EXAMPLE

Nova Corporation leases a deep field telescope to the British Science Institute under a five-year lease. The telescope cost Nova £500,000 to build, and should retain a £200,000 residual value at the end of the lease. The payments due under the lease are one payment of £99,139, payable at the end of each year. Nova's implicit interest rate is 10%. The present value multiplier for an ordinary annuity of 1 for five periods at 10% interest is 3.79079. The present value multiplier for £1 due in five years at 10% interest is 0.62092.

Nova recognizes the transaction with the following entries:
- *Revenue.* This is the £375,815 present value of the lease payments (calculated as £99,139 × 3.79079 present value factor).
- *Cost of goods sold.* This is the asset cost of £500,000, less the £124,184 present value of the residual value of the telescope (calculated as £200,000 × 0.62092 present value factor), resulting in a cost of goods sold of £375,816.
- *Lease receivable.* This is the £495,695 sum of the lease payments, plus the residual value of £200,000, for a total receivable of £695,695.

- *Unearned interest.* This is the lease receivable of £695,695, minus the £375,815 present value of the lease payments, minus the £124,184 present value of the residual value of the telescope, or £195,696.

Based on this information, Nova documents the initial leasing transaction with the following entry:

	Debit	Credit
Lease receivable	695,695	
Cost of goods sold	375,816	
Revenue		375,815
Telescope asset		500,000
Unearned revenue		195,696

Nova then calculates the annual amount of interest income that it should recognize, based on the following table:

Payment Timing	Lease Obligation	Payment	Interest Income	Balance Paydown
Year 1	£500,000	£99,139	£50,000	£49,139
Year 2	450,861	99,139	45,086	54,053
Year 3	396,808	99,139	39,681	59,458
Year 4	337,350	99,139	33,735	65,404
Year 5	271,946	99,139	27,193	71,946
Residual value	200,000			

Operating Leases

When a lessor enters into a leasing arrangement that is classified as an operating lease, it should recognize the income from this arrangement on a straight-line basis over the term of the lease, unless some other method of recognition more closely adheres to the time pattern over which the benefit derived from the asset declines. The straight-line basis is the default form of income recognition, even if the receipts from lease payments do not follow the same pattern.

Any costs incurred to earn leasing income are charged to expense. The primary cost so recognized is likely to be depreciation expense. The manner of calculating depreciation expense should be the same as the lessor uses for similar assets. Any costs incurred by the lessor to negotiate and arrange a lease are to be added to the capitalized cost of a leased asset, and depreciated over the term of the lease.

If a manufacturer or dealer lessor enters into an operating lease, it cannot recognize a selling profit at the inception of the lease, since it has not sold the underlying asset (as was the case for a financing lease).

Sale and Leaseback Transactions

As the name implies, a sale and leaseback transaction involves the lease of an asset to a lessor, after which the selling party leases the asset back from the lessor. This transaction usually arises in order to shift a large amount of cash to the seller of the property. A lessor is willing to engage in such a transaction in order to earn interest income on the financing aspect of the transaction. The accounting for a sale and leaseback arrangement is as follows:

- *Profit recognition (financing lease).* If classified as a financing lease, the seller-lessee must amortize any gain on the sale over the term of the lease.
- *Profit recognition (operating lease).* If classified as an operating lease where the transaction was established at fair value, the seller-lessee can recognize any gain on the sale at once.
- *Sale price below fair value.* If the sale price is below the fair value of the asset, the seller-lessor recognizes the profit or loss at once. However, if future lease payments are below the market rate, the loss is amortized over the usage period.
- *Sale price above fair value.* If the sale price is above the fair value of the asset, the seller-lessor defers the gain and amortizes it over the usage period.

Determining whether an Arrangement Contains a Lease

Two entities may enter into an arrangement that does not take the legal form of a lease, but which shifts the right to use an asset between the parties. The following guidance applies to whether these arrangements should be classified as leases:

- *Basic guidelines.* A lease exists when the right to use an asset has been conveyed, and the use of a specific asset is required. Right of use is assumed to have been conveyed when the purchaser can operate the asset in the manner it chooses and controls the output or utility of the asset, can control physical access to the asset and controls the output or utility of the asset, or will probably take a significant amount of the output or utility of the asset.
- *Assessment period.* The assessment of the existence of a lease occurs at the inception of the arrangement. This assessment can only be revised at a later date if one of the following occurs:
  o A change in the terms of the arrangement
  o A change in the leased asset
  o A change in the dependence on a specific asset
  o A renewal option has been exercised or the parties have agreed to an extension
- *Separation of elements.* If it is determined that a lease does exist, lease accounting shall only be applied to that portion of an arrangement that is considered to be a lease, based on the relative fair values of the various elements of the arrangement.

EXAMPLE

Puller Corporation enters into a supply arrangement where it constructs a doorknob manufacturing facility next to the Baroque Door Company, and supplies doorknobs to Baroque from that facility. Puller maintains control over the facility, and is responsible for its maintenance. Puller is required to supply a certain minimum quantity of units per period, for which Baroque pays the amount stated in the purchase agreement. Puller has the right to divert unused capacity at the facility to production for other customers, which it routinely does.

This is not a leasing arrangement, because Baroque does not have the right to operate the facility in the manner it chooses, does not control physical access to the facility, and other entities will take a significant amount of the output of the facility.

Evaluating the Substance of Lease Transactions

Two parties may enter into an arrangement or group of arrangements that have the legal form of a lease, but whose effect may not result in a lease. For example, a sale and leaseback arrangement could be agreed to that is actually designed to create a tax advantage for one party without conveying the right to use the underlying asset. The following guidance applies to these situations:

- *Aggregation.* If there are a series of transactions that cannot be understood without reference to the entire group, treat them as a single transaction to determine whether a lease exists.
- *Substance of the arrangement.* Account for the transaction or group of transactions as a lease if the substance of the underlying arrangement indicates a lease (which means that the right to use an asset has been conveyed).
- *Conditions.* There may not be a lease:
  o If the primary reason for the arrangement is to achieve a certain tax result.
  o When the arrangement includes an option under which the terms are so favorable as to make its exercise nearly certain.
  o When funds are placed in an investment account to protect an investor, and the business cannot control the account; or when the only cash flows from an arrangement come from funds withdrawn from the investment account.
  o When there is only a remote risk of reimbursing a fee received from an investor, or of paying a guarantee or other obligation.

If a fee is transferred between the parties as part of a purported leasing arrangement, the fee should probably *not* be recognized immediately as income when:

- There are performance conditions, or an obligation to refrain from an activity.
- Use of the underlying asset is restricted.
- There is a non-remote chance that the fee must be reimbursed.

EXAMPLE

The Close Call Company sells its headquarters building to Wealth Management Corporation for £10,000,000 and agrees to lease the building back from Wealth Management. The arrangement requires Wealth Management to exercise a put option after 10 years at a price that essentially earns Wealth Management a return on investment of 2% over the prime rate for the term of the arrangement.

Since the risks and rewards of ownership have not passed to Wealth Management, the arrangement should not be considered a lease.

Operating Lease Incentives

When a lessee is negotiating an operating lease, it may demand an incentive, of which the following are examples:
- The lessor grants several months of free rent
- The lessor pays cash to the lessee to offset its move-in costs
- The lessor absorbs the cost of leasehold improvements
- The lessor pays off the remaining payments on a lease to which the lessee is a party

All lease incentives should be considered an integral part of a leasing arrangement. This means that:
- *Lessee accounting.* The lessee should recognize the benefit of these incentives as a reduction of its rental expense over the term of the lease, typically on a straight-line basis.
- *Lessor accounting.* The lessor should recognize the cost of these incentives as a reduction of rental income over the term of the lease, typically on a straight-line basis.

In both cases, some other form of cost recognition than the straight-line basis is allowable if it more closely matches the time pattern over which the benefit of a leased asset is used.

EXAMPLE

The Close Call Company enters into a new lease arrangement for a warehouse, under which the lessor agrees to one year of free rent at the beginning of the lease period, followed by nine years of rent payments. The annual rent due to the lessor at the end of all years other than the first year is £100,000. The total consideration paid of £900,000 should be recognized over the full ten years of the lease arrangement.

Lease Disclosures by the Lessee

If a lessee has finance leases, it should disclose the following information in the notes that accompany its financial statements:

- *Carrying amount.* For each asset class, the ending net carrying amount of leased assets.
- *Contingent rent.* The amount of contingent rent expense recognized.
- *Descriptions.* General descriptions of material leasing arrangements, including the basis for paying contingent rent, the presence of any renewal, purchase, or escalation clauses, and leasing restrictions (such as on the payment of dividends or the extent of additional borrowings).
- *Reconciliation.* A reconciliation of the difference between total future minimum lease payments and their present value. Also state the total future minimum lease payments and their present values for the following periods: not later than one year, 1-5 years, and later than five years.
- *Subleases.* The total of future minimum sublease payments expected from non-cancellable subleases.

If a lessee has operating leases, it should disclose the following information in the notes that accompany its financial statements:

- *Descriptions.* General descriptions of significant leasing arrangements, including the basis for paying contingent rent, the presence of any renewal, purchase, or escalation clauses, and leasing restrictions (such as on the payment of dividends or the extent of additional borrowings).
- *Expenses.* The amount of lease and sublease payments recognized as expense in the period, along with separate disclosure of payments for contingent rent, subleases, and minimum lease payments.
- *Payments.* The total future minimum lease payments under non-cancellable leases for the following periods: not later than one year, 1-5 years, and later than five years.
- *Subleases.* The total of future minimum sublease payments expected from non-cancellable subleases.

Lease Disclosures by the Lessor

If a lessor has finance leases, it should disclose the following information in the notes that accompany its financial statements:

- *Contingent rent.* The amount of income recognized from contingent rents in the period.
- *Descriptions.* General descriptions of material leasing arrangements.
- *Reconciliation.* A reconciliation of the difference between the gross investment in the leases and the present value of minimum lease payments receivable. Also state the gross investment in the leases and the present value of minimum lease payments for the following periods: not later than one year, 1-5 years, and later than five years.

- *Residual values.* The amount of unguaranteed residual values benefiting the lessor.
- *Uncollectible payments.* The accumulated amount of the allowance for uncollectible minimum lease payment receivables.
- *Unearned income.* The amount of unearned interest income.

If a lessor has operating leases, it should disclose the following information in the notes that accompany its financial statements:

- *Contingent rent.* The amount of contingent rent income recognized.
- *Descriptions.* General descriptions of material leasing arrangements.
- *Payments.* The total future minimum lease payments under non-cancellable operating leases for the following periods: not later than one year, 1-5 years, and later than five years.

Other Disclosures

If there is an arrangement or group of arrangements whose substance calls for recognition as a lease, disclose the following information by arrangement or for each class of arrangement:

- *Description.* A description of the arrangement and its terms, the assets involved and any usage restrictions, the term of the arrangement, and which transactions are linked together.
- *Fees.* How any fees associated with the transaction are accounted for, the amount recognized in profit or loss, and where this information is located in the statement of comprehensive income.

Summary

Companies that are in the leasing business are well aware of the lease accounting rules set forth in this chapter, and so will usually structure the terms of a leasing arrangement to make it quite clear that a lease should be classified as either an operating or financing lease. Thus, it is rather unusual to be faced with an uncertain lease classification situation.

The accounting for finance leases is considerably more difficult than the accounting for operating leases, so it makes sense to adopt a detailed procedure that states exactly how these leases are supposed to be measured and recognized, along with templates for the journal entries to be used. Also, consider having a senior accountant review the initial accounting for every finance lease, to ensure that it is correct.

Chapter 30
Related Party Disclosures

Introduction

IFRS devotes an entire accounting standard to related party disclosures, which is somewhat unusual, because it does not mandate any accounting recordation – only the disclosure of information involving related party transactions. This chapter describes the nature of a related party transaction, and then itemizes the required disclosures for these types of transactions. The intent of these requirements is to draw particular attention to how the balance sheet and income statement may have been impacted by transactions with related parties, who might not otherwise have been willing to engage in the same transactions if they had not been related parties. This guidance applies to individual financial statements, as well as to the consolidated financial statements of a business.

IFRS Source Document

- IAS 24, *Related Party Disclosures*

Overview of Related Parties

A company may do business with a variety of parties with which it has a close association. These parties are known as related parties. Examples of related parties are:
- Other subsidiaries under common control
- Owners of a business, its key managers, and their families
- The parent entity
- Post-employment benefit plans for the benefit of employees
- An entity that provides key management personnel services to the reporting entity

Entities *not* considered to be related parties are lenders, trade unions, public utilities, government entities that do not control the business, entities that have a director or key manager in common, and fellow joint venturers who jointly control a venture.

There are many types of transactions that can be conducted between related parties, such as sales, asset transfers, leases, lending arrangements, guarantees, allocations of common costs, and the filing of consolidated tax returns.

The disclosure of related party information is considered useful to the readers of a company's financial statements, particularly in regard to the examination of changes in the financial results and financial position over time, and in comparison to the same information for other businesses.

Related Party Disclosures

In general, any related party transaction should be disclosed that would impact the decision making of the users of a company's financial statements. This involves the following disclosures:

- *General.* The nature of all related party relationships, even in the absence of any transactions between the parties, and the name of the ultimate controlling party (usually the parent entity).
- *Compensation.* The total amount of compensation for key management personnel, as well as for their short-term benefits, post-employment benefits, other long-term benefits, termination benefits, and any share-based payments. This is not necessary for management personnel services acquired from another entity.
- *Transaction level.* For specific related party transactions, the nature of the relationship, transaction terms and conditions, outstanding balances, commitments or guarantees, related collateral arrangements, provisions for related doubtful debts, and any related bad debt expense recognized during the period. These disclosures should be reported separately for the parent entity, any entities with joint control or influence over the business, subsidiaries, associates, joint ventures, key management personnel, and other related parties.
- *Key management personnel services.* The amounts incurred for key management personnel services from a separate management entity.
- *Government control.* Transaction-level disclosures are not required when the related party is a government entity that has control or influence over the business, or another entity over which the same government entity also exercises control or influence. Instead, disclose the name of the government entity and the nature of the relationship with it, as well as the nature and amount of those transactions considered significant. If a number of transactions are considered significant only if they are aggregated into a group, indicate the significance of these aggregated transactions (either numerically or descriptively). A transaction is considered to be more significant if it is of unusual size, contains non-market terms, is not a common transaction, is disclosed to either senior management or regulatory authorities, or requires the approval of shareholders.

Examples of transactions that may require related party disclosure are the purchase or sale of goods or property, rendering of services, provision of guarantees, and settlement of liabilities on behalf of another entity.

Depending on the transactions, it may be acceptable to aggregate some related party information by type of transaction.

When disclosing related party information, do not state or imply that the transactions were on an arm's-length basis, unless the claim can be substantiated.

EXAMPLE

During the year ended December 31, 20X2, the federal government provided Failsafe Containment Corporation with a £10,000,000 startup loan for the company's research into the development of a portable fusion reactor. The loan requires a single balloon payment in ten years, plus the payment of all accumulated interest on the maturity date. The government charges a fixed rate of 2% interest on the loan, as compared to the 9% rate that the company would otherwise have obtained from its lenders.

Summary

Related party transactions are surprisingly common, especially when the owners of a company are continually propping up a business with additional funding or granting favorable financing terms. Accordingly, this is a topic worthy of regular review, since there can be an ongoing series of related party transactions that must be disclosed.

Chapter 31
Events after the Reporting Period

Introduction

There will always be a continuing series of events that can impact the information incorporated into a company's financial statements, and some of them will occur after the reporting period. This chapter sets forth the general principles needed to determine whether the recognition of these subsequent events can be safely delayed until the next set of financial statements, or if the statements relating to the last accounting period must be revised to incorporate them.

IFRS Source Document

- IAS 10, *Events after the Reporting Period*

Overview of Events after the Reporting Period

An event after the reporting period is considered to be one that arises between the end of the reporting period and when the financial statements for that period are authorized for issuance. There are two types of these events:

- *Additional information.* An event provides additional information about conditions in existence at the end of a reporting period, including estimates used to prepare the financial statements for that period.
- *New events.* An event provides new information about conditions that did not exist at the end of a reporting period.

There are rare cases where a company may be required to submit its financial statements to its shareholders for approval. If so, the financial statements are considered to have been authorized for issuance on the date of issuance, rather than the shareholder approval date.

EXAMPLE

The Close Call Company completes its financial statements for the past year, to which the following dates apply:

- Draft statements completed on January 25
- Statements authorized for issuance by the board of directors on February 15
- Investment community notified of financial results on February 28
- Financial statements issued to shareholders on March 5
- Shareholders approve financial statements at annual meeting on March 15

The financial statements of Close Call were authorized for issuance on February 15, which is when they were approved by the board of directors.

IFRS states that the financial statements should include the effects of all events after the reporting period that provide additional information about conditions in existence during the reporting period. This rule requires that all entities evaluate subsequent events through the date when financial statements are available to be issued. Examples of situations calling for the adjustment of financial statements are:

- *Lawsuit.* If events take place before the date of the financial statements that trigger a lawsuit, and lawsuit settlement occurs after the reporting period, consider adjusting the amount of any contingent loss already recognized to match the amount of the actual settlement.
- *Bad debt.* If a company issued invoices to a customer before the date of the financial statements, and the customer goes bankrupt as a subsequent event, consider adjusting the allowance for doubtful accounts to match the amount of receivables that will likely not be collected.
- *Net realizable value.* If the business sells inventory after the reporting period at a low price, this indicates that the net realizable value of the inventory may have been low during the reporting period, which may call for a reduction in the carrying amount of those inventory items.

If there are subsequent events that provide new information about conditions that did not exist as of the date of the financial statements, these events should not be recognized in the financial statements. Examples of situations that do not trigger an adjustment to the financial statements if they occur after the date of the financial statements are:

- A business combination
- Changes in the value of investments after the end of the reporting period
- Changes in the value of assets due to changes in exchange rates
- Destruction of company assets
- Dividends declared after the reporting period
- Entering into a significant guarantee or commitment
- Sale of equity
- Settlement of a lawsuit where the events causing the lawsuit arose after the reporting period

The Going Concern Issue

IFRS mandates that a company should not prepare its financial statements under the assumption that it is a going concern, if events arise after the reporting period that indicate the business may no longer be a going concern. This scenario arises when management determines that it has no realistic alternative other than to liquidate the business or cease trading.

Disclosure of Events after the Reporting Period

A company should disclose the following information regarding events after the reporting period:

- The date when the financial statements were authorized for issuance
- Who gave the authorization for financial statement issuance

Also, if any party can amend the financial statements after issuance, disclose this point. Further, if information was received concerning conditions in existence at the end of the reporting period, update all disclosures accompanying the financial statements to include the effects of this information.

There may be situations where the non-reporting of a subsequent event would result in misleading financial statements. If so, disclose the nature of the event and an estimate of its financial effect (or a statement that no estimate can be made). Examples of such events are a major business combination, the destruction of a major facility, significant commitments, and the commencement of a major restructuring.

Summary

The recognition of subsequent events in financial statements can be quite subjective in many instances. Given the amount of time required to revise financial statements at the last minute, it is worthwhile to strongly consider whether the circumstances of a subsequent event can be construed as *not* requiring the revision of financial statements.

There is a danger in inconsistently applying the subsequent event rules, so that similar events do not always result in the same treatment of the financial statements. Consequently, it is best to adopt internal rules regarding which events will always lead to the revision of financial statements; these rules will likely require continual updating, as the business encounters new subsequent events that had not previously been incorporated into its rules.

Chapter 32
Insurance Contracts

Introduction

An insurer may sell a variety of insurance contracts to its policy holders. This chapter describes the accounting and disclosure requirements of insurers in regard to these insurance contracts, with a particular emphasis on the relevance and reliability of the information presented in an insurer's financial statements.

IFRS Source Document

- IFRS 4, *Insurance Contracts*

Overview of Insurance Contracts

An insurance contract arises when one party (the insurer) agrees to compensate another party if an uncertain future event causes losses for the other party. In essence, the insurer is being compensated for taking on a significant amount of the other party's risk. Examples of insurance contracts are:

Bid bonds	Medical insurance	Reinsurance contracts
Credit insurance	Performance bonds	Surety bonds
Disability insurance	Product liability insurance	Theft insurance
Fidelity bonds	Product warranties	Title insurance
Life insurance	Professional liability insurance	Travel assistance

Conversely, a contract that does not expose an insurer to any significant risk, or which shifts risk back to the policy holder, is not considered an insurance contract. Self-insurance is also not considered an insurance contract, since there is no agreement with a third party.

Within the following topics of this section, we address a variety of factors that influence the accounting by an insurer for its insurance contracts.

The following example shows the general accounting flow for a standard insurance contract.

EXAMPLE

Miner Insurance writes a number of insurance policies to mine operators and mine employees. The company commits to an insurance contract, under which it is paid £5,000 at once and for which it expects to pay a claim of £4,000 on the policy in three years. There is a

15% commission on the policy, which it is Miner's standard practice to pay immediately. Miner expects a 4% return on its investment of the initial £5,000 payment, less the £750 amount of the commission. The standard accounting policy of Miner is to ratably recognize the revenues and expenses related to an insurance contract over its term. Based on this information, Miner recognizes the following information over the three years of the contract:

	Year 1	Year 2	Year 3
Premium earned	£1,667	£1,667	£1,666
Claims expense	1,333	1,333	1,333
Commission expense	250	250	250
Underwriting profit	84	84	84
Investment return	170	170	170
Profit	£254	£254	£254

An alternative approach would have been to use the fair value method, under which Miner recognizes the full amount of the policy premium in the first reporting period, the present value of the expected claim, and the commission expense. Miner would recognize any actual returns generated from the investment of the initial contract payment in each successive year.

Reporting Issues

The following issues relate to how an insurer is to account for its insurance contracts:

- *Liability recognition.* Do not recognize a liability for possible future claims related to insurance contracts that do not yet exist at the end of the reporting period.
- *Liability adequacy test.* The insurer must complete the liability adequacy test, which is noted below.
- *Liability derecognition.* The insurer is not allowed to remove an insurance liability from its balance sheet unless the liability has been discharged or cancelled, or it has expired.
- *Offsetting.* The insurer cannot offset the assets and liabilities related to insurance contracts in the balance sheet. Instead, they must be separately stated. Also, it is not allowable to offset the revenue or expense from insurance contracts with the revenue or expense from reinsurance contracts.
- *Impairment review.* The insurer must periodically determine whether its reinsurance assets have become impaired.

Liability Adequacy Test

At the end of each reporting period, an insurer must assess whether it has recognized a sufficient amount of insurance liabilities, based on current estimates of the future cash flows expected from its insurance contracts. If the insurer determines that the amount of recognized liability is inadequate, it must recognize the shortfall in profit or loss in the current period.

The test must include the following minimum requirements:
- *Cash flows.* The test includes consideration of contractual cash flows, as well as cash flows from such related areas as claims handling costs and the cash flows from embedded options and guarantees.
- *Recognition.* The entire amount of any deficiency must be recognized in the current period.

If an insurer does not have accounting policies that incorporate the liability adequacy test, it must take the following steps to conduct the test:
1. Subtract deferred acquisition costs and related intangible assets from the carrying amount of the relevant insurance liabilities.
2. Determine whether the result of the first calculation is lower than the carrying amount required for all applicable provisions and contingent liabilities (see the Provisions, Contingent Liabilities and Contingent Assets chapter).
3. If the carrying amount of the liabilities calculated in the first step is less than the liability calculated in the second step, recognize the difference in profit or loss in the current period. The result will be either an increase in the carrying amount of the relevant insurance liabilities, or a reduction in the carrying amount of related deferred acquisition costs or intangible assets.

Reinsurance Impairment

If a reinsurance asset is impaired, the holder of this insurance (the *cedant*), reduces the carrying amount of the asset by the amount of impairment, and recognizes the loss at once in profit or loss. A reinsurance asset is only impaired under the following circumstances:
- There is objective evidence that the cedant may not receive the entire amount due to it under the terms of the reinsurance contract; and
- The cedant can reliably measure the amount of the shortfall.

Accounting Policy Changes

Quite a large number of accounting policies may relate to the accounting for insurance, and each of them can have an impact on the amounts recognized or the classification of balance sheet items. Here is a sampling of the transactions to which accounting policies could be applied:

Acquired contracts	Discretionary participation features	Premium renewals and lapses
Acquisition costs	Embedded guarantees	Premiums collected by agents
Cash flow discounting	Embedded options	Recovery costs
Claims handling costs	Fees to policy holders	Reinsurance held
Claims incurred	Liability adequacy tests	Underwriting pools
Coinsurance		Unearned premiums

It is allowable for an insurer to change the policies that it uses to account for its insurance contracts, but only if doing so results in no degradation of their relevance and reliability, while improving at least their relevance *or* reliability. The discussion of changes in accounting policy may encompass the following issues:

- *Interest rates.* It is permissible to change the method of measuring certain insurance liabilities in order to incorporate the effects of current market interest rates. This election does not have to be applied consistently to all similar insurance liabilities. When this method of measurement is changed, the insurer must continue to measure the designated liabilities in the same manner until they have been extinguished.

- *Existing practices.* It is allowable for an insurer to continue to measure insurance liabilities on an undiscounted basis, future management fees at an amount exceeding their fair value, or to use different accounting policies for its subsidiaries. However, *introducing* any of these practices is not allowed.

- *Prudence.* There is no need to introduce additional prudence into the review of insurance contracts where sufficient prudence already exists.

- *Future margins on investment.* It is not necessary for an insurer to alter its accounting policies in order to eliminate future investment margins. However, its financial statements may become less relevant and reliable if it adds an accounting policy that considers future investment margins in the measurement of insurance contracts. An example of such a policy is the use of a discount rate that is similar to the estimated return on assets. This issue can be avoided if other accounting policies altered at the same time have the effect of improving the relevance or reliability of the insurer's financial statements.

- *Shadow accounting.* It is allowable for an insurer to alter its accounting policies so that an unrealized gain or loss on an asset affects the measurement of liabilities in the same manner as a realized gain or loss.

EXAMPLE

Gulf Coast Insurance currently uses accounting policies that have been in place since the inception of the company, and which employ very prudent assumptions, ignore certain types of embedded options, and use a discount rate that was set without first referring to market conditions. Gulf Coast could replace these policies with ones that require the use of current estimates, a reasonable adjustment for policy risk, the incorporation of embedded options, and a current market discount rate. By doing so, the financial statements produced by Gulf Coast will not be any less reliable, and more relevant.

Acquired Contracts

An insurer may acquire insurance contracts through the transfer of a contract portfolio, or via a business combination. In both cases, the insurer should measure the acquired insurance assets and liabilities at their fair values.

In addition, an insurer is allowed to adopt a split presentation for the fair value of acquired contracts that shows:

1. A liability as measured under the insurer's current accounting policies; and
2. An intangible asset that is the difference between the fair value of the contracts acquired and the obligations assumed, and the liability measured in the first step.

The intangible asset just described is not subject to impairment testing (see the Impairment of Assets chapter).

Discretionary Participation Features

An insurance contract may contain a guaranteed element and a discretionary participation feature. A discretionary participation feature is a contractual right to receive additional benefits that are based in some manner on the investment returns or profits of the insurer. It is allowable to recognize the guaranteed and discretionary portions of these contracts separately from each other, in which case the guaranteed element must be classified as a liability. The discretionary portion may be classified as either a liability or a separate component of equity, or be split between the two.

If the two elements are combined for recognition purposes, the entire contract must be classified as a liability.

When the insurer receives premiums on these contracts, it can recognize the premiums as revenue without separating out any portion of the premiums that is associated with the equity component. Any resulting changes in the guaranteed and discretionary and liability-classified portions of the contracts must be recognized in profit or loss. If some elements of the discretionary features are classified in equity, allocate a portion of profit or loss to those elements.

Disclosure of Insurance Contracts

The disclosure of information pertaining to insurance contracts is designed to give the readers of an insurer's financial statements sufficient knowledge to understand the amount, timing, and uncertainty of the projected cash flows associated with insurance contracts. Given these targets, disclose the following information in the notes accompanying the financial statements:

- *Policies.* The accounting policies that are applied to insurance contracts and related items.
- *Recognition.* The recognized amounts of assets, liabilities, income, and expense from insurance contracts. This information appears within the financial statements.
- *Cedant-specific.* The gains and losses from the purchase of reinsurance, the amortization within the period of deferred gains and losses from the purchase of reinsurance, and the remaining unamortized amount.

- *Assumptions.* The process used to determine those assumptions having the greatest effect on the financial statement line items associated with insurance contracts.
- *Assumption changes.* The separate effects of any changes in those assumptions used in the measurement of insurance assets and liabilities.
- *Reconciliation.* A reconciliation of the changes in reinsurance assets, insurance liabilities, and deferred acquisition costs during the period.

There are a number of risks associated with insurance contracts, for which the following set of disclosures are required:

- *Risk management.* The objectives and processes used to manage insurance contract risk.
- *Insurance risk.* The insurer's sensitivity to insurance risk, where this risk is concentrated, how risk concentrations are determined, and the shared characteristic used to group each risk concentration. Examples of risk concentrations are geographical concentrations, any contracts that cover low-frequency, high-cost risks, or exposure to expected changes in trends, or the presence of significant legislative risks that could cause a large loss.
- *Historical comparison.* A comparison of actual claims to previous estimates. This disclosure should include the earliest material claim for which there is still uncertainty, though it is not necessary to make this disclosure if a claim is more than ten years old. This disclosure is not required for claims that will be resolved within one year.
- *Sensitivity analysis.* An analysis that reveals how changes in reasonably possible risk variables would impact profit or loss and equity, as well as the assumptions used in preparing this analysis, and any changes from the prior period. Alternatively, disclose qualitative information about the sensitivity of risk variables, as well as those contract terms that can have a material impact on the future cash flows of the insurer.

Summary

There is a considerable emphasis on accounting policies in the accounting for insurance contracts. Accordingly, it is useful to develop policies for every significant element of the accounting for insurance contracts, test them to see how changes will impact the financial statements, and also have the company's auditors review them for compliance with IFRS. In addition, these policies should be codified into the accounting department's training regimen, along with sample transactions to illustrate how the policies impact the financial statements. Once these policies have been properly deliberated, tested, and installed, it should not be necessary to adjust them, unless there is a fundamental change in the way the insurer does business.

Chapter 33
Agriculture

Introduction

IFRS provides guidance concerning agricultural activities, which span livestock, forestry, crops, orchards, fish farming, and related activities. The guidance in this chapter applies to biological assets on an ongoing basis, as well as to agricultural produce when it is harvested.

IFRS Source Document

- IAS 41, *Agriculture*

Accounting for Agriculture

Agriculture covers many activities involving the enhancement of living animals and plants, in order to increase their quantity or quality. A business should recognize a biological asset only if all of the following conditions are true:
- The business controls the asset;
- Future economic benefits related to the asset will flow to the business; and
- Either the fair value or cost of the asset can be measured in a reliable manner.

A biological asset should be measured when it is initially recognized, as well as at the end of each reporting period. The measurement should use the fair value of the asset, less any costs to sell. Fair value may not differ appreciably from cost when little biological transformation has yet taken place, or if the biological transformation has little impact on price. For example, the initial growth of a hardwood tree may be minimal, resulting in no real change in value for a number of years.

When agricultural produce is harvested, the measurement should also be at the fair value of the asset, less any costs to sell. This measurement only takes place when the produce is harvested. Subsequent to harvesting, produce is treated as inventory.

For these measurements, fair value is considered to be based on the current market conditions in which market participants are willing to enter into transactions. Thus, the fair value of a biological asset or agricultural produce is not necessarily the price at which an entity may have contracted to sell its assets at some point in the future.

When a biological asset is initially recognized at its fair value less costs to sell, any related gain or loss is recognized in profit or loss. The same accounting applies when there is a change in fair value from period to period.

EXAMPLE

A calf is born at Cud Farms, so Cud recognizes a gain of £500 that reflects the market value of a newborn calf. One year later, the price of the cow has risen to £2,200, so Cud recognizes a gain of £1,700 to account for the increase in fair value. One year after that, a glut of cows on the market drops the fair market value to £1,900, so Cud recognizes a loss of £300.

EXAMPLE

Spud Potato Farms harvests its Fall crop of potatoes, and recognizes a gain of £150,000 in profit or loss as soon as the harvest is complete.

It may not be possible to measure the fair value of a biological asset upon its initial recognition. If so, measure the asset at its cost, less any accumulated depreciation and accumulated impairment losses. If a fair value later becomes available on a reliable basis, the asset should be revalued at the fair value.

If a biological asset was initially measured at its fair value less costs to sell, it must continue to be measured in that manner until the asset is disposed of.

In all cases, agricultural produce must be measured at its fair value less costs to sell; this requirement is based on the assumption that fair values are always available for agricultural produce.

A government grant related to a biological asset should be recognized in profit or loss only when the following conditions are met:

- The grant is unconditional;
- All conditions associated with the grant have been met;
- The grant is measured at fair value less costs to sell; and
- The grant becomes receivable.

EXAMPLE

The local government issues a £100,000 grant to any farmer willing to operate a farm in an area formerly zoned for heavy industrial use. The grant stipulates that a farmer will be paid in full after having documented at least three consecutive years of farming on the same land. Given this condition, a farmer cannot recognize the grant until the required three-year period has elapsed.

Bearer Plants

A bearer plant is a plant that generates produce, such as an apple tree. The plant itself is not an agricultural product. A bearer plant has the following characteristics:

- Is used in the production of agricultural produce;
- Is expected to bear agricultural products for more than one season; and
- Is not likely to be sold as agricultural produce.

Thus, wheat is not a bearer plant, since it is routinely harvested. Trees can be treated as agricultural produce, if the intent is to cut them down to produce lumber. An apple tree is considered a bearer plant, even though it may eventually be cut down and sent to a lumber mill; since its use as lumber is a secondary application.

Agriculture Disclosures

A business engaged in agriculture should disclose the following information in the notes accompanying its financial statements:

- *Commitments*. Any commitments to develop or acquire biological assets.
- *Gain or loss*. The aggregate gain or loss recognized in the reporting period from the initial recognition of biological assets and agricultural produce, and from changes in the fair value less costs to sell of biological assets.
- *Groupings*. Describe each group of biological assets, such as groups of mature and immature assets. Mature assets have reached a state in which they can be harvested or can sustain ongoing harvests. IFRS encourages a quantified description that can help in assessing the timing of future cash flows. A suggested grouping is for consumable biological assets, which are those assets to be harvested or sold. Another possible grouping is bearer biological assets, which are self-regenerating assets, such as fruit trees and grape vines.
- *Nature of activities*. The nature of the activities required for each group of biological assets.
- *Quantities*. The physical quantities of each group of biological assets at the end of the reporting period, as well as the amount produced during the period.
- *Reconciliation*. A reconciliation of the carrying amounts of biological assets between the beginning and end of the period, including gains and losses on changes in fair value less costs to sell, increases caused by purchases, decreases caused by sales and items held for sale, decreases caused by harvests, increases caused by business combinations, foreign exchange differences, and other issues.
- *Restricted title*. The carrying amounts of those biological assets whose titles are restricted, and those amounts pledged as security.
- *Risk management*. Any financial risk management strategies applied to agricultural activity.

EXAMPLE

Cud Farms discloses the following information in the notes accompanying its financial statements:

Cud Farms produces goat milk for a number of local school districts. At year-end, Cud held 320 goats able to produce milk and 150 kids being raised to produce milk in the future. During the year ended 20X2, the company produced 88,000 gallons of goat milk, with a fair value less costs to sell of £230,000. The fair value of milk is based on quoted prices in the local area.

The company is exposed to changes in the price of goat milk. There is no expectation of reduced milk prices in the near future, so the company does not engage in derivative transactions to offset this risk. The management team reviews the milk price forecast on a weekly basis to determine the ongoing need for more active financial risk management.

If the fair values of biological assets cannot be measured reliably, disclose the following information:

- *Conversion to fair value.* If it becomes possible to measure assets at fair value during the period, describe these assets, explain why fair value can now be measured, and the impact of the change.
- *Depreciation.* The depreciation method used to ratably reduce the cost of the assets.
- *Description.* A description of the assets.
- *Estimates.* The range of estimates within which the fair value is likely to be (if possible).
- *Explanation.* An explanation of why fair value cannot be measured in a reliable manner.
- *Gains or losses.* The gains or losses recognized on the disposal of biological assets measured at cost, as well as a reconciliation for the period that includes impairment losses, reversals of impairment losses, and depreciation.
- *Gross amounts.* The gross carrying amount and accumulated depreciation as of the beginning and end of the reporting period.
- *Useful lives.* The useful lives incorporated into depreciation calculations.

If the entity has received government grants, disclose the nature of these grants recognized in the period, any unfulfilled conditions related to outstanding grants, and any significant decreases that are expected in the amount of future government grants.

Summary

Agriculture is one of the few areas in which IFRS allows a business to recognize gains and losses from self-generated assets. In agriculture, a gain can be recognized as soon as produce is harvested, while the initial recognition of a gain on a biological asset is a similar situation. In most businesses, no gain or loss can be recognized in profit or loss until a sale transaction has been completed with a third party.

Chapter 34
Government Grants

Introduction

A government may provide a variety of assistance to entities operating within its borders, perhaps to alter their activities to meet the goals of the government, or perhaps simply to provide economic assistance during difficult financial circumstances. In this chapter, we discuss how to account for, present, and disclose the various forms of government assistance that a business may receive.

IFRS Source Documents

- IAS 20, *Accounting for Government Grants and Disclosure of Government Assistance*
- SIC 10, *Government Assistance – No Specific Relation to Operating Activities*

Accounting for Government Grants

When a business receives a government grant, it must account for the receipt of an asset or the reduction of a liability. Also, the business needs to report in its financial statements the extent to which the grant or other assistance has altered its financial results; otherwise the intrusion of government assistance makes it difficult to compare the results and condition of the company from period to period.

The essential accounting for a government grant is that it should not be recognized unless there is reasonable assurance that the business will receive the grant and will comply with any associated conditions. Simply receiving a grant is not sufficient grounds for recognizing it, since the government may demand the return of the funds if the company does not comply with the associated conditions. The recognition of a government grant in profit or loss should be spread over the periods during which the business expects to recognize the expenses that the grant is designed to offset. These expenses may relate to the conditions associated with the grant. For example, a government may issue funds to a business in exchange for the training of certain employees; if so, the amount of the grant is recognized in proportion to the amount of expense recognized that relates to employee training.

EXAMPLE

Nascent Corporation receives a grant of land from the local city government that has a fair value of £1,000,000, on the condition that the company builds a factory on the premises. Accordingly, Nascent recognizes the fair value of the land over the 30-year useful life of the factory.

EXAMPLE

A federal disaster relief agency pays £10,000,000 to a major teaching hospital whose primary facility was destroyed in a flash flood, to assist it in rebuilding. Two years of construction work will be required to rebuild the facility at a cost of £25,000,000 in the first year and £18,000,000 in the second year. Based on this expenditure pattern, the hospital should recognize the £10,000,000 as noted in the following table:

Year	Projected Expenditures	Proportion of Total Expenditures	Allocation to Grant
1	£25,000,000	58%	£5,800,000
2	18,000,000	42%	4,200,000
	£43,000,000	100%	£10,000,000

If a government issues a grant that is intended to compensate a business for expenses already incurred, or to give immediate financial support with no future expenditures required by the recipient, the business can recognize the grant in profit or loss as soon as it becomes a valid receivable. In such a case, the recipient should fully disclose the amount and reason for the receipt, to keep from misleading investors regarding a sudden improvement in its reported results.

The following additional rules may apply to government grants:

- *Below-market interest rate.* If a government issues a loan that has a below-market interest rate, treat the rate difference from the market rate as a government grant.

- *Depreciable assets.* If a grant is related to a depreciable asset, recognize the grant in profit or loss over the periods when depreciation will be recognized, and in the same proportions that depreciation will be recognized. Thus, if depreciation is recognized using the straight-line method, use the same approach for the recognition of the grant.

- *Forgivable loan.* If a government issues a forgivable loan and there is reasonable assurance that the business will meet the associated conditions required to forgive the loan, treat it as a government grant. Otherwise, treat it as a loan.

- *Government assistance.* A government may give assistance, such as technical advice, on which it is difficult to assign a value. If so, it is best to avoid recognizing the assistance, but consider disclosing the nature of the assistance if not doing so would result in financial statements that are misleading.

- *Multiple conditions.* If there are multiple conditions associated with a government grant, it may be necessary to apportion parts of the grant to each condition, and recognize each apportioned element of the grant based on the company's compliance with each underlying condition.

EXAMPLE

A local government issues a grant of £500,000 to Luminescence Corporation, of which £400,000 is allocated to assistance with the construction of a new facility, and £100,000 to building a trail that skirts the premises of the property. Once the trail has been built, Luminescence will incur no ongoing trail maintenance obligation.

To account for the grant, the company recognizes the £400,000 portion of the grant as income over the 20-year useful life of the facility. The company can recognize the £100,000 portion of the grant as soon as it completes construction of the trail.

- *No conditions*. A government may elect to provide assistance to an entire industry sector or geographic region in which a company does business. If so, there may be no conditions associated with the extension of assistance. Under these circumstances, assistance given is considered a government grant for accounting purposes.
- *Non-monetary grant*. IFRS encourages the recognition of non-monetary grants by the recipient at their fair value, though it is also acceptable to record such a grant at some nominal amount.
- *Repayment*. Circumstances may dictate that a business must repay a grant to a government. If so, this is considered a change in accounting estimate, which is accounted for on a prospective basis. When accounting for a repayment, first offset the payment against any of the deferred credit that is still unamortized. If doing so does not completely offset the payment, recognize the remaining amount in profit or loss. If a repayment relates to a specific company asset against which the grant was originally offset, increase the carrying amount of the asset by the amount of the repayment. In the latter case, the increase in asset carrying amount will increase the amount of depreciation; the cumulative amount of depreciation related to the increase in carrying amount that would have been recognized to date if the grant had not been issued should be recognized at once in profit or loss.

EXAMPLE

Hegemony Toy Company receives a £150,000 grant from a local government, to be used in the construction of a new factory within the boundaries of the granting government entity. Hegemony offsets the grant against the £5,000,000 construction cost of the new factory, resulting in a net carrying amount of £4,850,000 that will be depreciated over the projected 20-year life of the factory. One year later, the granting government finds that Hegemony did not comply with all of the requirements of the grant, and demands immediate repayment. Hegemony does so, which increases the gross carrying amount of the factory to £5,000,000. In addition, Hegemony must also recognize the additional £7,500 of depreciation expense that it would have recognized if the grant had not occurred.

Government Grant Presentation

When a government entity issues a grant to a business, either in cash or as a non-monetary asset, the recipient should report the grant in its balance sheet using one of the following methods:

- *Deferred income approach.* Recognize the grant as deferred income, and recognize it in profit or loss over the useful life of the asset. Under this approach, the grant is recognized in an "other income" line item in the income statement.
- *Asset deduction.* Deduct the amount of the grant from the carrying amount of the related asset, which results in a reduced amount of depreciation recognition over the life of the asset.

EXAMPLE

Domicilio Corporation receives a grant of £100,000 from a local government that is to be applied toward the development of an on-site solar power generation facility at its corporate headquarters. Domicilio accounts for the grant by deducting it from the £600,000 carrying amount of the solar facility, which will reduce the amount of depreciation recognized by the company over the projected 20-year useful life of the facility.

Government Grant Disclosures

It may be necessary to disclose the amount and nature of a grant in order to give the reader of a company's financial statements a better understanding of the financial results and financial position being presented. If a grant has an unusual impact on a particular line item in the financial statements, it may be useful to disclose this effect. In particular, the following disclosures should be made in the notes accompanying the financial statements:

- *Accounting policy.* The nature of the policy under which the company accounts for government grants, as well as how the information is presented in the financial statements.
- *Conditions.* Any unfulfilled conditions associated with government assistance that has been recognized in the financial statements.
- *Grant descriptions.* The nature of the grants recognized by the business. Also note other types of government assistance benefiting the business.

Summary

An organization may take the easy approach to recording the value of a non-monetary grant at a nominal amount. Doing so is certainly efficient, but does a disservice to the users of its financial statements, who have no idea that the business may have just received a substantial asset that could be of benefit for years to come. Accordingly, if it is possible to obtain a fair value without too much effort, consider assigning a fair value to non-monetary assets received as grants.

Chapter 35
Regulatory Deferral Accounts

Introduction

Rate regulation occurs when an independent regulator oversees and approves the prices charged by a business entity to its customers. This circumstance most commonly occurs when there is a monopoly, or utility services are being provided.

Regulatory deferral accounts contain balances that might not normally be recognized as assets or liabilities, but which are expected to be included in the basis for prices that a rate regulator will allow an entity to charge to its customers. Examples of these costs are purchase price variances, project cancellation costs, and the cost of natural disasters. In some countries, the standard-setting bodies either require or permit rate-regulated entities to capitalize certain expenditures that would normally be charged to expense, with the same deferral treatment for certain types of income. These costs are later charged to expense to match the associated rate increases.

In this chapter, we address the accounting for, presentation of, and disclosures related to regulatory deferral accounts.

IFRS Source Documents

- IFRS 14, *Regulatory Deferral Accounts*

Accounting for Regulatory Deferral Accounts

If an entity has already included in regulatory deferral accounts expenditures that would normally have been charged to expense under other IFRS standards, it is permissible to continue using its existing accounting policies for the treatment of these expenditures. This means that existing policies for the recognition, measurement, impairment, and derecognition of these accounts can continue to be used. These policies can only be changed if doing so makes the financial statements more relevant or reliable for users.

This accounting is limited to first-time adopters that have already recognized regulatory deferral account balances in their financial statements. If they follow the requirements noted here during their initial adoption of IFRS, they can continue to follow the requirements in later periods.

Regulatory Deferral Account Presentation

In general, regulatory deferral accounts must be presented in separate line items in the statement of financial position. Further, if there are changes in these accounts, the resulting expense changes must be noted in separate line items in the statement of profit or loss or other comprehensive income. More specifically, the presentation requirements for regulatory deferral accounts in the financial statements are as follows:

Statement of Changes in Financial Position

- Present a separate line item in the statement of financial position for the aggregate amount of all regulatory deferral account debit balances.
- Present a separate line item in the statement of financial position for the aggregate amount of all regulatory deferral account credit balances.
- The preceding two lines items are not to broken down into current or long-term classifications. Instead, they are to be separated by interposing subtotals for all other line items prior to the presentation of the deferral accounts.
- When there is a deferred tax asset or liability resulting from the recognition of regulatory deferral account balances, pair these items for presentation purposes with the related regulatory deferral accounts. Do not present them within the total deferred tax asset or liability for the entity.

Profit or Loss

- Present in the other comprehensive income section the net movement in these account balances during the reporting period. Use separate line items to present this information for changes in items that will not be later reclassified to profit or loss, and which will later be reclassified to profit or loss.
- Present in profit or loss in a separate line item any remaining net movement in the regulatory deferral account balances for the reporting period, with the exception of items that are not included in profit or loss. This line item should be separated from other income and expense line items by interposing subtotals for all of these other line items prior to the presentation of this line item.

Other

- When there is a discontinued operation or a disposal group that must be presented separately, do not move the related regulatory deferral account balances and their changes to the separate presentations. Instead, continue to present this information in the standard locations.
- When calculating earnings per share, present an additional set of earnings per share information that excludes any changes in the regulatory deferral account balances.

Regulatory Deferral Account Disclosures

Generally, the disclosure of regulatory deferral accounts includes an explanation of those amounts in the financial statements that are caused by rate regulation, which will assist users in understanding the amounts, timing, and uncertainty of future cash flows related to these accounts. More specifically:

- *Nature of information.* The nature of the rate regulation that establishes allowable prices, and the risks associated with this regulation. Identify the rate regulators, and whether the regulator is a related party. Further, note how the future recovery of each type of deferred account by risks and uncertainties, such as changes in customer demand or future regulatory actions.

- *Effects of regulation.* The effects of rate regulation on the financial results, position, and cash flows of the entity. This includes the following items:
  - The basis under which deferred account balances are recognized and derecognized, how they are initially and subsequently measured, and how they are assessed for impairment.
  - For each class of account balance, reconcile the beginning and ending carrying amounts in a table. This may include the amount recognized in the period, any amounts recognized in the period, impairments, items acquired through a business combination, and so forth.
  - The rate of return or discount rate used to indicate the time value of money, which applies to each deferral account.
  - The remaining periods over which it is expected that the remaining account balances will be recovered or amortized.

- *Income taxes.* The impact of rate regulation on the amount and timing of income tax recognition as they apply to current and deferred taxes. Also note any regulatory deferral account balance that relates to taxation, and the movement in that account balance.

- *Subsidiaries.* If there is a subsidiary or joint venture that has rate-regulated activities and which uses regulatory deferral accounts, disclose the amounts in these accounts and net changes in the balances.

- *Non-recoverability.* When a deferral account balance is no longer fully recoverable or reversible, disclose the issue, the reason for non-recoverability or non-reversibility, and the associated amount of the account balance reduction.

Summary

A more expansive accounting standard is eventually expected to be issued that more fully addresses the concerns of regulated entities. In the meantime, this standard is designed to provide a short-term solution to the problem of how to deal with deferral accounts that would otherwise likely have to be charged to expense when an entity adopts IFRS.

Chapter 36
Mineral Resources

Introduction

This chapter addresses several accounting aspects of mining operations that are completely unique to this activity – specifically, the possible capitalization of exploration and evaluation costs, as well as the designation of stripping costs as either fixed assets, inventory, or expenses.

IFRS Source Documents

- IFRS 6, *Exploration for and Evaluation of Mineral Resources*
- IFRIC 20, *Stripping Costs in the Production Phase of a Surface Mine*

Accounting for Mineral Resources

A mining company essentially engages in the exploration for and extraction of mineral resources. The focus of this section is on the exploration phase, which is considered to include not only the initial exploration for minerals, but also the evaluation of whether the resulting mineral deposits can be extracted.

Certain expenditures in the exploration and evaluation phase should be recorded as assets, rather than being charged to expense as incurred. Examples of expenditures that could be recorded as assets are:

- Evaluation of the commercial viability and technical feasibility of mineral extraction
- Exploration rights
- Exploratory drilling and trenching
- Sampling
- Studies in the geological, topographical, geochemical, and related areas

The primary IFRS guidance regarding these activities is that exploration and evaluation assets initially be recorded at their cost. The subsequent accounting for exploration and evaluation assets is to apply either the *cost model* or the *revaluation model* to them. See the Property, Plant, and Equipment chapter for more information. Once the evaluation of a mineral property has been completed, it is possible that a capitalized exploration asset will then be considered impaired, because it is not economically feasible or technologically viable to extract the minerals. Impairment should be recognized when the carrying amount of such an asset exceeds its estimated recoverable amount. The following circumstances are indicators that impairment testing should be employed:

- Exploration in the area has not yielded commercially viable mineral quantities, so further exploration is to be discontinued.
- Substantive additional exploration expenditures are not planned.
- The right to explore has or is about to expire, and will not be renewed.
- Though development will proceed, the carrying amount of the asset will probably not be recovered.

It is possible that a business may also have to recognize a liability for the eventual restoration of a property because of its mining activities.

To properly account for the exploration and extraction of mineral resources, a mining business should create an accounting policy that specifies which expenditures are to be applied to the exploration and evaluation area, and then apply the policy consistently. There should be an additional policy for allocating assets to cash-generating units in order to assess them for impairment (see the Impairment of Assets chapter). It is allowable to subsequently change these policies, if doing so makes the financial statements of the business more reliable and relevant to users of the information.

The guidance in this section does not apply to expenditures incurred prior to exploration activities, as occurs before a business has secured the rights to explore a designated area. Also, this section does not apply to the extraction phase, which is after extraction feasibility has been demonstrated.

Accounting for Stripping Costs

In a surface mining operation, a mining company usually needs to remove a layer of waste materials (called *overburden*) before reaching the targeted mineral deposit. The removal of overburden is called *stripping*.

There are several options for the accounting for stripping costs incurred during the development phase of a mine, which are:

- *Treat as inventory.* If there is usable ore in the overburden, record the stripping cost as inventory.
- *Treat as fixed asset.* If there is no usable ore in the overburden, capitalize the stripping cost into the cost of the mine, along with an allocation of directly attributable overhead costs, and then depreciate it. The usual form of depreciation is the units of production method, though another method can be used if it is more appropriate. This option is only available if the stripping cost will probably result in improved access to the underlying ore, the business can identify the ore to which access will be improved, *and* costs associated with accessing that particular ore body can be measured reliably.
- *Charge to expense.* If the preceding two options are not applicable, charge the stripping cost to expense as incurred.

EXAMPLE

Pensive Corporation's gravel pit operation, Pensive Dirt, removes overburden from a gravel pit at a cost of £400,000. Pensive expects to extract 1,000,000 tons of gravel, which results in a depreciation rate of £0.40 per ton (1,000,000 tons ÷ £400,000 cost). During the first quarter of activity, Pensive Dirt extracts 10,000 tons of gravel, which results in the following depreciation expense:

£0.40 depreciation cost per ton × 10,000 tons of gravel = £4,000 depreciation expense

There may be cases where a modest amount of inventory can be extracted from overburden, while the remainder of the overburden contains no usable minerals. In this case, it is acceptable to allocate the cost of stripping between inventory and the asset derived from stripping costs. The allocation should be based on a relevant production measure, such as:

- The proportion of waste extracted in comparison to the expected proportion
- The proportion of ore extracted in comparison to the expected proportion
- The cost of inventory produced in comparison to the expected cost

Once any stripping costs have been capitalized, they are depreciated, revalued, and/or evaluated for impairment, just like any other fixed asset.

Mineral Resources Presentation

Any exploration and evaluation assets should be consistently classified as either tangible or intangible fixed assets. For example, drilling rights can be considered an intangible asset, while a drilling rig is considered a tangible asset.

When exploration and evaluation expenditures are recorded as assets, classify these assets in a separate line item in the balance sheet.

Mineral Resources Disclosures

A mining entity should separately disclose the following information in the notes that accompany its financial statements, or within the financial statements:

- *Policies*. The accounting policies related to the recognition of exploration and evaluation assets.
- *Mineral resources line items*. The amounts of revenues, expenses, operating cash flows, investing cash flows, assets, and liabilities arising from mineral resources exploration and evaluation.

Summary

This chapter has focused on the treatment of expenditures incurred during the exploration for mineral resources and the removal of overburden. For more general information about the ongoing accounting for fixed assets and impairment testing, please refer to the Property, Plant, and Equipment chapter and the Impairment of Assets chapter.

Chapter 37
Service Concessions

Introduction

A company may be brought in by a government to either service existing infrastructure or to develop and operate entirely new infrastructure, with the intent of providing a service to the public. For example, a company may build and operate a toll road, or it may operate an existing airport facility. These arrangements typically incorporate performance standards, systems for adjusting prices charged, and requirements for resolving disputes. The underlying infrastructure is handed back to the government after the period covered by the arrangement has been completed. This chapter describes the accounting by a business that is operating under a service concession arrangement, where the granting government controls the services to be provided and the prices that may be charged, and owns a significant residual interest in the infrastructure at the end of the arrangement.

IFRS Source Documents

- IFRIC 12, *Service Concession Arrangements*
- SIC 29, *Service Concession Arrangements - Disclosures*

Overview of Service Concessions

A service concession arrangement is one in which a business essentially gives the public access to major infrastructure facilities, such as:

Airports	Highways	Telecommunication networks
Bridges	Park operations	Tunnels
Ferry terminals	Parking facilities	Water treatment facilities

Under a service concession arrangement, a business typically receives a right to be paid within a fee structure in exchange for the incurrence of an obligation to provide services to the public.

Arrangements that are *not* considered service concessions typically involve outsourcing the internal services of a government entity, such as meal service, janitorial service, building maintenance, and computer systems support.

When a business enters into a service concession arrangement, it should follow these rules when accounting for transactions:

- *Borrowing costs.* Borrowing costs incurred by the business as part of its service concession arrangement are charged to expense as incurred. However, if the borrowing costs relate to a contractual right to receive an intangible asset (such as a license), capitalize these costs during the construction phase of the asset, and amortize them over the term of the arrangement.

- *Consideration paid.* A business may be cast in the role of either constructing, upgrading, or maintaining infrastructure, or of providing a public service. If it is providing more than one of these services, it should allocate the consideration paid to each service, based on their fair values. See the Revenue chapter regarding how these payments are to be recognized.
- *Construction services.* If a business is constructing or upgrading infrastructure assets for a government entity, it treats the arrangement as a construction contract. The accounting for construction contracts is described in the Construction Contracts chapter.
- *Fixed assets.* A business does not own the infrastructure that it operates, and so does not recognize it as a fixed asset.
- *Intangible asset.* If a business receives a right to charge users for the service it is providing, the business should recognize an intangible asset. See the following example.
- *Obligation to restore infrastructure.* If the business undertakes to restore infrastructure to a certain condition or level of serviceability, it should recognize a liability in the amount of the estimated expenditure required to do so.
- *Retainable assets.* A government entity may provide a business with assets as part of a service concession that the business is allowed to dispose of as it wishes. These assets are not to be accounted for as a government grant, but rather as assets measured at their fair values, with an offsetting liability for unfulfilled obligations assumed. These obligations are then charged to expense as the obligations are fulfilled.
- *Services revenue.* If services are provided to users, account for them as service revenue. This accounting is described in the Revenue chapter.

EXAMPLE

Rio Shipping enters into an agreement with the port authority of Southport to construct a ferry terminal and be the exclusive provider of ferry service to all surrounding cities and towns for the next 10 years. Rio constructs the terminal at a direct cost of £10,000,000, which is reimbursed by the port authority. Rio should recognize an intangible asset, which is the right to collect fees from customers using the ferry service. The amount of this intangible asset to recognize is the fair value of the consideration receivable in exchange for the construction oversight services provided.

Rio estimates the fair value of the consideration received to be the £400,000 cost of construction supervision plus an 8% profit margin. This results in a recognized intangible asset of £432,000. Rio then amortizes the intangible asset over the ten years of the service concession on a straight-line basis, which is £43,200 of amortization per year.

Rio collects payments from ferry users as they make use of the ferry services, so the company can recognize revenue from these payments as they are received.

Service Concession Disclosures

Both the operator and the grantor of a service concession should disclose the following information in the notes accompanying their financial statements, either for each individual concession or in aggregate for each class of concession arrangement:

- *Classification.* How the arrangement has been classified for reporting purposes.
- *Concession changes.* Any changes in the arrangement during the reporting period.
- *Description.* A description of the service concession arrangement.
- *Options.* The terms of any options to renew or terminate the arrangement.
- *Rights and obligations.* Any rights involving the use of assets, as well as any obligations to provide services, acquire or build property, or return assets at the end of the arrangement.
- *Terms.* Significant terms of the arrangement that may affect the future cash flows of the parties, such as the duration of the concession and the conditions under which prices are adjusted.

In addition, the business should disclose the amount of revenues and expenses recognized in the period that relate to the concession.

Summary

Service concession arrangements can be quite complex, especially when a business is required to provide ongoing maintenance and infrastructure upgrades, is subject to a variety of price alteration rules, and intangible assets are recognized as part of an arrangement. Under these circumstances, it is best to develop formal procedures for how to account for each arrangement, have them approved in advance by the company's auditors, and monitor transactions on an ongoing basis. Without this level of oversight, there is a substantial risk that the accounting for service concession arrangements will go awry.

Chapter 38
Other Topics

Introduction

The topics covered in this chapter are of some importance to those entities impacted by them, but are not broad enough to require coverage in separate chapters. The topics relate to the liability for waste electrical and electronic equipment, hedging a net investment in a foreign operation, distributing non-cash assets to the owners of a business, and swapping financial liabilities for equity instruments.

IFRS Source Documents

- IFRIC 6, *Liabilities arising from Participating in a Specific Market – Waste Electrical and Electronic Equipment*
- IFRIC 16, *Hedges of a Net Investment in a Foreign Operation*
- IFRIC 17, *Distributions of Non-cash Assets to Owners*
- IFRIC 19, *Extinguishing Financial Liabilities with Equity Instruments*

Liabilities from Waste Electrical and Electronic Equipment

The European Union issued the Directive on Waste Electrical and Electronic Equipment, which contains regulations that deal with the collection, treatment, recovery, and disposal of waste equipment. In the directive, decommissioning activities for private households are split into "new" waste occurring after August 13, 2005 and historical waste before that date. The directive requires the producers of household equipment to pay decommissioning costs for historical waste if they were operating in this market during a period to be specified by each member state of the European Union. Payments are based on the proportionate share of each producer in the relevant markets, by type of equipment.

If a producer participated in a market to which the directive applies, and did so during the measurement period approved by a member state of the European Union, it should recognize a decommissioning liability once the measurement period has been clarified.

EXAMPLE

Broadcast Radio sells emergency short-wave radios for personal use. During 2004, it achieved a market share of 8%. Its market share suffers thereafter, reaching 1% in 2006. The company exits the market at the beginning of 2007. A member state passes legislation in 2007, mandating that decommissioning liability will be assigned based on 2007 market shares. Since Broadcast is no longer in the market during the measurement period, it is assigned no liability.

Hedges of a Net Investment in a Foreign Operation

A business may have invested in a foreign operation, which could be classified as a subsidiary, associate, joint venture, or branch. Depending on its relationship with the foreign operation, a business may be required to translate the results of that operation into its own currency for reporting purposes. In these situations, it is entirely possible that ongoing differences in the exchange rates applicable to the business and its foreign operation will require the recognition of a gain or loss in other comprehensive income. These gains or losses are recognized in profit or loss whenever the business disposes of its net investment in the foreign operation.

The managers of a business may want to negate these foreign exchange gains and losses by establishing hedges. A hedge is officially established when a link is recognized between the net investment in a foreign operation and a hedging instrument. The following accounting issues relate to these hedging situations:

- *Hedge holdings.* A hedging instrument for a net investment in a foreign operation can be held by any entity within a group.
- *Hedging cap.* The amount of the hedge is capped at the carrying amount of the net assets of the foreign operation reported in the consolidated financial statements of the parent entity.
- *Hedging relationship qualification.* If hedging of a net investment in a foreign operation is contemplated at several levels of a consolidated business, be aware that only one hedging relationship qualifies for hedge accounting in the consolidated financial statements of the entity. In order to recognize hedge accounting by a higher level parent, any hedge accounting applied at a lower level must be reversed.
- *Hedge dependency.* The amount of net assets that can be hedged is dependent upon the existence of any hedge accounting by a lower-level parent within the organization.
- *Effectiveness assessment.* When assessing the effectiveness of a hedge of a net investment in a foreign operation, compare the functional currency of the hedged risk and the functional currency of the *parent* entity (which may not be the currency of the entity in the group where the hedge is held).
- *Intermediate-level parent.* If there is an intermediate-level parent of a foreign operation, this has no effect on the risk of the parent, since the parent still experiences foreign exchange risk in its consolidated financial statements.
- *Disposal recognition method.* When a foreign operation is disposed of, any hedging gains or losses in other comprehensive income should be recognized in profit or loss. The method for doing so can affect the amount included in the foreign exchange reserve for a specific foreign operation. Consequently, the corporate parent should have a policy for consistently using either the step-by-step method or the direct method of consolidation. The step-by-step method requires that the financial statements of a foreign operation first be translated into the functional currency of any intermediate parent and then into the functional currency of the ultimate parent, while the

direct method translates the financial statements directly into the functional currency of the ultimate parent.

EXAMPLE

Pianoforte International is the ultimate parent company; it presents its consolidated financial statements in pounds. Pianoforte has a wholly-owned subsidiary, Keyboard Deluxe, which reports its consolidated results in Euros. Keyboard, in turn, owns Ivory Keys, which reports its results in U.S. dollars. The £25,000,000 investment by Pianoforte in Keyboard includes an equivalent £5,000,000 investment in Ivory Keys.

The ultimate parent, Pianoforte, wants to hedge the foreign exchange risk associated with its £5,000,000 investment in Ivory Keys. The amount of the hedge can be equal to or less than the £5,000,000 net investment. To do so, Keyboard borrows $6,200,000, which is the dollar equivalent of the £5,000,000 investment. Pianoforte can designate the borrowing as a hedge of the pound/dollar spot exchange rate associated with the net investment in Ivory Keys. This transaction is allowable for hedge accounting purposes.

Keyboard could also use the hedge in its own consolidated financial statements, since it owns the hedging instrument.

For more information about hedging, see the Financial Instruments chapter.

Distributions of Non-cash Assets to Owners

A business may sometimes issue non-cash assets to its owners, perhaps through a dividend. The terms of the dividend may allow recipients to choose between a cash and non-cash payout. The relevant accounting is as follows:

- *Recognition date.* Recognize the related liability to pay the distribution on the dividend declaration date, which is usually when the board of directors authorizes the distribution.
- *Measurement.* Measure the liability at the fair value of the assets to be distributed. If the owners have a choice of accepting a cash or non-cash distribution, base the amount of the liability on the probability of the percentage of each option that will be chosen. The carrying amount of this payable is to be adjusted over time as the fair values of the underlying assets change, with the offset to the adjustment being recorded in equity.
- *Dividend settlement.* When a dividend is paid out, the business recognizes any difference between the carrying amount of the assets distributed and the amount of the dividend payable in profit or loss. This difference is presented in a separate line item in the income statement.

A business issuing non-cash assets should disclose the following information in the notes accompanying its financial statements:

- *Balances*. The beginning and ending balances of the dividend payable.
- *Carrying amount*. Any changes in the carrying amount of the dividend payable.
- *Late declaration*. If a non-cash dividend is declared after the reporting period but before the financial statements have been authorized for issuance, state the nature of the non-cash item, its carrying amount and fair value, and the method used to measure fair value.

Extinguishing Financial Liabilities with Equity Instruments

A borrower and a lender may sometimes elect to renegotiate a financial liability and replace it with the equity of the borrower, so that the lender now becomes a shareholder of the borrower. The accounting by the borrower in this situation is as follows:

- *Form of payment*. The issuance of equity in exchange for a financial liability is considered to be consideration paid, and results in the removal of the liability from the records of the borrower, if it has been paid in full. If there is a difference between the amount of the consideration paid and the carrying amount of the related liability, recognize it in profit or loss.
- *Equity measurement*. The equity issued in exchange for a liability should be measured at its fair value. If fair value cannot be measured, measure the equity at the fair value of the liability being extinguished. Recognize the equity instruments on the date when the liability is extinguished.
- *Terms modifications*. If some of the liability still remains and its terms have been modified, allocate the consideration paid between the extinguished and surviving portions of the liability. If the terms have been substantially modified, extinguish the old liability and create a new liability to reflect the new terms. If a gain or loss is recognized on the terms modification, present it in a separate line item in the income statement.

Glossary

A

Accounting policy. A principle, convention, rule, or practice used in preparing financial statements.

Accounting profit. The profit recorded for a reporting period, prior to the deduction of income taxes.

Acquiree. The entity that an acquirer gains control of in a business combination.

Acquirer. The entity that gains control of an acquiree in a business combination.

Active market. A market with sufficiently high frequency and volume to provide ongoing pricing information.

Actuarial gains and losses. A change in the present value of the obligations associated with a defined benefit plan, caused by changes in actuarial assumptions and actual experience.

Agricultural produce. Products harvested from biological assets, examples of which are wool, cotton, milk, grapes, and picked fruit.

Amortization. The systematic charge to expense of the cost of an intangible asset over its useful life.

Antidilution. Either an increase in earnings per share or a decline in loss per share when the assumption is made that ordinary shares are issued.

Asset ceiling. The present value of any economic benefits available as plan refunds or reductions in future contributions to a benefit plan.

Associate. An entity over which another party exercises significant influence.

B

Basic earnings per share. The earnings for an accounting period divided by the ordinary shares outstanding during that period.

Bearer plant. A living plant that is used in the production of agricultural produce.

Biological assets. A living plant or animal, examples of which are sheep, dairy cattle, fruit trees, and vines.

Borrowing costs. Interest and related costs associated with the borrowing of cash.

Business combination. An event in which an acquirer gains control of another business.

C

Carrying amount. The recognized amount of an asset, less accumulated depreciation and accumulated impairment losses.

Cash. The sum total of all cash on hand and demand deposits.

Cash equivalent. A short-term, very liquid investment that is easily convertible into a known amount of cash, and which is so near its maturity that it presents an insignificant risk of a change in value because of changes in interest rates.

Cash flows. The inflow or outflow of cash and cash equivalents.

Cash-generating unit. An asset group whose cash inflows are mostly independent of the cash inflows of other assets.

Cedant. The holder of a reinsurance contract.

Change in accounting estimate. A change that adjusts the carrying amount of an asset or liability, or the subsequent accounting for it. It results from new information.

Chief operating decision maker. A person who is responsible for making decisions about resource allocations to the segments of a business, and for evaluating those segments.

Close family members. The children, spouse, domestic partner, step-children, or dependents of a person who has control or significant influence over a business.

Consolidated financial statements. The combined financial statements of a group of entities, presented as the financial results, financial position, and cash flows of a single entity.

Construction contract. A contract under which an asset or group of interrelated assets will be constructed.

Constructive obligation. An obligation derived from the past practices, policies, or statements of a business that create an expectation that an obligation will be settled.

Contingent asset. A possible asset that may arise from past events, which will be confirmed by a future event not entirely under the control of an entity.

Contingent liability. A possible liability that may arise from past events, which will be confirmed by a future event not entirely under the control of an entity.

Contingent rent. A variable lease payment that is based on a future amount, such as a percentage of future sales or a future price index.

Contract. An agreement between parties that results in rights and obligations by the parties.

Cost approach. A valuation derived from the amount required to replace the service capacity of an asset.

Cost plus contract. A construction contract under which the contractor is reimbursed for allowable costs, plus either a percentage of costs incurred or a fixed fee.

Costs to sell. Those costs directly attributable to the disposal of an asset.

Credit risk. The risk that the counterparty to a financial instrument will not discharge an obligation, triggering the recognition of a loss by the other party.

Current cost. The current replacement cost or market price of an item.

Current service cost. The increase in the present value of a defined benefit obligation that is caused by employee service in the current period.

D

Deductible temporary difference. A temporary difference that will result in deductible amounts in future periods.

Deferred tax asset. The amount of income taxes recoverable in future periods that relate to deductible temporary differences, tax loss carryforwards, and tax credit carryforwards.

Deferred tax liability. The amount of income taxes payable in future periods that relate to taxable temporary differences.

Defined benefit plan. A post-employment benefit plan in which the amount of benefits to be provided is stated, but not the amount of funding required to achieve the designated benefits.

Defined contribution plan. A post-employment benefit plan in which the amount of contributions to the plan is stated, but not the amount of benefits that will eventually be paid out as a result of these contributions.

Depreciation. The systematic charge to expense of the cost of an asset over its useful life.

Derecognition. The elimination of an asset or liability from an entity's balance sheet.

Derivative. A contract whose value changes in relation to an outside value, requiring a small initial investment (if any), and which is settled on a future date.

Development. The application of research results to new products or processes before production begins.

Diluted earnings per share. The earnings for an accounting period divided by the ordinary shares outstanding during that period and all potential ordinary shares.

Dilution. When earnings per share is reduced by the assumption that all potential ordinary shares are converted to ordinary shares.

Direct method. A format of the statement of cash flows that presents specific cash flows in the operating activities section of the report.

Discontinued operation. A component of an entity that is either held for sale or which has been disposed of.

Discretionary participation feature. A contractual right to receive additional benefits that are based in some manner on the investment returns or profits of the insurer.

Disposal costs. Those costs incurred to dispose of an asset or cash-generating unit.

Disposal group. A group of assets and liabilities to be disposed of in a single transaction.

E

Economic life. The period over which an asset is expected to be economically usable, or the number of production units expected to be generated by it.

Effective interest rate. The interest rate that a borrower actually pays, based on the frequency of debt compounding, fees, points paid or received, transaction costs, and premiums or discounts.

Equity instrument. A contract that yields a residual interest in an entity.

Equity method. Accounting for an investment by adjusting the initial investment amount for changes in the investor's share of the investee's net assets.

Events after the reporting period. Events arising between the end of the reporting period and when the financial statements for that period are authorized for issuance.

Exchange rate. The ratio at which a unit of one currency can be exchanged for another currency.

Exploration and evaluation expenditures. Expenditures arising from the exploration for and evaluation of mineral resources prior to the point when it is demonstrated that mineral extraction is feasible and viable.

F

Fair value. The price paid in an orderly market transaction to sell an asset or transfer a liability.

Finance lease. A lease under which the risks and rewards of ownership are shifted to the lessee.

Financial asset. An asset that is either cash, equity in another entity, a contractual right to receive cash or other financial assets, or to exchange such assets and liabilities under potentially favorable conditions.

Financial guarantee contract. A contract under which the issuer must reimburse the holder for any losses caused by non-payments by a third party under a lending arrangement.

Financial instrument. Any contract that creates a financial asset for one party and a financial liability or equity instrument for the counterparty.

Financial liability. A liability that is an obligation to deliver cash or another financial asset, or to exchange financial assets or liabilities under potentially unfavorable terms.

Financing activities. Any actions that alter the size and composition of contributed equity or borrowings.

Fixed price contract. A construction contract under which the contractor accepts a fixed contract price.

Foreign currency. A currency other than the functional currency being used by an entity.

Forgivable loan. A loan for which the lender is prepared to waive repayment under certain circumstances.

Functional currency. The currency used in the primary economic environment in which a business operates. This is the environment in which an entity primarily generates and expends cash.

G

Goodwill. The residual asset arising from the future economic benefits of a business combination, which is not identified as a separate asset.

Government assistance. Government action to provide benefits to qualifying entities.

Government grant. Resources transferred by a government to an entity in return for compliance with certain conditions.

Grant date. The date on which an entity and the recipient of a share-based payment arrangement mutually arrive at the terms and conditions of the arrangement.

Guaranteed benefits. An obligation by an insurer to pay benefits to which a policyholder has an unconditional right.

Guaranteed residual value. That portion of the residual value of a leased asset that is guaranteed by the lessee.

H

Harvest. The separation of produce from a biological asset, or the termination of the life of a biological asset.

Hedge effectiveness. The extent to which variations in the cash flows or fair value of a hedged item are offset by variations in the cash flows or fair value of a hedging instrument.

Hedging instrument. A derivative, financial asset, or financial liability whose cash flows or fair value are expected to offset changes in the cash flows or fair value of a hedged item.

Held for trading. A financial asset or liability that is acquired for the purpose of generating a short-term profit, or which is a derivative.

Historical cost. Costing based on measures of historical prices, without subsequent restatement.

I

Impracticable. When it is not possible to apply a requirement, despite having made a reasonable effort to do so.

Income approach. A valuation derived from the discounted present value of future cash flows.

Indirect method. A format of the statement of cash flows that uses accrual-basis accounting as part of the presentation of cash flow information.

Insurance asset. The net contractual rights of an insurer under an insurance contract.

Insurance liability. The net contractual obligations of an insurer under an insurance contract.

Intangible asset. A non-monetary asset that lacks physical substance, and from which economic returns are expected for more than one period.

Interim financial report. A financial report containing a complete or condensed set of financial statements.

Interim period. A financial reporting period that is shorter than a full fiscal year.

Intrinsic value. The difference between the fair value of those shares that a party has a right to receive and the amount it must pay for the shares.

Investing activities. The acquisition and disposal of long-term assets, as well as other assets not considered to be cash equivalents.

Investment property. Property held with the intent of earning rental income or capital appreciation.

J

Joint arrangement. An arrangement in which several parties exercise joint control under a contractual arrangement.

Joint operation. A joint arrangement in which the participating parties have rights to the assets and obligations for the liabilities of the arrangement.

Joint venture. A joint arrangement in which the participating parties have rights to the net assets of the arrangement.

K

Key management personnel. Those managers having the authority and responsibility for planning, controlling, and directing the activities of a business.

L

Lease. An agreement under which the lessor conveys the right to use an asset to the lessee in exchange for one or more payments.

Lease term. The non-cancellable period of a lease, plus any additional lease term options that it is reasonably certain the lessee will exercise.

Levy. A tax or fee imposed by a government entity.

Liquidity risk. The risk that a business will not have sufficient cash to meet its obligations under a financial instrument.

M

Market approach. A valuation derived from similar market transactions.

Market condition. A condition upon which the terms of an equity instrument are based.

Market risk. The risk that changes in market prices will cause the future cash flows related to a financial instrument to fluctuate.

Master netting arrangement. A contractual arrangement to settle multiple financial transactions with a single counterparty on a net basis.

Material. An individual or collective omission from or misstatement of financial statements that could influence the decisions of users.

Monetary items. Money and items to be received or paid in money.

N

Non-cancellable lease. A lease that can be cancelled only under an unlikely condition, with the permission of the lessor, if replaced by a new lease, or with such a large payment that it is unlikely to be paid.

Non-controlling interest. That portion of the equity in a business that is not held by its parent.

Notes. Information that accompanies the financial statements, and which provide narrative descriptions, as well as information that is in disaggregated form or in addition to what is presented in the financial statements.

O

Obligating event. An event that essentially gives an entity no choice other than to settle an obligation.

Onerous contract. A contract that requires the incurrence of costs that will exceed the benefits derived from it.

Operating activities. The primary revenue-generating activities of a business.

Operating cycle. The time span from the acquisition of an asset to its realization in cash or cash equivalents.

Operating lease. Any lease other than a finance lease.

Operating segment. A component of a business that earns revenue and incurs expenses, for which separate financial information is available, and which is regularly evaluated by the chief operating decision maker in regard to resource allocations and performance assessment.

Ordinary share. An equity instrument that is subordinate to all other types of equity instruments.

Other comprehensive income. Items that are excluded from net income, such as gains and losses from financial statement translation, the effective portion of gains and losses on hedging instruments, and the remeasurement of defined benefit plans.

Owner-occupied property. Property held and to be used for production or administrative purposes.

P

Parent. An entity that controls other entities.

Past service cost. The change in present value of a defined benefit obligation for services performed by employees in prior periods. This amount can change when the underlying plan is altered or there is a significant reduction in the number of employees who will receive coverage under the plan.

Performance obligation. A contractual promise to transfer goods or services to a customer.

Potential ordinary share. Securities that can be converted to ordinary shares, such as options, warrants, and convertible securities.

Presentation currency. The currency in which a business prepares its financial statements.

Prior period error. A misstatement or omission in the financial statements for a prior period caused by the misuse or nonuse of information that was available when the statements were issued.

Profit or loss. The total amount of income minus expenses, not including any elements of other comprehensive income.

Progress billing. Billings for work performed on a contract.

Property, plant and equipment. Tangible items to be used in multiple periods, and which are used for production, rental, or administration.

Provision. A liability whose timing or amount is uncertain.

Puttable instrument. A financial instrument that allows its holder the option to put the instrument back to the issuer for cash or some other financial instrument.

Q

Qualifying asset. An asset requiring a significant time period to prepare for its intended use.

R

Rate regulation. A controlled process for establishing the prices that can be charged to customers, which is overseen by a rate regulator.

Reclassification adjustment. Items formerly recognized in other comprehensive income that are reclassified to profit or loss.

Recoverable amount. The greater of an asset's value in use and its fair value less costs to sell.

Reinsurance assets. The contractual rights of a cedant under a reinsurance contract.

Reinsurance contract. Insurance issued by one insurer to another to compensate for possible losses that may be incurred on the insurance contracts issued by the latter insurer.

Related parties. Those joint ventures, associates, principal owners, key management personnel, post-employment benefit plans for the benefit of employees, close family members of principal owners and managers, and other parties having control or significant influence over a business.

Related party transaction. A transaction in which there is a transfer of assets or liabilities between the reporting entity and a related party, even in the absence of a price related to the transaction.

Reload feature. The automatic granting of additional share options that occurs whenever an option holder exercises previously-granted options and uses shares to satisfy the exercise price.

Research. Investigations designed to gain new knowledge.

Residual value. The estimated amount currently obtainable from an asset disposal, less disposal costs, if it were in the condition expected at the end of its useful life.

Retention. That portion of a progress billing not paid until all contractually-specified conditions and defects have been rectified.

Retrospective application. The application of a new accounting policy to prior financial statements.

Revenue. Income generated by the ordinary activities of an entity.

S

Separate financial statements. The financial statements of a parent entity, in which investments are recorded at their cost or as financial instruments.

Service cost. A combination of current service cost, past service cost, and gains or losses on settlement.

Settlement. A transaction that terminates any further obligations by an employer under a defined benefit plan.

Share option. A contract that gives its holder the right, but not the obligation, to acquire the shares of an entity at a certain price, and within a certain period of time.

Significant influence. Having the power to participate in the financial and operating policy decisions of an investee.

Spot exchange rate. The exchange rate between two currencies that is available for immediate delivery.

Structured entity. An entity that has been structured in such a manner that voting rights are not the key determinant of who controls it.

Subsidiary. An entity over which control is exercised by another entity.

T

Tax base. The amount attributed to an asset or liability for tax purposes.

Taxable profit. The profit for a reporting period that is determined using the rules of the relevant taxation authority, upon which income taxes are calculated.

Taxable temporary difference. A temporary difference that will result in taxable amounts in future periods.

Temporary difference. A difference between the tax base and carrying amount of an asset or liability.

Total comprehensive income. The net change in equity during a period, not including transactions with owners. This is essentially the total amount of profit or loss and other comprehensive income.

Transaction costs. The fees and commissions, levies, taxes, and duties related to a transaction.

U

Useful life. Either the expected period over which an asset will be used, or the number of production units expected to be obtained from the asset.

V

Value in use. The present value of the cash flows expected from an asset or cash-generating unit.

Vest. The accrual of non-forfeitable rights.

Index

413

414

15249438R00240

Printed in Great Britain
by Amazon